The Beads

Danish Archaeological Investigations on Failaka, Kuwait

FAILAKA | DILMUN
THE SECOND MILLENNIUM SETTLEMENTS

volume 5
The Beads

by Ann Andersson

Jutland Archaeological Society

Moesgaard Museum, Denmark
National Council for Culture, Arts and Letters, Kuwait

Failaka | Dilmun
The Second Millennium Settlements
volume 5
The Beads

ISBN 978-87-93423-72-5
ISSN 0107-2854

Jutland Archaeological Society Publications vol. 17:5

Edition: Flemming Højlund
Design: Louise Hilmar
Photos and drawings: Ann Andersson
English revision: Sharon E. Rhodes
Printed by Stibo Complete, Horsens, Denmark

Published by Jutland Archaeological Society in cooperation with Moesgaard Museum and the National Council for Culture, Arts and Letters, Kuwait

Distributed by Aarhus University Press
Finlandsgade 29
DK-8200 Aarhus N
www.unipress.dk

The publication is funded by the Carlsberg Foundation

Contents

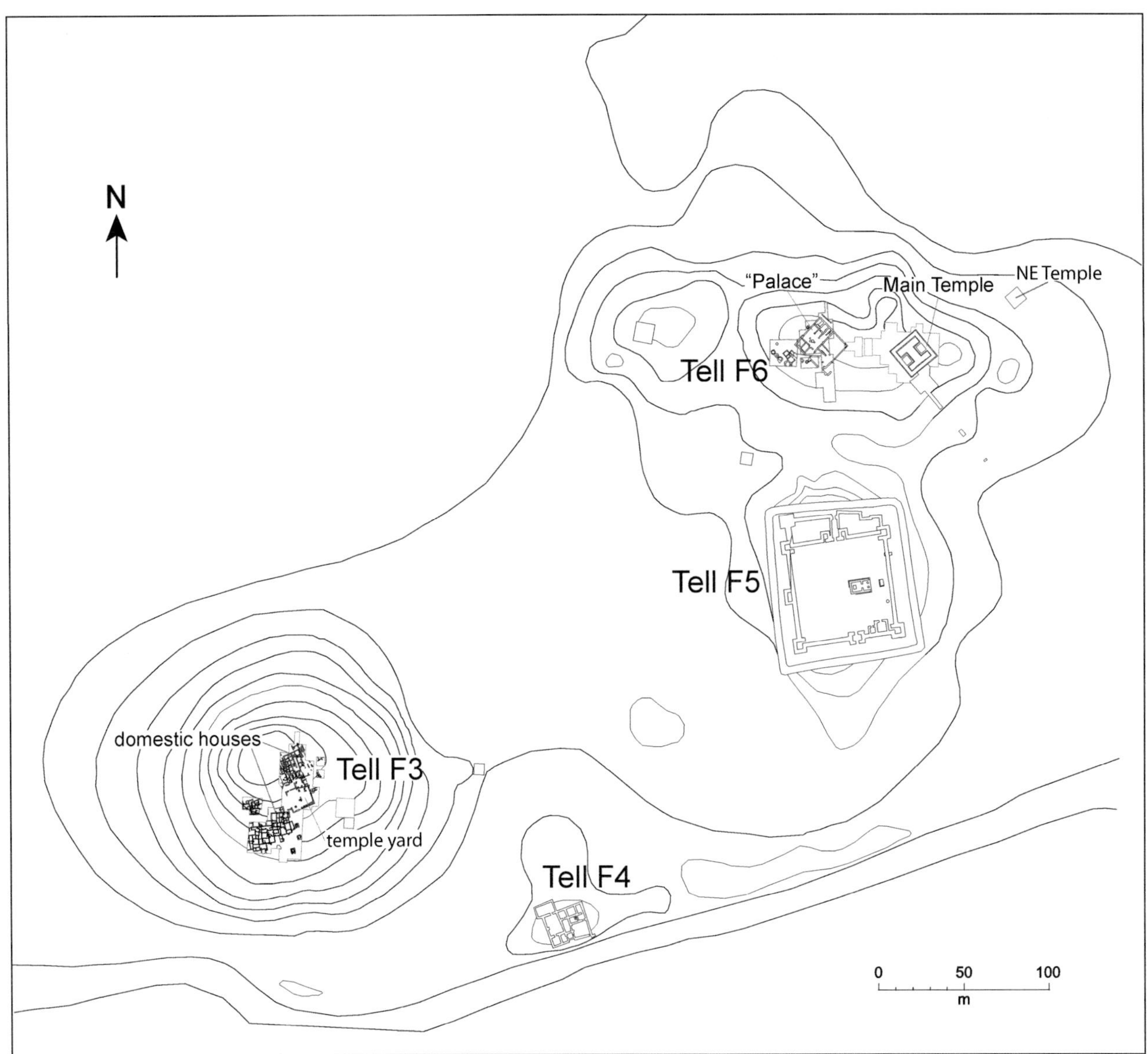

Fig. 1. Map of Tell F3 and Tell F6.

1. Introduction

The beads presented in this volume were recovered from excavations carried out in Tell F3 and Tell F6 on the island of Failaka in Kuwait by the Danish Archaeological Mission between 1958 and 1963. The architecture uncovered dates to the 2nd millennium BC and consists of several phases of domestic architecture along with a small temple courtyard in Tell F3 and a large production and storage installation called the "Palace" in Tell F6 (figs. 1 and 2). The architectural remains and their dating have since been published (Kjærum & Højlund 2013), along with material studies of stamp seals (Kjærum 1983), pottery (Højlund 1987), and stone vessels (Hilton 2014).

The corpus of beads from the 1958-1963 investigations consists of 167 beads from Tell F3 and 348 beads from Tell F6, a total of 515 beads. Originally, the material from the Danish excavations included 114 additional beads, but they were lost during the Iraqi invasion of Kuwait in 1990. Thus, the combined number of beads from the Danish 1958-1963 excavations would have amounted to 629 beads.

The lost beads were registered under Kuwait National Museum numbers KM 374 (n=53), KM 375 (n=40) and KM 376 (n=21). The National Museum of Kuwait kindly provided photographic documentation of these beads and therefore it was possible to determine that they resemble the rest of the bead assemblage with respect to forms and materials. Apart from their being attributed to Tell F3 or Tell F6, there is no information on their archaeological contexts.

The excavations were continued at Tell F3 and Tell F6 in 1973-74 by the Johns Hopkins University whereby fifteen further beads were found (Howard-Carter 1984).

In 1984-85, French excavations uncovered a temple in Tell F6 east of the "Palace"; this produced further fifty-one beads (Calvet and Pic 1986 p. 66-72).

In 2008-2012 the Kuwaiti-Danish Archaeological Mission to Failaka resumed excavations at Tell F6, and during these excavations 200 beads were recovered and subsequently published (Andersson 2016).

Kuwaiti-Danish excavations continued at Tell F3 in 2012-2017 bringing a further twenty-seven beads to light (Andersson 2021). The total number of beads found at Tell F3 and Tell F6 from 1958 to 2017 thus amounts to 922.

The available 515 beads found during the 1958-1963 excavations are the object of the present work and are referred to as the assemblage in the following pages. They are kept in the Kuwait National Museum, and they were studied by the author during several stays on Failaka (2009-2019) as a member of the Kuwaiti-Danish Archaeological Mission to Failaka directed by Dr Flemming Højlund. Final preparation of the manuscript was made in 2022.

This study uses two parallel systems for numbering the beads, the Danish field number and the Kuwait National Museum number. The field number consists of a tell prefix, F3 or F6, combined with letters or a number (e.g. F3.ei and F6.60) (cf. Højlund 1987 p. 8-9). A field number can be assigned to a single bead or a group of beads, up to fifteen, from the same context. Any information attached to the field number (trench, find level and horizontal coordinates, along with a description of form and material) was registered in paper-based documentation ("white registration cards"), stored at Moesgaard Museum. The registration system used by the Kuwait National Museum consists of the prefix KM, followed by a number (e.g. KM1681), which is usually assigned to a group of finds, from one to sixty-one beads. Each KM number has been registered in paper-based documentation ("blue registration cards") and photographed by the staff of the Kuwait National Museum, which has provided invaluable information.

The present study of the beads deriving from the 1958-1963 excavations consists of a typology (Chapter 2), a classification of materials (Chapter 3) and an analysis of the dating and distribution of the beads (Chapter 4). Manufacturing techniques including perforation and use-wear will also be considered (Chapter 5). In a final discussion, the bead corpus from Tell F3 and Tell F6 will be compared with similar material from contemporary sites on Failaka and in Bahrain, along with some thoughts on connections and trade relations that may be inferred from the materials and forms in the bead assemblage (Chapter 6). Relevant information on each bead as well as photos and drawings are listed in a catalogue (Chapter 7).

All drawings and photos are reproduced in full size (1:1).

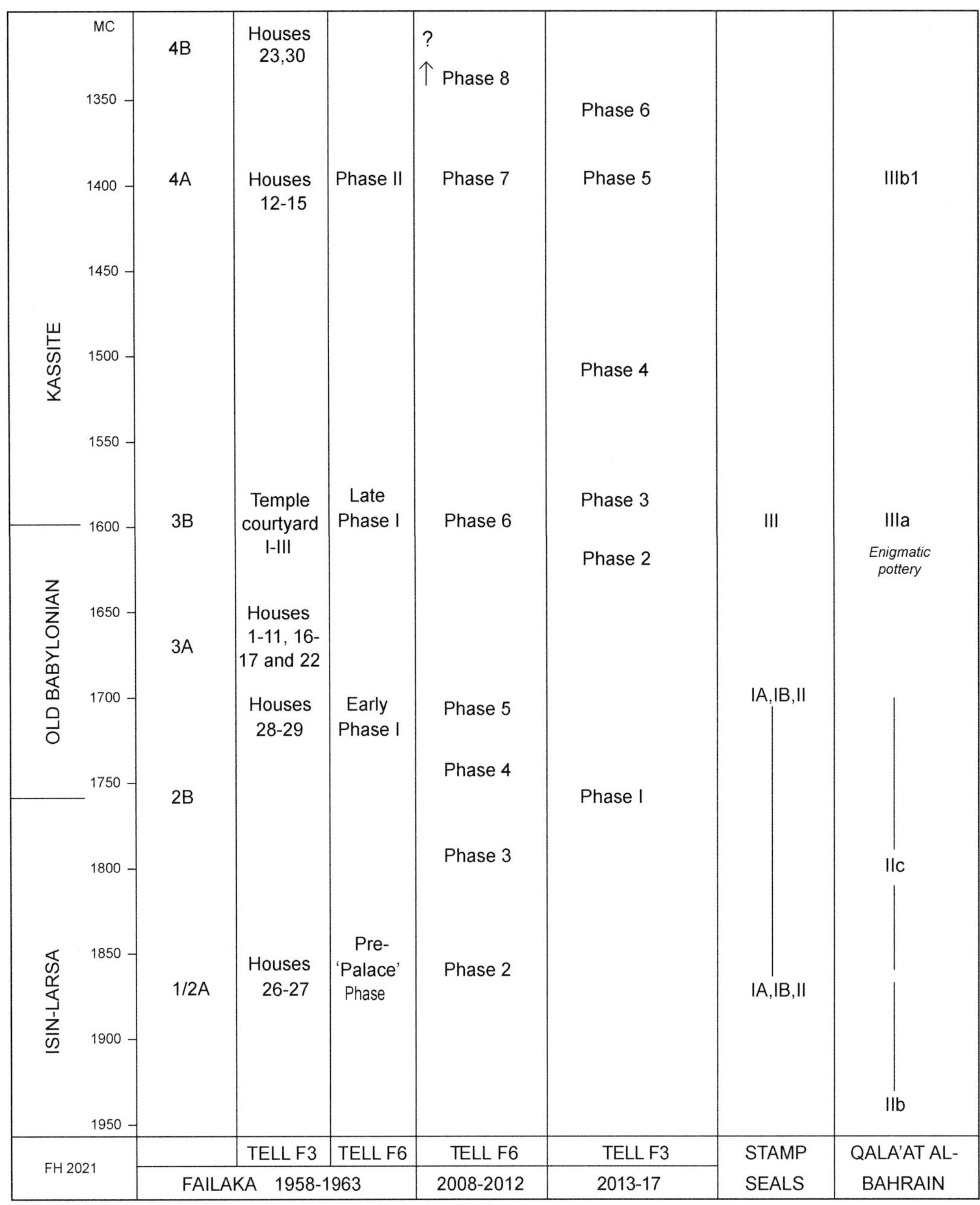

Fig. 2. Chronological chart for the 2nd millennium BC in the upper Arabian Gulf (Højlund & Hilton 2021 fig. 50).

Acknowledgements

We must thank the National Council for Culture, Arts and Letters, who has generously supported the Kuwaiti-Danish Archaeological Mission to Failaka through its Secretary Generals, Mr Ali Hussain Al-Youha and his successor Mr Kamel Al-Abdul Jalil. Warm thanks are also extended to the staff at the National Museum of Kuwait, who has been helpful and attentive throughout the process of this study, especially Directors of Antiquities and Museums Mr Shehab A.H. Shehab and Dr Sultan Al-Dowaish, Director of Excavations Dr Hamad Al-Mutairi and Superintendent Mr Talal Al-Saei.

The author is indebted to Dr Flemming Højlund and Dr Steffen Terp Laursen from Moesgaard Museum and to the entire team of the Kuwaiti-Danish Archaeological Mission to Failaka, especially Ms Anna Hilton and Ms Aiysha Abu-Laban. I would also like to thank Mr Jonathan Rose Andersen, Conservator Ms Helle Strehle and Ms Hélène David-Cuny for their kind help throughout this study. Thanks are also due to an anonymous reviewer for insightful comments.

The publication of this volume was supported by the Carlsberg Foundation.

2. Typology

The assemblage of beads found during the 1958-1963 excavations in Tell F3 and Tell F6 being treated in this volume has been classified with the aid of Horace C. Beck's seminal study *Classification and Nomenclature of Beads and Pendants* (Beck 1928). Beck's study provides a system of classification and a fixed terminology for the description of beads and pendants that is flexible and accounts for the main part of the form variations within the assemblage (figs. 3, 4 and 5). Other typological systems, like the one used by Leonard Woolley for the Ur bead assemblage, would not cover the form variations in the Failaka assemblage (Woolley 1934 p. 366-375). Using Beck's classification system, the typology is based on a form combination of profiles and cross sections (i.e. the longitudinal and transverse sections in Beck's terminology). Other parameters such as decoration are here regarded as a secondary feature.

This has resulted in a bead typology consisting of nineteen form types and an additional group (varia) containing forms that are rare or, for one reason or another, do not easily fit within Beck's system. Each of the nineteen form types based on geometric shape has been further subdivided following Beck's length classification, which considers the relative proportions between length and diameter of the beads. This subdivides the form types into four groups of disc, short, standard and long beads. A *disc bead* is a regular bead[1] in which the length is less than one-third the diameter. A *short bead* is a regular bead in which the length is more than one-third the diameter, and less than nine-tenths the diameter. A *standard bead* is a regular bead in which the diameter is approximately the same as the length, that is, a bead which has a length of more than nine-tenths and less than one and one-tenth times the diameter. A *long bead* is a regular bead in which the length is more than one and one-tenth times the diameter (Beck 1928 p. 4).

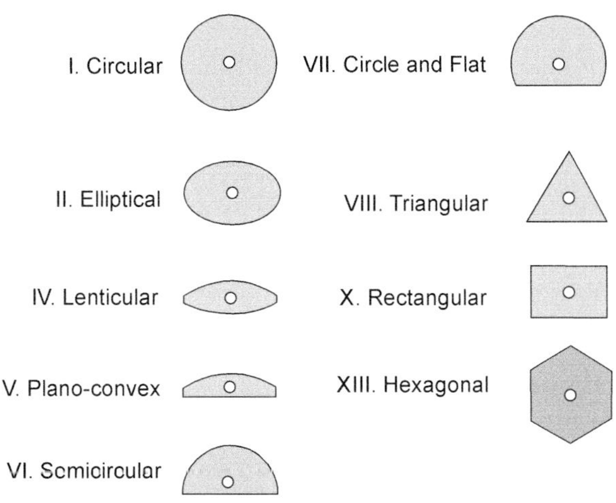

Fig. 3. Schematic representation of cross sections, Tell F3 and Tell F6.

Below, the twenty bead form types found in the 1958-1963 assemblage are presented. When relevant, each section will offer an overview of materials, size distribution and a paragraph highlighting beads of special interest (such as beads with notable decoration or made of rare materials).

In general, most form types represented in the assemblage are generic forms, like spheres (n=137, 26.6%), barrels (n=136, 26.4%), different forms of bicones (i.e. regular bicones, n=5, 1%; convex bicones, n=1, 0.2%; truncated bicones n=58, 11.2%; truncated convex bicones n=15, 2.9%) and cylinders with circular cross section (n=40, 7.7%). These forms make up 76% (n=392) of the assemblage. The rest of the beads consist of varia or of forms with elliptical, lenticular, plano-convex, semi-circular, circle and flat, triangular, rectangular, and hexagonal cross section, which occur in much smaller numbers (fig. 6).

Spheres with circular cross section (figs. 7-9, 76-211)

Spheres with circular cross section (fig. 7) make up 26.6% of the assemblage (n=137) (fig. 6).[2] Of these, 6.4% come from Tell F3 (n=33), while 20.3% (n=104) come from Tell F6. Within this category, oblates (I.B.1.a.) are by far the largest group with 123 beads (89.8%), while only a small part (n=14, 10.2%) can be classified as standard circular spheres (I.C.1.a.) (fig. 8).

Materials. Combining oblates and standard circular spheres (I.B.1.a. and I.C.1.a.) from Tell F3 and Tell F6, 19.7% (n=27) are made of artificial materials (glass, faience and paste), 78.8% (n=108) are made of mineral materials (agate, carnelian, jasper, lapis lazuli, rock crystal and turquoise) and 1.5% (n=2) are made of organic materials, that is, pearl (fig. 9). Carnelian is the most common of the mineral materials (n=88, 64.2%).

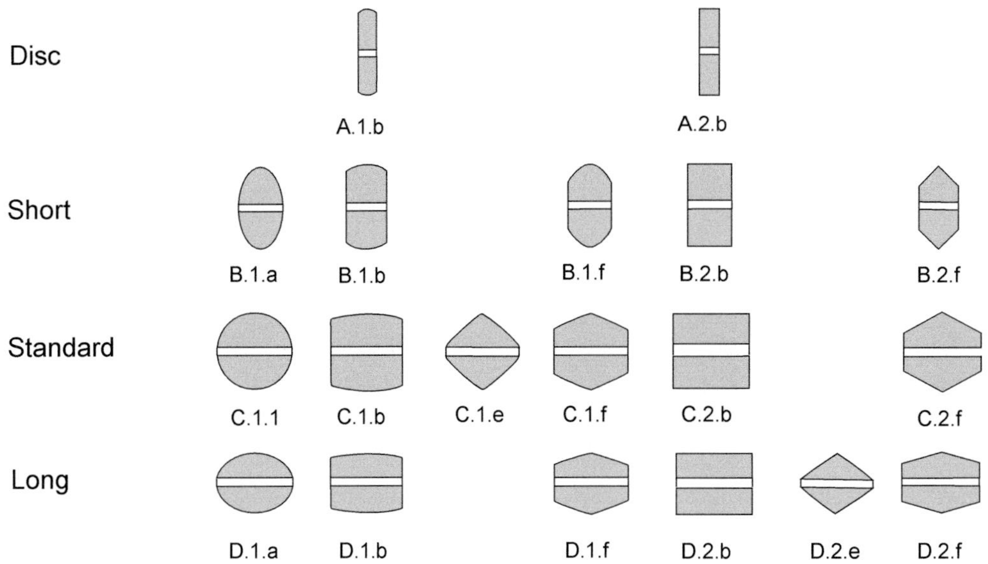

Fig. 4. Schematic representation of profiles, Tell F3 and Tell F6.

Cross section / Profile[1]	I. Circular	II. Elliptical	IV. Lenticular	V. Plano-convex	VI. Semicircular	VII. Circle and flat	VIII. Triangular	X. Rectangular	XIII. Hexagonal	Total
1.a. Spherical	137	3	2	-	-	-	-	-	-	142
1.b. Barrel	136	4	23	3	17	29	5	4	6	227
1.e. Convex bicone	1	-	-	-	-	-	-	-	-	1
1.f. Truncated convex bicone	15	-	4	-	-	-	-	-	-	19
2.b. Cylinder	40	-	5	-	-	-	-	-	-	45
2.e. Bicone	5	-	-	-	-	-	-	-	-	5
2.f. Truncated bicone	59	-	-	-	-	-	-	-	-	59
Total	**393**	**7**	**34**	**3**	**17**	**29**	**5**	**4**	**6**	**498**
%	76.3	1.2	6.6	0.6	3.3	5.7	1	0.8	1.2	96.7
1. Not including the group of Varia (17 beads)										

Fig. 5. Frequency of beads by cross sections and profiles, Tell F3 and Tell F6.

Beck Typology	Tell F3	%	Tell F6	%	Total	%
Spheres with circular cross sections (I.B.1.a. and I.C.1.a.)	**33**	6.4	**104**	20.3	**137**	26.6
Spheres with elliptical cross sections (II.B.1.a. and II.C.1.a.)	-	-	**3**	0.6	**3**	0.6
Spheres with lenticular cross section (IV.B.1.a.)	-	-	**2**	0.4	**2**	0.4
Barrels with circular cross sections (I.A.1.b., I.B.1.b., I.C.1.b. and I.D.1.b.)	**38**	7.3	**98**	19.1	**136**	26.4
Barrels with elliptical cross sections (II.D.1.b.)	**2**	0.4	**2**	0.4	**4**	0.8
Barrels with lenticular cross sections (IV.B.1.b., IV.C.1.b. and IV.D.1.b.)	**8**	1.5	**15**	2.9	**23**	4.4
Barrels with plano-convex cross sections (V.B.1.b. and V.C.1.b.)	-	-	**3**	0.6	**3**	0.6
Barrels with semi-circular cross section (VI.C.1.b. and VI.D.1.b.)	**10**	2	**7**	1.3	**17**	3.3
Barrels with circle and flat cross sections (VII.C.1.b. and VII.D.1.b.)	**14**	2.4	**15**	2.9	**29**	5.6
Barrels with triangular cross sections (VIII.D.1.b.)	**4**	0.8	**1**	0.2	**5**	1.0
Barrels with rectangular cross sections (X.C.1.b. and X.D.1.b.)	**2**	0.4	**2**	0.4	**4**	0.8
Barrels with hexagonal cross sections (XIII.D.1.b.)	**4**	0.8	**2**	0.4	**6**	1.2
Convex bicones with circular cross sections (I.C.1.e.)	**1**	0.2	**-**	-	**1**	0.2
Truncated convex bicones with circular cross sections (I.B.1.f.)	**9**	1.7	**6**	1.2	**15**	2.9
Truncated convex bicones with lenticular cross sections (IV.C.1.f. and IV.D.1.f.)	**1**	0.2	**3**	0.6	**4**	0.8
Bicones with circular cross sections (I.D.2.e.)	**4**	0.8	**1**	0.2	**5**	1.0
Truncated bicones with circular cross sections (I.B.2.f., I.C.2.f. and I.D.2.f.)	**11**	2.1	**48**	9.4	**59**	11.4
Cylinders with circular cross sections (I.B.2.b., I.C.2.b., I.D.2.b. and unidentified cylinder fragments)	**14**	2.7	**26**	5.0	**40**	7.7
Cylinders with lenticular cross sections (IV.D.2.b.)	**2**	0.4	**3**	0.6	**5**	1.0
Varia.	**10**	1.9	**7**	1.4	**17**	3.3
Total	**167**	**32**	**348**	**68**	**515**	**100**

Fig. 6. Distribution of beads by type, Tell F3 and Tell F6.

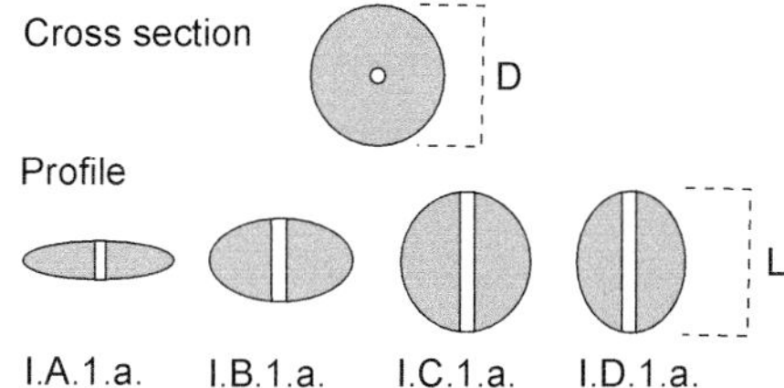

Fig. 7. Schematic representation of disc to long spheres with circular cross section.

Form Type	F3	F6	Total	%
Oblate disc/Circular (I.A.1.a.)	-	-	-	-
Oblate/Circular (I.B.1.a.)	31	92	**123**	89.8
Circular/Circular (I.C.1.a.)	2	12	**14**	10.2
Ellipsoid/Circular (I.D.1.a.)	-	-	-	-
Total	**33**	**104**	**137**	100
%	24.5	75.5	100	-

Fig. 8. Distribution of spheres with circular cross section, Tell F3 and Tell F6.

Form Type	Material	F3	F6	Total	%
I.B.1.a.	**Artificial**	**2**	**22**	**24**	**17.5**
	Faience	1	9	10	7.3
	Glass	1	10	11	8.0
	Paste	0	3	3	2.2
	Mineral	**29**	**68**	**97**	**70.8**
	Agate	3	2	5	3.6
	Carnelian	18	60	78	56.9
	Jasper	5	2	7	5.1
	Lapis lazuli	2	0	2	1.5
	Rock crystal	1	2	3	2.2
	Turquoise	0	2	2	1.5
	Organic	**0**	**2**	**2**	**1.5**
	Pearl	0	2	2	1.5
I.C.1.a.	**Artificial**	**0**	**3**	**3**	**2.2**
	Glass	0	3	3	2.2
	Mineral	**2**	**9**	**11**	**8.0**
	Carnelian	1	8	9	6.5
	Jasper	1	1	2	1.5
Total	-	**33**	**104**	**137**	**100**
%	-	24.5	75.5	100	-

Fig. 9. Distribution of spheres with circular cross section by tell and material.

Jasper is significantly less frequent (n=9, 6.6%) and lapis lazuli, rock crystal and turquoise appear only in very low numbers (n=2, n=1 and n=2, respectively).

Size. The size distribution of oblates and standard spheres from the assemblage is based on the lengths and diameters of 128 beads.[3] The size range within this bead group is significant, spanning from lengths of 2.70 to 18.90 mm and diameters between 3.50 and 21.80 mm.[4]

The two largest spheres come from Tell F3 and are made of jasper and lapis lazuli (figs. 102 and 105), which are among the rarer materials in the assemblage. Generally, the larger spheres (with diameters of 15-21.80 mm, n=12) are made of less common mineral materials (i.e. agate, jasper, rock crystal and turquoise, figs. 86, 99, 162 and 140), while only one of the larger spheres is made of carnelian (fig. 159). Artificial materials, such as glass and faience, are also represented among the larger spheres (figs. 97, 104, 126, 163 and 204). In comparison, the midsized spheres (diameters between 10-14.20 mm, n=32) are also made of a variety of mineral (agate, carnelian, jasper and rock crystal, n=18) and artificial materials (faience, glass and paste, n=14). Smaller spheres (diameters between 3.5-9.90 mm, n=93) are made predominantly of carnelian (n=80), along with much smaller numbers of other mineral (agate, lapis lazuli and turquoise, n=3), artificial (faience, glass and paste, n=8) and organic materials (natural pearls, n=2).

Beads of special interest. Fig. 106 stands out among the spheres as a standard, circular carnelian bead with five incised, vertical lines. Incised decoration is very rare in the assemblage.[5] Two similar faience beads found in trench D2 (figs. 124 and 135), are badly preserved, but both show remains of thin red vertical stripes on a yellow core. An oblate, faience bead with circular cross section found at Tell F6 also has a characteristic decoration preserved on its surface (fig. 194). The outer layer of the bead appears white with yellow spots distributed evenly across the surface. The exposed core is whitish beige and similar to a quantity of badly preserved faience beads (cf. chapter 3 p. 33). Fig. 126 is a large, fragmented glass bead decorated with a single white wavy line, the only one of its kind found in the assemblage. Two pierced pearls (figs. 191 and 192) are noteworthy. As a material used for beads, pearls are rare in the assemblage and at contemporary sites (cf. chapter 3 p. 32).

Spheres with elliptical cross section (figs. 10-12, 212-214)

Only three beads have been identified as circular beads with elliptical cross section (figs. 10, 212, 213 and 214), making up 0.6% of the assemblage (fig. 6). They all come from Tell F6 (fig. 11).

Materials. The spheres with elliptical cross section are all made of glass (fig. 12). While the glass of two of the beads (figs. 212 and 213) is quite badly preserved, the last bead (fig. 214) has retained hints of its original dark blue and white colouring.

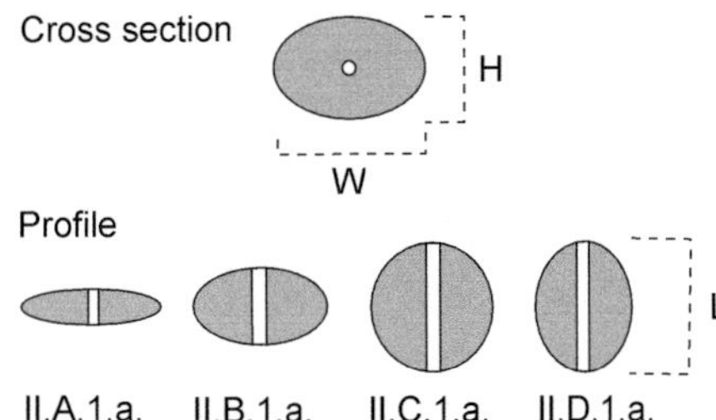

Fig. 10. Schematic representations of disc to long spheres with elliptical cross section.

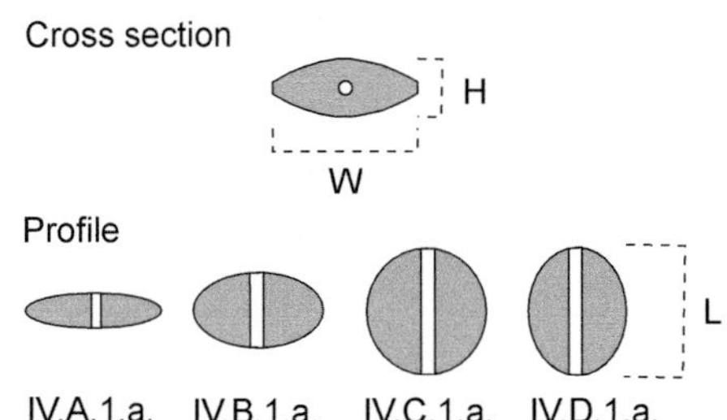

Fig. 13. Schematic representation of disc to long spheres with lenticular cross section.

Form Type	F3	F6	Total	%
Oblate disc/Elliptical (II.A.1.a)	-	-	-	-
Oblate/Elliptical (II.B.1.a)	-	2	2	66.6
Circular/Elliptical (II.C.1.a)	-	1	1	33.3
Ellipsoid/Elliptical (II.D.1.a)	-	-	-	-
Total	-	-	**3**	**100**
%	-	100	100	-

Fig. 11. Distribution of spheres with elliptical cross section, Tell F3 and Tell F6.

Form Type	F3	F6	Total	%
Oblate disc/ Lenticular (IV.A.1.a)	-	-	-	-
Oblate/Lenticular (IV.B.1.a)	-	2	2	100
Circular/Lenticular (IV.C.1.a)	-	-	-	-
Ellipsoid/Lenticular (IV.D.1.a)	-	-	-	-
Total	-	**2**	**2**	**100**
%	-	100	100	-

Fig. 14. Distribution of spheres with lenticular cross section, Tell F3 and Tell F6.

Form Type	Material	F3	F6	Total	%
II.B.1.a.	**Artificial**	**0**	**2**	**2**	**66.6**
	Glass	0	2	2	66.6
II.C.1.a.	**Artificial**	**0**	**1**	**1**	**33.3**
	Glass	0	1	1	33.3
Total	-	**0**	**100**	**1**	**100**
%	-	0	100	100	-

Fig. 12. Distribution of spheres with elliptical cross section by tell and material.

Form Type	Material	F3	F6	Total	%
IV.B.1.a.	**Artificial**	**0**	**1**	**1**	**50**
	Paste	0	1	1	50
	Mineral	**0**	**1**	**1**	**50**
	Turquoise	0	1	1	50
Total	-	**0**	**2**	**2**	**100**
%	-	0	100	100	-

Fig. 15. Distribution of spheres with lenticular cross section by tell and material.

Size. Of the three beads representing this bead type, two are fragmented. Fig. 214 is extremely large compared to the other two, estimated to have been 31.00 x 31.40 mm (L x W), when intact. The other beads are significantly smaller, with fig. 212 being 8.60 x 10.00 mm (L x D) and fig. 213 being 12.30 x 16.40 mm (L x D).

Beads of special interest. Fig. 214 is a so-called eye-bead. On one surface it is decorated with a white ring around a circle of blue to light brown colour, and it is reminiscent of an eye. Different forms of eye-beads are found in a variety of shapes, sizes and materials (e.g. glass and agate) in the assemblage. Among these are two glass beads (figs. 380 and 382) classified as short and standard barrels with plano-convex cross section and two agate beads classified under varia, that is, figs. 572-573.

Spheres with lenticular cross section (figs. 13-15, 215-216)

Only two beads in the assemblage are identified as spheres with lenticular cross section (figs. 13, 215 and 216), corresponding to 0.4% of the assemblage (fig. 6). They were both recovered from Tell F6 (fig. 14).

Materials. The two spheres with lenticular cross section are made of an artificial material identified as blue paste (fig. 215) and a mineral material (fig. 216) identified as turquoise (fig. 15).

Size. The two spheres with lenticular cross section are of relatively equal size, fig. 216 being only slightly smaller (L 10.50 x W 13.20 mm) than fig. 215 (L 14.30 x W 16.50 mm).

Beads of special interest. Beads of this form are rare in the assemblage and so are the materials they are made of. Combined turquoise and blue paste make up less than 2% of the assemblage (fig. 66). The blue colour of the paste bead (fig. 215) suggests that it might be an imitation of lapis lazuli (cf. chapter 3 p. 34).

Barrels with circular cross section (figs. 16-18, 217-352)

Barrels with a circular cross section (fig. 16) make up 26.6% of the assemblage (n=136) (fig. 6). Of these c. 27.7% (n=38) come from Tell F3 and c. 72% (n=98) from Tell F6. Within this group, long barrels are by far the largest group with 109 beads (I.D.1.b.; 80.1%), while disc barrels (I.A.1.b.; n=3, 2.2%), short barrels (I.B.1.b.; n=8, 5.9%) and standard barrels (I.C.1.b.; n=16, 11.8%) are infrequent (fig. 17).[6]

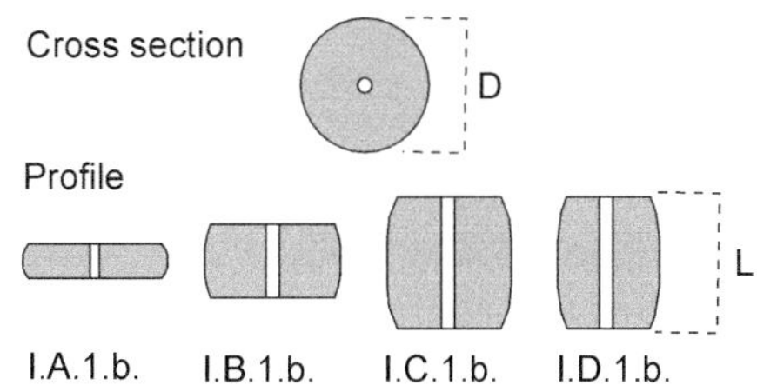

Fig. 16. Schematic representation of barrels with circular cross section.

Form Type	F3	F6	Total	%
Disc Barrel/Circular (I.A.1.b)	2	1	3	2.2
Short Barrel/Circular (I.B.1.b)	2	6	8	5.9
Standard Barrel/ Circular (I.C.1.b)	4	12	16	11.8
Long Barrel/Circular (I.D.1.b)	30	79	109	80.1
Total	**38**	**98**	**136**	**100**
%	28	72	100	-

Fig. 17. Distribution of barrels with circular cross section, Tell F3 and Tell F6.

Materials. Combining disc, short, standard and long barrels from Tell F3 and Tell F6, the vast majority (n=106, 78.1%) are made of mineral materials (fig. 18). A little more than a third of the barrels are made of carnelian (n=52, 38.6%), while agate (n=29, 21%) and jasper (n=18, 13.4%) occur less frequently. Artificial materials (n=27, 19.8%) are represented by glass (n=26, 19.1%) and paste (n=1, 0.7%), while organic materials (shell) constitute only 2.2% (n=3). Generally, there appears to be a greater variety of mineral materials among

Form Type	Material	F3	F6	Total	%
I.A.1.b.	**Organic**	**2**	**1**	**3**	**2.2**
	Shell	2	1	3	2.2
I.B.1.b.	**Mineral**	**2**	**6**	**8**	**5.9**
	Agate	1	0	1	0.7
	Carnelian	0	6	6	4.5
	Jasper	1	0	1	0.7
I.C.1.b.	**Mineral**	**4**	**11**	**15**	**11.1**
	Carnelian	4	11	15	11.1
	Artificial	0	1	1	0.7
	Paste	0	1	1	0.7
I.D.1.b.	**Mineral**	**27**	**56**	**83**	**61.1**
	Agate	10	16	26	19.1
	Calcite	1	1	2	1.4
	Carnelian	8	23	31	23
	Chlorite	0	2	2	1.4
	Hematite	0	1	1	0.7
	Jasper	6	11	17	12.7
	Lapis Lazuli	1	1	2	1.4
	Porphyry	0	1	1	0.7
	Unidentified	1	0	1	0.7
	Artificial	2	24	26	19.1
	Glass	2	24	26	19.1
Total	-	**37**	**99**	**136**	**100**
%	-	27.7	72.3	100	-

Fig. 18. Distribution of barrels with circular cross section by tell and material.

long barrels with circular cross section at Tell F6. In addition to agate, carnelian and jasper, there are lone examples of calcite, chlorite, hematite, and porphyry. A few long barrel beads are made of lapis lazuli (n=2, 1.4%). Moreover, all the glass barrel beads with circular cross section are long beads and the vast majority (n=24) were found at Tell F6. However, this impression might be skewed by the fact that long barrels with circular cross section is by far the largest group within this form type (n=109, 80.1%). The majority of the disc, short and standard barrel beads with circular cross section (n=27) are made of carnelian (n=21), shell (n=3) along with single examples of agate, jasper and paste.

Size. The size distribution of barrel beads with circular cross section is based on 105 beads.[7] There is a substantial range in the size of the beads the length measurements of which range from 3.50 to 31.60 mm, while diameter measurements lie between 3.80 and 29.50 mm.[8]

However, the size of a number of the stone beads from Tell F6 are noteworthy. Fig. 316 is a fragmented calcite bead preserved to a length of 24.90 mm. The estimate of the original length of the bead is 44.90 mm, which would make the bead, in its original form, one of the longest in the assemblage. A long barrel made of hematite (fig. 286) is also noteworthy, due to its size (28.1 mm in length). Fig. 326 is a long barrel made of porphyry with a length of 31.6 mm. Other noteworthy long, stone beads are fig. 314, a jasper bead with a length of 30.2 mm and fig. 315, a semi-drilled bead made of agate with a length of 25.1 mm. From Tell F3, a couple of beads are likewise notable due to their size. Fig. 266 is a long jasper bead of 28.7 mm and fig. 259 is an agate bead of 24.5 mm in length.

All the barrel beads with circular cross section made of glass are classified as long beads (I.D.1.b.) and many are fragmented and in poor condition. However, the preserved sizes of the fragmented glass beads indicate that their original sizes would have been quite long, many between 30 and 40 mm in length (see for instance figs. 296, 302, 305, 320 and 339).

Beads of special interest. The shell barrel discs or so-called shell rings (figs. 217, 218 and 219) may not be beads in the conventional sense, but are likely pieces of personal adornment, that may have been worn as parts of belts (Pulak 2008 p. 327. Frifelt 1991 p. 184).[9] The shell ring cut from a pearl oyster shell (fig. 219) is unique in the assemblage, due to its material, as the other two shell rings are cut from conus shells. Most shell rings found in archaeological contexts in the Gulf and Mesopotamia are made of conus shells.

A blue paste, standard barrel bead (fig. 239) is noteworthy, due to its rare material. Likewise, a long barrel bead made of porphyry (fig. 326), a fragmented long barrel bead made of calcite (fig. 316) and a long barrel made of hematite (fig. 286) are rare materials in the assemblage. Fig. 253, a long barrel made of lapis lazuli and perforated twice, horizontally, is unique. It may have functioned as a spacer in a piece of jewellery composed of multiple strings.

Barrels with elliptical cross section (figs. 19-21, 353-356)

Barrels with elliptical cross section (fig. 19) are represented by a small number of beads (n=4), which make up c. 0.8% of the assemblage (fig. 6); they are distributed evenly between Tell F3 and Tell F6 (fig. 20) and occur only in long form.

Materials. The four beads are made of different mineral materials, including agate, limestone, milky quartz and a mineral material simply classified as quartz (fig. 21).

Size. The four beads occur in quite different sizes, ranging from 9.70 to 26.50 mm in length and 7.50-14.50 mm in diameter.[10]

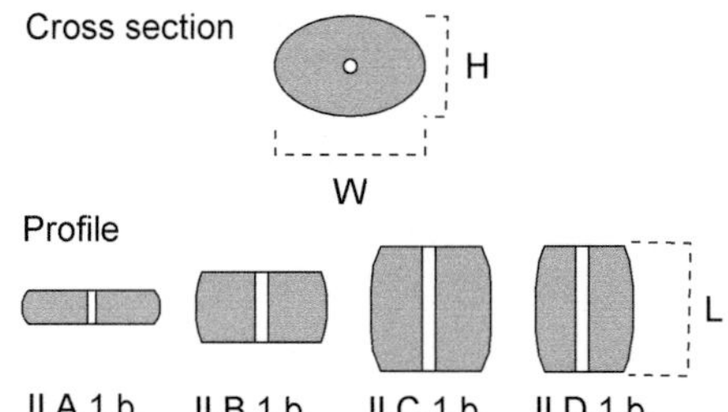

Fig. 19. Schematic representation of disc to long barrels with elliptical cross section.

Form Type	F3	F6	Total	%
Disc Barrel/Elliptical (II.A.1.b)	-	-	-	-
Short Barrel/Elliptical (II.B.1.b)	-	-	-	-
Standard Barrel/ Elliptical (II.C.1.b)	-	-	-	-
Long Barrel/Elliptical (II.D.1.b)	2	2	4	100
Total	**2**	**2**	**4**	**100**
%	50	50	100	-

Fig. 20. Distribution of barrels with elliptical cross section, Tell F3 and Tell F6.

Form Type	Material	F3	F6	Total	%
II.D.1.b.	**Mineral**	**2**	**2**	**4**	**100**
	Agate	0	1	1	25
	Limestone	0	1	1	25
	Milky quartz	1	0	1	25
	Quartz	1	0	1	25
Total	-	**2**	**2**	**4**	**100**
%	-	50	50	100	-

Fig. 21. Distribution of barrels with elliptical cross section by tell and material.

Barrels with lenticular cross section (figs. 22-24, 357-379)

Approximately 4.4% of the bead assemblage (fig. 6) are barrels with lenticular cross section (n=23) (fig. 22).[11] A small number are short and standard beads, but the majority are long barrels. Most were found at Tell F6 (n=15, 65.2%), while a smaller number was recovered from Tell F3 (n=8, 34.8%) (fig. 23).

Materials. All but two are made of mineral materials, primarily agate and carnelian (n=12, 52.1%; n=5, 22.1%, respectively), with singular examples of jasper, lapis lazuli, limestone, porphyry (Tell F6) and quartz (Tell F3) (fig. 24). As noted in the section on barrels with circular cross sections, there appears to be a greater variety of materials in barrels with lenticular cross

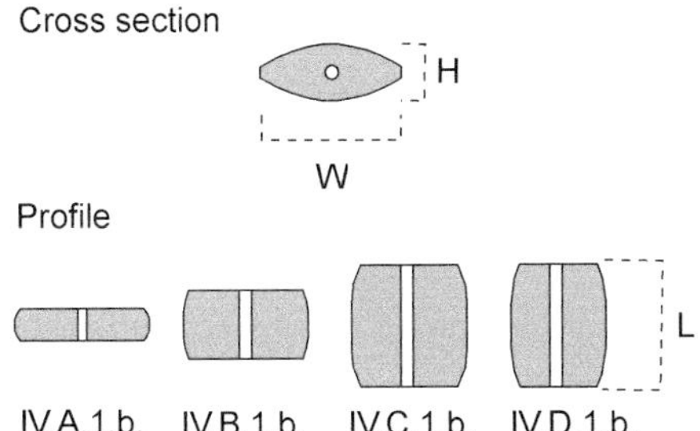

Fig. 22. Schematic representation of disc to long barrels with lenticular cross section.

Form Type	F3	F6	Total	%
Disc Barrel/ Lenticular (IV.A.1.b.)	-	-	-	-
Short Barrel/ Lenticular (IV.B.1.b.)	-	1	1	4.3
Standard Barrel/ Lenticular (IV.C.1.b.)	-	4	4	17.2
Long Barrel/ Lenticular (IV.D.1.b.)	8	10	18	78.5
Total	**8**	**15**	**23**	**100**
%	34.8	65.2	100	-

Fig. 23. Distribution of barrels with lenticular cross section, Tell F3 and Tell F6.

Form Type	Material	F3	F6	Total	%
IV.B.1.b.	**Mineral**	**0**	**1**	**1**	**4.3**
	Agate	0	1	1	4.3
IV.C.1.b.	**Mineral**	**0**	**3**	**3**	**12.9**
	Agate	0	3	3	12.9
	Organic	0	1	1	4.3
	Shell(Unid.)	0	1	1	4.3
IV.D.1.b.	**Mineral**	**8**	**9**	**17**	**74.2**
	Agate	4	4	8	34.9
	Carnelian	3	2	5	22.1
	Jasper	0	1	1	4.3
	Limestone	0	1	1	4.3
	Porhyry	0	1	1	4.3
	Quartz	1	0	1	4.3
	Organic	**0**	**1**	**1**	**4.3**
	Fossilized coral	0	1	1	4.3
Total	-	**8**	**15**	**23**	100
%	-	34.2	65.2	100	-

Fig. 24. Distribution of barrels with lenticular cross section by tell and material.

sections at Tell F6 than at Tell F3. A single bead (Tell F6) is made of a unique material tentatively identified as fossilized coral and classified under organic materials (fig. 370).

Size. The size distribution is based on seventeen beads.[12] Their lengths vary from 5.30 to 39.50 mm, and their widths are between 6.50 and 23.30 mm.[13] Some are notably larger than the rest. The largest example (LxW 39.50x23.50 mm) (fig. 364) and a fragmented bead (fig. 367), which would have been of similar size (LxW est. 38.00x25.00 mm), both come from Tell F3. Fig. 368 is also among the largest barrels with lenticular cross section. Generally, most of the larger beads of this type come from Tell F3 (see also figs. 362, 364 and 365), while fewer come from Tell F6 (figs. 376, 377 and 378). However, the smaller beads of this form type are found mainly at Tell F6.

Beads of special interest. Fig. 363 is a barrel with lenticular cross section with four vertical facets on each side. Even though the facets are not particularly prominent, they have been made deliberately. Facetted beads are rare in the assemblage.

One bead (fig. 370), tentatively identified as fossilized coral, is a unique material in the assemblage. The material looks like grey stone, with white chalky deposits running diagonally through the bead. Fig. 377 is made of another rare material identified as porphyry.

One small agate bead (fig. 357) finds parallels at Ur (in the early part of the Ur III period, c. 2100 BC) in a rich grave (P.G. 1422), where a group of similar beads were excavated (Maxwell-Hyslop 1971 p. 65-68 and pl. 48a-b)[14] and at Susa.[15] The similar beads from Ur and Susa demonstrate standardization in the production of these types of beads, intentionally creating a pattern, where half of the bead is white and the other half is dark brown to black. The same grave at Ur contains a parallel for fig. 364, although the bead from Ur is adorned with gold caps (Maxwell-Hyslop 1971 p. 68 and pl. 48c). Again, the pattern and colour scheme of the natural agate appears to be utilized similarly in the two bead examples, suggesting aesthetic standardization. An additional parallel for the same bead comes from Ur (grave P.G. 1847, Burial R).[16]

Barrels with plano-convex cross section (figs. 25-27, 380-382)

A small number of beads (fig. 25), corresponding to c. 0.6% (n=3) of the assemblage (fig. 6), have been classified as barrels with plano-convex cross section. The beads, occurring in short and standard forms, all come from Tell F6 (fig. 26).

Materials. The beads are all made of artificial materials identified as glass (fig. 27). They are either extremely fragmented, or the material is very badly preserved. One of the beads (fig. 381) shows hints of an original dark blue colour, now almost completely white from deterioration.

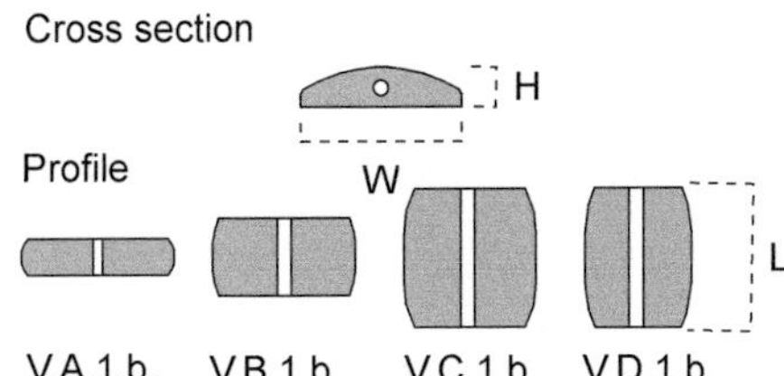

Fig. 25. Schematic representation of disc to long barrels with plano-convex cross section.

Form Type	F3	F6	Total	%
Disc Barrel/plano-convex (V.A.1.b.)	-	-	-	-
Short Barrel/plano-convex (V.B.1.b.)	-	1	1	33.3
Standard Barrel/ plano-convex I (V.C.1.b.)	-	2	2	66.6
Long Barrel/plano-convex (V.D.1.b.)	-	-	-	-
Total	**0**	**3**	**3**	**100**
%	0	100	100	-

Fig. 26. Distribution of barrels with plano-convex cross section, Tell F3 and Tell F6.

Form Type	Material	F3	F6	Total	%
V.B.1.b.	**Artificial**	**0**	**1**	**1**	**33.3**
	Glass	0	1	1	33.3
V.C.1.b.	**Artificial**	**0**	**2**	**2**	**66.6**
	Glass	0	2	2	66.6
Total	-	**0**	**3**	**3**	**100**
%	-	0	100	100	-

Fig. 27. Distribution of barrels with plano-convex cross section by tell and material.

Size. The three beads are all of equal length (20.00 mm) and vary only slightly in their widths (23.00-26.00 mm).[17]

Beads of special interest. The beads (figs. 380 and 382) are "eye-beads" (cf. p. 25) decorated on the convex surface with a white ring around a dark circle, but the glass is so badly preserved that the original colour cannot be determined.

Barrels with semi-circular cross section (figs. 28-30, 383-399)

Only a small number of barrels with semi-circular cross section (fig. 28) were found in the assemblage (n=17, 3.3%) (fig. 6). The beads mostly occur in long form, but one is a standard bead. They are relatively equally divided between Tell F3 (n=10, 58.8%) and Tell F6 (n=7, 41.2%) (fig. 29).

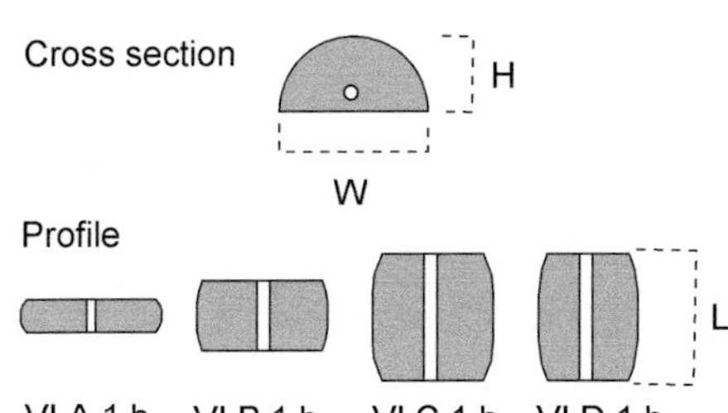

Fig. 28. Schematic representation of disc to long barrels with semi-circular cross section.

Form Type	F3	F6	Total	%
Disc Barrel/semi-circular (VI.A.1.b.)	-	-	-	-
Short Barrel/semi-circular (VI.B.1.b.)	-	-	-	-
Standard Barrel/ semi-circular (VI.C.1.b.)	-	1	1	5.9
Long Barrel/semi-circular (VI.D.1.b.)	10	6	16	94.1
Total	**10**	**7**	**17**	**100**
%	58.8	41.2	100	-

Fig. 29. Distribution of barrels with semi-circular cross section, Tell F3 and Tell F6.

Form Type	Material	F3	F6	Total	%
VI.C.1.b.	**Mineral**	**0**	**1**	**1**	**5.9**
	Jasper	0	1	1	5.9
VI.D.1.b.	**Mineral**	**10**	**6**	**16**	**94.1**
	Agate	2	0	2	11.7
	Jasper	0	3	3	17.7
	Limestone	2	0	2	11.7
	Milky quartz	4	1	5	29.5
	Rose quartz	1	0	1	5.9
	Quartz	0	1	1	5.9
	Unidentified stone	1	1	2	11.7
Total	-	**10**	**7**	**17**	**100**
%	-	58.8	41.2	100	-

Fig. 30. Distribution of barrels with semi-circular cross section by tell and material.

Materials. All barrels with semi-circular cross section are made of mineral materials, most are made of milky quartz (n=5, 29.5%), followed by jasper (n=4, 23.6%) and agate (n=2, 11.7%) (fig. 30). The rest of the barrels with semi-circular cross section consist of single examples of rose quartz and quartz, two beads made of lime-stone and two beads made of different unidentified stone types.

Size. The size distribution of this bead type is based on sixteen beads.[18] Their lengths are between 18.60 and 34.00 mm, while their widths are between 13.60 and 21.10 mm.[19] Again, the larger beads of this type come from Tell F3, while the smaller examples were found at Tell F6. One bead from Tell F3 is significantly larger than the others (fig. 391).

Barrels with circle and flat cross section (figs. 31-33, 400-428)

Barrels with circle and flat cross section (fig. 31) make up 5.6% (n=29) of the assemblage (fig. 6). All, except one standard barrel bead, are long barrels; they are distributed equally between Tell F3 (n=14) and Tell F6 (n=15) (fig. 32).

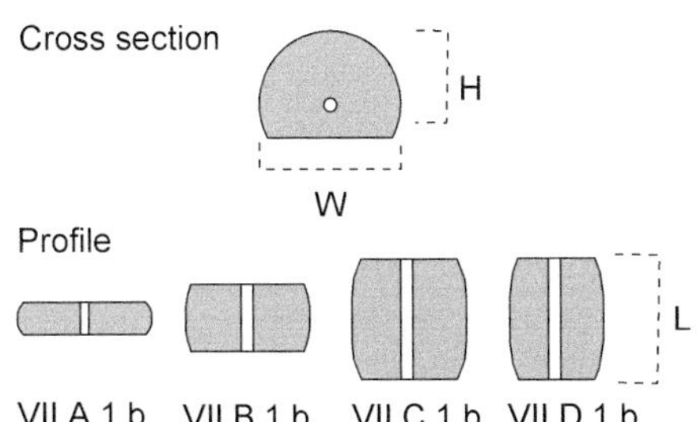

Fig. 31. Schematic representation of disc to long barrels with circle and flat cross section.

Form Type	F3	F6	Total	%
Disc Barrel/circle and flat (VII.A.1.b)	-	-	-	-
Short Barrel/circle and flat (VII.B.1.b)	-	-	-	-
Standard Barrel/ circle and flat (VII.C.1.b)	0	1	1	3.4
Long Barrel/circle and flat (VII.D.1.b)	14	14	28	96.6
Total	**14**	**15**	**29**	**100**
%	48.3	51.7	100	-

Fig. 32. Distribution of barrels with circle and flat cross section, Tell F3 and Tell F6.

Form Type	Material	F3	F6	Total	%
VII.C.1.b.	**Mineral**	**0**	**1**	**1**	**3.4**
	Jasper	0	1	1	3.4
VII.D.1.b.	**Artificial**	**1**	**0**	**1**	**3.4**
	Faience	1	0	1	3.4
	Mineral	**13**	**14**	**27**	**93.2**
	Agate	6	3	9	31.1
	Chlorite	1	0	1	3.4
	Jasper	3	3	6	20.7
	Lapis Lazuli	0	1	1	3.4
	Limestone	3	4	7	24.2
	Milky quartz	0	2	2	7
	Unidentified stone	0	1	1	3.4
Total	-	**14**	**15**	**29**	**100**
%	-	48.3	51.7	100	-

Fig. 33. Distribution of barrels with circle and flat cross section by tell and material.

Materials. Most are made of mineral materials (n=27, 96.6%) and only one from artificial material, that is faience (3.4%) (fig. 33). Agate, jasper and limestone are highly represented (n=9, 31.1%, n=7, 27.6% and n=7, 27.6%, respectively), while milky quartz is represented by only two beads (7%). A single bead of chlorite comes from Tell F3, while a single bead of lapis lazuli and a bead made of an unidentified stone material come from Tell F6.

Size. The size distribution is based on twenty-eight beads.[20] Their lengths are between 7.90 and 36.70 mm, while their widths vary from 8.70 to 22.50 mm.[21]

Barrels with triangular cross section (figs. 34-36, 429-433)

Five beads are classified as barrels with triangular cross section (fig. 34). They correspond to 1% of the assemblage (fig. 6) and are all long form variants of this bead type. Four (80%) come from Tell F3, while one comes from Tell F6 (20%) (fig. 35).

Materials. Each of these beads is made of different mineral materials, most of which are relatively common in the assemblage (i.e. agate, jasper, milky quartz and quartz). One is made of an unidentified stone material (fig. 36).

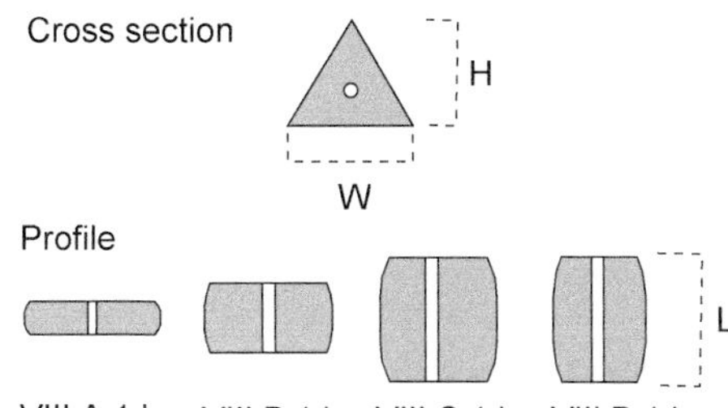

Fig. 34. Schematic representation of disc to long barrels with triangular cross section.

Form Type	F3	F6	Total	%
Disc Barrel/triangular (VIII.A.1.b)	-	-	-	-
Short Barrel/ triangular (VIII.B.1.b)	-	-	-	-
Standard Barrel/ triangular (VIII.C.1.b)	-	-	-	-
Long Barrel/ triangular (VIII.D.1.b)	4	1	5	5
Total	**4**	**1**	**5**	**100**
%	80	20	100	-

Fig. 35. Distribution of barrels with triangular cross section, Tell F3 and Tell F6.

Form Type	Material	F3	F6	Total	%
VIII.D.1.b.	Mineral	4	1	5	100
	Agate	1	0	1	20
	Jasper	1	0	1	20
	Milky quartz	1	0	1	20
	Quartz	1	0	1	20
	Unidentified stone	0	1	1	20
Total	-	**4**	**1**	**5**	**100**
%	-	80	20	100	-

Fig. 36. Distribution of barrels with triangular cross section by tell and material.

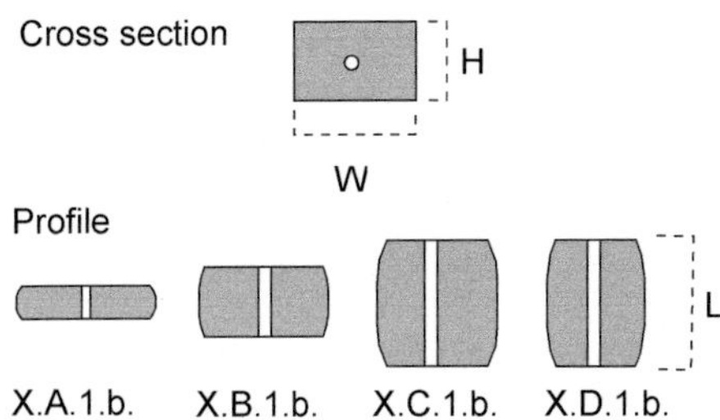

Fig. 37. Schematic representation of disc to long barrels with rectangular cross section.

Size. The size ranges between 15.50 and 25.00 mm in length and 9.50 and 16.50 mm in width.[22]

Barrels with rectangular cross section (figs. 37-39, 434-437)

A few beads (n=4, 0.8%) of the assemblage (fig. 6) are classified as barrels with rectangular cross section (fig. 37). One is a standard bead, while three are long barrels with rectangular cross section. They are evenly distributed between Tell F3 (n=2, 50%) and Tell F6 (n=2, 50%) (fig. 38).

Form Type	F3	F6	Total	%
Disc Barrel/rectangular (X.A.1.b)	-	-	-	-
Short Barrel/ rectangular (X.B.1.b)	-	-	-	-
Standard Barrel/ rectangular (X.C.1.b)	-	1	1	25
Long Barrel/rectangular (X.D.1.b)	2	1	3	75
Total	**2**	**2**	**4**	**100**
%	50	50	100	-

Fig. 38. Distribution of barrels with rectangular cross section, Tell F3 and Tell F6.

Materials. All are made of mineral materials, two from agate (n=2, 50%), while chrysoprase, that is, green chalcedony (25%) and sandstone (25%) are present in single examples (fig. 39).

Size. The three complete beads have lengths between 17.00 and 22.50 mm.[23] Their widths are between 10.00 and 17.60 mm.[24]

Form Type	Material	F3	F6	Total	%
X.C.1.b.	**Mineral**	**0**	**1**	**1**	**25**
	Agate	0	1	1	25
X.D.1.b.	**Mineral**	**2**	**1**	**3**	**75**
	Agate	0	1	1	25
	Calcite	1	0	1	25
	Chrysoprase	1	0	1	25
Total	-	**2**	**2**	**4**	**100**
%	-	50	50	100	-

Fig. 39. Distribution of barrels with rectangular cross section by tells and materials.

Barrels with hexagonal cross section (figs. 40-42, 438-443)

Only a few beads of the assemblage (n=6, 1.2%), all long beads, are classified as barrels with hexagonal cross section (figs. 6 and 40). Four were found at Tell F3 (66.6%), while two were recovered from Tell F6 (33.3%) (fig. 41). This form type may be divided into two subgroups, as the four carnelian beads (figs. 440-443) are all of the same distinct type, while the last two beads (figs. 438-439) represent different forms.

Materials. All are made of mineral materials, primarily carnelian (n=4, 60%), with single occurrences of calcite and chlorite (fig. 42).

Size. Combining the measurements of the two complete, similar carnelian beads (figs. 440 and 443) and the size estimate of the fragmentary bead of the same type (fig. 442), these three beads appear to be of similar size with lengths between 14.80 and 21.00 mm and widths between 12.80 and 13.40 mm. The last bead included in this small group of similar carnelian beads fig. 441, although very fragmentary, is significantly larger than the rest with an estimated original size of 36.90 x 19.80 mm (L x W). The last two beads (figs. 438-439) are of equal length, but their widths are smaller (i.e. 9.00 mm).

Beads of special interest. Fig. 441 stands out from the rest due to its large size and decorative incised lines. Not only is incised decoration very rare in the bead assemblage of Failaka, but the quality and precision of these incisions differ from the other examples, which are rougher and appear to have been made less skilfully (cf. figs. 106 and 505 and chapter 5 p. 42-43). The calcite

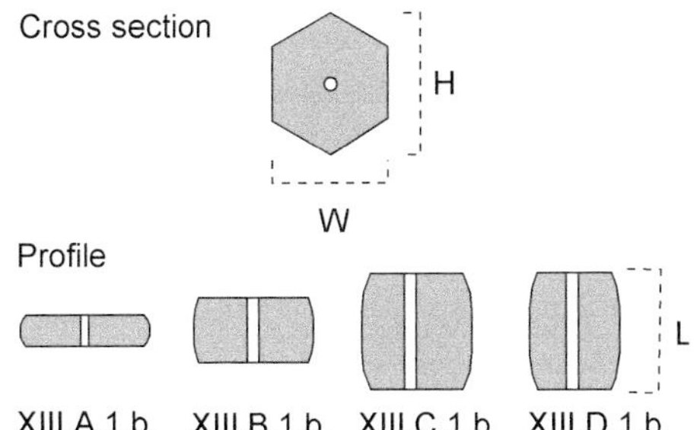

Fig. 40. Schematic representation of disc to long barrels with hexagonal cross section.

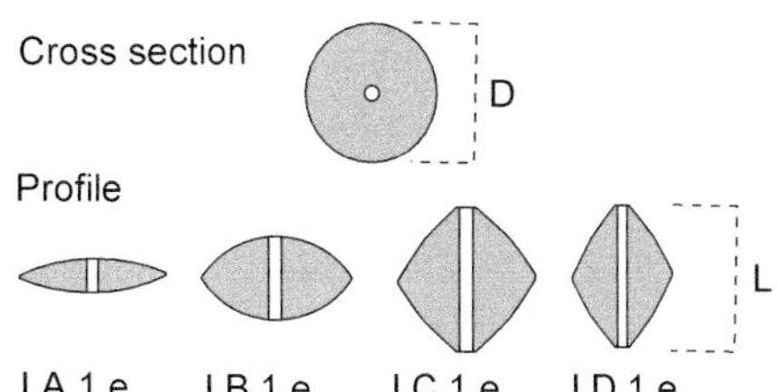

Fig. 43. Schematic representation of disc to long convex bicones with circular cross section.

Form Type	F3	F6	Total	%
Disc Barrel/hexagonal (XIII.A.1.b.)	-	-	-	-
Short Barrel/hexagonal (XIII.B.1.b.)	-	-	-	-
Standard Barrel/ hexagonal (XIII.C.1.b.)	-	-	-	-
Long Barrel/hexagonal (XIII.D.1.b.)	4	2	6	100
Total	**4**	**2**	**6**	**100**
%	66.6	33.3	100	-

Fig. 41. Distribution of barrels with hexagonal cross section, Tell F3 and Tell F6.

Form Type	F3	F6	Total	%
Convex bicone disc/ Circular (I.A.1.e)	-	-	-	-
Short convex bicone/ Circular (I.B.1.e)	-	-	-	-
Standard convex bicone /Circular (I.C.1.e)	1	-	1	100
Long convex bicone / Circular (I.D.1.e)	-	-	-	-
Total	**1**	-	**1**	**100**
%	100	-	100	-

Fig. 44. Distribution of convex bicones with circular cross section, Tell F3 and Tell F6.

Form Type	Material	F3	F6	Total	%
XIII.D.1.b.	**Mineral**	**4**	**2**	**6**	**100**
	Calcite	1	0	1	20
	Carnelian	2	2	4	60
	Chlorite	1	0	1	20
Total	-	**4**	**2**	**6**	**100**
%	-	66.6	33.3	100	-

Fig. 42. Distribution of barrels with hexagonal cross section by tell and material.

Form Type	Material	F3	F6	Total	%
I.C.1.e.	**Mineral**	**1**	**0**	**1**	**100**
	Carnelian	1	0	1	100
Total	-	**1**	**0**	**1**	**100**
%	-	100	0	100	-

Fig. 45. Distribution of convex bicones with circular cross section by tell and material.

and chlorite beads (figs. 438-439) do not appear to be finished beads (cf. chapter 5 p. 41), as one is a blank and the other appears only rudimentarily polished. It is likely, that their hexagonal cross section was not intended for the final bead but rather that they were meant to be further shaped and polished into barrels with circular cross section.

Convex bicones with circular cross section (figs. 43-45, 444)

Only one bead belongs to this type (figs. 43-44 and 444), accounting for 0.2% of the assemblage (fig. 6). It was found at Tell F3.

Material. This bead is made of carnelian (fig. 45).

Size. The fragmented bead is similar in size to many of the other bicone forms with a length of 8.00 mm.

Truncated convex bicones with circular cross section (figs. 46-48, 445-459)

The small number of this type (n=15), making up 2.9% of the assemblage (figs. 6 and 46), are distributed fairly evenly between Tell F3 (n=9) and Tell F6 (n=6) (fig. 47).

Materials. Most are made of faience, all similar in appearance (n=9, 60%), while a smaller number is made of carnelian (n=6, 40%). The two different materials are distributed fairly equally between Tell F3 and Tell F6 (fig. 48).

Size. The size range is significant: from 2.40 to 10.60 mm in length and between 4.70 and 18.50 mm in diameter.[25] The faience beads appear to be standardized forms as they are all of similar size, while the largest difference in dimensions lies within the group of carnelian beads (between 2.40 x 4.70 mm and 6.30 x 13.00 mm in L x D).

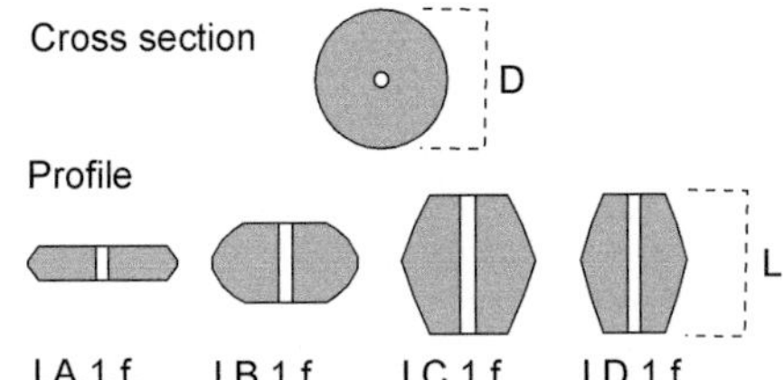

Fig. 46. Schematic representation of disc to long truncated convex bicones with circular cross section.

Form Type	F3	F6	Total	%
Truncated convex bicone Disc/Circular (I.A.1.f)	-	-	-	-
Short truncated convex bicone/Circular (I.B.1.f)	9	6	15	100
Standard truncated convex bicone/Circular (I.C.1.f)	-	-	-	-
Long truncated convex bicone/Circular (I.D.1.f)	-	-	-	-
Total	**9**	**6**	**15**	**100**
%	60	40	100	-

Fig. 47. Distribution of truncated convex bicones with circular cross section, Tell F3 and Tell F6.

Form Type	Material	F3	F6	Total	%
I.B.1.f.	**Artificial**	**6**	**3**	**9**	**60**
	Faience	6	3	9	60
	Mineral	**3**	**3**	**6**	**40**
	Carnelian	3	3	6	40
Total	-	**9**	**6**	**15**	**100**
%	-	60	40	100	-

Fig. 48. Distribution of truncated convex bicones with circular cross section by tell and material.

Beads of special interest. The type includes a distinctive group of faience beads (n= 9), found at both Tell F3 (n=6) and Tell F6 (n=3). They are fairly well preserved, but the white coatings of the original surfaces have worn off, exposing a yellowish to brown core. Vertical stripe patterns highlighted by a reddish brown to dark brown colour create a slightly gadrooned appearance (see for instance fig. 452). Three of the beads are dated to period 4B (figs. 446-447 and 451) and the other beads were found in contexts dating to period 1 (fig. 456), period 2-4A (fig. 455) or from unknown contexts (figs. 449, 452, 453 and 457) (cf. chapter 4).

Truncated convex bicones with lenticular cross section (figs. 49-51, 460-463)

Only a few beads belong to this type[26] (n=4, 0.8%) (figs. 6 and 49); they come from both Tell F6 (n=2, 50%) and Tell F3 (n=2, 50%) (fig. 50).

Materials. The four beads are made of mineral materials, agate (n=2), turquoise (n=1) and lapis lazuli (n=1) (fig. 51).

Size. The size range is considerable, falling between 8.60 and 25.00 mm in length and 8.60 and 25.00 mm in width.[27] Three of these beads are of nearly equal size (figs. 461-463), while the last (fig. 460) is significantly larger (25.00 x 25.00 mm in L x W).

Beads of special interest. The large lapis lazuli bead (fig. 460) is notable among the beads of this type and in the assemblage due to its size and material. It exhibits extensive string wear and seems to have been worn and curated for a long time before it was deposited at Tell F6. Lapis lazuli is quite rare in the 1958-1963

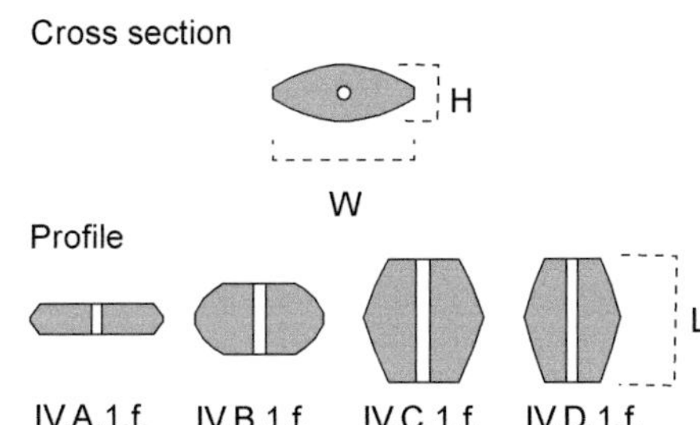

Fig. 49. Schematic representation of truncated convex bicones with lenticular cross section.

Form Type	F3	F6	Total	%
Truncated convex bicone Disc/Lenticular (IV.A.1.f)	-	-	-	-
Short truncated convex bicone/Lenticular (IV.B.1.f)	-	-	-	-
Standard truncated convex bicone/ Lenticular (IV.C.1.f)	0	2	2	50
Long truncated convex bicone/Lenticular (IV.D.1.f)	1	1	2	50
Total	**1**	**3**	**4**	**100**
%	25	75	100	-

Fig. 50. Distribution of truncated convex bicones with lenticular cross section, Tell F3 and Tell F6.

Form Type	Material	F3	F6	Total	%
IV.C.1.f.	**Mineral**	**0**	**2**	**2**	**50**
	Turquoise	0	1	1	25
	Lapis Lazuli	0	1	1	25
IV.D.1.f.	**Mineral**	**1**	**1**	**2**	**50**
	Agate	1	1	2	50
Total	-	**1**	**3**	**4**	**100**
%	-	25	75	100	-

Fig. 51. Distribution of truncated convex bicones with lenticular cross section by tell and material.

assemblage (n=12, 2.3%, fig. 3.1) and at other Bronze Age excavations at Failaka, for example, the Slovakian excavations at Al-Khidr (n=0), the French excavations of the temple at Tell F6 (n=2) and the Johns-Hopkins excavations at Tell F6 (n=1).

In the present assemblage, lapis lazuli is usually used for beads of smaller dimensions, excepting fig. 460, the unusually large cylinder with lenticular cross section (fig. 569) and a large sphere with circular cross section (fig. 105). Likewise, a truncated convex bicone, with lenticular cross section (fig. 461) and made of turquoise, is notable for its rare material both in this assemblage and other bead assemblages from Failaka. This bead has a good parallel from a possibly disturbed Temple I context at the Barbar temples (Andersen & Højlund 2003 p. 316, fig. 817).

Bicones with circular cross section (figs. 52-54, 464-468)

This type is rare (n=5, 1%), and they are all long variants (figs. 6 and 52). Four (0.8%) come from Tell F3, while one was recovered from Tell F6 (0.2%) (fig. 53).

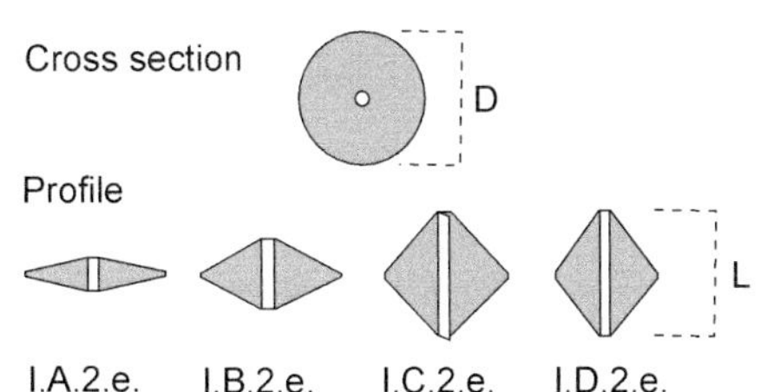

Fig. 52. Schematic representation of disc to long bicones with circular cross section.

Form Type	F3	F6	Total	%
Bicone Disc/Circular (I.A.2.e)	-	-	-	-
Short Bicone/Circular (I.B.2.e)	-	-	-	-
Standard Bicone / Circular (I.C.2.e)	-	-	-	-
Long Bicone /Circular (I.D.2.e)	4	1	5	100
Total	-	-	-	**100**
%	80	20	100	-

Fig. 53. Distribution of bicones with circular cross section, Tell F3 and Tell F6.

Form Type	Material	F3	F6	Total	%
I.D.2.e	**Minerals**	**4**	**1**	**5**	**100**
	Agate	1	0	1	20
	Carnelian	3	1	4	80
Total	-	**4**	**1**	**5**	**100**
%	-	80	20	100	-

Fig. 54. Distribution of bicones with circular cross section by tell and material.

Materials. They are all made of mineral materials, namely carnelian (n=4, 80%) and agate (n=1, 20%) (fig. 54).

Size. There is a notable range of sizes between the smallest bead (10.80 x 6.80 mm, L x D) (fig. 467) and the largest bead (19.80 x 11.00 mm, L x D) (fig. 466).[28]

Truncated bicones with circular cross section (figs. 55-57, 469-527)

This type occurs in short, standard and long proportions and makes up 11.4% (n=59) of the assemblage (figs. 6 and 55). Standard and long beads are most frequent (n=26, 44% and n=28, 47.5% respectively), while short truncated bicones are relatively rare (n=5, 8.5%). The majority of this type was found at Tell F6 (n=48, 81.3%), while a smaller number was found at Tell F3 (n=11, 18.7%) (fig. 56).

Materials. They are predominantly made of carnelian (n=54, 91.5%). The only other mineral materials present are agate and amethyst (n=4, 6.8%). One short, truncated bicone is made of an organic material identified as bone (n=1, 1.7%) (fig. 57).

Size. The size distribution of complete beads is based on fifty-seven examples.[29] There is a significant size range, with the smallest bead measuring 4.70 x 6.20 mm (L x D) and the largest measuring 16.40 x 7.30 mm

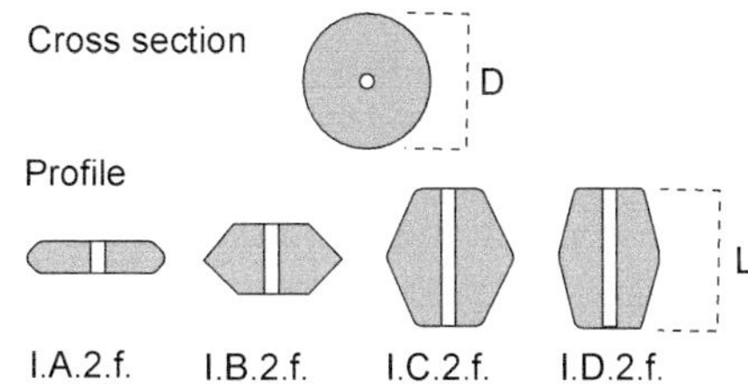

Fig. 55. Schematic representation of disc to long truncated bicones with circular cross section.

Form Type	F3	F6	Total	%
Truncated Bicone Disc/ Circular (I.A.2.f.)	-	-	-	-
Short Truncated Bicone/Circular (I.B.2.f.)	1	4	5	8.5
Standard Truncated Bicone/ Circular (I.C.2.f.)	2	24	26	44
Long Truncated Bicone/ Circular (I.D.2.f.)	8	20	28	47.5
Total	**11**	**48**	**59**	**100**
%	18.7	81.3	100	-

Fig. 56. Distribution of truncated bicones with circular cross section, Tell F3 and Tell F6.

Form Type	Material	F3	F6	Total	%
I.B.2.f.	**Mineral**	**0**	**4**	**4**	**6.8**
	Carnelian	0	4	4	6.8
	Organic	**1**	**0**	**1**	**1.7**
	Bone	1	0	1	1.7
I.C.2.f.	**Mineral**	**2**	**24**	**26**	**44.0**
	Carnelian	2	24	26	44.0
I.D.2.f.	**Mineral**	**8**	**20**	**28**	**47.5**
	Agate	1	2	3	5.1
	Amethyst	1	0	1	1.7
	Carnelian	6	19	24	40.7
Total	-	**11**	**48**	**59**	**100**
%	-	18.7	81.3	100	-

Fig. 57. Distribution of truncated bicones with circular cross section by tell and material.

(L x D).[30] Most of the beads have lengths between 5.00 and 7.00 mm (n=32, 56.1%), while their diameters generally lie between 5.00 and 7.00 mm (n=39, 68.4%). Unfortunately, the beads that would have certainly been the largest (figs. 501 and 506) are fragmented. The original size of fig. 501 is estimated to have been 38.20 x 8.30 (L x D), while fig. 506 is estimated to have been 38.80 x 7.70 mm (L x D).

Beads of special interest. The two fragmentary, long truncated bicone beads made of carnelian (figs. 501 and 506), both found at Tell F3, have been identified as fragments of so-called "Indus bicones". Indus bicones are exceptionally long truncated bicone beads and drilling these beads would have required a craftsperson of exceptional expertise, normally associated with the Indus region and the Harappan civilization. The characteristic Indus bicones were produced between 2450 to 1900 BC at Chanhu-Daro, but similar production took place at other large urban centres in the Indus region, such as Harappa (c. 2600-1900 BC) and Mohenjo-daro (Lankton 2003 p. 35. Kenoyer 2005 p. 165, fig. 4). The time between this period and the first settlement at Tell F3, along with the fragmented state of the beads suggest that they may have been curated for some time, before being deposited on Failaka. However, the bead with one end still intact (fig. 506), does not show extensive string wear. While one long truncated bicone bead (fig. 501) was found in an unknown context, the other (fig. 506) was found in a possible period 4A/4B context (c. 1400-1300 BC) (fig. 2). This leaves an interval of c. 1150 years from the time that the beads could have been first manufactured in the Indus region to the latest date of final deposition at Tell F3 at Failaka.

Another noteworthy, long truncated bicone is made of carnelian and has vertical incised lines at each end spiralling around the bead (fig. 505). Incised decoration on beads is rare on Failaka (cf. chapter 5 p. 42-43).

A carnelian bead (fig. 474) has remains of a copper rod stuck in the perforation, which may indicate that the bead was originally strung on a copper wire.

Finally, a short truncated bicone bead made of bone (fig. 469) is noteworthy due to its material, which is very rare in the assemblage.

Cylinders with circular cross section (figs. 58-60, 528-563)

This type is relatively frequent, consisting of 8.1% (n=40) of the assemblage (figs. 6 and 58).[31] The majority (n=29, 72.5%) are long cylinders (fig. 59). These come from both Tell F3 (n=11) and Tell F6 (n=18). The rest of the cylinders with circular cross section consist of short cylinders (n=6, 15%), standard cylinders (n=1, 2.5%) and cylinder fragments of uncertain length (n=4, 10%).

Materials. This type is primarily made of mineral materials (n=24, 60%), that is carnelian (n=12), lapis lazuli (n=5), agate (n=3), jasper (n=1), hematite (n=1), and rock crystal (n=1) (fig. 60). Several of the lapis lazuli beads in the assemblage are classified as cylinders (n=5, 1% of the assemblage), but the majority are small and crude (e.g. figs. 530, 545, 551 and 560) and may have been reworked from larger lapis lazuli objects (cf. chapter 3 p. 31). Artificial materials (n=13, 32.5%) are represented by faience (n=2) and glass (n=11). Lastly, organic materials (n=3, 7.5%) have been identified as bone and ivory, while one remains unidentified.

Size. The size distribution is based on twenty-six beads.[32] The range of sizes is considerable, the smallest being 2.50 x 5.60 mm (L x D) and the largest 35.90 x 4.50 mm (L x D).[33] The cylinders have rather different appearances, as some are very fine and slim with nicely polished surfaces (e.g. figs. 539, 547, 552, 555, 562-563), while others are "squat" with thick walls and rougher surfaces (e.g. figs. 535, 542-544, 546 and 561). The finer examples are found at Tell F6, while the cruder ones are mainly found at Tell F3.

Beads of special interest. Like other very long beads in the assemblage, such as longer barrels and bicones (e.g. "Indus" bicones), the very long and slim cylinder (fig. 562), classified as a "long cylinder", is noteworthy because of the time and expertise needed to drill the perforation. Furthermore, the bead was worked and polished into a cylinder with very thin walls, adding to the impression of a bead of exceptional quality. Such long cylinder beads can, for instance, be found at the

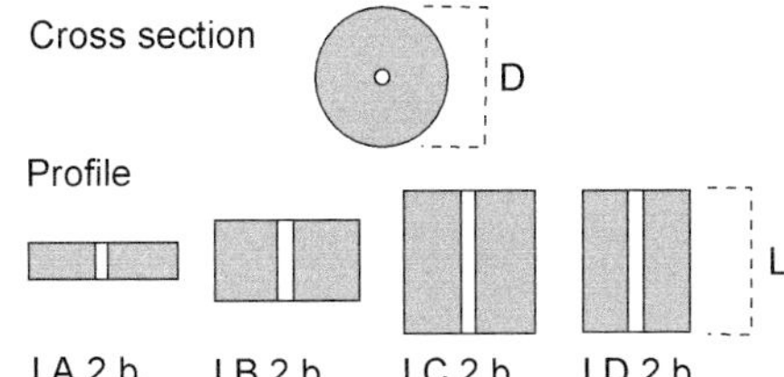

Fig. 58. Schematic representation of cylinders with circular cross section.

Form Type	F3	F6	Total	%
Cylinder Disc /Circular (I.A.2.b.)	0	0	0	-
Short Cylinder/Circular (I.B.2.b.)	2	4	6	15
Standard Cylinder/ Circular (I.C.2.b.)	1	0	1	2.5
Long Cylinder/Circular (I.D.2.b.)	11	18	29	72.5
Unidentified Cylinder/ Circular (fragments)	0	4	4	10
Total	**14**	**26**	**40**	**100**
%	35	65	100	-

Fig. 59. Distribution of cylinders with circular cross section, Tell F3 and Tell F6.

Form Type	Material	F3	F6	Total	%
I.B.2.b.	**Mineral**	**2**	**3**	**5**	**12.5**
	Carnelian	1	1	2	5
	Hematite	1	0	1	2.5
	Lapis Lazuli	0	1	1	2.5
	Smoky quartz	0	1	1	2.5
	Artificial	0	1	1	2.5
	Glass	0	1	1	2.5
I.C.2.b.	**Organic**	**1**	**0**	**1**	**2.5**
	Ivory	1	0	1	2.5
I.D.2.b.	**Mineral**	**8**	**11**	**19**	**47.5**
	Agate	1	2	3	7.5
	Carnelian	4	6	10	25
	Jasper	1	0	1	2.5
	Lapis Lazuli[1]	1	31	4	10
	Rock crystal	1	0	1	2.5
	Organic	**1**	**1**	**2**	**5**
	Bone	1	0	1	2.5
	Unidentified	0	1	1	2.5
	Artificial	**2**	**6**	**8**	**20**
	Faience	1	1	2	5
	Glass	1	5	6	15
Fragments	**Artificial**	**0**	**4**	**4**	**10**
	Glass	0	4	4	10
Total	-	**14**	**26**	**40**	**100**
%	-	35	65	100	-

1 One of the lapis lazuli cylinders has a gold cap at one end (F6.639, fig. 554).

Fig. 60. Distribution of cylinders with circular cross section by tell and material.

Royal Cemetery at Ur in Akkadian or Ur III contexts (c. 2350-2000 BC) and at Susa. The long slim cylinder (Woolley's type 5 "tubular") is described as five times more common in the Early Cemetery, than in the Late Cemetery (Woolley 1934 p. 371). Shorter slim cylinders, comparable to the Failaka examples (figs. 539, 547, 552, 555 and 563), can also be found at Ur and Susa (these examples are dated between c. 2100-1750 BC).[34] One finely shaped lapis lazuli cylinder bead (fig. 554) has a gold cap preserved at one end and might originally have been fitted with gold caps at both ends. Gold capped beads were in fashion from the Ur III period into the Kassite period (Maxwell Hyslop 1971 p. 68).

A long faience cylinder bead with an incised lattice pattern (fig. 557) is the only one in the assemblage and finds parallels at Uruk (Limper 1988, catalogue numbers F217-221). Here similar beads are described as reproductions of Jemdet Nasr cylinder seals. These beads came into fashion in the middle of the 2nd millennium and continued in use until the second half of the 1st millennium. The best parallels for the Failaka bead come from Uruk (from a Neo-Babylonian context) and 13th century BC (Middle Elamite period) Choga Zanbil (Limper 1988 p. 19, fig. 218).

Cylinders with lenticular cross section (figs. 61-63, 564-566)

Only a few beads belong to this type (n=5),[35] making up c. 1% of the assemblage (figs. 6 and 61). They are distributed evenly between Tell F3 (n=2) and Tell F6 (n=3) (fig. 62).

Materials. These beads are primarily made of min-

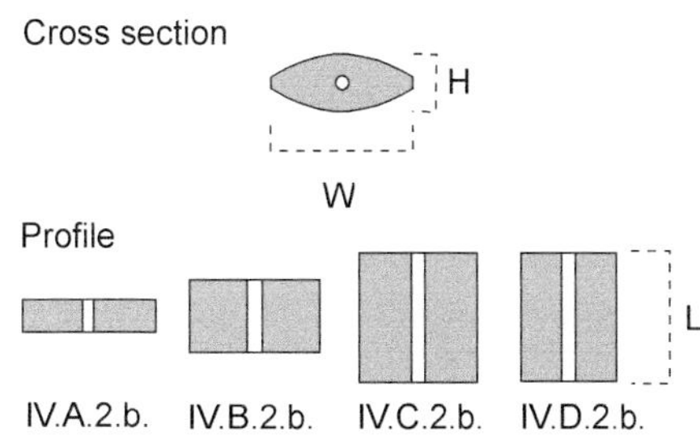

Fig. 61. Schematic representation of cylinders with lenticular cross section.

Form Type	F3	F6	Total	%
Cylinder Disc / Lenticular (IV.A.2.b.)	0	0	0	0
Short Cylinder/Circular (IV.B.2.b.)	0	0	0	0
Standard Cylinder/ Circular (IV.C.2.b.)	1	0	1	20
Long Cylinder/Circular (IV.D.2.b.)	1	3	4	80
Total	**2**	**3**	**5**	**100**
%	2	3	100	-

Fig. 62. Distribution of cylinders with lenticular cross section, Tell F3 and Tell F6.

Form Type	Material	F3	F6	Total	%
IV.C.2.b.	Mineral	1	0	1	20
	Agate	1	0	1	20
IV.D.2.b.	**Mineral**	**0**	**3**	**3**	**60**
	Agate	0	2	2	40
	Lapis Lazuli	0	1	1	20
	Artificial	**0**	**1**	**1**	**20**
	Faience	0	1	1	20
Total	-	**1**	**4**	**5**	**100**
%	-	20	80	100	-

Fig. 63. Distribution of cylinders with lenticular cross section by tell and material.

eral materials (fig. 63). Three are made of agate (figs. 567, 570-571), while one large bead is made of lapis lazuli (fig. 569). The last bead is a rather well-preserved faience bead (fig. 568).

Size. The size distribution is based on four complete beads.[36] Three are relatively similar in length and width (figs. 567-568 and 570), while one is slightly longer (fig. 571). The last bead is a remarkably large, albeit fragmentary, lapis lazuli bead (fig. 569), which would have been 40.00 x 35.50 mm (L x W) at minimum.

Beads of special interest. A faience bead (fig. 568) has a polychrome surface decorated by many applied spots of colour in reddish brown, light brown, yellowish white and greyish black. This bead is the best example in the assemblage of a faience bead with its surface still preserved (cf. chapter 3 p. 33).

Varia (figs. 64-65, 567-588)

The group of varia consists of a small number of beads (n=17, 3.3%), whose forms and/or decoration occur rarely (such as different forms of pendants, eye-beads and figurative beads) or which cannot be easily categorized according to Beck's typological classification (such as an "S-shaped bead") (fig. 6). They have been subdivided into figurative (n=4), geometric (n=7) or pendant (n=6) beads (fig. 64), but they have little in common in terms of form, material and size.

Figurative. Fig. 575 is fragmented, and it is difficult to reconstruct its original shape, but the form might be an animal-shape to be classified within Beck's types XXXII-XXXV (Beck 1928 p. 36-39). A single bead (fig. 574) has been classified as "vase-shaped", that is Beck's type XXIX.A.15. (Beck 1928 p. 32), possibly a stylized pomegranate as seen in the Uruk bead assemblage (Limper 1988 p. 36-37 and 188, especially figs. 384-386). Two of the beads are so-called eye-beads made of agate (figs. 572-573), in which the banded stone is shaped, presumably to resemble the iris and the white of an eye. The two eye-beads are different form types, but both are classified under XLVI.A.1.a. (Beck 1928 p. 41-46).

Geometric. Fig. 576 is a short truncated bicone with a rectangular cross section (X.B.2.f.) made of carnelian (Beck 1928 p. 6).[37] Fig. 577 is a short truncated bicone with a hexagonal cross section and seven facets at each end (XIII.B.2.f.), also made of carnelian. Fig. 579 is a collared ellipsoid (I.D.1.a.) made of extremely badly preserved glass; the bead is light grey with only a slight hint of light green colour at its core and remains of a brown coating on its surface. Fig. 578 is a collared gold melon bead (XXIII.A.3.a.). The bead originally had a core made of another material (perhaps clay or bitumen), which has since disappeared so that only the gold foil remains. Fig. 582 is a cornerless cube (XIX.A.1.) made of carnelian. Fig. 581 is a slightly S-shaped bead with a rectangular cross section made of carnelian. Fig. 580 is a long barrel bead with elliptical cross section (II.D.1.b.) made of a fragile, greyish, unburnt clay with incised lines crisscrossing its surface, creating a sort of "net" decoration.

Pendants. This group includes two cone pendants (n=2, figs. 587-588) and different types of drop pendants (n=3, figs. 584-586). The two types are best classified under *"drop pendants with rounded ends"* (XXII.B.2.b.) and *"cone pendants perforated at the large end"* (XXII.B.5.b.) (Beck

Form Type	F3	F6	Total	%
Figurative	**3**	**1**	**4**	**23.5**
Vase-shaped bead (XXX.A.15.)	1	0	1	5.9
Animal-shape (XXXII-XXXV.)	1	0	1	5.9
Eye-beads (XLVI.A.1.a.)	1	1	2	11.7
Geometric	**2**	**5**	**7**	**41.3**
Short truncated bicone/ Hexagonal (XIII.B.2.f.)	1	0	1	5.9
Short truncated bicone/ Rectangular (X.B.2.f.)	0	1	1	5.9
Collared ellipsoid bead (I.D.1.a.)	0	1	1	5.9
Collared melon bead (XXIII.A.3.b.)	0	1	1	5.9
Cornerless cube bead (XIX.A.1.)	0	1	1	5.9
"S-shaped" bead	0	1	1	5.9
Barrel bead with "net" decoration (II.D.1.b .)	1	0	1	5.9
Pendants	**5**	**1**	**6**	**35.2**
Cone pendants (XXII.B.5.b.)	1	1	2	11.7
Drop pendants (XXII.B.2.b.)	3	0	3	17.6
Oval shell "plate" pendant	1	0	1	5.9
Total	**10**	**7**	**17**	**100**
%	59	41	100	-

Fig. 64. Distribution of varia form types, Tell F3 and Tell F6.

Form Type	Material	F3	F6	Total	%
Figurative	**Mineral**	**3**	**1**	**4**	**23.5**
	Agate	2	1	3	17.7
	Turquoise	1	0	1	5.9
Geometric	**Mineral**	**1**	**3**	**4**	**23.5**
	Carnelian	1	3	4	23.5
	Artificial	**1**	**2**	**3**	**17.7**
	Clay	1	0	1	5.9
	Glass	0	1	1	5.9
	Gold	0	1	1	5.9
Pendants	**Mineral**	**4**	**1**	**5**	**29.4**
	Agate	1	1	2	11.8
	Carnelian	2	0	2	11.8
	Jasper	1	0	1	5.9
	Organic	**1**	**0**	**1**	**5.9**
	Shell (spiny oyster)	1	0	1	5.9
Total	-	**10**	**7**	**17**	**100**
%	-	59	41	100	-

Fig. 65. Distribution of varia form types distributed by tell and material.

1928 p. 22 and 24), along with an oval shell "plate" pendant (n=1, fig. 583).

Materials. The group of varia is made of many different materials. Most of these are mineral (n=13), with carnelian (n=6), agate (n=5), jasper (n=1) and turquoise (n=1) represented (fig. 65). Only one bead in the varia group is made of an organic material, that is a shell "plate" pendant, cut from a spiny oyster shell (*Spondylus exilis*). A few beads (n=3) in the varia group are made of artificial materials, which include unfired clay (n=1), glass (n=1) and, notably, a gold foil bead (n=1).

Size. Since the group of varia consists of different forms, there is no basis for a size comparison.

Beads of special interest. The shell "plate" pendant (fig. 583) is unique in the assemblage. No exact parallels have been found for this kind of pendant, but it does share similarities in material and form to *Spondylus* sp. shell ornaments found in tumuli graves at Al-Subiyah (mainland Kuwait) (Wygnanska 2015 p. 502-506). However, this style of shell ornament was popular in the Gulf region during the Neolithic and occurred infrequently in the following millennia. The presence of such an ornament in 2nd millennium contexts at Failaka may indicate that this shell "plate" pendant could have been inspired from an archaic style of shell ornaments.[38]

Two eye-beads of different forms made of agate have been found at Failaka. Eye-beads are found in Mesopotamia dating from the Early Dynastic III period, but agate eye-beads appear most frequently in the Kassite period and are chiefly associated with Babylonia (Campbell et al. 2017 p. 38. Clayden 2009 p. 41). Agate eye-beads in different forms have been found in Kish, Ur, Tepe Hissar, Babylon, Tell al-Rimah, Assur, Mari and Susa. One bead from Susa exhibits the same form, colour and stone banding, as one of the examples from Failaka (fig. 573).[39] The other eye-bead from Failaka (fig. 572) finds better parallels at Larsa (Old Babylonian period), Assur (Middle Assyrian period) and Choga Zanbil (Middle Elamite period) (Arnaud, Calvet & Huot 1979 p. 36, figs. 33 and 79. Limper 1988 p. 16).

The single short truncated bicone with a hexagonal cross section from Tell F3 (fig. 577) finds a close parallel at Qala'at al-Bahrain in a period IIb context (Højlund & Andersen 1994 p. 392, fig. 1959) as well as in a collection of facetted carnelian beads from Susa.[40]

Fig. 576 is a unique form in the assemblage and was recovered from Tell F6. The bead is made of carnelian. No exact parallel for this type of bead has been found in the Indus region. Instead, beads of this type are primarily known from Mesopotamian contexts. A large number of parallels are found at Ur in various graves.[41]

At Ur, the comparable beads made of both carnelian and lapis lazuli have been found at the Royal Cemetery. Here, the distribution of the "diamond" form type (Type 19 in Woolley's classification), is described as *"about equally divided between the two main cemeteries and are found in the Second Dynasty graves also"* (Woolley 1934 p. 371). The form type occurs in grave contexts dated to ED III (c. 2600-2350 BC) and the Akkadian period (c. 2350-2150 BC) (cf. Woolley 1934 p. 32. Pollock 1985 p. 139). In the Gulf, two similar beads have been discovered in Ras al-Khaimah, where they are found in an early 2nd-millennium tomb context at Qarn-al-Harf (Hilton pers. comm. 2021).

The Failaka assemblage contains a small number of cone and drop pendants (n=5). Two carnelian drop pendants found at Tell F3 (figs. 584 and 586) find similar form parallels at Uruk (here called double cone pendants, with most examples made of rock crystal) dated to the Jemdet Nasr period, the Kassite period and the Neo-Babylonian period. However, the Neo-Babylonian examples are thought to be reproductions of archaic forms, due to less skilful manufacture and more compact forms (Limper 1986 p. 42-43, figs. 453-461). The two carnelian cone pendants from Failaka are somewhat dissimilar in form, one being quite nicely shaped, perforated and polished (fig. 586), while the other is more uneven, less polished and less skilfully perforated (fig. 584).

One possible parallel, from Susa, has been identified for the two cone pendants (figs. 587-588).[42] The banding and colours of the stone material is also very similar to one of the cone pendants (i.e. fig. 587). The bead dates to the Middle Elamite period (c. 1500-1100 BC). The drop pendant bead (fig. 585) in the assemblage looks much like a polished and drilled pebble with a somewhat random shape and therefore no parallels have been identified.

A collared gold melon bead is unique in the assemblage (fig. 578). Gold in itself is very rare at Failaka and in the Dilmun Gulf bead assemblages in general. No gold beads have been found at Al-Khidr, the Tell F6 Temple or the Johns Hopkins excavations at Tell F6. Likewise, gold beads have not been found in Dilmun contexts in Bahrain, such as at the Saar settlement or in Sar al-Jisr burial mounds, the Barbar temples or Qala'at al-Bahrain (cf. chapter 3 p. 34). Parallels for this bead can be found in Mesopotamia, more specifically in the Dilbat (Tell al-Deylam) hoard. This is a hoard of gold jewellery found in a jar, which was deposited in no later than the early Kassite period (c. 1600 BC) (Maxwell-Hyslop 1971 p. 88-91 and pl. 61, 63a-64b). The seventeenth century BC has been proposed as the likely production date of the jewellery (Lilyquist 1994 p. 5). Part of the hoard is a gold necklace made of seven gold pendants and 188 beads of varying sizes. The smaller gold collared melon beads in particular are comparable to the Failaka example (see Maxwell-Hyslop 1971 pl. 63a-b).[43]

Fig. 582 is a cornerless cube bead made of carnelian, the form of which is usually associated with Roman and Early Islamic periods (Francis Jr. 2002 p. 110-111). The bead form became popular a few centuries BC and is common at sites in Europe and the Middle East from c. 1st century BC to c. 1200 AD. Many cornerless cube beads are made of glass, instead of stone. Francis Jr. suggests that very early beads of this form may have been made of stone (Francis Jr. 2002 p. 111). Lankton mentions cornerless cube beads as Roman forms made of lapis lazuli, carnelian or rock crystal (Lankton 2003 p. 64, fig. 7.1: no. 609). Cornerless cube beads are also found in the Early Islamic period, c. mid 8th century to 1200 AD (Lankton 2003 fig. 8.1: no. 644). It is possible that the cornerless cube bead from Tell F6 may be an intrusion, perhaps in relation to later stone plundering. No other bead forms in the Tell F3 or Tell F6 assemblage are explicitly later in date than the 2nd millennium BC.

3. Materials

The materials of the 1958-1963 bead assemblage from Tell F3 and Tell F6 have been divided into three groups: mineral, organic and artificial (fig. 66). The mineral materials are comprised of different types of semi-precious stone, such as different varieties of chalcedony (agate, carnelian, jasper, and moss agate) and quartz (rock crystal, milky quartz, and smoky quartz), and a range of other stone variants such as calcite, chlorite, lapis lazuli, turquoise and porphyry. The organic materials include bone, ivory, shells, and natural pearls, while the artificial materials consist of clay, glass, faience and paste. The mineral materials found in the Failaka bead assemblage were brought to the island, and a map of these materials' possible places of origin includes the Middle East, parts of the Mediterranean region, North Africa (i.e. Egypt), the Gulf region, Afghanistan and Pakistan (fig. 67). Most of the organic materials in the assemblage would have been available locally,[44] while the majority of artificial materials are thought to have been produced outside Failaka and transported to the island.

Mineral materials

Beads of mineral materials make up 80.6% (n=416) of the assemblage; 88% (n=147) of the beads from Tell F3 and 77.3% (n=269) of the beads from Tell F6.

Chalcedony

Chalcedony is a hard stone and a cryptocrystalline compact variety of silica.[45] In the assemblage this group covers the following varieties: agate, carnelian, chrysoprase, jasper and moss agate. Generally, the distinction between the different stone types follows the definitions proposed by Bishop et al. (2005 p. 130-133). Uniformly coloured transparent to subtranslucent chalcedony includes carnelian and chrysoprase, while agate is transparent to subtranslucent and *"characterized by curved bands or zones of differing colour"*. Jasper is an opaque chalcedony, most often in multiple colours distributed in spots or bands (Bishop et al. 2005 p. 130-133).

Agate occurs in the Failaka assemblage in a wide variety of colours, ranging from banded stone in white, black and brown to pink, orange, blue and red. Seventy-six beads of the assemblage (14.7%) have been identified as agate, of which thirty-six come from Tell F3 (n=36, 6.9%) and forty come from Tell F6 (n=40, 7.8%). Agate has been reported in the Gulf at al-Ghail (Jebel al-Ma'taradh) in Ras al-Khaimah (UAE) and is also widespread in neighbouring regions, such as Iran, Pakistan and India and in the more distant Anatolia, all of which are possible sources of the agate found at Failaka (Charpentier et al. 2017. Moorey 1994 p. 99. Law 2011).

Carnelian is described as a red to reddish brown variant of chalcedony (Bishop et al. 2005 p. 132), but on Failaka the hue of the stone may range from yellowish orange to reddish brown. Good quality carnelian is usually a bright red to reddish brown, translucent to subtranslucent and without impurities. Most of the mineral material at Tell F3 (n=60, 11.6%) and Tell F6 (n=171, 33.2%) is identified as carnelian. However, in several cases, the carnelian beads on Failaka are discoloured by a white opaque "film", which may also appear as opaque orange, but when beads are broken, one can see that this surface is superficial, cf. discoloured and fragmented beads in the 2008-2012 Tell F6 assemblage (Andersson 2016 p. 180, figs. 878, 936, 941, 943 and 996). This trait is observed in c. 70 (c. 30%) of the 231 carnelian beads found at Tell F3 and Tell F6 (see chapter 5 p. 43 for further discussion of the discolouration).

The origin place of carnelian is traditionally attributed to the Indus region (located in parts of modern Afghanistan, India and Pakistan), as the region has significant deposits of carnelian and was long renowned for the expertise of its bead-producing craftspeople. Both the craftspeople and their products may have travelled widely along the trade networks (Lankton 2003 p. 35. Kenoyer 1997 p. 272).

Sources of carnelian are also known in the Gulf itself, for instance at al-Ghail (Jebel al-Ma'taradh) in Ras al-Khaimah (UAE). The agate and carnelian sources at Jebel al-Ma'taradh were mined for bead production between the 6th and the 4th millennia and beads were probably produced for local consumption. It has also been suggested that a local production of beads may have taken place during the Bronze Age, due to the similarity of mineralogical characteristics

	Tell and phases / Materials	Tell F3 (all)	Phase 2	Phase 3A	Phase 3B	Phase 4A	Phase 4B	Unknown	Phase 3A/3B	Phase 4A/4B	Phase 3A/4A	Phase 3B/4B	Tell F6 (all)	Phase 1	Phase 2-4A	Unknown	Total	%
Minerals	***Chalcedony***																	**68.1**
	Agate	**36**	-	2	-	4	2	20	1	3	-	4	**40**	4	15	21	76	14.7
	Carnelian	**60**	-	5	2	2	9	36	1	3	1	1	**171**	9	53	109	231	44.8
	Chrysoprase	**1**	-	-	-	-	1	-	-	-	-	-	-	-	-	-	1	0.2
	Jasper	**19**	1	4	-	1	2	6	-	1	-	4	**23**	1	9	13	42	8.2
	Moss Agate	-	-	-	-	-	-	-	-	-	-	-	**1**	-	1	-	1	0.2
	Quartz																	**3.9**
	Amethyst	**1**	-	-	-	-	-	1	-	-	-	-	-	-	-	-	1	0.2
	Milky Quartz	**6**	-	-	-	-	1	4	-	1	-	-	**3**	-	2	1	9	1.7
	Rock Crystal	**2**	-	-	-	-	-	2	-	-	-	-	**2**	-	2	-	4	0.8
	Rose Quartz	**1**	-	-	-	-	-	-	-	-	-	1	-	-	-	-	1	0.2
	Smoky Quartz	-	-	-	-	-	-	-	-	-	-	-	**1**	-	-	1	1	0.2
	Quartz	**3**	-	-	-	-	-	2	-	1	-	-	**1**	-	-	1	4	0.8
	Other stone types																	**8.6**
	Calcite	**4**	-	-	-	-	2	2	-	-	-	-	**1**	-	-	1	5	1.0
	Chlorite	**2**	-	-	-	-	-	2	-	-	-	-	**2**	-	1	1	4	0.8
	Hematite	**1**	-	-	-	-	-	1	-	-	-	-	**1**	-	1	-	2	0.2
	Limestone	**5**	-	-	-	-	-	4	-	1	-	-	**5**	-	1	4	10	1.9
	Lapis Lazuli[1]	**4**	-	-	-	-	-	4	-	-	-	-	**8**	-	2	6	12	2.3
	Porphyry	-	-	-	-	-	-	-	-	-	-	-	**2**	-	1	1	2	0.4
	Turquoise	**1**	-	-	-	-	-	1	-	-	-	-	**4**	1	-	3	5	1.0
	Unid. stone types	**1**	-	-	-	-	1	-	-	-	-	-	**4**	-	1	3	5	1.0
Organic																		**2.4**
	Bone	**2**	-	1	-	-	-	1	-	-	-	-	-	-	-	-	2	0.4
	Fossilized coral	-	-	-	-	-	-	-	-	-	-	-	**1**	-	1	-	1	0.2
	Ivory	**1**	-	-	-	-	-	1	-	-	-	-	-	-	-	-	1	0.2
	Pearls	-	-	-	-	-	-	-	-	-	-	-	**2**	-	-	2	2	0.4
	Shell	**3**	1	-	-	-	-	2	-	-	-	-	**2**	1	-	1	5	1.0
	Unidentified	-	-	-	-	-	-	-	-	-	-	-	**1**	-	1	-	1	0.2
Artificial																		**17**
	Clay	**1**	-	-	-	-	-	1	-	-	-	-	-	-	-	-	1	0.2
	Faience	**9**	-	-	-	-	3	6	-	-	-	-	**14**	2	5	7	23	4.4
	Glass	**5**	-	-	-	1	-	4	-	-	-	-	**53**	6	37	10	58	11.2
	Gold	-	-	-	-	-	-	-	-	-	-	-	**1**	-	1	-	1	0.2
	Paste	-	-	-	-	-	-	-	-	-	-	-	**5**	-	3	2	5	1.0
Total		**167**	2	12	2	8	21	99	2	10	1	10	**348**	24	138	186	515	100
%		**32.4**	0.4	2.3	0.4	1.5	4.0	19.2	0.4	2	0.2	2	**67.6**	4.7	26.8	36.1	100	-

1 F6.639.2 bead is a composite bead made of Lapis Lazuli with a gold cap.

Fig. 66. Materials divided on tells and settlement periods.

of the Jebel al-Ma'taradh carnelian sources and the Bronze Age bead material from the UAE (Charpentier et al. 2017).

Another possible source is the Bushire peninsula in Iran (Brunet 2009 p. 60. Law 2011 p. 282. Vogt 1996 p. 96). Law considers the possibility of the Bandar Bushire source being an *"important source for consumers in ancient Mesopotamia."* (Law 2011 p. 282).[46] Carnelian can also be found as pebbles and in minor deposits (Moorey 1994 p. 97). Sources of carnelian are also reported in the central and eastern parts of Iran, Afghanistan, Yemen, Egypt and Anatolia (Law 2011 p. 282. Moorey 1994 p. 97). A carnelian source and production of carnelian beads is also attested at chalcolithic Tayma in Saudi Arabia by fragments of beads and drills (Hausleiter 2011 p. 109, fig. 7a. Kenoyer & Frenez 2018b p. 399).

Chrysoprase is a green chalcedony variant represented in one bead (n=1, 0.2%) from Tell F3 (fig. 435) (Bishop et al. 2005 p. 132). Deposits of chrysoprase has been found at Suhaila 2, near Jebel al-Ma'taradh. The material is otherwise not reported from the UAE and the Oman peninsula (Charpentier et al. 2017).

Jasper. Jasper is an opaque variant of chalcedony and is rarely uniformly coloured. Colours range from yellow, brown, green to grey-blue (Bishop et al. 2005 p. 132-

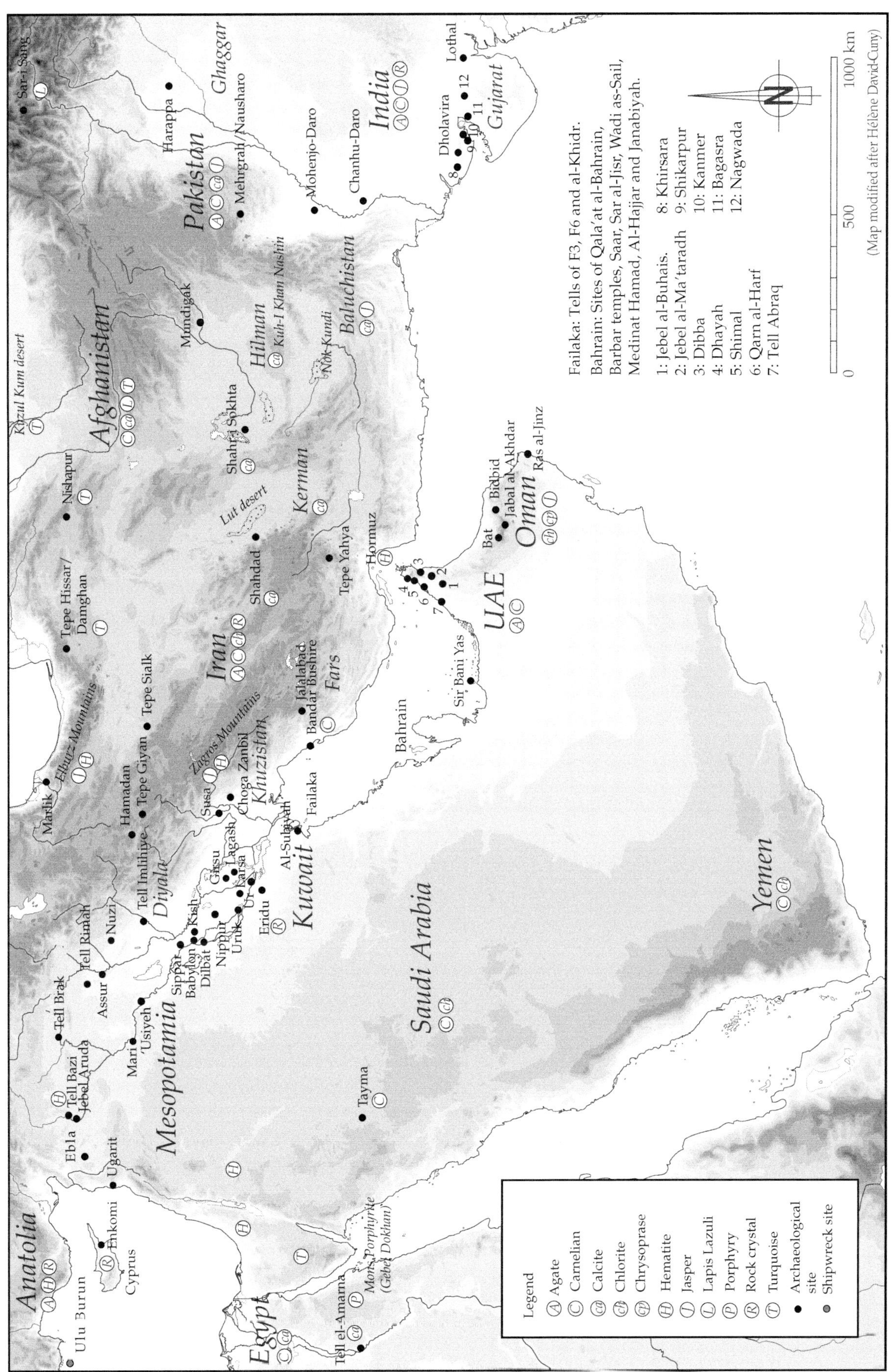

Fig. 67. Geographic map with possible sources of mineral materials of the Failaka bead assemblage and sites mentioned in the text.

133). A total of forty-two (8.2%) beads were identified as jasper. Of these, nineteen beads (3.6%) come from Tell F3 and twenty-three beads (4.6%) from Tell F6. Jasper is described as *"relatively frequent in the Near East as large outcrops or as washed sediments."* Jasper sources are reported in the mountainous zones of the southern Elburz and the central Zagros, the Makran coast of Baluchistan and in northern Oman (Moorey 1994 p. 98). Jasper is likewise widely available in the greater Indus region (Law 2011).

Moss agate generally ranges from a translucent to white matrix with irregular green to black markings (Bishop et al. 2005 p. 133); the only bead of this material, from Tell F6, has a white opaque matrix with black spots (0.2%) (fig. 292).

Quartz

Quartz is a crystalline (or macrocrystalline) variety of chalcedony, where individual crystals in the stone can be identified by the naked eye (Bishop et al. 2005 p. 130. Moorey 1994 p. 93-96). The different varieties of quartz are generally defined according to colour, but here a small part of the material has simply been identified as quartz; three beads from Tell F3 and one from Tell F6 (n=4, 0.8%).

Amethyst. One bead (n=1, 0.2%) (fig. 507) from Tell F3 is made of a quartz with a purple hue, that is, amethyst (Bishop et al. 2005 p. 130).

Milky quartz. Milky quartz is a translucent white quartz (Bishop et al. 2005 p. 130). Nine beads (n=9, 1.7%) from the assemblage are made of this material; six from Tell F3 (n=6, 1.1%) and three from Tell F6 (n=3, 0.6%).

Rock crystal. Four beads (n=4, 0.8%) are made of rock crystal, which is a transparent and colourless quartz (Bishop et al. 2005 p. 130); two from Tell F3 (n=2, 0.4%) (figs. 93 and 542) and two from Tell F6 (n=2, 0.4%) (figs. 134 and 140). Rock crystal may have arrived on Failaka from many different regions, such as India, Iraq (near Eridu), Iran, Anatolia and Cyprus (Moorey 1994 p. 95).

Rose quartz. One bead (n=1, 0.2%) from Tell F3 is identified as rose quartz, which is quartz with a rose-red to pink hue (Bishop et al. 2005 p. 130) (fig. 385).

Smoky quartz. One bead (n=1, 0.2%) from Tell F6 is made of smoky quartz, which is generally a smoky brown to black quartz (fig. 532).

Other stone types

Besides chalcedony and quartz variants, several other stone types have been identified in the assemblage. These include different types of soft stone (chlorite, limestone), medium-hard stone (calcite, hematite, lapis lazuli, turquoise) and hard stone (porphyry).

Calcite. Four beads and one bead blank are made of calcite (n=5, 1%). Four are from Tell F3 (n=4, 0.8%, figs. 268, 384, 436 and 438) and one is from Tell F6 (n=1, 0.2%, fig. 316). Calcite is a medium-hard stone type and two different kinds are present in the assemblage, i.e. a beige semi-translucent material (figs. 316 and 438) and a banded calcite of rather bad quality ranging in colour from semi-translucent beige over translucent orange to opaque dark brown (fig. 268, 384, 436). Calcite is also commonly classified as alabaster in archaeological literature.

Calcite is widely attested in Egypt. Quarries working in the Middle and New Kingdoms are found near Tell el-Amarna and between El Meniya and Wadi Asyut (Aston, Harrell and Shaw 2000 p. 59-60, fig. 2.a). Calcite sources are also found on the Iranian side of the Gulf, namely in the Hilman and Kerman provinces, close to the ancient sites of Shahr i-Sokhta and Shahdad. Sources are also confirmed in Afghanistan in the region of Kuh-I Khan Nashin and in Nok Kundi in Pakistan (Ciarla 1979 p. 321-324).

Chlorite. Chlorite is a soft stone generally characterized by a dark greyish green colour, occasionally appearing as black. It is fine-grained and has a vitreous or pearly lustre (Bishop et al. 2005 p. 126. Moorey 1994 p. 100). Only four beads are made of chlorite (Tell F3 n=2, 0.4%; Tell F6 n=2, 0.4%).[47] They correspond to Hilton's stone type 2 (fig. 342) and type 3 (figs. 336, 408 and 439), both of which are common in the stone vessel assemblage from Tell F3 and Tell F6 (Hilton 2014 fig. 15). The chlorite could have come from several different sources in Iran, the Oman Peninsula, Saudi Arabia and Yemen (Hilton 2014 p. 14).

Hematite. Only two beads (n=2, 0.4%) have been identified as hematite (figs. 286 and 528). No hematite was found in the bead assemblage of the 2008-2012 excavations of Tell F6 and only one hematite bead has been recorded in the 2012-2017 excavations at Tell F3 (Andersson 2016. 2021).

Other objects made of hematite have been recorded at Tell F3 and Al-Khidr, such as Mesopotamian weights, suggesting a northern provenience of at least some of the hematite objects at Failaka (Benediková

2008, fig. 105. Højlund in prep.). The same may be observed in Bahrain, where hematite weights of Mesopotamian style have been found at the Saar necropolis (Crawford 2000 figs. 100-103), in burials at Al-Hajjar site 2 and at Qala'at al-Bahrain (Højlund & Andersen 1994 p. 396-397, fig. 1990). See also a large fragment of worked hematite at Qala'at al-Bahrain (Højlund & Andersen 1997 fig. 109).

The exact source of the hematite found at Failaka is unknown. It may have come from Syria (the limestone plateau bordering Euphrates near Tell Bazi) and mountainous regions in Anatolia (Taurus) and Iran (Zagros and Elburz). The material is also reported to occur in Israel, Jordan and in Greece (at the island of Serifos) (Melein 2018 p. 19. Moorey 1994 p. 84). Southeast of Failaka, hematite can be found on the Iranian side of the Hormuz strait (at Hormuz Island), but it is unclear if this source was exploited in the late 3rd and 2nd millennia.

Lapis lazuli. Beads made of lapis lazuli (n=12, 2.3%) occur but rarely at Tell F3 (n=4, 0.8%) and Tell F6 (n=8, 1.5%). Lapis lazuli is also rare in other Bronze Age excavations at Failaka, for example, at Tell F3 (2012-2017 excavations) (n=1), Tell F6 (2008-2012 excavations) (n=2), Al-Khidr (n=0), the French Tell F6 temple excavation (n=2) and the Johns Hopkins excavation at Tell F6 (n=1) (Andersson 2016. 2021. Benediková 2010. Calvet & Pic 1986. Howard-Carter 1984).

Outcrops of lapis lazuli are traditionally ascribed only to the deposits of the Sar-I-Sang in the region of Badakhshan in Afghanistan (Hermann 1968). Casanova refers to deposits found in the Pamir mountains, that is, Ladjevar-Dara (Casanova 2008 p. 68), but Law's sulfur isotope analysis of lapis lazuli suggests that Badakhshan was the only exploited source (Law 2014). Even though the material originated in Afghanistan, unworked lapis lazuli was transported through intermediary markets to manufacturing sites across a wide region. Such manufacturing sites first appear in southern and central Asia and Iran. From the beginning of the 4th millennium to the beginning of the 3rd millennium manufacturing sites can be found at Mehrgarh, Mundigak, Sarazm and Tepe Hissar. During the 3rd millennium and the beginning of the 2nd millennium, manufacturing sites have been located at Shahdad, Tepe Hissar, Susa and Shahr-i Sokhta. Later manufacturing sites also appear in Syria and Mesopotamia during the 2nd millennium at sites like Ebla, Jebel Aruda, Larsa, Ur and likely also at Mari (Casanova 2008 p. 68).

Limestone. The beads identified as limestone (n=10, 1.9%) are generally made of the same pale pink opaque stone. Some occur with grey blurry veins, and some have pink to orange hues. They are found at both Tell F3 (n=5, c. 0.9%; figs. 387, 391, 401, 413-414) and Tell F6 (n=5, c. 0.9%; figs. 355, 418, 424, 427 and 546).

Porphyry. Two beads (n=2, 0.4%) from Tell F6 (fig. 326 and 377), have been identified as porphyry, a hard stone with a purplish hue and beige inclusions (also called Imperial Porphyry).

Purple porphyry is purported to have originated only in Egypt, at the Mons Porphyrites/Gebel Dokhan in the Eastern Desert, but usually the mining of the material is linked with the Roman period as the only two quarries discovered so far are dated to this period. The use of the stone is attested in Egypt in earlier periods (Predynastic and Early Dynastic periods), but the quarries supplying this material remain unknown (Aston, Harrell and Shaw 2000 p. 48). In Mesopotamia, the presence of porphyry is attested by two beads in burial contexts at Kish (Mackay 1925 p. 188).

Frenez has discussed the identification of Egyptian porphyry at Ras Al-Jinz RJ-2 in Oman (c. 2500-2000 BC), reconsidering the Egyptian origin of a stone vessel (Frenez 2021). Instead, the Indus Valley region is suggested as the area of origin for the stone vessel, based on the similarity of the stone material with Sang-e-Maryam fossiliferous limestone. Outcrops of this stone are found at several locations in the Indus Valley and objects made of it have been found at Indus civilization sites, such as Harappa and Dholavira. Whether direct or indirect, interaction between Oman and Egypt is only evidenced to have occurred much later, around the Ptolemaic period (Frenez 2021 p. 3). Mesopotamian contact with Egypt is, however, attested since the 4th millennium (Shaw & Nicholson 1995 p. 109. Stevenson 2013).

Turquoise. Four beads (n=4, 0.8%) in the assemblage, all from Tell F6 (figs. 118, 162, 216 and 461), are made of turquoise. Turquoise has not been reported from other Bronze Age excavations at Failaka and is generally reported to occur only rarely in Mesopotamia while being more common in Iran and Central Asia (Aruz 2008 p. 243). One turquoise bead is reported from the Barbar temples in Bahrain in a, possibly disturbed, Temple I context (Andersen & Højlund 2003 p. 316, fig. 817).

Sources of turquoise are present on the Sinai Peninsula, in Iran (Nishapur and Damgham mines in northeastern Iran), Afghanistan and the Kyzul Kum desert in Uzbekistan, but several of the mines have no firm evidence for ancient exploitation (Law 2011 p. 90. Moorey 1994 p. 101-103).

Unidentified stone materials. The materials of five beads (n=5, 1%) in the assemblage were unidentified. They come from both Tell F3 (n=1, 0.2%) and Tell F6 (n=4, 0.8%). Three of the beads appear to be made of the same characteristic black stone, two with white veins (figs. 250, 396 and 433), while the others differ from each other (figs. 375 and 421).

Organic materials

The organic materials in the assemblage consist of bone, ivory, pearls and shell. They represent only a small portion of the assemblage (n=12, 2.4%), equally divided between Tell F3 (n=6, 1.2%) and Tell F6 (n=6, 1.2%).

Bone. Two beads, both from Tell F3, have been identified as bone (figs. 468 and 538), but further identification of animal species is impossible due to the removal of diagnostic features.

Fossilized coral. One bead has been tentatively identified as fossilized coral (fig. 370). The bead is light grey with white veins. Both the grey stone and the white veins are chalky and porous. There are no parallels in other Dilmun bead assemblages. The identification as fossilized coral is due to its slight similarity to an Afghan bead, whose material was identified as fossilized coral (Lui 1995 p. 98, top photo). However, the bead from Failaka is rough in appearance and lacks the high polish of the Afghan bead. A stone material with a similar appearance has been discussed by Frenez, that is, a white-in-black fossiliferous limestone, tentatively identified as Waagenophillum (Frenez 2021, fig. 4). Originating at Jabal Al-Akhdar in Oman, the material is stated to have had some appeal from the Late Neolithic to the Iron Age, but it is rarely recognized at archaeological sites (Frenez 2021). Two Waagenophillum vessels (stone type 10) have been identified in the stone vessel assemblage at Failaka (Hilton 2014 p. 13). However, the stone material of the vessels at Failaka is described as extremely hard and compact.

Ivory. Only one fragmentary bead has been tentatively identified as ivory (fig. 534). The size of this object might also suggest it to be a fragmented, uncut seal. The material is very hard and dense in composition and dissimilar to the other organic materials (i.e. shell and bone) identified in the assemblage. It has a smooth and highly polished surface with small cracks. Ivory in this context could have originated from different animals (most likely elephant or hippopotamus) and different geographical regions (India, Africa and parts of the Middle East).

It is possible that the ivory could have come from Mesopotamia as there were elephants living in parts of the Middle East, including southern Iran, northern Iraq, southern Turkey and the Syrian Steppe between c. 1800 until c. 800/700 BC (Çakırlar & Ikram 2016 p. 180). Hippopotamuses could also be found across Egypt and the Levant. Likewise, the possibility that the ivory came from other tusk bearing animals found in the Middle East, such as wild boar and dugong, cannot be excluded. Dugong bones are present at Qala'at al-Bahrain and Saar (Beech 2010. Çakirla & Ikram 2016. Moorey 1994 p. 115-119).

According to Mesopotamian cuneiform sources, Dilmun was an intermediary in the ivory trade through the Gulf from the Indus region (Laursen & Steinkeller 2017 p. 68). For instance, merchants returning from Dilmun with ivory and ivory objects are mentioned in Ur texts dated to around 2000-1800 BC (Moorey 1994 p. 118-119).

Several elephant tusks, identified by Schreger lines, were found in the "Palace" at Tell F6 in a probable Period 4A context (c. 1400 BC) (Højlund in prep. Moorey 1994 p. 119).

Pearl. Two beads, both from Tell F6, are made of pierced pearls (figs. 191-192). Their find contexts and dating are unknown. In addition, two unpierced pearls were noted in the 1958-1963 Tell F6 excavation (Højlund in prep.), and two unpierced pearls were found in the 2008-2012 Tell F6 excavations (Højlund & Abu-Laban 2016 p. 223, fig. 1127a-b). For context, 14 unpierced pearls were found at the Saar settlement in Bahrain, where they were cautiously connected with pearl fishing activities (Killick & Moon 2005 p. 180). At Failaka, the presence of a small number of unpierced pearls along with substantial oyster shell deposits in the excavations (Tell F3 and Tell F6) may suggest fishing activities, centered on oyster exploitation. However, the pierced pearls point to the use of pearls as personal adornment, while no evidence for such use (i.e. pierced pearls) was found at Saar or other Dilmun sites in the Gulf (Carter 2012 p. 6-8).

Generally speaking, there is little archaeological evidence for the use of pearls as personal adornment in the 3rd to 2nd millennium and the interpretation of possible textual evidence for the use of pearls is still disputed (Carter 2012 p. 6-8). The term "fish-eye" occurs in Mesopotamian texts listing imports from Dilmun, and this term has long been understood as referring to oyster pearls (Campbell Thompson 1936) in relation to the enormous importance of pearl fishing in the Gulf throughout history (Carter 2012). Howard-Carter has argued against this interpretation by referring to the fact that the eyes of living fish are often extremely colourful and may rather resemble beads made of various types of semi-precious stone, such as agate eye-beads (Howard-Carter 1986 p. 305-306). It is, however, worth noting that the eyes of fish, once cooked, turn into a completely spherical, milky white, hard substance that is indeed very reminiscent of a real pearl, though without the shine and lustre of the latter. Additionally, Oppenheim noted that the word for "fish-eye" in the Ur texts did not include the determinative for stone (Oppenheim 1954 p. 7, note 6. Carter 2012 p. 8, note 13).

Shell. Five beads are made of three different kinds of shell. Two shell rings (figs. 217-218) are worked to such a degree that it is not possible to determine the exact type of shell, but it is likely a conus species, as the rings have the same appearance as these shells, and they occur naturally at Failaka. The third shell ring (fig. 219) has been identified as cut from a pearl oyster shell. The shell of a pendant with an attractive pink exterior and a beige interior (fig. 583) has been identified as a spiny oyster (*spondylus exilis*). Lastly, a bead from Tell F6 (fig. 359) has been worked extensively, removing any clear diagnostic features, but the colour and appearance point to conus shell.

Unidentified organic material. The material of one bead remains unidentified (fig. 559). The bead may be made of either bone or shell, but further identification of the material has not been possible.

Artificial materials

The artificial materials in the assemblage are generally badly preserved and have lost much of their original appearance. Due to the disintegrated state of the material, it is often difficult to distinguish between glass and faience.

Clay. Only one bead (n=1, 0.2%) was identified as made of clay (fig. 580), unlike the large number of clay beads found at the Saar settlement (Killick & Moon 2005 p. 181). They also occur in Excavation 519 at Qala'at al-Bahrain (Højlund & Andersen 1997 figs. 95-96). However, the single clay bead from Tell F3 does not resemble any of the clay beads from Saar or Qala'at al-Bahrain.

Faience. Faience beads are not especially abundant, they make up 4.4% (n=23) of the assemblage, nine at Tell F3 (1.7%) and fourteen at Tell F6 (2.7%). Most of the faience beads are badly preserved, having lost all their original surface. Two beads still retain some of their original appearance, suggesting that some of the faience beads had surfaces decorated in multiple nuances of white, yellow, red and dark grey. The surfaces seem to have been applied in blotches, creating a mosaic of different colours, or as spots on a uniform background (figs. 194 and 568). Other faience beads (n=9) have remains of a white surface and brown to reddish vertical lines on a yellowish-brown core (figs. 446-447, 449, 451-453, 455-457). Similarly, two beads show only the brown to reddish vertical lines and the yellowish-brown core (figs. 124 and 135).

During the 2008-2012 Tell F6 excavations, twenty-two faience beads were found. A good number of them were recovered from Phase 1 (n=9), fewer from Phase 7 (n=3), and most were found in disturbed contexts (n=10) (Andersson 2016). A number of faience beads were also found at the Tell F6 temple (n=19) (Calvet & Pic 1986). They are, however, not found at the early Dilmun settlement of Al-Khidr (Benediková 2010). They occur in small numbers at the Early Dilmun Saar settlement (n=4) (Killick & Moon 2005 p. 186) but are not reported from the burials at Saar (Ibrahim 1982 p. 36. Mughal 1983 p. 68). Faience beads (n=7) are reported from the Early Dilmun periods Ib-IIc (c. 2150-1700 BC) at Qala'at al-Bahrain Excavation 520 (Højlund & Andersen 1994 p. 391-392, figs. 1943-1946, 1948, 1950 and 1962), while one faience or glass bead from Excavation 519 is dated to period IIIb1 (c. 1400 BC) (Højlund & Andersen 1997 fig. 301).

Glass. Glass occurs at Tell F3 in small numbers (n=5, 1%), while it is more common at Tell F6 (n=53, 10.3%). The material makes up 11.3% (n=58) of the assemblage. Although the glass is very badly preserved, in some cases it has retained a hint of its original colour, making it possible to distinguish blue and turquoise glass. The blue glass has remains of a deep blue colour, usually only seen at the very core of fragmented beads. The beads have otherwise disintegrated into an opaque white, sometimes with a beige or brownish discolouration on the surface (see for instance figs. 104, 244-245 and 541). Fig. 548 is the best-preserved glass bead, where the deep blue colour can be seen in the dark brown disintegrated glass core. The turquoise glass beads occur only in a small number (n=4). All are fragmented pieces with beige or brownish discolouration. One comes from Tell F3 (fig. 540) and three from Tell F6 (figs. 556, 558 and 564). Some of the poorly preserved glass beads, which are generally discoloured into a white to greyish material, show traces of combed trail decoration (e.g. figs. 299, 327 and 335) and, in a few instances, traces of larger white, wavy bands (e.g. figs. 126, 289 and 295). Blue glass colour is mentioned in relation to some of the glass beads found at Tell F6 (Calvet & Pic 1986 fig. 27: nos. 111-112 and 142). The Johns Hopkins University excavations next to the "Palace" recovered one glass bead, described as a "blue glass cylinder/bead?" made of pale blue glass (Howard-Carter 1984 no. 1303). Glass beads are not found at the Early Dilmun settlements of Al-Khidr and Saar, nor in the burials at Saar (Ibrahim 1982 p. 36. Mughal 1983 p. 68), but three biconical glass beads were found in period Ib (c. 2100 BC) and one in period IIc (c. 1800 BC) at Qala'at al-Bahrain (Højlund & Andersen 1994 p. 391, figs. 1941-1942, 1963) and two glass beads derive from an Early Type burial mound in Wadi as-Sail (Højlund et al. 2008 p. 149, fig. 17a-b).

Gold. One bead (n=1, 0.2%) made of a thin gold foil (0.1 mm thick) was recovered from Tell F6 (fig. 578). It is a collared melon bead, which would likely have been formed around a core. Small clay fragments kept with the gold "shell" may derive from this core. Another bead classified as lapis lazuli has a gold cap added to one end (fig. 554).

Paste. The paste beads (n=5, 1%) in the assemblage are made of either blue (n=3, 0.6%; figs. 141, 146 and 215) or white paste (n=2, 0.4%; figs. 133 and 239). Blue paste has been found at the Saar settlement (Killick & Moon 2005 p. 186, fig. 5.11n), where it was tentatively suggested to have been made of ground lapis lazuli. Compared to the Saar bead, the paste beads from Failaka appear in somewhat brighter blue colours. It is not possible to definitively identify the colour component of the blue paste; it may be ground lapis lazuli, but other parallels are identified as Egyptian blue or blue frit. The blue paste beads may be cheaper copies of lapis lazuli beads.

4. Dating and distribution

Throughout the Bronze Age of Failaka stone was invariably used in the construction of buildings as it became apparent during the excavations of Tell F3 and Tell F6 (Kjærum & Højlund 2013). It is also evinced by the many stone plundering pits found in the tells. Countless pits have been dug into the two tells in search of building stones, resulting in a general disturbance of layers, architecture and finds. Since excavation was carried out in horizontal, artificial layers (Højlund 1987 p. 7), these disturbances were rarely recognized in the field, and it has therefore not been possible to produce a reliable chronology for the beads based on stratigraphic context information.

Pottery was much more plentiful in the finds than beads and analysed with the chronological methods, typology, find combination and stratigraphy, a pottery chronology was established that could be used to date the different architectural phases (Højlund 1987). In addition, it has been attempted to use the pottery to date the layers in which the beads were found (fig. 68), but these datings must be viewed with caution and can only indicate certain trends in the material (Højlund pers.com. 2022).

Tell F3

Tell F3 contained several complexes of small houses, sometimes with enclosed courtyards, dated to periods 2, 3A, and 4A, an open temple courtyard dated to period 3B, and a large residential unit dated to period 4B (figs. 69-70) (Kjærum & Højlund 2013 p. 11, 21).

The context information available for a bead normally states the trench in which the bead was found and, sometimes, a find level. Occasionally, precise horizontal coordinates are provided. Of the 167 beads recovered from Tell F3, 86.1% (n=144) can be assigned to one of fifty-three specific trenches or baulks, while 13.9% (n=23) can only be assigned to Tell F3 in general.

A total of forty-seven beads can be related to individual excavation layers in Tell F3 in which the accompanying pottery may indicate the date within the periods represented at Tell F3, that is, periods 2-4B (fig. 70). Of these forty-seven beads, two (1.2%) were found in contexts dating to period 2, twelve (7.2%) from period 3A, two (1.2%) from period 3B, nine (5.4%) from period 4A and twenty-two (13.2%) from period 4B. Since there is no certainty that the contexts are undisturbed, these datings should be treated with caution.

A number of beads (n=23) from Tell F3 were found in contexts that could not be assigned to individual periods. Instead, they may belong to one or the other of two periods represented at Tell F3. Of these, a small number come from successive periods, for instance, from periods 3A/3B (n=2) and periods 4A/4B (n=10) (fig. 70).

A similarly small number of beads come from layers in which pottery dating to non-successive periods were present, for example, periods 3A/4A (n=1) and periods 3B/4B (n=10). Additionally, a total of ninety-nine beads from Tell F3 come from unknown contexts (fig. 70).

The suggested dating of the beads does, however, give the impression that beads were infrequent in the period 2 occupation of Tell F3 (n=2). In period 3A (n=12), there may be a slight increase in the number of beads, but even with the possible addition of the periods 3A/3B (n=1) and periods 3A/4A beads (n=1), the number is still rather low (n=13 or 14) (fig. 70). Period 3B also has a low number of beads (n=2), but the addition of period 3A/3B (n=1) or 3B/4B (n=10) beads may alter the impression somewhat (from n=3 to n=13). For period 4A (n=9), the number of beads is again relatively low, with the possible addition of periods 3A/4A (n=1) and 4A/4B (n=9). The largest number of beads are ascribed to period 4B (n=22), with the possible addition of periods 3B/4B (n=10) and/or 4A/4B (n=9).

Of the 144 beads that could be located to a trench or an excavated baulk at Tell F3, thirty-two beads (c. 19%) were also provided with horizontal coordinates (fig. 69). The distribution shows a scatter of beads with no major concentrations. Most trenches provided only one to four beads but a few trenches, lying mainly in the northwest part of the excavation, provided seven to eleven beads (trenches AB, AF, AB/Y, Y, AN, AO, X and AE. The fairly high number of beads (n=14) found in Trench RM, is misleading, as the trench is very large compared to other excavation trenches at Tell F3.

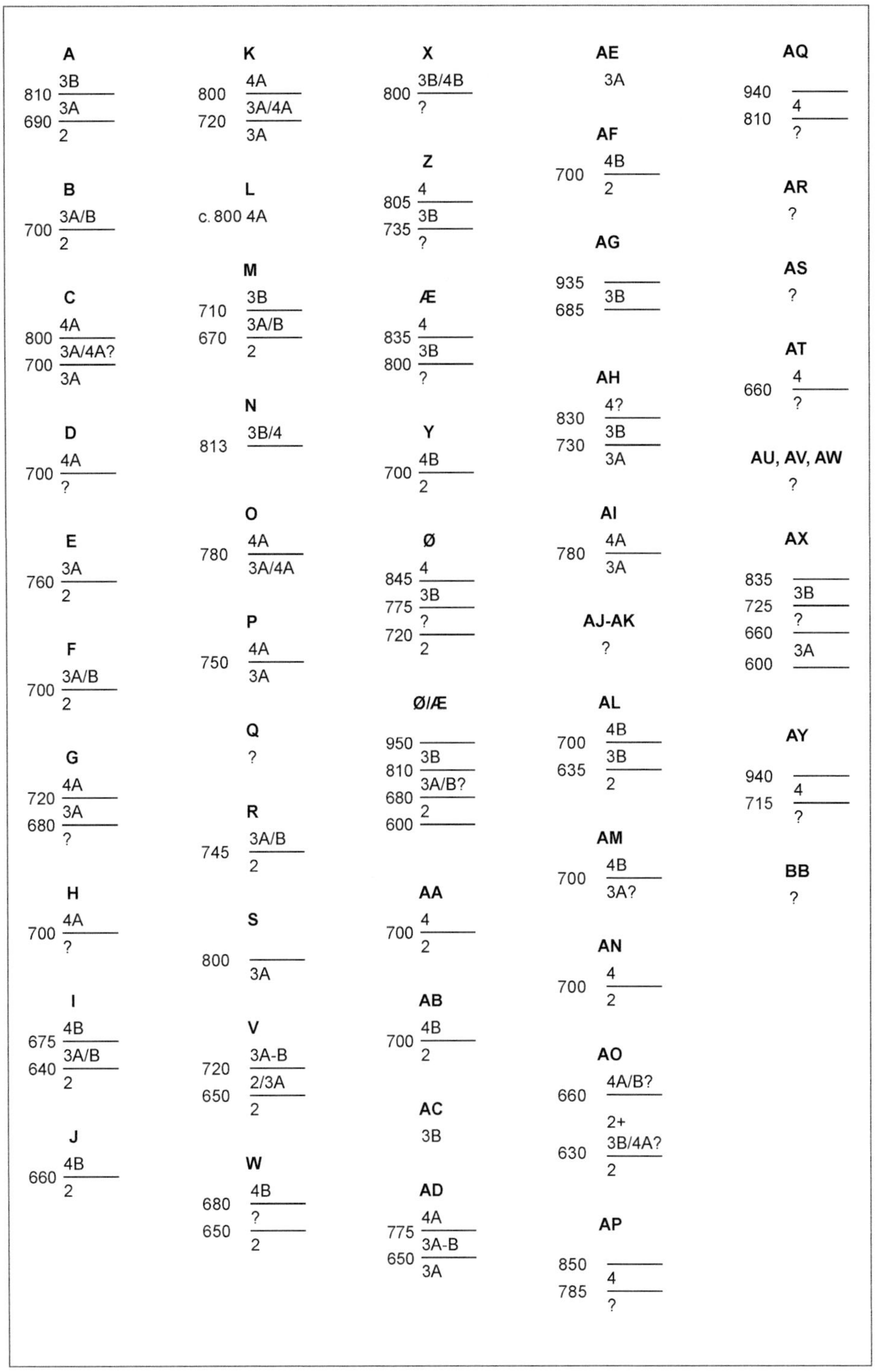

A: 3B / 810 — / 3A / 690 — / 2

B: 3A/B / 700 — / 2

C: 4A / 800 — / 3A/4A? / 700 — / 3A

D: 4A / 700 — / ?

E: 3A / 760 — / 2

F: 3A/B / 700 — / 2

G: 4A / 720 — / 3A / 680 — / ?

H: 4A / 700 — / ?

I: 4B / 675 — / 3A/B / 640 — / 2

J: 4B / 660 — / 2

K: 4A / 800 — / 3A/4A / 720 — / 3A

L: c. 800 4A

M: 3B / 710 — / 3A/B / 670 — / 2

N: 3B/4 / 813 —

O: 4A / 780 — / 3A/4A

P: 4A / 750 — / 3A

Q: ?

R: 3A/B / 745 — / 2

S: 800 — / 3A

V: 3A-B / 720 — / 2/3A / 650 — / 2

W: 4B / 680 — / ? / 650 — / 2

X: 3B/4B / 800 — / ?

Z: 4 / 805 — / 3B / 735 — / ?

Æ: 4 / 835 — / 3B / 800 — / ?

Y: 4B / 700 — / 2

Ø: 4 / 845 — / 3B / 775 — / ? / 720 — / 2

Ø/Æ: 950 — / 3B / 810 — / 3A/B? / 680 — / 2 / 600 —

AA: 4 / 700 — / 2

AB: 4B / 700 — / 2

AC: 3B

AD: 4A / 775 — / 3A-B / 650 — / 3A

AE: 3A

AF: 4B / 700 — / 2

AG: 935 — / 3B / 685 —

AH: 4? / 830 — / 3B / 730 — / 3A

AI: 4A / 780 — / 3A

AJ-AK: ?

AL: 4B / 700 — / 3B / 635 — / 2

AM: 4B / 700 — / 3A?

AN: 4 / 700 — / 2

AO: 4A/B? / 660 — / 2+ / 3B/4A? / 630 — / 2

AP: 850 — / 4 / 785 — / ?

AQ: 940 — / 4 / 810 — / ?

AR: ?

AS: ?

AT: 4 / 660 — / ?

AU, AV, AW: ?

AX: 835 — / 3B / 725 — / ? / 660 — / 3A / 600 —

AY: 940 — / 4 / 715 — / ?

BB: ?

Fig. 68. Tentative ceramic dating of excavated layers at Tell F3.

Tell F6

Tell F6 contained small-scale domestic architecture in the lowest levels dating to period 1, followed by a large production and storage installation, the "Palace", constructed in period 2 with major reoccupations in periods 3B and 4A (Kjærum & Højlund 2013 p. 99. Højlund & Abu-Laban 2016) (fig. 71). Of the 348 beads found at Tell F6, 72.1% (n=251) could be assigned to one of twenty-three specific trenches or baulks, while 27.9% (n=97) could only be assigned to Tell F6 in general.

Due to stone plundering, disturbance was far more extensive at Tell F6 than at Tell F3, making any attempt to date the beads extremely tentative and complicating any interpretation of the distribution pattern at Tell F6. Twenty-four beads were found below the earliest floor level of the "Palace" at level -1.55, that is, in the pre-"Palace" phase, and they can tentatively be dated to period 1 (fig. 72). This is a relatively high number, even though the excavation only reached this phase

Fig. 69. Plan of Tell F3 with bead distribution.

Period/ Trench	2	3A	3B	4A	4B	Unkn.	3A / 3B	4A / 4B	3A / 4A	3B / 4B	Total	%
A	-	2	-	-	-	-	-	-	-	-	**2**	1.2
C	-	-	-	-	-	1	-	-	-	-	**1**	0.6
D	-	-	-	3	-	-	-	-	-	-	**3**	1.8
E	1	-	-	-	-	-	-	-	-	-	**1**	0.6
F	-	-	-	-	-	4	-	-	-	-	**4**	2.4
G	-	-	-	-	-	1	-	-	-	-	**1**	0.6
H	-	-	-	3	-	-	-	-	-	-	**3**	1.8
I	1	-	-	-	1	-	1	-	-	-	**3**	1.8
J	-	-	-	-	4	-	-	-	-	-	**4**	2.4
K	-	-	-	2	-	1	-	-	1	-	**4**	2.4
M	-	-	2	-	-	-	-	-	-	-	**2**	1.2
P	-	-	-	1	-	-	-	-	-	-	**1**	0.6
RM	-	-	-	-	-	14	-	-	-	-	**14**	8.4
Baulk RM/S	-	-	-	-	-	1	-	-	-	-	**1**	0.6
X	-	-	-	-	-	1	-	-	-	8	**9**	5.4
Baulk N/X	-	-	-	-	-	1	-	-	-	2	**3**	1.8
Y	-	-	-	-	7	-	-	-	-	-	**7**	4.1
Z	-	-	-	-	-	2	-	-	-	-	**2**	1.2
Æ	-	-	-	-	-	3	-	-	-	-	**3**	1.8
Ø	-	-	-	-	-	3	-	-	-	-	**3**	1.8
Baulk Æ/Ø	-	-	-	-	-	3	-	-	-	-	**3**	1.8
AA	-	-	-	-	3	-	-	-	-	-	**3**	1.8
AB	-	-	-	-	1	10	-	-	-	-	**11**	6.6
AD	-	1	-	-	-	2	-	-	-	-	**3**	1.8
AE	-	9	-	-	-	-	-	-	-	-	**9**	5.4
Baulk AD/AE	-	-	-	-	-	1	-	-	-	-	**1**	0.6
AF	-	-	-	-	-	7	-	-	-	-	**7**	4.1
Baulk AB/AF	-	-	-	-	-	9	-	-	-	-	**9**	5.4
AI	-	-	-	-	-	1	-	-	-	-	**1**	0.6
AM	-	-	-	-	-	1	-	-	-	-	**1**	0.6
AN	-	-	-	-	6	1	-	-	-	-	**7**	4.1
AO	-	-	-	-	-	3	-	7	-	-	**10**	6.0
AP	-	-	-	-	-	1	-	-	-	-	**1**	0.6
AQ	-	-	-	-	-	-	-	1	-	-	**1**	0.6
Baulk AP/AQ	-	-	-	-	-	2	-	-	-	-	**2**	1.2
AR	-	-	-	-	-	1	-	-	-	-	**1**	0.6
AT	-	-	-	-	-	-	-	1	-	-	**1**	0.6
AV	-	-	-	-	-	2	-	-	-	-	**2**	1.2
No trench	-	-	-	-	-	23	-	-	-	-	**23**	13.9
Total	**2**	**12**	**2**	**9**	**22**	**99**	**1**	**9**	**1**	**10**	**167**	**100**
%	1.2	7.2	1.2	5.4	13.2	59.2	0.6	5.4	0.6	6.0	**100**	-

Fig. 70. The beads from Tell F3 divided by trench and settlement period.

in a few places, but intrusions from upper layers, due to stone plundering, may play a role. Furthermore, there is no guarantee that beads dating to period 1 from below the "Palace" have not intruded into the later layers. 142 beads derive from the layers above the earliest floor, that is, they can tentatively be referred to periods 2-4A or "Palace" phases I-II (fig. 72).

The beads found outside the "Palace" are ascribed to unknown contexts.

At Tell F6 as many as 251 beads could be located to a specific trench or baulk and, of these, 169 were provided with horizontal coordinates. The distribution pattern shows a high frequency of beads (eighteen to sixty-seven) in trench D2 (n=67, 19.2%), trench F2 (n=31, 8.9%), trench M2 (n=36, 10.3%), trench D1 (n=18, 5.2%) and trench F1 (n=24, 6.9%). In the remaining trenches smaller numbers of beads were found, that is one to eight (fig. 72).

Trench D2 covers all of room 3 and a smaller part of room 2, suggesting that these rooms (perhaps mainly room 3) were used to store beads, which may subsequently have been scattered to nearby trenches inside the walls of the "Palace". The beads do not seem to have been scattered outside the palace walls, as very small numbers of beads are found here.

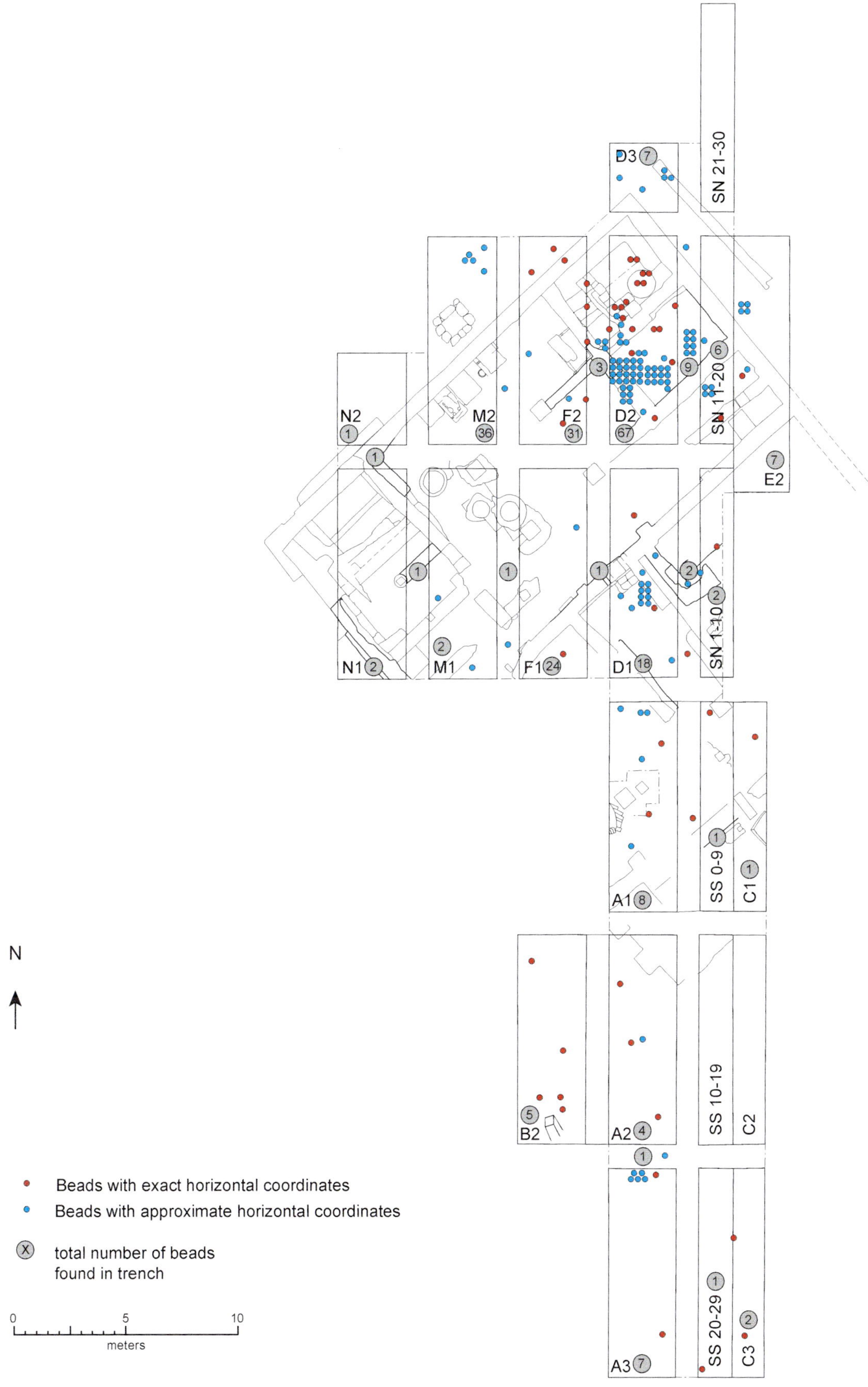

Fig. 71. Plan of Tell F6 with bead distribution. Horizontal coordinates locate beads at specific find spots i.e. "exact find spot of bead(s)" or refer to a larger area within a trench, i.e. "approximate find spot of bead(s)". In the latter case, the location has been placed at the central point of the given area. The original coordinates are listed in the catalogue.

Period/ Trenches	Period 1	Period 2-4A	Unkn.	Total	%
A1	1	7	-	8	2.3
A2	-	-	4	4	1.1
A3	-	-	7	7	2
A2/A3	-	1	-	1	0.3
B2	-	-	5	5	1.4
C1	-	1	-	1	0.3
C3	-	-	2	2	0.6
D1	1	14	3	18	5.2
D2	13	51	3	67	19.2
D3	-	-	7	7	2
E2	-	2	5	7	2
D2/E2	-	9	-	9	2.3
F1	-	15	9	24	6.9
D1/F1	1	-	-	1	0.3
F2	2	10	19	31	8.9
D2/F2	-	3	-	3	0.9
M1	-	2	-	2	0.6
F1/M1	1	-	-	1	0.3
M2	1	18	17	36	10.3
N1	-	-	2	2	0.6
M1/N1	-	-	1	1	0.3
N2	-	-	1	1	0.3
N1/N2	-	-	1	1	0.3
SN 1-10	-	2	-	2	0.6
D1/SN 1-10	-	2	-	2	0.6
SN 11-20	4	2	-	6	1.7
SS 0-9	-	1	-	1	0.3
SS 20-29	-	-	1	1	0.3
No trench	-	2	95	97	27.8
Total	**24**	**142**	**182**	**348**	**100**
%	6.9	40.8	52.3	100	-

Fig. 72. The beads from Tell F6 divided by trenches and settlement period.

5. Manufacture and use-wear

Stone beads

The bulk of the 1958-1963 assemblage consists of finished stone beads. Only a few roughouts, blanks or semi-drilled beads have been identified.

A few blanks were found at Tell F3 (n=2, figs. 252 and 438) and Tell F6 (n=2, figs. 211, 252 and 434), 0.8% of the assemblage. They are made of calcite, carnelian and agate (soft and hard stone) and are unperforated. Three have been polished (figs. 211, 252 and 434), while one (fig. 438) appears as a facetted roughout. It is uncertain whether the blanks and the roughout were made at Failaka or were imported along with the finished beads. No tools identified as drills have, however, been located at Tell F3 or Tell F6 (cf. the large collection of drills from Dholavira in Bisht 2015 p. 449-497, figs. 8.138-8.192a. Prabhakar 2015. Prabhakar et al. 2012).

One agate bead from Tell F6 is partially drilled (fig. 315). Again, it is not known if the drilling was done on Failaka or if the unfinished bead was brought to the island along with the finished beads.

It is uncertain whether the four chlorite beads (figs. 336, 408, 439 and 342), the calcite blank (fig. 438) and the four fragmented calcite beads (figs. 268, 316, 384 and 436) were made of reused vessel fragments, but any local production of beads made of these materials must have been minor in scale. Most of the beads in question are quite crudely fashioned.

There is some evidence of lapidary work taking place on the island. The study of the stone vessels from the 1958-1963 excavations on Failaka documents a local production of soft-stone vessels in a local style (the Failaka Figurative Style) in addition to the reuse of broken soft-stone vessels as pendants[48] and spindle whorls (Hilton 2014 p. 163). These consists of broken chlorite vessels, but a smaller component of broken calcite vessels are also present (Hilton 2014 p. 13). However, soft and medium-hard stone (like chlorite and calcite) are easier to cut and shape than hard stone types, out of which the beads from Failaka are primarily made.

The presence of lapidary activity involving hard stone is demonstrated by the 2012-2017 excavations at Tell F3, which recovered stone debitage along with lumps and chunks of raw material (flint, carnelian and jasper) in phases 1, 2, 4, 5 and 6 of the excavated area (period 2-4A). One of these small carnelian lumps, from phase 2, may even show the faint traces of a concentric drill (Hilton 2021 fig. 453). The import of carnelian as a raw material may be connected with the probable production of local style Dilmun seals at Tell F3 (Hilton 2021 p. 123-129). A minor production of hardstone beads in the same workshop may be indicated by a spherical bead blank made of jasper, recovered in phase 2 (period 3B) (Andersson 2021 p. 119).

The stone bead assemblage exhibits wide variation in quality in terms of the size of the beads and the work put into their shaping and polishing, including the drilling of the perforations. The carnelian beads may tentatively be divided into three different groups: 1) High-quality products with clear stylistic connections to the Indus, standardized forms or very long perforations (above 3 cm); 2) Medium-quality products with stylistic connections to the Indus, the Aegean and Mesopotamia, standardized forms and short to medium perforations (below 3 cm); and 3) Low-quality carnelian products with clear signs of being unfinished and short perforations, sometimes achieved by pecking rather than drilling.

Group 1 consists of a small number of beads (n=3, 0.6% of the total bead assemblage), including a long cylinder with a circular cross section (fig. 562) that has been carefully shaped with very thin walls and a long perforation, suggestive of the work of a highly skilled craftsperson. Two fragments of classic Indus bicone beads (figs. 501 and 506) also belong to the group of high-quality bead products. These beads most likely originated in the Indus area.

Group 2 makes up the vast majority of the carnelian beads in the assemblage and includes bead forms like barrels (I.A.1.b.-I.D.1.b.), truncated bicones (I.A.2.f-I.D.2.f) with circular cross section, truncated convex bicones with circular cross sections (I.B.1.f.), cylinders with circular cross sections (I.B.2.b.-I.D.2.b.) and spherical beads (I.B.1.a. and I.C.1.a.). These are generally smaller, well-made beads, relatively standardized in size and form, with nicely polished surfaces. Most of these beads are form types whose parallels are best known from the Indus region (see for instance Kenoyer 1991, fig. 5 on selected Harappan beads and pendant types, where types 1-6 are especially relevant). Other carnelian bead forms occur in significantly smaller numbers, such as barrels with hexagonal cross sections (XIII.D.1.b.). These also appear to be well made, standardized in size and form and with nicely polished surfaces, but their stylistic parallels are found in the Aegean.

In Group 3 a small number (n=4, 0.8%) of carnelian beads are crudely finished and exhibit particularly unfinished and irregularly facetted surfaces (e.g. figs. 114, 119, 137 and 337). These beads have not been polished and finished to the same standard as other carnelian beads in the assemblage. They appear to have been sawed off at both ends before being crudely shaped by chipping at one end. They were never ground nor finely polished, but they have been drilled. The crude carnelian beads all come from Tell F6. The appearance of these beads indicates that they are in an unfinished state or perhaps simply of low quality. They may either have been produced at Failaka (perhaps from reused material) or they may have arrived at the island along with the finished beads.

Different quality levels in carnelian bead assemblages are also observed at sites like Girsu (Tello) (600 beads dated c. 2600-2350 BC) and Susa (2000 beads of uncertain date) (Inizian 2000). A small proportion of beads in both assemblages consists of imports of high-quality Indus products (such as classical Indus bicones and etched carnelian beads). The most numerous beads consist of imported beads (spheres, bicones and cylinders) of relatively good quality in terms of raw material and polishing. Lastly, part of the bead material consists of locally produced beads of low quality or low-quality imports from other regions, such as the Iranian plateau or the Indus region (Inizian 2000).

The varying levels of quality observed at Girsu and Susa compares well with the carnelian component of the Failaka bead assemblage, although the number of stylistically distinct Indus beads is slightly higher at Girsu (nine classical long Indus bicones and one etched bead, c. 1.6% of the Girsu assemblage) and Susa (fourteen classical long Indus bicones and sixteen etched beads (c. 1.5% of the Susa assemblage) (Inizian 2000).

However, the Failaka bead assemblage also comprises other bead form types like barrels with semi-circular (VI.A.1.b.) or circle and flat cross section (VII.A.1.b.-VII.D.1.b.) or similar forms; these are generally larger, sometimes crude beads, made of hard stone types such as agate, jasper, limestone and milky quartz. They are not consistent in shape and are often not carefully shaped or polished, sometimes showing facets on the surface or unevenness in shape (e.g. examples such as figs. 383-384, 391, 401-402, 413-414, 418, 427 and 437). Additionally, these stone beads frequently show small striations on the surface indicating polishing direction and the use of abrasive material in polishing. These beads do not appear to be the products of highly skilled craftspeople, and it is unlikely that they originated in the Indus region. The variation in the Failaka stone bead assemblage suggests the import of beads of assorted quality, with a carnelian component of good quality, but very few "exceptional" or high-quality products.

Evidence of use-wear and stringing

The bead assemblage was evaluated by visual examination and not by microscope. The vast majority of the hard-stone beads show little signs of string wear on the edges of the drill hole and some surfaces still show traces of the final polishing, suggestive of products which were used only for a short amount of time or freshly manufactured products (cf. Kenoyer & Frenez 2018a p. 65). However, some hard-stone beads do show traces of extensive use-wear and string wear, suggesting that these beads were worn and curated for a long time, before entering the archaeological record (such as figs. 368, 375, 383, 428, 435, 460, 528 and 536).

Much of the surface damage and fractures occasionally seen on the hard-stone beads may be due to archaeological excavation rather than extensive use.

One bead was found with its drill hole blocked by a thick piece of corroded copper wire, c. 2 mm in diameter (fig. 474), indicating that the bead may have been originally strung on a wire thread. Another carnelian bead (fig. 440) may exhibit the same feature, as the perforation appears to be blocked by a corroded piece of copper. As the beads' perforations appear complete, the corroded copper cannot be the remains of a drill.

Incised decoration on hard-stone beads

The sole form of decoration on the hard-stone beads is incised decoration, seen only on three carnelian beads. One fragmented bead (fig. 441) is skilfully incised with clean straight lines. Smaller examples of this type of bead form are most at home in the Aegean region, both with and without incised decoration (cf. chapter 6 p. 53). A spherical bead (fig. 106) has five incised vertical lines making the bead somewhat reminiscent of a gadrooned bead, but the incision appears uneven and less skilfully executed than on fig. 441. It may be that an unskilled craftsperson attempted to make this spherical bead into a more desirable form. Gadrooned beads and melon beads were popular from the 3rd millennium onwards (Lankton 2003 p. 31). The last incised bead is a truncated bicone with a circular cross section and uneven diagonal lines incised around each end (fig. 505). Again, this decoration may be the creation of someone, who was not very skilled in hard-stone lapidary work. No parallels for this type of decoration have been found.

Discolouration of carnelian beads

Approximately 30% (n=70) of the carnelian beads from the Failaka 1958-1963 assemblage are discoloured by an opaque, white film covering their surfaces. This phenomenon has been observed in other bead assemblages, and two different explanations have been offered, either accidental overheating or alkaline soil conditions (Brunet 2009. Lankton 2003).

The discolouration may have occurred during an accidental overheating of the stone material, which likely happened during the manufacture of the beads. During this process, the carnelian was heated in order to bring out the red colour (Brunet 2009 p. 63. Inizian 2000). Such white opaque surfaces on beads have been observed at other sites in the Gulf, such as the Saar burial complex, Medinat Hamad burial mounds and Janabiyah (Bahrain), as well as Shimal and Dhayah (Ras al-Khaimah) and the Jebel al-Buhais necropolis (Sharjah) (Brunet 2009 p. 63. Crawford 2000 fig. 97. Jasim 2012 fig. 9. Mughal 1983. Srivastava 1991 pl. XLI.a: nos. 1, 3-5). The overheating and consequent discolouration is connected with less skilled craftspersons who would have had insufficient knowledge of the stone material and the heating treatment (Brunet 2009 p. 63). If the opaque, white surface is indeed a result of an accidental overheating, it might suggest that these beads would have been second-rate goods.

The discolouration on some of the fractured surfaces of the fragmented beads in the 2008-2012 Tell F6 assemblage suggests that they may have been heated after or during breakage (Andersson 2016 p. 180).

Lankton notes that ancient, hard-stone beads may be discoloured by soil conditions causing *"a natural etching by alkali in the soil"* (Lankton 2003 p. 69). Only part of the material at Failaka is discoloured, however, making this an implausible source of discolouration for the beads from Tell F3 and Tell F6. An explanation for this scenario would be if the discoloured beads were first deposited elsewhere and then reintroduced into circulation, only to be deposited at Failaka again at a later time. Similarly discoloured carnelian beads from the Mature Indus period are noted at Nausharo (c. 2800-2000 BC). At this site, different levels of expertise of bead making were noted in the assemblage and are attributed to a small local production (beads of lesser quality) and import of beads (beads of high quality and "exceptional" bead types) (Barthélemy de Saizieu 2000 figs. 4a-c, 6a, 7b). The overheating is not confined to bead products of lesser quality, but also occurs in beads of "fairly good", and "good quality". Overheating is also linked to the reshaping of fragmented beads of "exceptional quality" (Barthélemy de Saizieu 2000 fig. 8b).

Perforations

The perforations of 484 beads have been categorized by visual examination according to Beck's system (Beck 1928 p. 51-52, Pl. IV) (figs. 73-74). While Beck's system was originally intended for stone beads, beads of organic and artificial materials have also been categorized according to this classification. The perforations have been divided into five categories, that is, I and I.1 (n=4, 0.8%; type I n=1; type I.1 n=3), II (n=295, 57%), III (n=119, 23.2%), and IV (n=66, 12.8%). A single bead (fig. 253) with multiple perforations has been classified as Type X.a (n=1, 0.2%).

Perforation type I is a double cone bored from both ends with no attempt at a parallel hole (Beck 1928 pl. IV, type I). The I.1 subcategory of type I is a pecked perforation, creating a characteristic pecked conical depression (Kenoyer & Frenez 2018a p. 68). This type of perforation is found across Arabia (e.g. Oman), Egypt, Mesopotamia, the Indus Valley (at sites like Mohenjo-Daro, Chanhu-Daro, Dholavira, and Harappa) and China (Kenoyer & Frenez 2018a p. 68, figs. 6-7). The perforation technique is specifically attested at sites like Mari, Kish, Larsa, Ur, Tepe Sialk and Susa (Chevalier et al. 1982).

Perforation type II is a perforation drilled from both ends. The perforation appears with parallel sides or as slightly cone formed (Beck 1928 pl. IV, type II). In the Failaka assemblage, the perforations often have a marked meeting point, where the drillings from each end do not completely align. For most of the beads, the drillings meet at the middle of the bead or slightly off centre.

Perforation type III is a single cone perforation type (Beck 1928, pl. IV, type III). Beads were drilled from one end only, but the craftsperson was unable to keep the drill perfectly straight, creating a conical perforation with a larger diameter at the end where the drilling began and a smaller diameter at the exit of the perforation.

Perforation type IV is an approximately parallel perforation that is drilled from one end only (Beck 1928 pl. IV, type IV). Here the craftsperson has been able to keep the drill stable and straight while drilling.

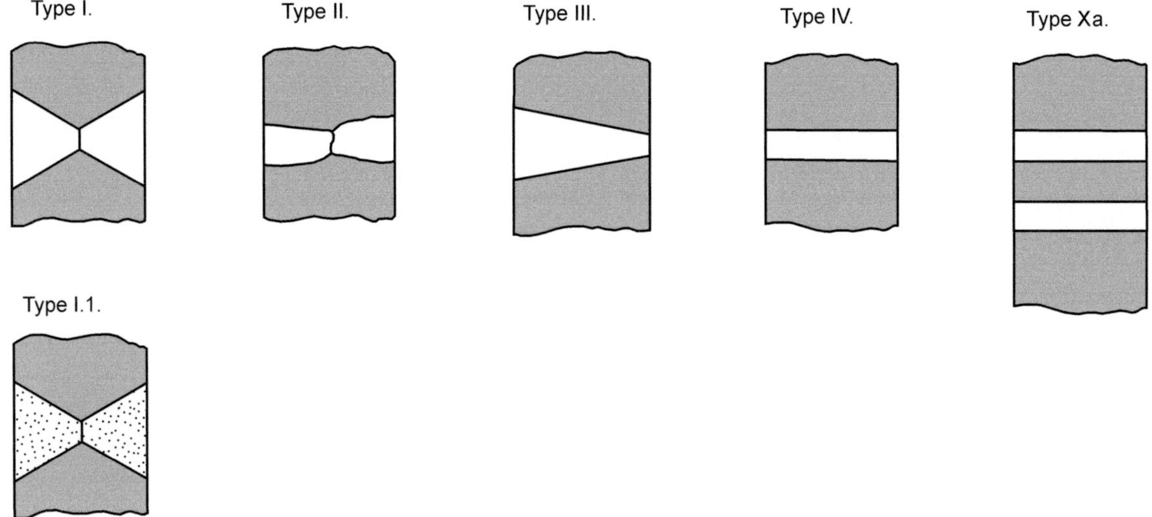

Fig. 73. Schematic representation of perforation types.

Perforation Type/Form Type	Type I/I.1	Type II	Type III	Type IV	Type X.a.	Semi-drilled	Blank	Unid.
Spheres with circular cross sections (I.B.1.a. and I.C.1.a.)	-	24	88	24	-	-	1	-
Spheres with elliptical cross sections (II.B.1.a. and II.C.1.a.)	-	1	-	1	-	-	-	1
Spheres with lenticular cross section (IV.B.1.a.)	-	1	-	-	-	-	-	1
Barrels with circular cross sections (I.A.1.b., I.B.1.b., I.C.1.b. and I.D.1.b.)	-	95	10	25	1	1	1	3
Barrels with elliptical cross sections (II.D.1.b.)	-	4	-	-	-	-	-	-
Barrels with lenticular cross sections (IV.B.1.b., IV.C.1.b. and IV.D.1.b.)	-	18	5	-	-	-	-	-
Barrels with plano-convex cross sections (V.B.1.b. and V.C.1.b.)	-	-	1	2	-	-	-	-
Barrels with semi-circular cross section (VI.C.1.b. and VI.D.1.b.)	-	16	1	-	-	-	-	-
Barrels with circle and flat cross sections (VII.C.1.b. and VII.D.1.b.)	-	28	-	1	-	-	-	-
Barrels with triangular cross sections (VIII.D.1.b.)	-	5	-	-	-	-	-	-
Barrels with rectangular cross sections (X.C.1.b. and X.D.1.b.)	-	3	-	-	-	-	1	-
Barrels with hexagonal cross sections (XIII.D.1.b.)	-	3	1	-	-	-	1	1
Convex bicones with circular cross sections (I.C.1.e.)	-	-	1	-	-	-	-	-
Truncated convex bicones with circular cross sections (I.B.1.f.)	-/2	4	1	8	-	-	-	-
Truncated convex bicones with lenticular cross sections (IV.C.1.f.)	-	3	-	-	-	-	-	1
Bicones with circular cross sections (I.D.2.e.)	-	5	-	-	-	-	-	-
Truncated bicones with circular cross sections (I.B.2.f., I.C.2.f. and I.D.2.f.)	-	56	2	1	-	-	-	-
Cylinders with circular cross sections (I.B.2.b., I.C.2.b., I.D.2.b. and unidentified cylinder fragments)	1/1	18	5	3	-	-	-	12
Cylinders with lenticular cross sections (IV.D.2.b.)	-	3	1	-	-	-	-	1
Varia	-/1	8	3	1	-	-	-	5
Total	**1/3**	**295**	**119**	**66**	**1**	**1**	**4**	**25**
%	0.8	57	23.2	12.8	0.2	0.2	0.8	5

Fig. 74. Distribution of perforation types by form.

	MOH's scale of hardness	Type I/I.1	Type II	Type III	Type IV	Type X.a.	Semi-drilled	Blank	Unid.	Total
Hard Stones										
Chalcedony										
Agate		-	61	9	-	-	1	2	2	75
Carnelian	6.5-7	1/3	142	82	1	-	-	1	1	231
Chrysoprase		-	1	-	-	-	-	-	-	1
Jasper		-	30	11	1	-	-	-	-	42
Moss Agate		-	1	-	-	-	-	-	-	1
Quartz										
Amethyst		-	1	-	-	-	-	-	-	1
Milky Quartz		-	9	-	-	-	-	-	-	9
Rock Crystal	7	-	3	1	-	-	-	-	-	4
Rose Quartz		-	1	-	-	-	-	-	-	1
Smoky Quartz		-	-	1	-	-	-	-	-	1
Quartz		-	4	-	-	-	-	-	-	4
Other stone types	7									
Porphyry		-	2	-	-	-	-	-	-	2
Total		1/3	255	104	2	-	1	3	3	**372**
%		0.2/0.6	62.3	25.1	0.4	-	0.2	0.6	0.6	90
Medium Hard stones										
Other stone types										
Calcite	3	-	4	-	-	-	-	1	-	5
Hematite	5.5-6.5	-	2	-	-	-	-	-	-	2
Lapis Lazuli	5-5.5	-	8	3	-	1	-	-	-	12
Limestone	3	-	10	-	-	-	-	-	-	10
Turquoise	5-6	-	2	1	-	-	-	-	2	5
Total		-	26	4	-	1	-	1	2	**34**
%		-	6.6	0.8	-	0.2	-	0.2	0.4	8.2
Soft Stones										
Other stone types										
Chlorite	2-2.5	-	4	-	-	-	-	-	-	4
Total		-	4	-	-	-	-	-	-	**4**
%		-	0.8	-	-	-	-	-	-	0.8
Unidentified Stone Types										
	?	-	5	-	-	-	-	-	-	5
Total		-	5	-	-	-	-	-	-	**5**
%		-	1	-	-	-	-	-	-	1
Total		1/3	290	108	2	1	1	4	5	**415**
%		0.2/0.6	70.9	26.1	0.4	0.2	0.2	0.8	1	100

Fig. 75. Perforations distributed on materials/Mohs hardness scale.

Perforation type X.a. is a perforation with multiple plane, parallel perforations (Beck 1928, pl. IV, type X.a.). In the case of the single bead with this type of perforation (fig. 253) both perforations are drilled from both ends, with perforations meeting at the middle.

A small number of beads (n=5) are labelled as blanks (n=4, 0.8%) or semi-drilled (n=1, 0.2%). Finally, some perforations are labelled as unidentified because of their fragmented state (n=25, 5%). Fig. 75 shows perforation types according to the stone types: soft, medium and hard.

The drillings observed vary greatly with regard to the size of the drill used, ranging in diameters from small (c. 1 mm) to large (c. 4 mm). It is assumed that the longer and thinner the drilling (and the harder the stone material), the more time would have been spent in the manufacture of a bead. The time used on the drillings in the production of beads is therefore often correlated with the value of the finished product.

Kenoyer's observations of bead production in modern bead workshops in India suggest *"that the time and effort needed to produce a single Harappan agate bead (three to eight days of drilling alone) or the large carnelian belts from Mohenjo-Daro (two to three years)"* (Kenoyer 2003 p. 18. 2008b p. 396). Few beads in the assemblage exhibit very long and thin drillings. Instead, the shorter thinner drillings are connected with smaller beads, which are generally made of hard stone (mainly carnelian). Larger and heavier beads (made of hard and medium-hard stone) generally have long, but large-diameter drillings.

Shell rings

Two of the shell rings found in the 1958-1963 assemblage are made of Conus shells wherein the apex of the shell was removed, and the shell was hollowed out and cut into slices. These slices, rings of shell were subsequently polished. The third shell ring is made of an oyster shell (i.e. a bivalve), wherein the shell has been cut, so as to remove the top portion and the ragged edge of the shell, and then polished.

Conus snails live in the sea around Failaka, and their shells wash ashore on the island. Oysters are also found near Failaka.

One Conus shell ring was found at later excavations at Tell F6 (2008-2012) (Andersson 2016 p. 183, fig. 883). The discovery of worked apexes of conus shells at Tell F6 (Andersson 2016 figs. 900, 927 and 972) and at Tell F3 in the 2012-2017 excavations (Andersson 2021, p. 118, figs. 423-425, 433-434, 437-439. Hilton, Andersson & Højlund 2021, p. 20, fig. 40) indicate a local production, as the apexes are considered a by-product of shell ring production. Two broken shell rings were also found in the 2012-2017 Tell F3 excavations (Andersson 2021 figs. 419, 432).

The low number of finished shell rings found at the island may indicate that the shell rings were exported. Since the production of shell rings was relatively simple and the raw material was available at Failaka, it may have been a profitable trade. At 3rd-millennium Ebla, 90% of the shell items found were made of shells that came from the Arabian Gulf or the Indian Ocean. At early 2nd-millennium 'Usiyeh a large quantity of shell items was found at Area A, among these 2509 shell rings, providing evidence of shell trade in the middle Euphrates region, which was most likely transported through the Gulf and South Mesopotamia (Oguchi 1992). An extensive trade in shell items coming through the Gulf from Oman and the Indus region has been documented as beginning as early as the 7th millennium (Gensheimer 1984).

Glass, faience and paste beads

Due to their very worn and fragmented state, it is difficult to assess the production techniques of the glass, faience and paste beads found at Failaka, but some observations can be mentioned.

Glass

Several of the glass beads are made around an inner "tube" forming the perforation and core of the bead. This is especially visible in a fragmented glass bead from Tell F6, where the shell of the bead has separated from the core (fig. 296). This feature is also seen in glass beads from the 14th century BC shipwreck of Ulu Burun, found off the coast of Anatolia, and in glass beads from Nuzi (Ingram 2005). Ingram notes that this opaque beige perforation deposit is likely a combination of calcite and clay, which is commonly found in wire-wound beads. In the wire-wound manufacture technique, the bead is formed by winding hot and malleable raw glass around a mandrel, which could then be further shaped with tools and paddles. This technique leaves striations around the bead axis in the glass material, observable by the naked eye, and becomes even more visible when the bead is deteriorated (Ingram 2005 p. 114).

Smaller glass oblate beads with circular cross section (I.B.1.a.) in the Failaka assemblage are reminiscent of beads from Ulu Burun, although the glass from Failaka is much more deteriorated. The beads from Ulu Burun retain some of their original blue colour, but in some instances, they also show visible striations in the glass or a glassy brownish surface (probably caused by deterioration, cf. Ingram 2005 p. 187-192), which is seen also in some of the glass beads from Failaka (figs. 125, 139, 160-161, 195-197). Notably, the tapered perforations observable in some of the spherical glass beads from Failaka are indicative of a tapered mandrel used in their production.

It has been possible to identify some decorative designs in the glass beads including trailed (cf. figs. 289, 299, 327 and 335) and banded designs (figs. 295 and 304). This kind of decoration can also be seen on glass beads from Nuzi (Vandiver 1983, fig. 3 lower left: trailed design). Banded designs were added by applying a different coloured glass to the bead. In the Failaka assemblage it is commonly a white glass applied to a bead in a darker colour. A large sphere in dark glass with a circular cross section exhibits an applied zig-zag design in white glass around the circumference of the bead (fig. 126). The same was the case with glass eye-beads, where the white of the "eye" was made by applying white glass (figs. 380 and 382). The glass eye-beads from Failaka are stylistically similar to examples found at Nuzi (Vandiver 1983 fig. 3: lower right).

Glass beads were probably first produced to copy and resemble stone beads, but glass in itself was valuable and became a prestige material in the 2nd millennium (Lankton 2003 p. 39-40, 45). Among the Failaka glass beads, a few large beads with white bands may be imitations of banded stone (figs. 126, 295, 304 and 548). The same is likely to be the case with a large bead with trailed/combed decoration (fig. 289). While many of the glass beads are deteriorated and now appear with dull, light brown surfaces (cf. figs. 285, 305, 319-320), they may have originally had vibrant colours. A long glass barrel bead with a circular cross section could be an imitation of a long Indus style bicone bead, due to its form and length (40 mm) (fig. 339).

Faience

Some of the faience beads found in the Failaka assemblage are standardized in form (figs. 446-447, 449, 451-453, 455-457), suggesting that they may have been produced in large quantities. They have remains of a white surface glaze and traces of decoration applied to this surface. This suggests a moulded faience core, with the addition of further coatings of glaze and decoration. Two other decorated faience beads (figs. 124 and 135) are quite fragile and worn, with visible air bubbles in the matrix. They are made of faience with a dark yellow core and red vertical stripes. One of the beads (fig. 124) retains some of its original surface, suggesting that it may originally have been white with red stripes.

Paste

The few paste beads in the assemblage appear to be moulded, as the perforations show no signs of being drilled. Sometimes beads were moulded around a flammable material such as sticks, strings or straws, which would burn away when the bead was fired. The paste beads from Failaka occur in blue and white colours. The blue paste may be made of either ground lapis lazuli, Egyptian blue or blue frit.

Fig. 215 has form parallels identified as made of Egyptian blue, a mixture of quartz, lime, a copper compound and an alkali flux. The other blue paste beads are made of a similar material (figs. 141, 146 and 239). Egyptian blue was produced in both Egypt and Mesopotamia in the second half of the 2nd millennium BC (Moorey 1994 p. 187. Hatton et al. 2008 p. 1591-1592, 1603). Given the geographical proximity to Mesopotamia, it may be the most likely origin for the Egyptian blue on Failaka.

Evidence of use-wear and stringing

Use-wear has also been observed on some beads made of glass, faience and paste, but generally it has been hard to evaluate, due to the bad state of preservation of most of the artificial materials. A few beads show significant signs after string-wear (e.g. figs. 215, 382 and 568) and some beads show use-wear on surfaces, where the beads would have rubbed against other ornaments strung on the same string (figs. 446-447, 449, 451-453, 455-457).

6. Discussion

The Bronze Age settlement on Failaka, Tell F3 and Tell F6, has, from its discovery in 1958, been seen in connection with the sea trade between Dilmun and Mesopotamia (Glob 1968. Bibby 1969). This is partly due to the position of the settlement on a small island midway between Bahrain and the South Mesopotamian cities and partly due to a variety of objects found on the island, which can be shown to have been imported from faraway places. It is in the context of this discussion that the beads presented in this volume find their value in terms of historical interpretation.

The beads are a group of objects, which, by the nature of their materials, are almost all foreign to Failaka and thus testify to relations between Failaka and distant places. The sheer number of beads found at Tell F3 and Tell F6 compared to other Dilmun sites is exceptional and indicative of the volume of trade that must have passed through this site.

Dating individual beads found during the 1958-1963 excavations have not been possible due to insufficient stratigraphical information (cf. p. 35), but the indications of dating, given by the pottery contexts of the beads, suggest that they occurred in all periods of occupation identified at Tell F3 and Tell F6, that is periods 1-4B. This is corroborated by the results of the 2012-2017 excavations in Tell F3 (Andersson 2021) and by the 2008-2012 excavations in Tell F6 which, in addition, provided information about the presence of beads on Failaka in the preceding Ur III period (Andersson 2016).

A total of 922 beads have been found at Tell F3 and Tell F6 in excavations carried out there between 1958 and 2017 by various expeditions. The number is much larger than what has been found on other contemporary Early Dilmun sites, compare, for example, the twelve beads at Al-Khidr on Failaka (not counting shell rings and apices), thirty beads from Qala'at al-Bahrain, eleven beads from the Barbar Temples and 104 beads from Saar Settlement.[49]

There is a great deal of typological similarity between the beads in the Failaka assemblage and those found at the above-mentioned Early Dilmun sites. The Failaka assemblage contains identical parallels with most of the beads from these other Early Dilmun sites (cf. from *Al-Khidr*: Benediková 2010 figs. 67f, 90a, 104a-c, e, and 107c-f; from *Qala'at al-Bahrain*: Højlund & Andersen 1994 p. 391-393, figs. 1941-1965 and Højlund & Andersen 1997 p. 36, figs. 95-96, from the *Barbar Temples*: Andersen & Højlund 2003 p. 316-317, figs. 815, 817, 820-827 and 830, from *Saar Settlement*: Killick & Moon 2005 p. 176-177, 181-186, figs. 5.7s and 5.9-5.11) as well as from the Bahrain burial mounds (Højlund 2007 figs. 115, 133, 149, 157-158, 180-181, and 187-188. Ibrahim 1982 pl. 56. Mughal 1983 figs. 28-29. Srivastava 1991 figs. 58-59A, pl. XLI-XLII).

However, there is a marked difference between the Failaka assemblage and the other Early Dilmun settlements in terms of the proportion of beads made of semi-precious materials relative to the beads made of materials traditionally considered less valuable, such as clay and shell. Glass is also conspicuously absent or rare at most other Dilmun sites.

At Tell F3 and Tell F6 on Failaka, 80% of the beads are made of mineral materials: varieties of hard stone, such as agate, carnelian, jasper, moss agate, rock crystal, milky quartz, smoky quartz, calcite, chlorite, lapis lazuli, turquoise, limestone and porphyry. At Al-Khidr, the corresponding figure is 16.6%, at Qala'at al-Bahrain 46.6%, and at Saar Settlement 41.3%.

These statistics may indicate that the bead assemblage found on Failaka is related to the position of the island on the trade route to Mesopotamia, whereas the beads found on the other sites mentioned are rather an expression of local consumption.

Accordingly, the clay beads so common at the Saar Settlement have been interpreted as the cheap local imitation of expensive hard-stone beads (Killick & Moon 2005 p. 181). They are made of clay in a dull pink colour, suggesting that they may imitate red stone, such as carnelian or agate. Clay or terracotta beads are common in the Indus region, for instance at Harappa, where they are also interpreted as imitations of stone (Kenoyer 2005 p. 159).

That nearly all the beads found at the Barbar Temple (90,9%, n=10) are semi-precious (carnelian, lapis lazuli, limestone and turquoise) and in addition exceptional in size, may be due to the religious context (Andersen & Højlund 2003 p. 316-317).

The remarkable number of beads found at Tell F3 and Tell F6 may suggest that large volumes of beads were loaded onto and off boats at the site. This may have been how trade between Dilmun and Mesopotamia was normally organized. Alternatively, it could perhaps also be attributed to a more random barter exchange which took place during encounters on Failaka in connection with the service, maintenance and repair of the cargo fleet.

At Tell F3, the beads are scattered over the excavated trenches with no apparent or substantial concentrations. This suggests that most of the beads here must either have been lost by accident or that they may represent small caches of wealth stashed away by the inhabitants of Tell F3 and, subsequently, forgotten or lost.

In Tell F6 there is a clear concentration of beads around rooms 2-3 of the "Palace", suggesting that this was a preferred place to store beads. Due to the difficulties involved in interpreting the stratigraphical conditions, it is not clear, however, if the concentration represents a single hoard of beads lost when the building was abandoned and later scattered during stone plundering or if they represent an accumulation of beads lost over time.

There is a marked difference in the quantity of beads found in the two tells. At Tell F3 a surface of 1511 m^2 was excavated, resulting in the find of 167 beads or an average of c. 0.11 bead per m^2. At Tell F6 a surface of 617 m^2 was excavated resulting in the find of 348 beads or an average of c. 0.56 bead per m^2. Given that the trenches were generally deeper in Tell F3 than in Tell F6, the frequency of beads does seem considerably higher in Tell F6 than in Tell F3.

Such numbers are difficult to compare since they are dependent on several variables that cannot all be controlled, but at least the excavations of Tell F3 and Tell F6 compared here took place at the same time and were supervised by the same team of archaeologists, and sieving of the excavated deposits was a standard procedure, documented both in the diaries and photos (e.g. Højlund 2008 p. 31 upper: Tell F3 with three sieves in the background. Kjærum & Højlund 2013 figs. 4, 14, 72, and 77: Tell F3 with sieves in the background and figs. 130, 139-141: Tell F6 with sieves in the background).

According to the excavation documentation, 197 beads, or 38% of the assemblage, were recovered from sieving the excavated deposits at Tell F3 and Tell F6.

The conclusion must be that a far greater number of beads were handled and thereby accidentally lost at Tell F6 than at Tell F3.

The proximity of the temple to the "Palace" might give rise to the notion that the beads found in the "Palace" were part of temple equipment, for example, for the adornment of cult statues. However, the lack of other such temple-related articles in the "Palace" makes this interpretation less likely, the more so since the other finds in the building suggest exclusively mundane production and storage (Kjærum & Højlund 2013 p. 105). Thus, the interpretation of the beads as having been lost during storage in the building seems a more likely alternative.

The great number of beads found inside the "Palace" contrasts with the low number (n=11) found immediately west of the "Palace" by the Johns Hopkins investigations in trenches FH3-5 and 9 (Howard-Carter 1984. Kjærum & Højlund 2013 fig. 131) and at the nearby temple excavated by the French expedition (n=51). Although comparing these numbers is problematic because of different excavation methods (cf. Højlund & Abu-Laban 2016 p. 261, note 23), they do seem to corroborate that activities involving beads mainly took place inside the "Palace" walls.

Originally, the excavators of the large building in Tell F6 interpreted it as a palace with administrative functions (Glob 1968 p. 132. Kjærum 1986 p. 79). This interpretation rested on the size of the building (c. 500 m^2) which is considerable when compared to the small houses at Tell F3 (c. 12-50 m^2), and its general structure, especially the long corridor that leads to an inner gate giving access to a large, pillared hall. The building, however, has many features suggesting that it was used for the manufacture and storage of fluids (Kjærum & Højlund 2013 p. 105). The present interpretation of the many beads found in the "Palace" as having been stored there supports the general interpretation of the building as a storage facility. The proximity of the "Palace" and the temple and their distance from the domestic Tell F3 all suggest that both the "Palace" and temple were under public, probably royal, authority.

In cuneiform sources from South Mesopotamia, trade in semi-precious beads – in addition to copper and ivory – from the southeast, from the lands of *Magan* and *Meluhha,* through Dilmun to Mesopotamia is amply documented (Oppenheim 1954. Laursen & Steinkeller 2017).

The active Dilmun trade through the Gulf waters, in the late 3rd and early 2nd millennium, is also documented by small Dilmun campsites or way stations between Bahrain and the Northern Emirates (Carter 2003 fig. 1). The survey of these sites shows evidence of Dilmun activity in the form of Dilmun pottery, stone-lined pits and sometimes larger structures. Recent excavations at Sir Bani Yas have confirmed the presence of a substantial way station at this island (Al

Kaabi & Al Meqbali 2018). This route between Qala'at al-Bahrain and Tell Abraq could be traced stretching for 755 km, where the shortest distance between the way stations is 35 km and the longest distance is 145 km (Carter 2013 table 3). Further up the Gulf, the route would probably have hugged the Iranian side of the Gulf, of which Bandar Bushire is a likely place for a way station (Carter 2013 p. 130).

The beads found at Failaka are likely evidence of this trade, as it is doubtful that they came to this small island as a result of a local demand for luxuries. Even though some of the beads may have been the private possessions of the inhabitants on the island, it is more likely that the majority of them were trade goods tied to the complex network of long-distance sea trade. Beads must have been only one of the commodities transported and stored at the "Palace" at Tell F6.

It is probable that the land of *Meluhha*, that is, the Indus Valley civilization, was the place of origin of a good deal of the semi-precious stone beads found along the shores of Dilmun and on Failaka. Excavations at large Indus cities, such as Mohenjo-Daro, Chanhu-Daro, Harappa, and Dholavira, have produced an abundance of beads in a large variety of materials including workshops where all stages of the production can be followed (cf. *Mohenjo Daro*: Mackay 1938 p. 495-522, 546-556, pl. 134-139. *Chanhu-Daro*: Mackay 1943 p. 199-214, pl. 79-87. *Harappa*: Vats 1940 p. 392-442, pl. 128-137. *Dholavira*: Bisht 2015 p. 416-497, figs. 8.81-8.131). Additionally, recent excavations in Gujarat have uncovered small-scale sites, among these Kanmer, Bagasra, Shikarpur, and Khirsara, which also took part in the production of hard-stone beads (Uesugi 2018 p. 30).

Parallels to many of the stone bead types found along the Gulf shores can be found in the corpus published from the Indus region, but the variety is larger here and includes beads of a higher quality in terms of size, material and execution than those found in the late 3rd- to 2nd-millennium Gulf corpus. Generally, large Indus cities had expert craftspeople producing high quality products, while smaller Indus settlements accommodated bead production of poorer quality and simultaneously imported high-quality beads from the larger Indus cities (Barthélemy de Saizieu 2000). In the Indus sphere, beads of different qualities were targeted at different consumers and were produced for different functions. Bead products of high quality (such as the classical Indus bicones and small beads of high quality) were produced by a few qualified craftspeople responding to the limited demand of elites and religious institutions. These beads were generally not intended for commercial purposes (Roux & Matarasso 2000).

Archaeological data also indicates that bead production at the larger cities varied. Bead making at Lothal, Mohenjo-Daro, Harappa, Dholavira and Nagwada focused on the production of beads of small and medium dimensions, while preforms for classic long Indus bicones have only been found at Chanhu-Daro (Roux & Matarasso 2000). Within the Indus sphere there was marked regional variation in the nature and scale of bead production, as for instance exemplified between the regions of Gujarat and the Ghaggar Valley. Where the region of Gujarat generally produced longer beads, sites in the Ghaggar valley produced shorter beads. This regional variation is tied to uneven access to stone sources and skilled craftspeople in the two regions (Uesugi 2018 p. 32).

As such, the civilization of the Mature Harappan period (c. 2600-1900 BC) produced products with different qualities, which were likely sold to merchants and entered the trade bound for the Gulf and Mesopotamia. During the decline of the Indus civilization in the Late Harappan period (1900-1300 BC), bead production continued, but with some significant changes in the applied drilling technology ("Ernestite" constricted cylindrical drills were no longer used) and the disappearance of distinctive high-quality beads, such as long, bicone carnelian beads (Possehl 1996 p. 159-160, fig. 13. Kenoyer & Frenez 2018b p. 401) and carnelian beads with etched decoration (De Waele & Haerinck 2006 p. 32. Prabhakar 2018 p. 475ff, figs. 3, 5, 8-9).

The few probable Mature Harappan period beads found at Failaka, like the long Indus bicones (figs. 501 and 506) are fragmented and may be remnants of the earliest bead trade at the island. Such characteristic long Indus bicone beads moved widely along trade networks, as they are not only found in Mesopotamia (at Ur, Kish, Girsu, Mari, Tell Brak and Ebla) and Iran (Susa, Jalalabad and Marlik) but also in Anatolia and the Aegean (at Hattusa-Bogazköy and Troy) (Chakrabarti & Moghadam 1977. Ludvik et al. 2014. Ludvik et al. 2015. Peyronel 2015).

Carnelian beads with etched decoration are completely absent at Failaka, while several examples have been found in Bahrain (Medinat Hamad and Sar al-Jisr) and other sites in the wider Gulf region in contexts dated to the Early Bronze Age (De Waele & Haerinck 2006 p. 33-35, table 1. Aruz 2008 p. 243, fig. 74. Frenez 2018 p. 392 and fig. 35.10. Kenoyer & Frenez 2018a). The scarcity of carnelian beads with etched decoration in the Gulf after this period has been linked to the decline of the Indus Civilization in the first part of the 2nd millennium (De Waele & Haerinck 2006 p. 32, 35-36). This may also explain their absence at Dilmun Failaka, since this settlement post-dates the Mature Harappan period. Alternatively, it may be a result of the fact that the etched beads from Bahrain were mostly recovered from graves which do not occur at Failaka. Otherwise, the distribution of etched carnelian beads (although in small numbers) reached all the way from the Indus to the Aegean (Aruz 2008 p. 242 and fig. 74).

Carnelian is traditionally attributed to the Indus region and, stylistically, a large part of the carnelian beads from Failaka are forms that would be at home in the Indus. This is especially true of such standardized form types as barrels with circular cross section (n= 86, 16.6%), truncated convex bicones with circular cross sections (n= 4, 0.2%) and truncated bicones with circular cross sections (n= 54, 10.4%), making up about 27.9% of the assemblage (n= 144). Likewise, a small number (n=4, 0.2%) of long slender carnelian cylinders (cf. figs. 539, 552, 562-563) would also have required a very skilled lapidary craftsperson to produce. The form type is known in the Indus, although it is not very common (Kenoyer 2016 p. 206).

It has been suggested that a production of long Indus carnelian bicones could have taken place in South Babylonia by Indus immigrants around 2350-2150 BC. Faceted long Indus carnelian bicones, drilled with Indus type drill technology, have been found at Ur, but this type is not found in the Indus region and have therefore been proposed as a possible local production (Lankton 2003 p. 35-37. Kenoyer 2008a p. 25-26), possibly linked to Meluhhan craft specialists working in Mesopotamia.

Initial interpretation of textual evidence (Parpola et al. 1977), suggesting the presence of a "Meluhhan village" in the Ur III period of South Babylonia (Girsu/Lagash province) has since been re-examined by Steinkeller, who finds the textual evidence for an actual Meluhhan settlement insufficient (Laursen & Steinkeller 2017 p. 79-82).

The low number of lapis lazuli beads found at Failaka are either quite small or look very worn, suggesting some curation of the beads and possibly reduced access to the material (Lankton 2003 p. 39. Moorey 1994 p. 8). However, one sphere (fig. 105) and one lenticular barrel (fig. 460) are exceptionally large.

While the lapis lazuli found at Failaka must ultimately originate from mines in Afghanistan, it is less obvious from which direction the lapis lazuli beads would have come. Lapis lazuli was primarily traded through either a northern or a southern land route to Mesopotamia. The northern route travelled through Damghan, Hamadan and the Diyala region, while the southern route travelled via Shahr-i Sokhta, the Lut desert, Shahdad, Fars and Khuzistan (De Waele & Haerinck 2006 p. 32). Despite the Indus region being connected with lapis lazuli in Mesopotamian textual sources, lapis lazuli was not a popular material in the Harappan sphere, and similarly few objects made of the material have been found in Iran. Lapis lazuli seems to have been directed toward the Mesopotamian markets and production places and distributed further to Egypt and the Mediterranean region (Aruz 2008 p. 242-243. Law 2014).

The possibility that stone beads were manufactured along the Gulf has sometimes been entertained. During the 3rd and 2nd millennia production of vessels in soft stone was a large-scale industry in southeast Arabia and Iran. The round stamp seals of Dilmun type, cut in soft stone, were similarly produced at Bahrain and Failaka and there is ample proof of production of pendants and spindle whorls made of reused soft-stone vessels on Failaka in the 2nd millennium (Ciarli 1990 p. 480. Hilton 2014 p. 163).

Conversely, there is little evidence of hard-stone bead production along the Gulf in the 3rd millennium when such goods are largely believed to have come from the Indus region. However, it has been suggested that a local production of beads took place in the UAE during the 2nd millennium (Brunet 2009 p. 65. Charpentier et al. 2017).

A study by Kenoyer and Frenez on hard-stone beads from Oman concludes that *"there is very little evidence for the production of hard-stone beads such as carnelian from any sites in Oman"* during the 3rd and 2nd millennia and that part of the bead material does come from the Indus region. However, the authors also stress *"that many carnelian beads found in Oman come from other sources and that it is important to broaden our study of ancient trade networks to include areas such as Afghanistan, Iran, Yemen, Egypt, and Anatolia."* (Kenoyer and Frenez 2018a p. 74). This fits well with Kenoyer's analysis of the drill holes in a small sample of carnelian beads from the 2008-2012 excavations at Tell F6, which showed that a variety of drills were used and that this did not point to an exclusive Indus origin of the carnelian beads at the island (Kenoyer 2016).

The Failaka hard stone beads (mainly carnelian) of differing quality in terms of production and raw material, may suggest that the bulk of the beads coming through the Dilmun trading station were not first-class trade goods. The varying quality of production and raw materials could indicate that the beads may have been produced at several different workshops, perhaps in different geographic regions.

Some evidence of hard-stone industry on Failaka was found in the 2012-2017 excavations at Tell F3. A number of carnelian chips dating to periods 2-4A (c. 1800-1400 BC) (Hilton 2021) testify to some kind of production, perhaps of stamp seals in Style II or III (cf. Kjærum 1983 nos. 330 and 353 = David-Cuny & Neyme 2016 p. 66 and p. 189. Højlund & Abu-Laban 2016 figs. 743-744). A spherical bead blank made of jasper was also recovered in a period 3B context during the 2012-2017 excavations at Tell F3 (Andersson 2021 p. 125, fig. 418).

The number of unpierced, hard-stone bead blanks and semi-drilled beads in the 1958-1963 assemblage is low (n=4 and n=1, respectively) and while they can be explained as accidental imports arriving along with the finished beads, it is at least a possibility that they represent a minor local production.

The Failaka bead assemblage exhibits differences in use-wear. A small part of the beads shows extensive string wear and look worn, probably as a result of long use. The majority of the beads, however, show very little sign of wear and may be freshly manufactured products.

Many of the form types in the Failaka assemblage are commonly found during all of the 2nd millennium and widely across the western and south Asian regions, but some specific types are more restricted in terms of dating and stylistic parallels point to their origin in certain geographical regions. A few of the Failaka stone beads have late 3rd-millennium Mesopotamian parallels. These include a large agate bead (fig. 364) with close parallels – in form, size and material (including the banding of the stone, which the craftsperson carefully exploited to create the pattern of the bead) – at the Royal Cemetery at Ur (Woolley 1934 p. 185, pl. 132, PG/1422; p. 195, pl. 147, PG/1847). This type of bead likely dates to the 3rd millennium and was either curated for some time before it was deposited on Failaka or, again, may represent a very early phase of the bead trade there.

One bead (fig. 576) has many parallels in graves at Ur dated to ED III (c. 2600-2350 BC) and the Akkadian period (c. 2350-2150 BC) (cf. Woolley 1934 p. 32. Pollock 1985 p. 139). In the Gulf, similar beads have been found at Ras al-Khaimah, where two parallels have been found in an early 2nd-millennium tomb context at Qarn-al-Harf (Hilton pers. comm. 2021).

Nicely shaped barrels with semi-circular or circle and flat cross sections made of agate and jasper (figs. 389, 397-399, 407 and 412) have good parallels in the second half of the 3rd millennium (Lankton 2003 p. 35). A comparable example was found at the Tell F6 temple (Calvet and Pic 1986 p. 19, fig. 127).

The barrels with semi-circular or circle and flat cross sections made of less colourful stone, such as limestone and milky quartz, are larger and bulkier and have parallels in Bahrain in a context dated c. 1950 BC (Andersen & Højlund 2003 p. 316, figs. 820 and 822). A comparable bead in a black stone was found at the F6 temple (Calvet and Pic 1986 p. 19, fig. 129). Such bead forms can also be found in Mesopotamian contexts, for example, at 'Usiyeh (type 27, B148-B150), where they are generally larger than other form types (made of agate). Parallels of white calcite and black serpentine belonging to the Akkadian period (c. 2350-2150 BC) are found at Tell Brak (Mallowan 1947 p. 256-257, Pls. LXXXV: no. 11 and LXXXVI: no. 2. Oguchi 1998 p. 60). At Uruk, the form is found in contexts dating from the Uruk period to the Parthian period (Limper 1988 cat. nos. F142-143, F145, F147, F149). While comparable bead forms in banded agate can be found at Harappa, dated to the Late Harappan period (c. 1900-1700 BC), the larger, cruder and bulkier beads do not seem to be part of the Indus repertoire (cf. Kenoyer 2005 fig. 7). This would suggest that such beads were produced in other regions. The use of less colourful stone for part of the Failaka beads of this kind may indicate that these beads were not goods of premium quality.

With respect to the beads made of faience, glass and paste, the direction from which they may have come to Failaka is less certain, and we must consider the possibility that some were produced on the island.

The uppermost settlement phase in the northern part of Tell F3 (Houses 30 and 23) contained a significant amount of glazed pottery and faience dating to period 4B (Højlund 1987 fig. 619) and cylinder seals of faience and glass have been found distributed all over Tell F3 (Kjærum 1983 no. 375ff).

However, at Failaka, glass, faience and paste beads are found mainly at Tell F6 (n=53, n=5 and n=5, respectively), while they are less frequent at Tell F3 (glass n=5 and faience n=9, and no paste beads) (fig. 3.1). Thus, the distribution of glass, faience and paste beads at Failaka does not support a local production of such beads at Tell F3.

It is unlikely, that the glass beads at Failaka could have come from the Indus region as glass bead production is not reported to have become common until

c. 1450-1200 BC. If Harappans knew of glassmaking at an earlier stage, this knowledge must have been lost during the decline of the Indus civilization (Kanungo 2008 p. 1024-1025).

In comparison, faience was produced much earlier in the Indus Valley region and evidence of faience production is attested at Harappa from the Early to the Late Harappan period (c. 2800-1300 BC) (Kanungo 2008 p. 1024. Kenoyer 2005 tables 1 and 3).

However, faience is not frequently attested in the 1958-1963 assemblage (n=14). No faience beads were found in the Johns Hopkins University excavations at Tell F6, but the French temple excavations did recover faience beads (n=19) from 2nd- to 1st-millennium contexts (Howard Carter 1984. Calvet & Pic 1986). No stylistic parallels for the 1958-1963 Failaka faience beads have been identified in the Indus region.

In the mid-2nd-millennium, production of glass and faience beads became very common in Mesopotamia. Parallels to most of the Failaka glass and faience beads can be found at Mesopotamian sites and accordingly, a northern provenience is likely. A distinctive group of faience beads (figs. 446-447, 449, 451-453, 455-457) compares well with late 2nd millennium faience beads at Uruk with parallels found in a wide region stretching between Hattusa-Bogazköy (Anatolia) and Choga Zanbil (Iran) (Limper 1988 p. 20, 125-126, cat. nos. F222-F224). Although the Failaka glass beads are badly preserved, it has been possible to identify some of their original designs, which find parallels from 2nd-millennium Nuzi (Vandiver 1983 figs. 1 and 3). The decorative designs of the glass and faience beads include trailed designs (cf. figs. 130, 299, 327 and 335), zig-zag designs (cf. fig. 126) and banded designs (cf. figs. 295 and 304). Additionally, the glass eye-beads found on Failaka have good parallels in Mesopotamia, for instance at Tell Khaiber and Nuzi (Campbell et al. p. 38 and fig. 18. Vandiver 1983 p. 242, fig. 3: lower right). Such glass eye-beads first appears in the middle of the 2nd millennium (Clayden 2009 p. 44).

Some of the wire-wound spherical beads at Failaka find good parallels in the 2nd millennium material from Ulu Burun, which would also point to a mid-2nd-millennium date for this part of the bead material.

Some of the hard-stone bead forms in the assemblage may also primarily belong to the later part of the 2nd millennium. One example of this is the barrel with a hexagonal cross section (figs. 440, 442-443) otherwise called an amygdaloid bead (Ludvik et al. 2015 p. 10-11, figs. 5.d-e) and described by Lankton as typical of the Late Bronze Age (c. 1600-1200 BC) (Lankton 2003 p. 40). It is found in all of the Aegean but especially popular in the southeastern part of this region (Pieniążek 2012 p. 505-506). Parallels can be found, for instance, at Maroni, Enkomi (Cyprus), Ialysus (Rhodes), Troy and Bersik-Tepe (Anatolia), but also northern Syria, (i.e. Ugarit, Minet el-Beida and Emar) and central Syria (i.e. Mari). A fourth example of the same form type is fragmented (fig. 441), but a great deal larger than the other three examples from Failaka and has incised lines running down the length of the bead. The bead form with incised lines can be found at Troy, Cyprus, Rhodes and Ugarit (Ludvik et al. 2015 p. 10-11, figs. 4d-e and 5d-e. Pieniążek 2012 p. 505-506, pl. CXXVd. Pieniążek & Kozal 2014 p. 193-194, fig. 3).[50]

Other examples of late 2nd millennium stone beads on Failaka are the agate eye-beads which are characteristic of the Kassite period in Babylonia (Campbell et al. 2017 p. 38). The bead type may also testify to the far reach of the networks in question, with a widespread distribution from Cyprus to Anatolia, across Mesopotamia to different regions in Iran and through the Gulf with the examples found at Failaka and in Oman (Clayden 2009 p. 41. Frenez et al. 2021). Though eye-beads occur in the Indus region they are different in form, colour and materials (Kenoyer 2013).

The symbolic meaning and value of eye-beads are indicated by inscribed examples interpreted as high-status artefacts linked to kingship and which served a religious function. While uninscribed examples can be found outside Mesopotamia, inscribed examples are found mainly in Mesopotamia (Clayden 2009 p. 55). An inscribed eye-bead was, however, recently reported from an Iron Age (1300-600 BC) collective tomb at Dibbā al-Bayah, Oman, which represents the southernmost cuneiform inscription in the Gulf and the only cuneiform inscription in southeastern Arabia. The inscription dates to the Kassite period (Frenez et al. 2021).

With these examples in mind, there is some evidence of beads (both faience, glass and carnelian) moving from Mesopotamia and even from the Aegean (probably through Mesopotamia) to Failaka in the latter part of the 2nd millennium.

It appears that the beads with likely Indus Valley provenience dates to the late 3rd and early 2nd millennium, which may indicate that some of the beads were curated for a long time before finally entering the archaeological record at Failaka (due to their being found in later period contexts) or that they were simply lost at the island and later disturbed through building activities and the extensive stone plundering of the Bronze Age tells. These beads may also be the remnants of the very first bead trade coming through Failaka. Bead material with Mesopotamian stylistic parallels, which mainly date to the late 3rd millennium, may represent beads produced locally in Mesopotamia from imported semi-precious raw material.[51] If these are not curated beads deposited at a later time at Failaka, this would suggest that some bead material was also arriving at the island from the north in the early phases of the bead trade. But still, a major part of the Failaka bead assemblage consists of carnelian beads with forms typical of the Indus region (especially, barrels with circular cross section, bicones with circular cross sections, long slender cylinders with spherical cross sections).

Some of the bead material with likely Mesopotamian and Aegean provenience (mainly faience, glass and a small number of distinctive carnelian beads: barrels with a hexagonal cross section) dates to the latter part of the 2nd millennium. This might signify a directional change in trading networks over time, influenced by the decline of the Indus Valley civilization and the geopolitical integration of Mesopotamia and Dilmun. At least, the Aegean style beads indicate that "branches" of the trade network reached toward the northwest (probably through Mesopotamia). Compared to other bead assemblages in the Gulf, the proximity of Failaka to the Mesopotamian markets may have increased the occurrence of Mesopotamian style bead products and the new prestige material of the late 2nd millennium: glass.

7. Catalogue

The bead catalogue presented below is arranged firstly according to bead type, context and field number and secondly according to material and dimensions.

The *bead types* are listed by length (i.e. disc, short, standard or long), profile and cross-section form according to Beck's classification (Beck 1928) (cf. p. 9). The *field number system* includes a tell prefix listed in front of the field number. Next the KM number is listed. The *context* is listed by trench, then by period (i.e. Tell F3: periods 2, 3A, 3B, 4A, 4B, 3A/3B, 4A/4B, 3A/4A or 3B/4B and Tell F6: periods 1 or 2-4A), vertical level and horizontal coordinates. The approximate datings given here should be approached with caution (cf. p. 35). *Dimensions* are given in mm and the following abbreviations have been used: (*L*) Length; (*D*) Diameter; (*W*) Width and (*H*) Height. In the case of fragmented beads, the preserved measurements are given (*pres.*) and when possible, an estimate of the original dimensions (*est.*). Next the *material* and the *condition* of the beads (i.e. complete or fragmented) is noted. *Perforations* are described according to Beck's classification (i.e. I, II, III and IV, with the addition of the subvariant I.1.) and the diameter of the perforation (*PD*) is given in mm.

All drawings and photos are reproduced in full size (1:1).

Spheres with circular cross section (figs. 76-211)

I.B.1.a. Short oblates with circular cross section (figs. 76-197)

No. F3.å, KM 1681 (fig. 76). *Context:* Trench A; 3A/3B; Between level 7.85 and 8.15; Found in sieve. *Type:* Short oblate/Circular; I.B.1.a. *Dimensions:* L 5.50, D 7.30 mm. *Material:* Carnelian. *Condition:* Complete. *Perforation:* Type II; PD 1.90 mm.

No. F3.ei, KM 1681 (fig. 77). *Context:* Trench F; Unknown; Found in sieve. *Type:* Short oblate/Circular; I.B.1.a. *Dimensions:* L 6.80, D 7.70 mm. *Material:* Carnelian. *Condition:* Complete. *Perforation:* Type III; PD 2.10-2.70 mm.

No. F3.hu, KM 1681 (fig. 78). *Context:* Trench F; Unknown; Found in sieve. *Type:* Short oblate/Circular; I.B.1.a. *Dimensions:* L 9.20, D 12.90 mm. *Material:* Agate. *Condition:* Complete. *Perforation:* Type III; PD 2.70-3.50 mm.

No. F3.ais, KM 1681 (fig. 79). *Context:* Trench I I; 4A; level 7.65; No information. *Type:* Short oblate/Circular; I.B.1.a. *Dimensions:* L 9.20, D 14.20 mm. *Material:* Jasper. *Condition:* Complete. *Perforation:* Type III; PD 2.30-2.80 mm.

No. F3.145, KM 1683 (fig. 80). *Context:* Trench RM; Unknown; Between level 8.25-8.75 and 8.60-9.10; 40.00-58.00N/0.00-5.00W. *Type:* Short oblate/Circular; I.B.1.a. *Dimensions:* L 3.80, D 8.80-9.50 mm. *Material:* Lapis lazuli. *Condition:* Complete. *Perforation:* Type II; PD 2.50-3.90 mm.

No. F3.251.2, KM 1683 (fig. 81). *Context:* Trench RM; Unknown; Found in sieve. *Type:* Short oblate/Circular; I.B.1.a. *Dimensions:* L 7.30, D 8.30 mm. *Material:* Carnelian. *Condition:* Complete. *Perforation:* Type III; PD 2.00-2.70 mm.

No. F3.259, KM 1681 (fig. 82). *Context:* Trench RM; Unknown; level 8.01; 41.30N/1.10W. *Type:* Short oblate/Circular; I.B.1.a. *Dimensions:* L 9.60, D 11.20 mm. *Material:* Carnelian. *Condition:* Complete. *Perforation:* Type II; PD 2.10 mm.

No. F3.pw, KM 1681 (fig. 83). *Context:* Trench X; 3B/4B; level 8.37; 53.40N/5.25E. *Type:* Short oblate/Circular; I.B.1.a. *Dimensions:* L 8.90, D 12.30 mm. *Material:* Jasper. *Condition:* Complete. *Perforation:* Type III; PD 1.80-2.10 mm.

No. F3.rg, KM 1681 (fig. 84). *Context:* Trench X; Unknown; Found in sieve. *Type:* Short oblate/Circular; I.B.1.a. *Dimensions:* L 11.40, D 13.60 mm. *Material:* Agate. *Condition:* Complete. *Perforation:* Type II; PD 2.90-3.20 mm.

No. F3.cab, KM 1681 (fig. 85). *Context:* Trench Y; 4B; level 9.37; No information. *Type:* Short oblate/Circular; I.B.1.a. *Dimensions:* L 8.20, D 12.20 mm. *Material:* Carnelian. *Condition:* Complete. *Perforation:* Type II; PD 2.50-2.70 mm.

No. F3.qå, KM 1681 (fig. 86). *Context:* Trench Y; 4B; level 7.27; 65.50N/0.80W. *Type:* Short oblate/Circular; I.B.1.a. *Dimensions:* L 14.00, D 17.90 mm. *Material:* Agate. *Condition:* Complete. *Perforation:* Type III; PD 3.20-3.60 mm.

No. F3.vw, KM 1681 (fig. 87). *Context:* Trench Ø; Unknown; Found in sieve. *Type:* Short oblate/Circular; I.B.1.a. *Dimensions:* L 5.60, D 5.90 mm. *Material:* Carnelian. *Condition:* Complete. *Perforation:* Type II; PD 1.30-2.00 mm.

No. F3.så, KM 1681 (fig. 88). *Context:* Baulk between trench Æ and Ø; Unknown; Found in sieve. *Type:* Short oblate/Circular; I.B.1.a. *Dimensions:* L 7.30, D 8.70 mm. *Material:* Carnelian. *Condition:* Complete. *Perforation:* Type III; PD 1.60-2.60 mm.

No.F3.zø.1, KM 1681 (fig. 89). *Context:* Trench AB; Unknown; Found in sieve. *Type:* Short oblate/Circular; I.B.1.a. *Dimensions:* L 4.80, D 5.90 mm. *Material:* Carnelian. *Condition:* Complete. *Perforation:* Type II; PD 1.30 mm.

No.F3.zø.2, KM 1681 (fig. 90). *Context:* Trench AB; Unknown; Found in sieve. *Type:* Short oblate/Circular; I.B.1.a. *Dimensions:* L 6.00, D 9.00 mm. *Material:* Carnelian. *Condition:* Complete. *Perforation:* Type III; PD 2.40-3.00 mm.

No. F3.æn.1, KM 1681 (fig. 91). *Context:* Baulk between Trench AB and AF; Unknown; Found in sieve. *Type:* Short oblate/Circular; I.B.1.a. *Dimensions:* L 6.90, D 8.30 mm. *Material:* Carnelian. *Condition:* Complete. *Perforation:* Type III; PD 2.00-2.40 mm.

No. F3.æn.2, KM 1681 (fig. 92). *Context:* Baulk between Trench AB and AF; Unknown; Found in sieve. *Type:* Short oblate/Circular; I.B.1.a. *Dimensions:* L 7.80, D 9.30 mm. *Material:* Carnelian. *Condition:* Complete. *Perforation:* Type III; PD 2.30-2.90 mm.

No. F3.æn.6, KM 1683 (fig. 93). *Context:* Baulk between Trench AB and AF; Unknown; Found in sieve. *Type:* Short oblate/Circular; I.B.1.a. *Dimensions:* L 6.90, D 13.70 mm. *Material:* Rock crystal. *Condition:* Complete. *Perforation:* Type III; PD 1.60-2.70 mm.

No. F3.øm, KM 1681 (fig. 94). *Context:* Trench AE; Unknown; Found in sieve. *Type:* Short oblate/Circular; I.B.1.a. *Dimensions:* L 5.60, D 8.10 mm. *Material:* Carnelian. *Condition:* Complete. *Perforation:* Type III; PD 1.70-2.30 mm.

No. F3.ås.1, KM 1681 (fig. 95). *Context:* Trench AE; Unknown; Found in sieve. *Type:* Short oblate/Circular; I.B.1.a. *Dimensions:* L 5.60, D 7.40 mm. *Material:* Carnelian. *Condition:* Complete. *Perforation:* Type III; PD 1.70-2.50 mm.

No. F3.yå.1, KM 1681 (fig. 96). *Context:* Trench AF; Unknown; Found in sieve. *Type:* Short oblate/Circular; I.B.1.a. *Dimensions:* L 7.30, D 8.30 mm. *Material:* Carnelian. *Condition:* Complete. *Perforation:* Type III; PD 1.70-2.60 mm.

No. F3.yå.4, KM 1704 (fig. 97). *Context:* Trench AF; Unknown; Found in sieve. *Type:* Short oblate/Circular; I.B.1.a. *Dimensions:* L 11.60, D 20.00 mm. *Material:* Faience. *Condition:* Fragmented. *Perforation:* Type IV; PD 8.50 mm.

No. F3.axn, KM 1681 (fig. 98). *Context:* Trench AN; 4B; level 7.01; 76.00N/7.00E. *Type:* Short oblate/Circular; I.B.1.a. *Dimensions:* L 8.70, D 12.30 mm. *Material:* Jasper. *Condition:* Complete. *Perforation:* Type II; PD 3.00-3.20 mm.

No. F3.axw, KM 1681 (fig. 99). *Context:* Trench AN; Unknown; Found in sieve. *Type:* Short oblate/Circular; I.B.1.a. *Dimensions:* L 11.80, D 15.90 mm. *Material:* Jasper. *Condition:* Complete. *Perforation:* Type III; PD 3.20-3.80 mm.

No. F3.aze, KM 1681 (fig. 100). *Context:* Trench AN; 4B; level 7.80; No information. *Type:* Short oblate/Circular; I.B.1.a. *Dimensions:* L 4.60, D 5.60 mm. *Material:* Carnelian. *Condition:* Complete. *Perforation:* Type III; PD 1.30-2.00 mm.

No. F3.bde, KM 1681 (fig. 101). *Context:* Baulk between Trench AN and I; Unknown; Found in sieve. *Type:* Short oblate/Circular; I.B.1.a. *Dimensions:* L 5.30, D 6.40 mm. *Material:* Carnelian. *Condition:* Complete. *Perforation:* Type II; PD 1.50

No. F3.bhe, KM 1681 (fig. 102). *Context:* Trench AO; Unknown; Found in sieve. *Type:* Short oblate/Circular; I.B.1.a. *Dimensions:* L 18.90, D 21.80 mm. *Material:* Jasper. *Condition:* Complete. *Perforation:* Type III; PD 2.70-3.20 mm.

No. F3.atn.2, KM 1681 (fig. 103). *Context:* No provenience; Unknown; Found in sieve. *Type:* Short oblate/Circular; I.B.1.a. *Dimensions:* L 6.80, D 8.80 mm. *Material:* Carnelian. *Condition:* Complete. *Perforation:* Type III; PD 1.70-2.50 mm.

No. F3.apq, KM 1681 (fig. 104). *Context:* No provenience; Unknown; Found in sieve. *Type:* Short oblate/Circular; I.B.1.a. *Dimensions:* L 12.70, D 18.00 mm. *Material:* Glass. *Condition:* Fragmented. *Perforation:* Type IV; PD 4.00 mm.

No. F3.gæ, KM 1681 (fig. 105). *Context:* No provenience; Unknown; level 7.43; No information. *Type:* Short oblate/Circular; I.B.1.a. *Dimensions:* L 16.00, D 21.50 mm. *Material:* Lapis Lazuli. *Condition:* Complete. *Perforation:* Type II; PD 2.50-3.00 mm.

No. F3.yl.1, KM 1673 (fig. 106). *Context:* No provenience; Unknown; No information. *Type:* Short oblate/Circular; I.B.1.a. *Dimensions:* L 7.70, D 8.70 mm. *Material:* Carnelian. *Condition:* Complete. *Perforation:* Type III; PD 1.60-2.50 mm.

No. F6.60, KM 1698 (fig. 107). *Context:* Trench A1; 2-4A; level 0.29; 4.85S/2.20W. *Type:* Short oblate/Circular; I.B.1.a. *Dimensions:* L 4.30, D 5.30 mm. *Material:* Carnelian. *Condition:* Complete. *Perforation:* Type III; PD 1.60-2.20 mm.

No. F6.66, KM 1698 (fig. 108). *Context:* Trench A1; 2-4A; level 0.16; 1.80S/1.70W. *Type:* Short oblate/Circular; I.B.1.a. *Dimensions:* L 11.60, D 13.90 mm. *Material:* Carnelian. *Condition:* Complete. *Perforation:* Type III; PD 1.90-3.00 mm.

No. F6.128, KM 1698 (fig. 109). *Context:* Trench A1; 2-4A; level -0.62; 2.50S/2.50W. *Type:* Short oblate/Circular; I.B.1.a. *Dimensions:* L 6.20, D 7.30 mm. *Material:* Carnelian. *Condition:* Complete. *Perforation:* Type III; PD 1.50-2.40 mm.

No. F6.1048, KM 1698 (fig. 110). *Context:* Trench A1; 2-4A; level -0.32; 0-10S/0-0.5W. *Type:* Short oblate/Circular; I.B.1.a. *Dimensions:* L 7.00, D 7.90 mm. *Material:* Carnelian. *Condition:* Complete. *Perforation:* Type III; PD 1.70-2.60 mm.

No. F6.111, KM 1698 (fig. 111). *Context:* Trench A2; 2-4A; level -0.38; 17.80S/1.80W. *Type:* Short oblate/Circular; I.B.1.a. *Dimensions:* L 7.20, D 9.40 mm. *Material:* Carnelian. *Condition:* Complete. *Perforation:* Type III; PD 1.50-2.20 mm.

No. F6.204, KM 1698 (fig. 112). *Context:* Trench B2; 2-4A; level 0.35; 11.20S/7.40W. *Type:* Short oblate/Circular; I.B.1.a. *Dimensions:* L 6.30, D 7.30 mm. *Material:* Carnelian. *Condition:* Complete. *Perforation:* Type III; PD 1.90-2.60 mm.

No. F6.205, KM 1698 (fig. 113). *Context:* Trench B2; 2-4A; level 0.00; 17.00S/7.00W. *Type:* Short oblate/Circular; I.B.1.a. *Dimensions:* L 6.40, D 7.90 mm. *Material:* Carnelian. *Condition:* Complete. *Perforation:* Type III; PD 1.80-2.40 mm.

No. F6.220, KM 1698 (fig. 114). *Context:* Trench B2; 2-4A; level 0.01; 15.00S/6.00W. *Type:* Short oblate/Circular; I.B.1.a. *Dimensions:* L 3.70, D 5.60 mm. *Material:* Carnelian. *Condition:* Complete. *Perforation:* Type III; PD 1.70-2.20 mm.

No. F6.236, KM 1698 (fig. 115). *Context:* Trench SS 0-9; 2-4A; level -0.10; 0.50S/0.50E. *Type:* Short oblate/Circular; I.B.1.a. *Dimensions:* L 5.80, D 7.50 mm. *Material:* Carnelian. *Condition:* Complete. *Perforation:* Type II; PD 1.70 mm.

No. F6.431.1, KM 1694 (fig. 116). *Context:* Trench D1; 2-4A; level 0.16; 4.00-5.50N/2.00-3.00W. *Type:* Short oblate/Circular; I.B.1.a. *Dimensions:* L 6.20, D 8.90 mm. *Material:* Carnelian. *Condition:* Complete. *Perforation:* Type III; PD 2.10-2.50 mm.

No. F6.431.2, KM 1694 (fig. 117). *Context:* Trench D1; 2-4A; level 0.16; 4.00-5.50N/2.00-3.00W. *Type:* Short oblate/Circular; I.B.1.a. *Dimensions:* L 7.00, D 8.50 mm. *Material:* Carnelian. *Condition:* Complete. *Perforation:* Type III; PD 2.10-2.90 mm.

No. F6.914, KM 1694 (fig. 118). *Context:* Trench D1; 1; level -2.04; 8.00N/3.00W. *Type:* Short oblate/Circular; I.B.1.a. *Dimensions:* L 5.00, D 6.50 mm. *Material:* Turquoise. *Condition:* Complete. *Perforation:* Type II; PD 1.50 mm.

No. F6.355, KM 1698 (fig. 119). *Context:* Trench D2; 2-4A; level -0.13; 17.10N/3.30W. *Type:* Short oblate/Circular; I.B.1.a. *Dimensions:* L 4.00, D 6.10 mm. *Material:* Carnelian. *Condition:* Complete. *Perforation:* Type III; PD 1.60-2.40 mm.

No. F6.357, KM 1698 (fig. 120). *Context:* Trench D2; 2-4A; level -0.15; 12.00-13.00N/1.00-4.00W. *Type:* Short oblate/Circular; I.B.1.a. *Dimensions:* L 5.20, D 6.50 mm. *Material:* Carnelian. *Condition:* Complete. *Perforation:* Type III; PD 1.50-2.20 mm.

No. F6.362.4, KM 1698 (fig. 121). *Context:* Trench D2; 2-4A; level -0.59; 14.00-15.00N/3.50-4.00W. *Type:* Short oblate/Circular; I.B.1.a. *Dimensions:* L 4.40, D 5.70 mm. *Material:* Carnelian. *Condition:* Complete. *Perforation:* Type III; PD 1.80-2.40 mm.

No. F6.362.5, KM 1698 (fig. 122). *Context:* Trench D2; 2-4A; level -0.59; 14.00-15.00N/3.50-4.00W. *Type:* Short oblate/Circular; I.B.1.a. *Dimensions:* L 5.10, D 6.30 mm. *Material:* Carnelian. *Condition:* Complete. *Perforation:* Type III; PD 1.70-2.50 mm.

No. F6.362.6, KM 1694 (fig. 123). *Context:* Trench D2; 2-4A; level -0.59; 14.00-15.00N/3.50-4.00W. *Type:* Short oblate/Circular; I.B.1.a. *Dimensions:* L 6.70, D 8.30 mm. *Material:* Carnelian. *Condition:* Complete. *Perforation:* Type II; PD 1.50-1.60 mm.

No. F6.362.2, KM 1694 (fig. 124). *Context:* Trench D2; 2-4A; level -0.59; 14.00-15.00N/3.50-4.00W. *Type:* Short oblate/Circular; I.B.1.a. *Dimensions:* L 6.50, D 8.00 mm. *Material:* Faience. *Condition:* Complete. *Perforation:* Type IV; PD 3.00-3.60 mm.

No. F6.362.1, KM 1560 (fig. 125). *Context:* Trench D2; 2-4A; level -0.59; 14.00-15.00N/3.50-4.00W. *Type:* Short oblate/Circular; I.B.1.a. *Dimensions:* L 8.00, D 11.20 mm. *Material:* Glass. *Condition:* Complete. *Perforation:* Type IV; PD 4.30 mm.

No. F6.362.3, KM 1698 (fig. 126). *Context:* Trench D2; 2-4A; level -0.59; 14.00-15.00N/3.50-4.00W. *Type:* Short oblate/Circular; I.B.1.a. *Dimensions:* L 12.30, D 17.20 mm. *Material:* Glass. *Condition:* Fragmented. *Perforation:* Type IV; PD 5.40 mm.

No. F6.393.3, KM 1694 (fig. 127). *Context:* Trench D2; 2-4A; level -0.96; 14.00-15.00N/3.50-4.00W. *Type:* Short oblate/Circular; I.B.1.a. *Dimensions:* L 4.10, D 5.90 mm. *Material:* Carnelian. *Condition:* Complete. *Perforation:* Type III; PD 1.70-2.20 mm.

No. F6.393.2, KM 1694 (fig. 128). *Context:* Trench D2; 2-4A; level -0.96; 14.00-15.00N/3.50-4.00W. *Type:* Short oblate/Circular; I.B.1.a. *Dimensions:* L 6.10, D 7.50 mm. *Material:* Carnelian. *Condition:* Complete. *Perforation:* Type III; PD 1.90-2.60 mm.

No. F6.393.1, KM 1694 (fig. 129). *Context:* Trench D2; 2-4A; level -0.96; 14.00-15.00N/3.50-4.00W. *Type:* Short oblate/Circular; I.B.1.a. *Dimensions:* L 6.50, D 7.70 mm. *Material:* Carnelian. *Condition:* Complete. *Perforation:* Type III; PD 1.80-2.30 mm.

No. F6.400.1, KM 1694 (fig. 130). *Context:* Trench D2; 2-4A; level -1.10; 19.00N/3.00W. *Type:* Short oblate/Circular; I.B.1.a. *Dimensions:* L 9.00, D 10.90 mm. *Material:* Faience. *Condition:* Fragmented. *Perforation:* Type IV; PD 2.90 mm.

No. F6.406.1, KM 1694 (fig. 131). *Context:* Trench D2; 2-4A; level -1.08; 13.00-15.00N/1.25-4.00W. *Type:* Short oblate/Circular; I.B.1.a. *Dimensions:* L 5.10, D 7.00 mm. *Material:* Carnelian. *Condition:* Complete. *Perforation:* Type III; PD 1.90-2.30 mm.

No. F6.406.2, KM 1694 (fig. 132). *Context:* Trench D2; 2-4A; level -1.08; 13.00-15.00N/1.25-4.00W. *Type:* Short oblate/Circular; I.B.1.a. *Dimensions:* L 5.80, D 7.20 mm. *Material:* Carnelian. *Condition:* Complete. *Perforation:* Type III; PD 2.00-2.60 mm.

No. F6.408.2, KM 1556 (fig. 133). *Context:* Trench D2; 2-4A; level -1.03; 18.40N/2.20W. *Type:* Short oblate/Circular; I.B.1.a. *Dimensions:* L 8.00, D 10.50 mm. *Material:* Paste. *Condition:* Fragmented. *Perforation:* Type IV; PD 2.60 mm.

No. F6.417.1, KM 1694 (fig. 134). *Context:* Trench D2; 2-4A; Between level -0.46 and -1.08; 13.00-15.00N/1.25-4.00W. *Type:* Short oblate/Circular; I.B.1.a. *Dimensions:* L 10.60, D 13.30 mm. *Material:* Rock crystal. *Condition:* Complete. *Perforation:* Type II; PD 3.60-3.80 mm.

No. F6.417.3, KM 1694 (fig. 135). *Context:* Trench D2; 2-4A; Between level -0.46 and -1.08; 13.00-15.00N/1.25-4.00W. *Type:* Short oblate/Circular; I.B.1.a. *Dimensions:* L 5.90, D 9.50 mm. *Material:* Faience. *Condition:* Complete. *Perforation:* Type IV; PD 3.60 mm.

No. F6.417.2, KM 1694 (fig. 136). *Context:* Trench D2; 2-4A; Between level -0.46 and -1.08; 13.00-15.00N/1.25-4.00W. *Type:* Short oblate/Circular; I.B.1.a. *Dimensions:* L 12.00, D 13.70 mm. *Material:* Glass. *Condition:* Complete. *Perforation:* Type IV; PD 2.10 mm.

No. F6.465, KM 1694 (fig. 137). *Context:* Trench D2; 1; level -1.59; 16.00N/3.00W. *Type:* Short oblate/Circular; I.B.1.a. *Dimensions:* L 5.70, D 7.50 mm. *Material:* Carnelian. *Condition:* Complete. *Perforation:* Type III; PD 1.90-2.90 mm.

No. F6.502.1, KM 1694 (fig. 138). *Context:* Trench D2; 1; level -1.74; 15.00-16.00N/3.00-4.00W. *Type:* Short oblate/Circular; I.B.1.a. *Dimensions:* L 9.00, D 10.40 mm. *Material:* Glass. *Condition:* Complete. *Perforation:* Type IV; PD 2.70 mm.

No. F6.620, KM 1694 (fig. 139). *Context:* Trench D2; 1; level -1.98; 14.50N/1.20W. *Type:* Short oblate/Circular; I.B.1.a. *Dimensions:* L 7.80, D 12.50 mm. *Material:* Glass. *Condition:* Complete. *Perforation:* Type IV; PD 4.10 mm.

No. F6.1014, KM 1698 (fig. 140). *Context:* Trench D2; 2-4A; level -1.10; 16.00-17.00N/3.00-4.00W. *Type:* Short oblate/Circular; I.B.1.a. *Dimensions:* L 12.90, D 15.50 mm. *Material:* Rock crystal. *Condition:* Complete. *Perforation:* Type II; PD 2.30 mm.

No. F6.508, KM 1694 (fig. 141). *Context:* Trench D3; 2-4A; level 0.21; 23.00-24.00N/2.00-3.00W. *Type:* Short oblate/Circular; I.B.1.a. *Dimensions:* L 4.30, D 4.20 mm. *Material:* Paste. *Condition:* Complete. *Perforation:* Type IV; PD 1.80 mm.

No. F6.514, KM 1694 (fig. 142). *Context:* Trench D3; 2-4A; level -0.01; 21.00-24.00N/3.00-4.00W. *Type:* Short oblate/Circular; I.B.1.a. *Dimensions:* L 8.80, D 11.40 mm. *Material:* Agate. *Condition:* Complete. *Perforation:* Type III; PD 1.20-2.40 mm.

No. F6.590.4, KM 1694 (fig. 143). *Context:* Baulk between Trench D2 and E2; 2-4A; level -1.28; 14.50-16.00/0.00-1.00W. *Type:* Short oblate/Circular; I.B.1.a. *Dimensions:* L 8.00, D 9.70 mm. *Material:* Carnelian. *Condition:* Complete. *Perforation:* Type III; PD 2.20 mm.

No. F6.590.2, KM 1714 (fig. 144). *Context:* Baulk between Trench D2 and E2; 2-4A; level -1.28; 14.50-16.00/0.00-1.00W. *Type:* Short oblate/Circular; I.B.1.a. *Dimensions:* L 2.90, D 5.40 mm. *Material:* Faience. *Condition:* Complete. *Perforation:* Type IV; PD 1.60-2.30 mm.

No. F6.590.1, KM 1694 (fig. 145). *Context:* Baulk between Trench D2 and E2; 2-4A; level -1.28; 14.50-16.00/0.00-1.00W. *Type:* Short oblate/Circular; I.B.1.a. *Dimensions:* L 8.90, D 11.60 mm. *Material:* Faience. *Condition:* Complete. *Perforation:* Type IV; PD 2.80 mm.

No. F6.590.3, KM 1714 (fig. 146). *Context:* Baulk between Trench D2 and E2; 2-4A; level -1.28; 14.50-16.00/0.00-1.00W. *Type:* Short oblate/Circular; I.B.1.a. *Dimensions:* L 2.70, D 3.50 mm. *Material:* Paste. *Condition:* Complete. *Perforation:* Type IV; PD 2.10 mm.

No. F6.608.2, KM 1694 (fig. 147). *Context:* Trench SN 11-20; 1; level -1.75; 13.00-14.00N/0.00-1.00E. *Type:* Short oblate/ Circular; I.B.1.a. *Dimensions:* L 5.20, D 6.10 mm. *Material:* Carnelian. *Condition:* Complete. *Perforation:* Type III; PD 1.60-2.20 mm.

No. F6.608.1, KM 1694 (fig. 148). *Context:* Trench SN 11-20; 1; level -1.75; 13.00-14.00N/0.00-1.00E. *Type:* Short oblate/ Circular; I.B.1.a. *Dimensions:* L 6.80, D 7.70 mm. *Material:* Carnelian. *Condition:* Complete. *Perforation:* Type III; PD 1.90-2.80 mm.

No. F6.953.2, KM 1698 (fig. 149). *Context:* Trench F1; 2-4A; level -0.99; No information. *Type:* Short oblate/Circular; I.B.1.a. *Dimensions:* L 6.80, D 7.90 mm. *Material:* Carnelian. *Condition:* Complete. *Perforation:* Type III; PD 1.80-2.50 mm.

No. F6.969, KM 1698 (fig. 150). *Context:* Trench F1; Unknown; Found in sieve. *Type:* Short oblate/Circular; I.B.1.a. *Dimensions:* L 7.30, D 10.10 mm. *Material:* Carnelian. *Condition:* Complete. *Perforation:* Type II; PD 2.30 mm.

No. F6.981, KM 1698 (fig. 151). *Context:* Trench F1; 2-4A; No deeper than level -0.71; Found in sieve. *Type:* Short oblate/ Circular; I.B.1.a. *Dimensions:* L 8.60, D 11.40 mm. *Material:* Carnelian. *Condition:* Complete. *Perforation:* Type II; PD 1.90 mm.

No. F6.998, KM 1698 (fig. 152). *Context:* Trench F1; Unknown; level -0.81; 6.00-9.00N/4.00-7.00W. *Type:* Short oblate/Circular; I.B.1.a. *Dimensions:* L 7.80, D 9.10 mm. *Material:* Carnelian. *Condition:* Complete. *Perforation:* Type III; PD 1.90-2.70 mm.

No. F6.1091, KM 1698 (fig. 153). *Context:* Trench F1; Unknown; Found in sieve. *Type:* Short oblate/Circular; I.B.1.a. *Dimensions:* L 7.20, D 8.90 mm. *Material:* Carnelian. *Condition:* Complete. *Perforation:* Type III; PD 1.70-2.60 mm.

No. F6.634, KM 1694 (fig. 154). *Context:* Trench F2; 2-4A; level 0.22; 19.00N/6.00W. *Type:* Short oblate/Circular; I.B.1.a. *Dimensions:* L 6.90, D 8.20 mm. *Material:* Carnelian. *Condition:* Complete. *Perforation:* Type III; PD 1.80-2.50 mm.

No. F6.639.2, KM 1694 (fig. 155). *Context:* Trench F2; Unknown; Between level -1.72 and -0.98; Found in sieve. *Type:* Short oblate/Circular; I.B.1.a. *Dimensions:* L 4.60, D 5.90 mm. *Material:* Carnelian. *Condition:* Complete. *Perforation:* Type III; PD 1.50-2.20 mm.

No. F6.652, KM 1694 (fig. 156). *Context:* Trench F2; 2-4A; level -0.31; 18.00N/5.00W. *Type:* Short oblate/Circular; I.B.1.a. *Dimensions:* L 10.50, D 13.30 mm. *Material:* Jasper. *Condition:* Complete. *Perforation:* Type III; PD 2.30-2.50 mm.

No. F6.656.1, KM 1694 (fig. 157). *Context:* Trench F2; 2-4A; level -0.71; 15.00-16.00N/4.50W. *Type:* Short oblate/Circular; I.B.1.a. *Dimensions:* L 5.60, D 7.80 mm. *Material:* Carnelian. *Condition:* Complete. *Perforation:* Type III; PD 1.90-2.40 mm.

No. F6.678, KM 1694 (fig. 158). *Context:* Trench F2; Unknown; No information. *Type:* Short oblate/Circular; I.B.1.a. *Dimensions:* L 6.80, D 9.90 mm. *Material:* Carnelian. *Condition:* Complete. *Perforation:* Type III; PD 2.00-2.80 mm.

No. F6.705, KM 1694 (fig. 159). *Context:* Trench F2; 2-4A; level -1.30; 15.00N/7.50W. *Type:* Short oblate/Circular; I.B.1.a. *Dimensions:* L 12.40, D 15.50 mm. *Material:* Carnelian. *Condition:* Complete. *Perforation:* Type III; PD 1.90-3.60 mm.

No. F6.746, KM 1702 (fig. 160). *Context:* Trench F2; 1; level -1.69; 11.00-15.00N/5.50-6.00W. *Type:* Short oblate/Circular; I.B.1.a. *Dimensions:* L 7.20, D 10.50 mm. *Material:* Glass. *Condition:* Fragmented. *Perforation:* Type IV; PD 2.60 mm.

No. F6.760, KM 1694 (fig. 161). *Context:* Trench F2; 1; level -1.69; 15.50N/5.00W. *Type:* Short oblate/Circular; I.B.1.a. *Dimensions:* L 8.00, D 10.70 mm. *Material:* Faience. *Condition:* Fragmented. *Perforation:* Type IV; PD 2.50 mm.

No. F6.938, KM 1694 (fig. 162). *Context:* Trench F2; Unknown; Found in sieve. *Type:* Short oblate/Circular; I.B.1.a. *Dimensions:* L 12.00, D 15.80 mm. *Material:* Turquoise. *Condition:* Complete. *Perforation:* Type III; PD 2.20-2.80 mm.

No. F6.800.1, KM 1694 (fig. 163). *Context:* Trench M2; 2-4A; Found in sieve above level -1.07. *Type:* Short oblate/Circular; I.B.1.a. *Dimensions:* L 13.90, D 18.00 mm. *Material:* Glass. *Condition:* Complete. *Perforation:* Type IV; PD 2.90 mm.

No. F6.880.1, KM 1694 (fig. 164). *Context:* Trench M2; 2-4A; Found in sieve above level -1.07. *Type:* Short oblate/Circular; I.B.1.a. *Dimensions:* L 4.50, D 6.20 mm. *Material:* Carnelian. *Condition:* Complete. *Perforation:* Type III; PD 1.50-2.30 mm.

No. F6.880.2, KM 1694 (fig. 165). *Context:* Trench M2; 2-4A; Found in sieve above level -1.07. *Type:* Short oblate/Circular; I.B.1.a. *Dimensions:* L 6.80, D 8.20 mm. *Material:* Carnelian. *Condition:* Complete. *Perforation:* Type III; PD 2.20-2.80 mm.

No. F6.1083, KM 1698 (fig. 166). *Context:* Baulk between Trench M1 and N1; Unknown; Found in sieve. *Type:* Short oblate/Circular; I.B.1.a. *Dimensions:* L 8.60, D 10.40 mm. *Material:* Carnelian. *Condition:* Complete. *Perforation:* Type III; PD 2.10-3.10 mm.

No. F6.944.1, KM 1698 (fig. 167). *Context:* No provenience; Unknown; Found in sieve. *Type:* Short oblate/Circular; I.B.1.a. *Dimensions:* L 6.40, D 8.00 mm. *Material:* Carnelian. *Condition:* Complete. *Perforation:* Type III; PD 1.90-2.50 mm.

No. F6.944.2, KM 1698 (fig. 168). *Context:* No provenience; Unknown; Found in sieve. *Type:* Short oblate/Circular; I.B.1.a. *Dimensions:* L 7.20, D 9.10 mm. *Material:* Carnelian. *Condition:* Complete. *Perforation:* Type III; PD 2.10-3.10 mm.

No. F6.944.3, KM 1698 (fig. 169). *Context:* No provenience; Unknown; Found in sieve. *Type:* Short oblate/Circular; I.B.1.a. *Dimensions:* L 8.40, D 8.90 mm. *Material:* Carnelian. *Condition:* Complete. *Perforation:* Type III; PD 1.90-2.80 mm.

No. F6.945.3, KM 1698 (fig. 170). *Context:* No provenience; Unknown; Found in sieve. *Type:* Short oblate/Circular; I.B.1.a. *Dimensions:* L 6.40, D 9.40 mm. *Material:* Agate. *Condition:* Complete. *Perforation:* Type III; PD 2.10-3.00 mm.

No. F6.945.4, KM 1691 (fig. 171). *Context:* No provenience; Unknown; Found in sieve. *Type:* Short oblate/Circular; I.B.1.a. *Dimensions:* L 3.80, D 4.80 mm. *Material:* Carnelian. *Condition:* Complete. *Perforation:* Type III; PD 1.70-2.20 mm.

No. F6.945.2, KM 1698 (fig. 172). *Context:* No provenience; Unknown; Found in sieve. *Type:* Short oblate/Circular; I.B.1.a. *Dimensions:* L 5.80, D 9.00 mm. *Material:* Carnelian. *Condition:* Complete. *Perforation:* Type II; PD 1.80 mm.

No. F6.945.5, KM 1698 (fig. 173). *Context:* No provenience; Unknown; Found in sieve. *Type:* Short oblate/Circular; I.B.1.a. *Dimensions:* L 6.20, D 7.90 mm. *Material:* Carnelian. *Condition:* Complete. *Perforation:* Type III; PD 1.80-2.50 mm.

No. F6.945.1, KM 1698 (fig. 174). *Context:* No provenience; Unknown; Found in sieve. *Type:* Short oblate/Circular; I.B.1.a. *Dimensions:* L 6.80, D 8.10 mm. *Material:* Carnelian. *Condition:* Complete. *Perforation:* Type II; PD 1.80-1.90 mm.

No. F6.1094, KM 1698 (fig. 175). *Context:* No provenience; Unknown; Found in sieve. *Type:* Short oblate/Circular; I.B.1.a. *Dimensions:* L 5.30, D 7.30 mm. *Material:* Carnelian. *Condition:* Complete. *Perforation:* Type III; PD 1.60-2.50 mm.

No. F6.1102A, KM 1698 (fig. 176). *Context:* No provenience; Unknown; Found in sieve. *Type:* Short oblate/Circular; I.B.1.a. *Dimensions:* L 5.60, D 8.60 mm. *Material:* Carnelian. *Condition:* Complete. *Perforation:* Type III; PD 1.90-2.70 mm.

No. F6.1167, KM 1698 (fig. 177). *Context:* No provenience; Unknown; Found in sieve. *Type:* Short oblate/Circular; I.B.1.a. *Dimensions:* L 7.40, D 8.50 mm. *Material:* Carnelian. *Condition:* Complete. *Perforation:* Type III; PD 1.90-2.60 mm.

No. F6.1184, KM 1694 (fig. 178). *Context:* No provenience; Unknown; Found in sieve. *Type:* Short oblate/Circular; I.B.1.a. *Dimensions:* L 6.80, D 8.30 mm. *Material:* Carnelian. *Condition:* Complete. *Perforation:* Type III; PD 2.00-2.70 mm.

No. F6.1240, KM 1698 (fig. 179). *Context:* No provenience; Unknown; Found in sieve. *Type:* Short oblate/Circular; I.B.1.a. *Dimensions:* L 7.60, D 9.20 mm. *Material:* Carnelian. *Condition:* Complete. *Perforation:* Type III; PD 2.10 mm.

No. F6.1241.1, KM 1698 (fig. 180). *Context:* No provenience; Unknown; Found in sieve. *Type:* Short oblate/Circular; I.B.1.a. *Dimensions:* L 10.70, D 12.40 mm. *Material:* Jasper. *Condition:* Complete. *Perforation:* Type III; PD 1.80-2.00 mm.

No. F6.1244, KM 1698 (fig. 181). *Context:* No provenience; Unknown; Found in sieve. *Type:* Short oblate/Circular; I.B.1.a. *Dimensions:* L 5.20, D 7.40 mm. *Material:* Carnelian. *Condition:* Complete. *Perforation:* Type III; PD 1.50-2.30 mm.

No. F6.without no.1, KM 1687 (fig. 182). *Context:* No provenience; Unknown; No information. *Type:* Short oblate/Circular; I.B.1.a. *Dimensions:* L 4.60, D 7.50 mm. *Material:* Carnelian. *Condition:* Complete. *Perforation:* Type III; PD 1.80-2.50 mm.

No. F6.without no.2, KM 1687 (fig. 183). *Context:* No provenience; Unknown; No information. *Type:* Short oblate/Circular; I.B.1.a. *Dimensions:* L 5.50, D 6.90 mm. *Material:* Carnelian. *Condition:* Complete. *Perforation:* Type III; PD 1.40-2.10 mm.

No. F6.without no.3, KM 1687 (fig. 184). *Context:* No provenience; Unknown; No information. *Type:* Short oblate/Circular; I.B.1.a. *Dimensions:* L 5.60, D 7.80 mm. *Material:* Carnelian. *Condition:* Complete. *Perforation:* Type III; PD 1.80-2.50 mm.

No. F6.without no.4, KM 1687 (fig. 185). *Context:* No provenience; Unknown; No information. *Type:* Short oblate/Circular; I.B.1.a. *Dimensions:* L 5.70, D 7.80 mm. *Material:* Carnelian. *Condition:* Complete. *Perforation:* Type III; PD 1.90-2.50 mm.

No. F6.without no.5, KM 1687 (fig. 186). *Context:* No provenience; Unknown; No information. *Type:* Short oblate/Circular; I.B.1.a. *Dimensions:* L 6.00, D 8.60 mm. *Material:* Carnelian. *Condition:* Complete. *Perforation:* Type III; PD 1.80-2.60 mm.

No. F6.without no.6, KM 1679 (fig. 187). *Context:* No provenience; Unknown; No information. *Type:* Short oblate/Circular; I.B.1.a. *Dimensions:* L 6.20, D 7.00 mm. *Material:* Carnelian. *Condition:* Complete. *Perforation:* Type II; PD 1.70-1.80 mm.

No. F6.without no.7, KM 1687 (fig. 188). *Context:* No provenience; Unknown; No information. *Type:* Short oblate/Circular; I.B.1.a. *Dimensions:* L 6.70, D 8.00 mm. *Material:* Carnelian. *Condition:* Complete. *Perforation:* Type III; PD 1.70-2.40 mm.

No. F6.without no.8, KM 1687 (fig. 189). *Context:* No provenience; Unknown; No information. *Type:* Short oblate/Circular; I.B.1.a. *Dimensions:* L 7.30, D 9.20 mm. *Material:* Carnelian. *Condition:* Complete. *Perforation:* Type III; PD 1.60-2.60 mm.

No. F6.without no.9, KM 1679 (fig. 190). *Context:* No provenience; Unknown; No information. *Type:* Short oblate/Circular; I.B.1.a. *Dimensions:* L 7.60, D 9.10 mm. *Material:* Carnelian. *Condition:* Complete. *Perforation:* Type III; PD 1.70-2.90 mm.

No. F6.without no.15, KM 1666 (fig. 191). *Context:* No provenience; Unknown; Found in sieve. *Type:* Short oblate/ Circular; I.B.1.a. *Dimensions:* L 4.50, D 6.70 mm. *Material:* Pearl. *Condition:* Complete. *Perforation:* Type II; PD 2.20 mm.

No. F6.without no.25, KM 1666 (fig. 192). *Context:* No provenience; Unknown; Found in sieve. *Type:* Short oblate/ Circular; I.B.1.a. *Dimensions:* L 7.30, D 8.90 mm. *Material:* Pearl. *Condition:* Complete. *Perforation:* Type II; PD 2.00 mm.

No. F6.without no.10, KM 1679 (fig. 193). *Context:* No provenience; Unknown; No information. *Type:* Short oblate/ Circular; I.B.1.a. *Dimensions:* L 8.00, D 12.60 mm. *Material:* Faience. *Condition:* Complete. *Perforation:* Type IV; PD 4.00 mm.

No. F6.without no.11, KM 1694 (fig. 194). *Context:* No provenience; Unknown; No information. *Type:* Short oblate/ Circular; I.B.1.a. *Dimensions:* L 9.00, D 11.30 mm. *Material:* Faience. *Condition:* Fragmented. *Perforation:* Type IV; PD 2.50 mm.

No. F6.without no.12, KM 1694 (fig. 195). *Context:* No provenience; Unknown; No information. *Type:* Short oblate/ Circular; I.B.1.a. *Dimensions:* L 6.30, D 9.00 mm. *Material:* Glass. *Condition:* Fragmented. *Perforation:* Type III; PD 2.70 mm.

No. F6.without no.13, KM 1694 (fig. 196). *Context:* No provenience; Unknown; No information. *Type:* Short oblate/ Circular; I.B.1.a. *Dimensions:* L 7.40, D 9.50 mm. *Material:* Glass. *Condition:* Fragmented. *Perforation:* Type III; PD 3.50-4.00 mm.

No. F6.without no.14, KM 1694 (fig. 197). *Context:* No provenience; Unknown; No information. *Type:* Short oblate/ Circular; I.B.1.a. *Dimensions:* L 7.90, D 10.00 mm. *Material:* Glass. *Condition:* Complete. *Perforation:* Type III; PD 3.40 mm.

I.C.1.a. Standard circular with circular cross section (figs. 198-211)

No. F3.gx, KM 1681 (fig. 198). *Context:* Trench M; 3B; level 7.60; No information. *Type:* Standard circular/Circular; I.C.1.a. *Dimensions:* L 7.80, D 8.20 mm. *Material:* Carnelian. *Condition:* Complete. *Perforation:* Type III; PD 1.70-2.50 mm.

No. F3.qb, KM 1681 (fig. 199). *Context:* Trench X; 3B/4B; Between level 8.73 and 8.25; Found in sieve. *Type:* Standard circular/Circular; I.C.1.a. *Dimensions:* L 10.20, D 10.80 mm. *Material:* Jasper. *Condition:* Complete. *Perforation:* Type III; PD 2.20-2.50 mm.

No. F6.447.1, KM 1689 (fig. 200). *Context:* Trench D1; 2-4A; level -0.26; 4.00-5.00N/2.00-3.00W. *Type:* Standard circular/ Circular; I.C.1.a. *Dimensions:* L 7.60, D 8.00 mm. *Material:* Carnelian. *Condition:* Complete. *Perforation:* Type III; PD 1.90-2.60 mm.

No. F6.362.8, KM 1694 (fig. 201). *Context:* Trench D2; 2-4A; level -0.59; 14.00-15.00N/3.50-4.00W. *Type:* Standard circular/ Circular; I.C.1.a. *Dimensions:* L 6.60, D 6.80 mm. *Material:* Carnelian. *Condition:* Complete. *Perforation:* Type III; PD 1.40-2.30 mm.

No. F6.362.7, KM 1590 (fig. 202). *Context:* Trench D2; 2-4A; level -0.59; 14.00-15.00N/3.50-4.00W. *Type:* Standard circular/ Circular; I.C.1.a. *Dimensions:* L 10.00, D 10.50 mm. *Material:* Glass. *Condition:* Complete. *Perforation:* Type IV; PD 2.80 mm.

No. F6.417.4, KM 1559 (fig. 203). *Context:* Trench D2; 2-4A; Between level 0.46 and -1.08; 13.00-15.00N/1.25-4.00W. *Type:* Standard circular/Circular; I.C.1.a. *Dimensions:* L 8.30, D 9.00 mm. *Material:* Glass. *Condition:* Fragmented. *Perforation:* Type IV; PD 180 mm.

No. F6.482, KM 1694 (fig. 204). *Context:* Trench D2; 1; level -1.60; 16.00-16.50N/3.00-4.00W. *Type:* Standard circular/ Circular; I.C.1.a. *Dimensions:* L 17.90, D 17.40 mm. *Material:* Glass. *Condition:* Fragmented. *Perforation:* Type IV; PD 3.20 mm.

No. F6.629, KM 1694 (fig. 205). *Context:* Trench D2; Unknown; Found in sieve. *Type:* Standard circular/Circular; I.C.1.a. *Dimensions:* L 7.60, D 8.40 mm. *Material:* Carnelian. *Condition:* Complete. *Perforation:* Type II; PD 2.00 mm.

No. F6.1090, KM 1698 (fig. 206). *Context:* Trench M1; 2-4A; level -0.74; 1.00-2.00N/9.00-11.00W. *Type:* Standard circular/ Circular; I.C.1.a. *Dimensions:* L 9.40, D 10.30 mm. *Material:* Jasper. *Condition:* Complete. *Perforation:* Type III; PD 1.80-2.20 mm.

No. F6.854.3, KM 1694 (fig. 207). *Context:* Trench M2; 1; level -1.98; 18.00-20.00N/9.00-11.00W. *Type:* Standard circular/ Circular; I.C.1.a. *Dimensions:* L 6.60, D 7.20 mm. *Material:* Carnelian. *Condition:* Complete. *Perforation:* Type II; PD 1.60 mm.

No. F6.1064, KM 1698 (fig. 208). *Context:* Trench N1; Unknown; Found in sieve. *Type:* Standard circular/Circular; I.C.1.a. *Dimensions:* L 6.60, D 6.80 mm. *Material:* Carnelian. *Condition:* Complete. *Perforation:* Type III; PD 1.60-2.40 mm.

No. F6.944.4, KM 1698 (fig. 209). *Context:* No provenience; Unknown; Found in sieve. *Type:* Standard circular/Circular; I.C.1.a. *Dimensions:* L 5.00, D 5.30 mm. *Material:* Carnelian. *Condition:* Complete. *Perforation:* Type III; PD 1.40-2.10 mm.

No. F6.1187, KM 1698 (fig. 210). *Context:* No provenience; 2-4A; level -0.98; No information. *Type:* Standard circular/ Circular; I.C.1.a. *Dimensions:* L 3.30, D 3.50 mm. *Material:* Carnelian. *Condition:* Complete. *Perforation:* Type II; PD 1.20-1.30 mm.

No. F6.1212, KM 1668 (fig. 211). *Context:* No provenience; Unknown; Found in sieve. *Type:* Standard circular/Circular; I.C.1.a. *Dimensions:* L 7.30, D 7.30 mm. *Material:* Carnelian. *Condition:* Complete. *Perforation:* Blank.

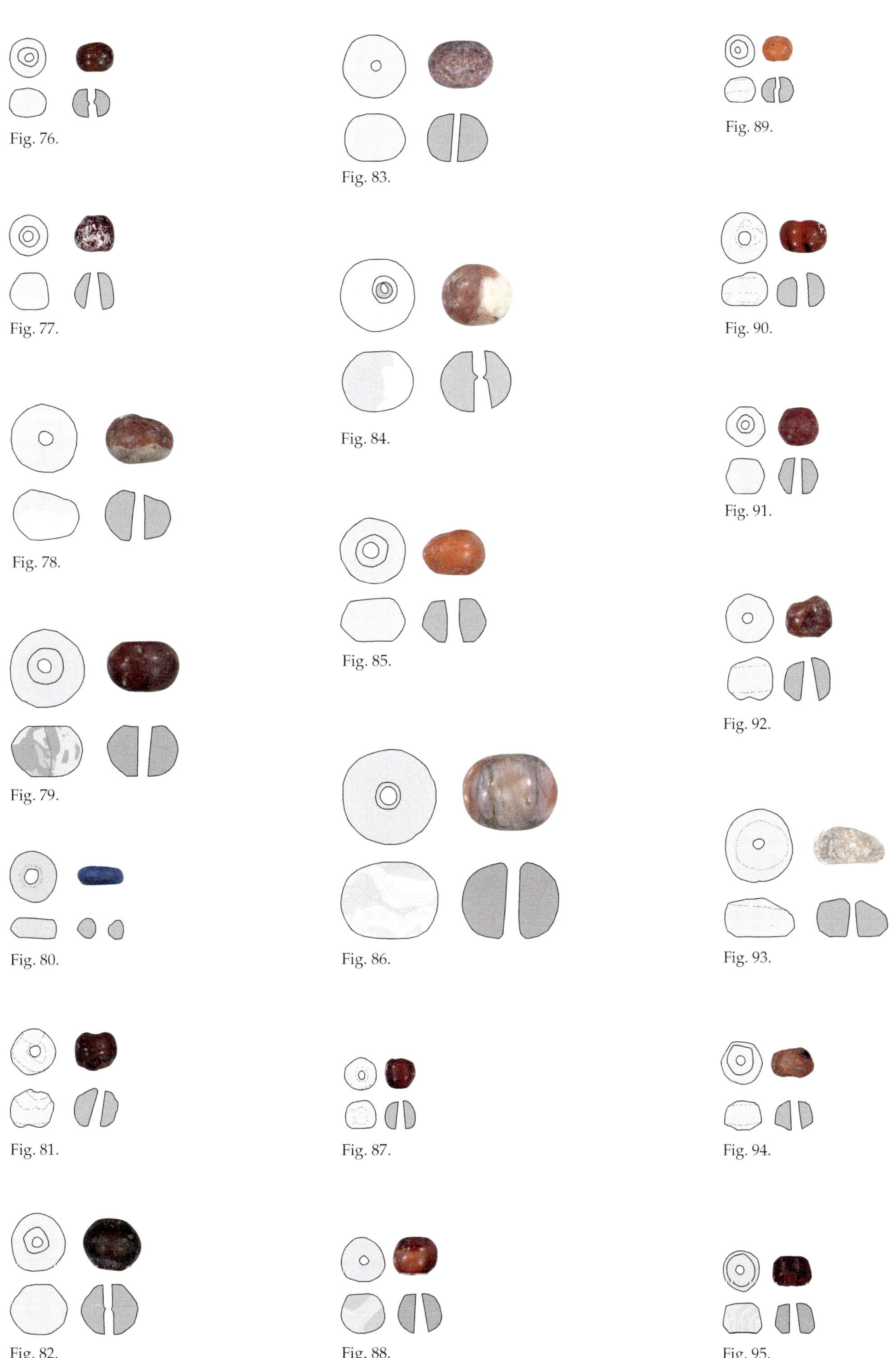

Fig. 76.

Fig. 77.

Fig. 78.

Fig. 79.

Fig. 80.

Fig. 81.

Fig. 82.

Fig. 83.

Fig. 84.

Fig. 85.

Fig. 86.

Fig. 87.

Fig. 88.

Fig. 89.

Fig. 90.

Fig. 91.

Fig. 92.

Fig. 93.

Fig. 94.

Fig. 95.

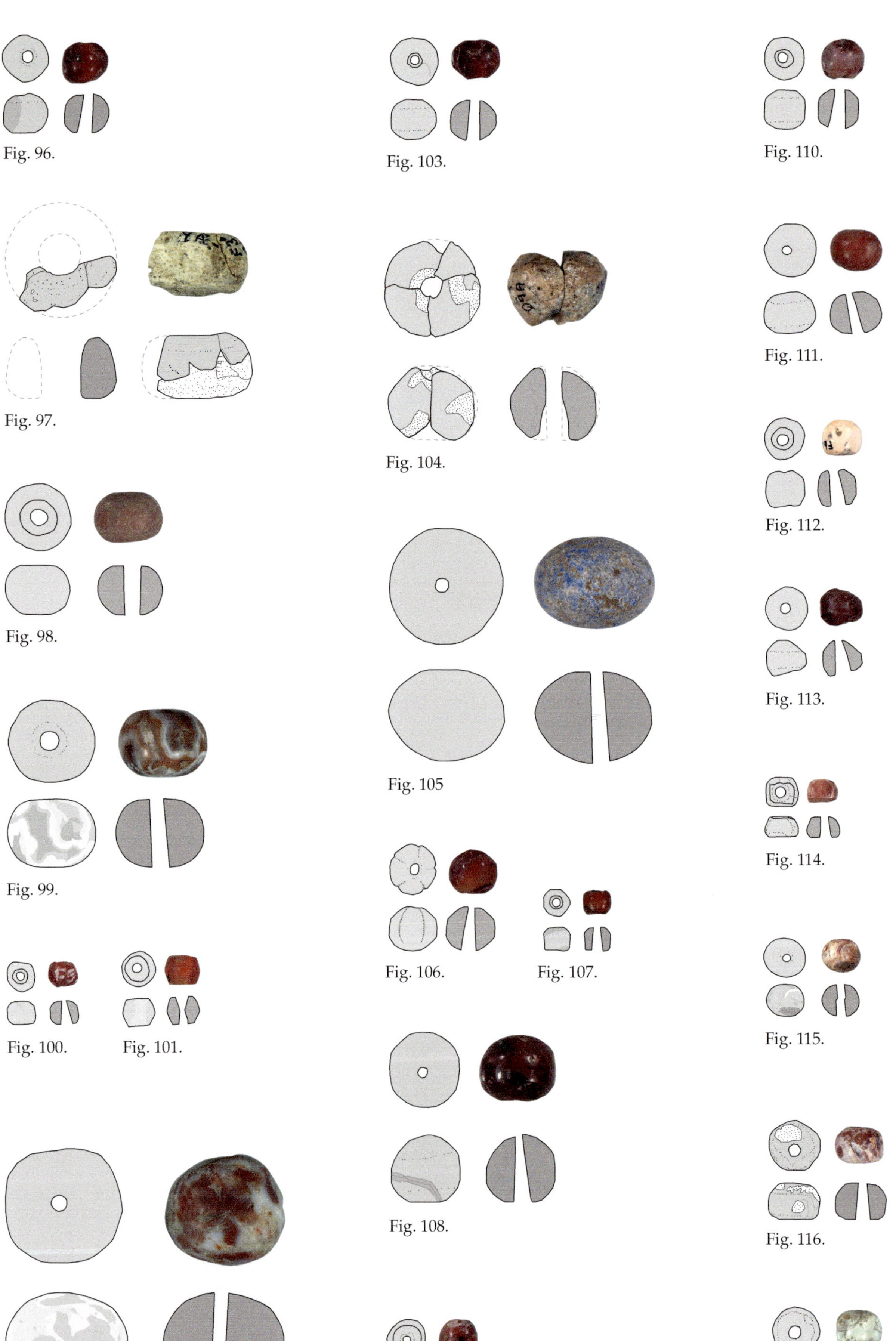

Fig. 96.

Fig. 97.

Fig. 98.

Fig. 99.

Fig. 100.

Fig. 101.

Fig. 102.

Fig. 103.

Fig. 104.

Fig. 105

Fig. 106.

Fig. 107.

Fig. 108.

Fig. 109.

Fig. 110.

Fig. 111.

Fig. 112.

Fig. 113.

Fig. 114.

Fig. 115.

Fig. 116.

Fig. 117.

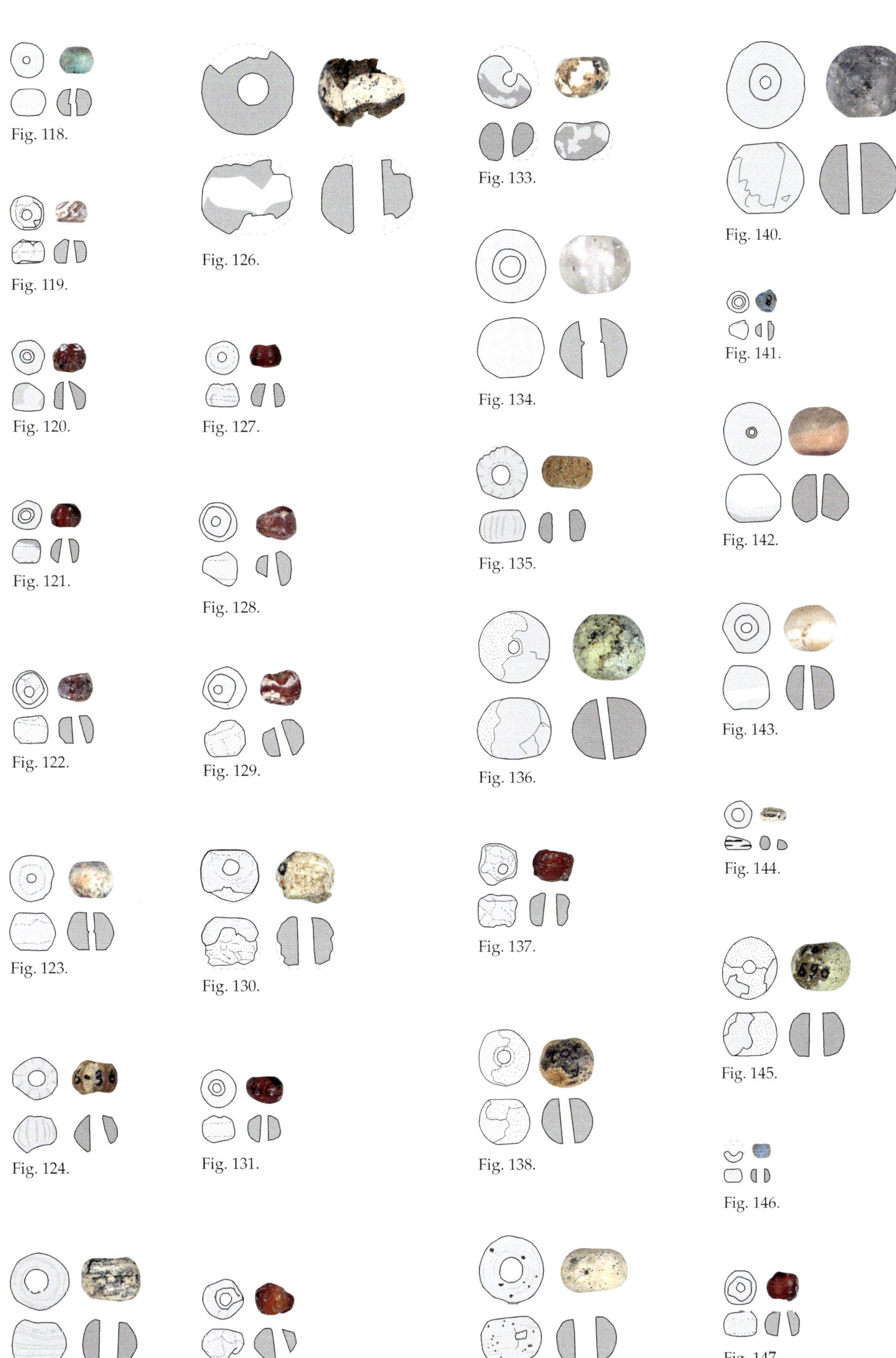

Fig. 118.

Fig. 119.

Fig. 120.

Fig. 121.

Fig. 122.

Fig. 123.

Fig. 124.

Fig. 125.

Fig. 126.

Fig. 127.

Fig. 128.

Fig. 129.

Fig. 130.

Fig. 131.

Fig. 132.

Fig. 133.

Fig. 134.

Fig. 135.

Fig. 136.

Fig. 137.

Fig. 138.

Fig. 139.

Fig. 140.

Fig. 141.

Fig. 142.

Fig. 143.

Fig. 144.

Fig. 145.

Fig. 146.

Fig. 147.

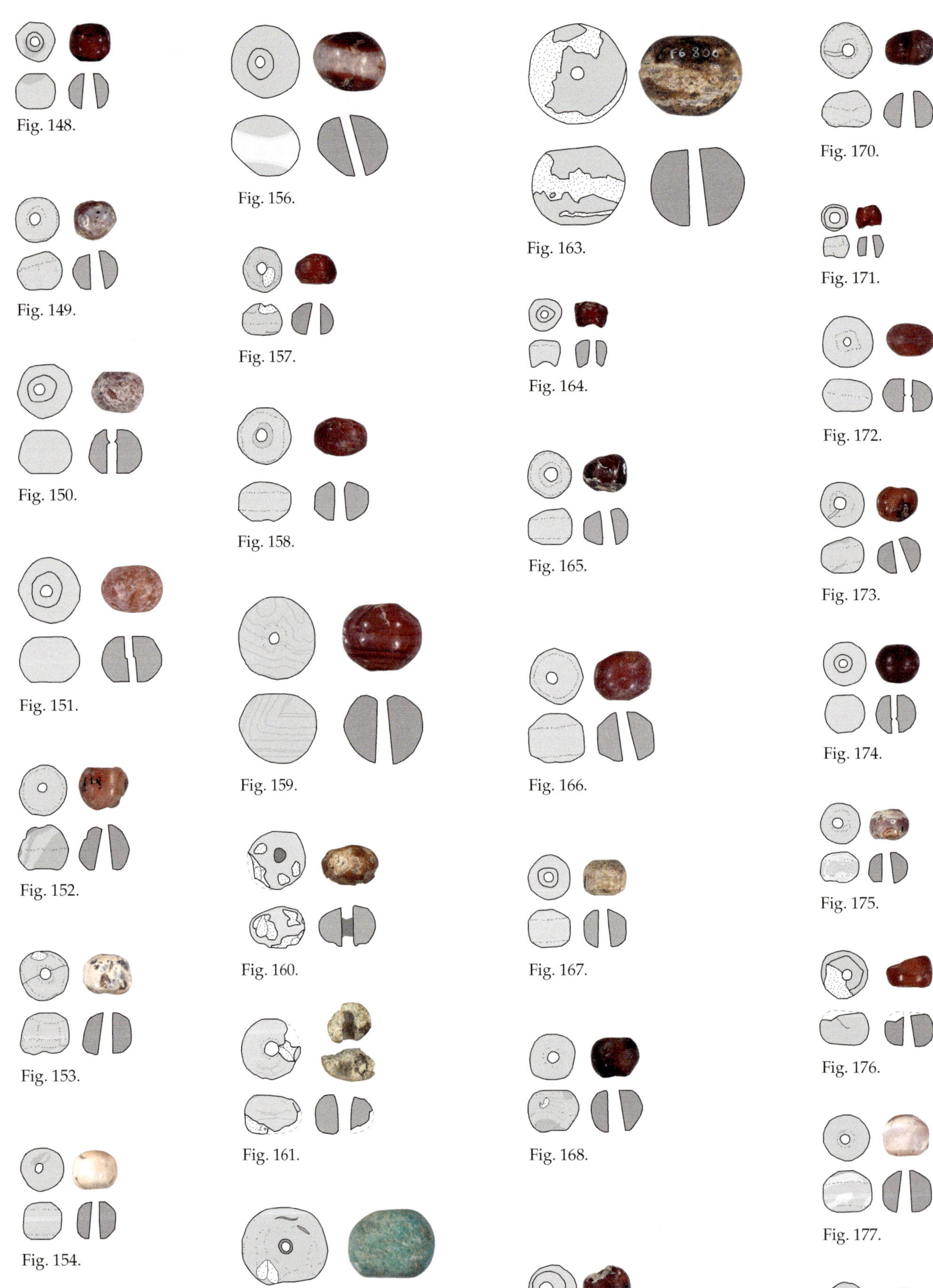

Fig. 148.

Fig. 149.

Fig. 150.

Fig. 151.

Fig. 152.

Fig. 153.

Fig. 154.

Fig. 155.

Fig. 156.

Fig. 157.

Fig. 158.

Fig. 159.

Fig. 160.

Fig. 161.

Fig. 162.

Fig. 163.

Fig. 164.

Fig. 165.

Fig. 166.

Fig. 167.

Fig. 168.

Fig. 169.

Fig. 170.

Fig. 171.

Fig. 172.

Fig. 173.

Fig. 174.

Fig. 175.

Fig. 176.

Fig. 177.

Fig. 178.

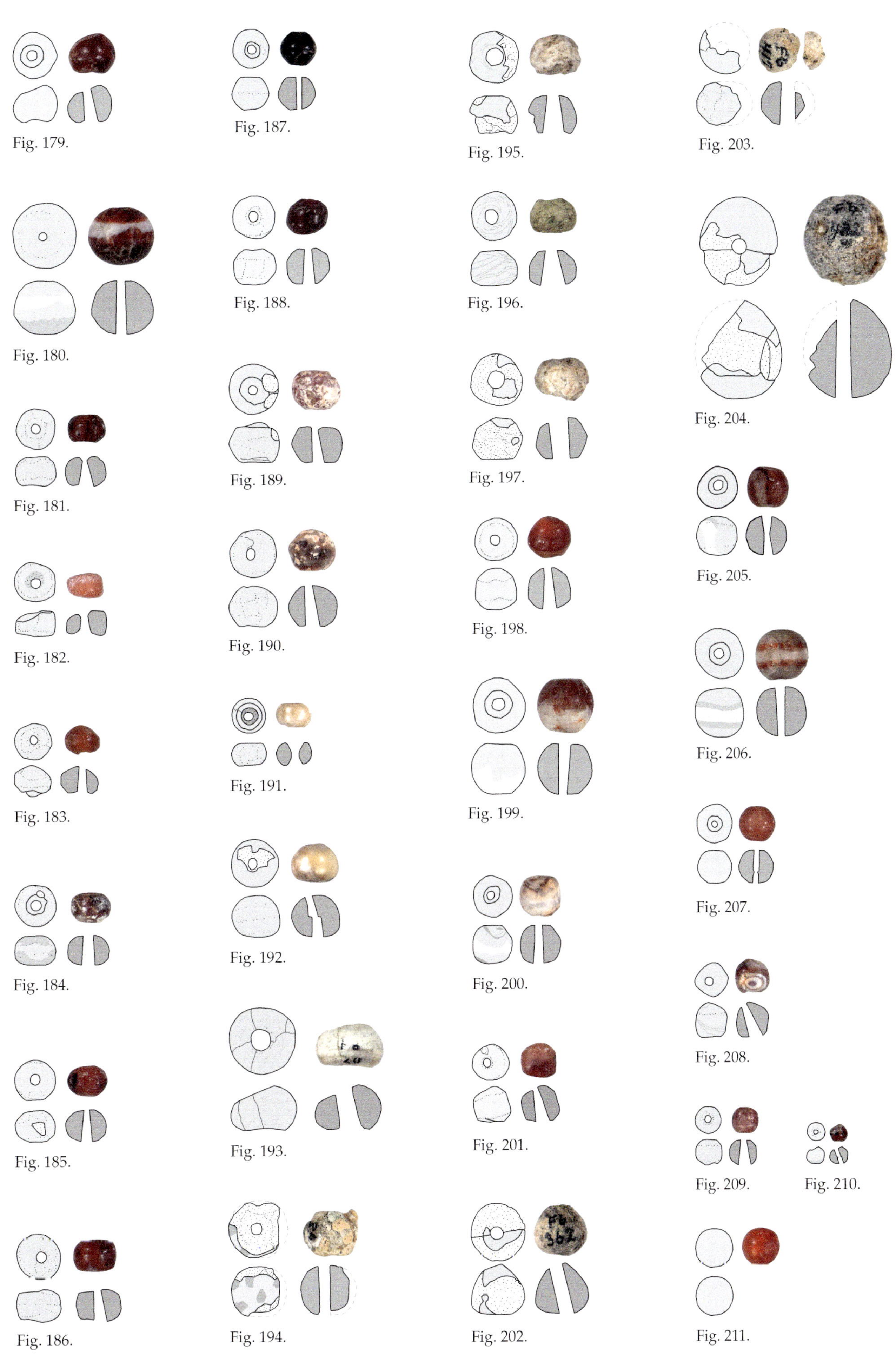

Fig. 179.

Fig. 180.

Fig. 181.

Fig. 182.

Fig. 183.

Fig. 184.

Fig. 185.

Fig. 186.

Fig. 187.

Fig. 188.

Fig. 189.

Fig. 190.

Fig. 191.

Fig. 192.

Fig. 193.

Fig. 194.

Fig. 195.

Fig. 196.

Fig. 197.

Fig. 198.

Fig. 199.

Fig. 200.

Fig. 201.

Fig. 202.

Fig. 203.

Fig. 204.

Fig. 205.

Fig. 206.

Fig. 207.

Fig. 208.

Fig. 209.

Fig. 210.

Fig. 211.

Spheres with elliptical cross section (figs. 212-214)

II.B.1.a. Short oblate with elliptical cross section (figs. 212-213)

No. F6.396.3, KM 1562 (fig. 212). *Context:* Trench D2; 2-4A; level -0.96; 14.00-15.00N/3.50-4.00W. *Type:* Short oblate/ Elliptical; II.B.1.a. *Dimensions:* L 8.60, W 7 20, H 5.50 mm. *Material:* Glass. *Condition:* Fragmented. *Perforation:* Type IV; PD 2.50 mm.

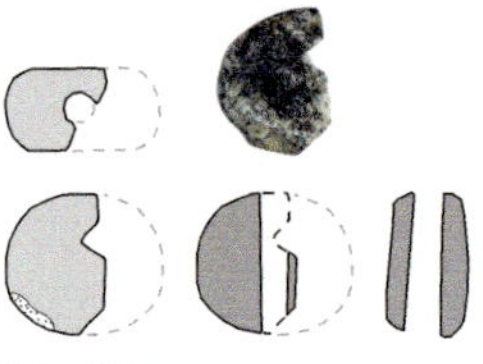

Fig. 212.

No. F6.1169, KM 1688 (fig. 213). *Context:* No provenience; Unknown; Found in sieve. *Type:* Short oblate/Elliptical; II.B.1.a. *Dimensions:* L 12.30, W 16.40, H 6.40 mm. *Material:* Glass. *Condition:* Complete. *Perforation:* Type II; PD 2.40-3.00 mm.

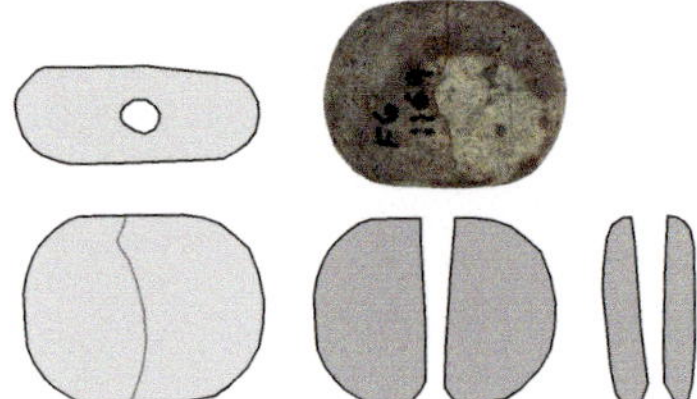

Fig. 213.

II.C.1.a. Standard spheres with elliptical cross section (fig. 214)

No. F6.417.9, KM 1559 (fig. 214). *Context:* Trench D2; 2-4A; Between level -0.46 and -1.08; 13.00-15.00N/1.25-4.00W. *Type:* Standard circular/Elliptical; II.C.1.a. *Dimensions:* L 30.00, W 17.90, H 7.90 mm. *Material:* Glass. *Condition:* Fragmented. *Perforation:* Not preserved. PD 3.00 mm.

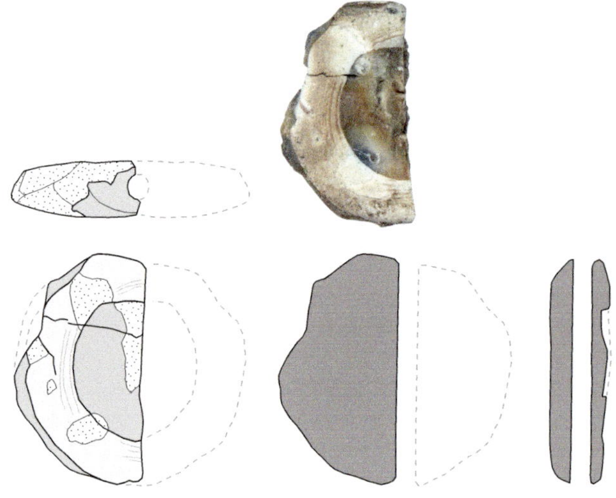

Fig. 214.

Spheres with lenticular cross section (figs. 215-216)

IV.B.1.a. Short oblate with lenticular cross section

No. F6.283, KM 1724 (fig. 215). *Context:* Trench D2; 2-4A; level 0.33; 12.25N/2.00W. *Type:* Short Oblate/Lenticular; IV.B.1.a. *Dimensions:* L 14.00, W 16.00, H 4.00 mm. *Material:* Paste. *Condition:* Complete. *Perforation:* Type Unid.; PD 1.00-1.50 mm.

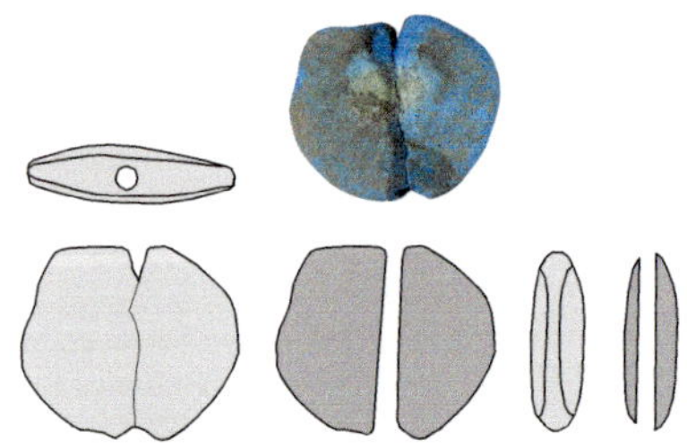

Fig. 215.

No. F6.458.2, KM 1688 (fig. 216). *Context:* Trench E2; 2-4A; level -0.35; 16.00-18.00N/1.50-3.00E. *Type:* Short Oblate/ Lenticular; IV.B.1.a. *Dimensions:* L 10.50, W 13.20, H 3.80 mm. *Material:* Turquoise. *Condition:* Complete. *Perforation:* Type II; PD 1.30 mm.

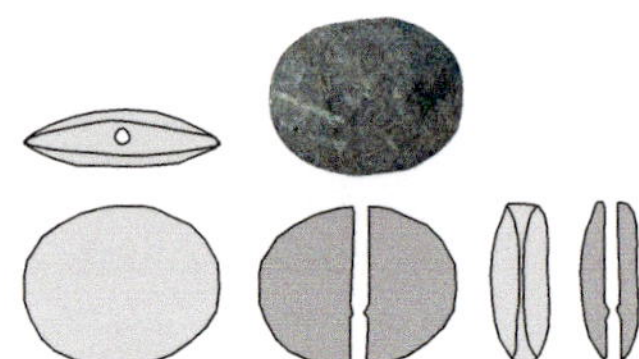

Fig. 216.

Barrels with circular cross section (figs. 217-352)

I.A.1.b. Disc barrels with circular cross section (figs. 217-219)

No. F3.ba, KM 1506 (fig. 217). *Context:* No provenience; Unknown; No information. *Type:* Disc barrel/Circular; I.A.1.b. *Dimensions:* L 4.00, D 23.20 mm. *Material:* Shell (Conus). *Condition:* Complete. *Perforation:* - ; PD 13.80-14.60 mm.

No. F3.bbg, KM 1496 (fig. 218). *Context:* Trench I; 2; Between level 6.23 and 6.01; No information. *Type:* Disc barrel/Circular; I.A.1.b. *Dimensions:* L 3.50, D 23.80-25.20 mm. *Material:* Shell (Conus). *Condition:* Complete. *Perforation:* - ; PD 11.00-12.00 mm.

No. F6.509, KM 1665 (fig. 219). *Context:* Trench D1; 2-4A, level -0.97; 4.00-5.00N/3.00-4.00W. *Type:* Disc barrel/Circular; I.A.1.b. *Dimensions:* L 4.00-7.10, D 29.50 mm. *Material:* Shell (pearl oyster). *Condition:* Complete. *Perforation:* - ; PD 16.40-17.30 mm.

I.B.1.b. Short barrels with circular cross section (figs. 220-227)

No. F3.165, KM 1681 (fig. 220). *Context:* Trench RM; Unknown; Between level 8.60 and 8.25; 40.00-58.00N/0.00-5.00W. *Type:* Short barrel/Circular; I.B.1.b. *Dimensions:* L 8.80, D 12.30 mm. *Material:* Agate. *Condition:* Complete. *Perforation:* Type II; PD 2.60 mm.

No. F3.265.3, KM 1681 (fig. 221). *Context:* Trench RM; Unknown; Found in sieve. *Type:* Short barrel/Circular; I.B.1.b. *Dimensions:* L 9.60, D 14.40 mm. *Material:* Jasper. *Condition:* Complete. *Perforation:* Type II; PD 3.10 mm.

No. F6.936.5, KM 1631 (fig. 222). *Context:* Trench F2; Unknown; Found in sieve. *Type:* Short barrel/Circular; I.B.1.b. *Dimensions:* L 5.20, D 6.10 mm. *Material:* Carnelian. *Condition:* Complete. *Perforation:* Type II; PD 1.60 mm.

No. F6.854.1, KM 1691 (fig. 223). *Context:* Trench M2; 1; level -1.98; 18.00-20.00N/9.00-11.00W. *Type:* Short barrel/Circular; I.B.1.b. *Dimensions:* L 5.30, D 6.60 mm. *Material:* Carnelian. *Condition:* Complete. *Perforation:* Type II; PD 1.50 mm.

No. F6.867, KM 1691 (fig. 224). *Context:* Trench M2; Unknown; Found in sieve; 17.00-20.00N/8.00-11.00W. *Type:* Short barrel/Circular; I.B.1.b. *Dimensions:* L 6.30, D 7.30 mm. *Material:* Carnelian. *Condition:* Complete. *Perforation:* Type II; PD 1.80 mm.

No. F6.945.6, KM 1691 (fig. 225). *Context:* No provenience; Unknown; Found in sieve. *Type:* Short barrel/Circular; I.B.1.b. *Dimensions:* L 5.30, D 6.20 mm. *Material:* Carnelian. *Condition:* Complete. *Perforation:* Type II; PD 1.70 mm.

No. F6.945.7, KM 1691 (fig. 226). *Context:* No provenience; Unknown; Found in sieve. *Type:* Short barrel/Circular; I.B.1.b. *Dimensions:* L 6.10, D 7.00 mm. *Material:* Carnelian. *Condition:* Complete. *Perforation:* Type III; PD 1.80-2.60 mm.

No. F6.without no.16, KM 1687 (fig. 227) *Context:* No provenience; Unknown; No information. *Type:* Short barrel/Circular; I.B.1.b. *Dimensions:* L 6.90, D 7.80 mm. *Material:* Carnelian. *Condition:* Complete. *Perforation:* Type II; PD 2.00 mm.

I.C.1.b. Standard barrels with circular cross section (figs. 228-243)

No. F3.æn.4, KM 1685 (fig. 228). *Context:* Baulk between AB and AF; Unknown; No information. *Type:* Standard barrel/Circular; I.C.1.b. *Dimensions:* L 4.30, D 4.40 mm. *Material:* Carnelian. *Condition:* Complete. *Perforation:* Type II; PD 1.30 mm.

No. F3.æn.3, KM 1685 (fig. 229). *Context:* Baulk between AB and AF; Unknown; No information. *Type:* Standard barrel/Circular; I.C.1.b. *Dimensions:* L 5.40, D 5.80 mm. *Material:* Carnelian. *Condition:* Complete. *Perforation:* Type II; PD 1.90-2.10 mm.

No. F3.aig.1, KM 1685 (fig. 230). *Context:* Trench K; 4A; Between level 8.50 and 9.40. *Type:* Standard barrel/Circular; I.C.1.b. *Dimensions:* L 6.00, D 6.00 mm. *Material:* Carnelian. *Condition:* Complete. *Perforation:* Type II; PD 1.80-2.00 mm.

No. F3.251.1, KM 1685 (fig. 231). *Context:* Trench RM; Unknown; Found in sieve. *Type:* Standard barrel/Circular; I.C.1.b. *Dimensions:* L 6.20, D 6.40 mm. *Material:* Carnelian. *Condition:* Complete. *Perforation:* Type II; PD 1.40 mm.

No. F6.502.2, KM 1691 (fig. 232). *Context:* Trench D2; 1; level -1.74; 15.00-16.00N/3.00-4.00W. *Type:* Standard barrel/Circular; I.C.1.b. *Dimensions:* L 5.50, D 5.90 mm. *Material:* Carnelian. *Condition:* Complete. *Perforation:* Type II; PD 1.80 mm.

No. F6.936.2, KM 1631 (fig. 233). *Context:* Trench F2; Unknown; Found in sieve. *Type:* Standard barrel/Circular; I.C.1.b. *Dimensions:* L 6.50, D 6.20 mm. *Material:* Carnelian. *Condition:* Complete. *Perforation:* Type II; PD 1.80 mm.

No. F6.847.5, KM 1691 (fig. 234). *Context:* Trench M2; Unknown; Found in sieve. *Type:* Standard barrel/Circular; I.C.1.b. *Dimensions:* L 5.90, D 6.40 mm. *Material:* Carnelian. *Condition:* Complete. *Perforation:* Type II; PD 2.10 mm.

No. F6.851.3, KM 1691 (fig. 235). *Context:* Trench M2; Unknown; Found in sieve. *Type:* Standard barrel/Circular; I.C.1.b. *Dimensions:* L 6.80, D 6.60 mm. *Material:* Carnelian. *Condition:* Complete. *Perforation:* Type II; PD 1.50-2.40 mm.

No. F6.880.3, KM 1691 (fig. 236). *Context:* Trench M2; 2-4A; Found in sieve no deeper than level -1.07. *Type:* Standard barrel/Circular; I.C.1.b. *Dimensions:* L 5.70, D 6.30 mm. *Material:* Carnelian. *Condition:* Complete. *Perforation:* Type II; PD 2.10-2.40 mm.

No. F6.880.4, KM 1691 (fig. 237). *Context:* Trench M2; 2-4A; Found in sieve no deeper than level -1.07. *Type:* Standard barrel/Circular; I.C.1.b. *Dimensions:* L 6.30, D 6.60 mm. *Material:* Carnelian. *Condition:* Complete. *Perforation:* Type II; PD 2.20-2.60 mm.

No. F6.246, KM 1691 (fig. 238). *Context:* Trench SS 20-29; 1; level -1.69; 28.70S/0.20E. *Type:* Standard barrel/Circular; I.C.1.b. *Dimensions:* L 7.10, D 7.00 mm. *Material:* Carnelian. *Condition:* Complete. *Perforation:* Type II; PD 2.10-2.50 mm.

No. F6.944.5, KM 1698 (fig. 239). *Context:* No provenience; Unknown; Found in sieve. *Type:* Standard barrel/Circular; I.C.1.b. *Dimensions:* L 4.00, D 4.30 mm. *Material:* Paste. *Condition:* Complete. *Perforation:* Type IV; PD 1.70 mm

No. F6.945.9, KM 1691 (fig. 240). *Context:* No provenience; Unknown; Found in sieve. *Type:* Standard barrel/Circular; I.C.1.b. *Dimensions:* L 6.10, D 6.10 mm. *Material:* Carnelian. *Condition:* Complete. *Perforation:* Type II; PD 1.70 mm.

No. F6.945.8, KM 1691 (fig. 241). *Context:* No provenience; Unknown; Found in sieve. *Type:* Standard barrel/Circular; I.C.1.b. *Dimensions:* L 6.80, D 7.20 mm. *Material:* Carnelian. *Condition:* Complete. *Perforation:* Type II; PD 1.90-2.20 mm.

No. F6.without no.20, KM 1687 (fig. 242). *Context:* No provenience; Unknown; No information. *Type:* Standard barrel/Circular; I.C.1.b. *Dimensions:* L 6.50, D 6.40 mm. *Material:* Carnelian. *Condition:* Complete. *Perforation:* Type II; PD 1.50 mm.

No. F6.without no.19, KM 1687 (fig. 243). *Context:* No provenience; Unknown; No information. *Type:* Standard barrel/Circular; I.C.1.b. *Dimensions:* L 7.00, D 7.20 mm. *Material:* Carnelian. *Condition:* Complete. *Perforation:* Type II; PD 2.00-2.30 mm.

I.D.1.b. Long barrels with circular cross section (figs. 244-352)

No. F3.abh, KM 1693 (fig. 244). *Context:* Trench D; 4A; Between level 8.27 and 8.67; No information. *Type:* Long barrel/Circular; I.D.1.b. *Dimensions:* L 16.30, D 11.00 mm. *Material:* Glass. *Condition:* Fragmented. *Perforation:* Type IV; PD 2.70 mm.

No. F3.abv, KM 1690 (fig. 245). *Context:* Trench D; 4A; Between level 7.67 and 7.97; No information. *Type:* Long barrel/Circular; I.D.1.b. *Dimensions:* L 14.90, D 8.40 mm. *Material:* Glass. *Condition:* Fragmented. *Perforation:* Type IV; PD 2.00 mm.

No. F3.aif, KM 1693 (fig. 246). *Context:* Trench G; Unknown; No information. *Type:* Long barrel/Circular; I.D.1.b. *Dimensions:* L 13-10, D 8.50 mm. *Material:* Jasper. *Condition:* Fragmented. *Perforation:* Type III; PD 3.20 mm.

No. F3.ahf.1, KM 1693 (fig. 247). *Context:* Trench H; 4A; level 7.99; 37.10N/10.55W. *Type:* Long barrel/Circular; I.D.1.b. *Dimensions:* L 19.00, D 9.50 mm. *Material:* Agate. *Condition:* Complete. *Perforation:* Type II; PD 2.40-2.70 mm.

No. F3.ahf.2, KM 1693 (fig. 248). *Context:* Trench H; 4A; level 7.99; 37.10N/10.55W. *Type:* Long barrel/Circular; I.D.1.b. *Dimensions:* L 24.30, D 11.30 mm. *Material:* Agate. *Condition:* Complete. *Perforation:* Type II; PD 3.20-3.50 mm.

No. F3.in, KM 1685 (fig. 249). *Context:* Trench I; 4B; level 7.13; No information. *Type:* Long barrel/Circular; I.D.1.b. *Dimensions:* L 10.50, D 6.80 mm. *Material:* Carnelian. *Condition:* Complete. *Perforation:* Type II; PD 1.50 mm.

No. F3.jd, KM 1693 (fig. 250). *Context:* Trench J; 4B; level 7.21; 75.40N/3.30E. *Type:* Long barrel/Circular; I.D.1.b. *Dimensions:* L 16.00, D 7.20 mm. *Material:* Unidentified stone (black stone with white vein). *Condition:* Complete. *Perforation:* Type II; PD 2.30 mm.

No. F3.aig.2, KM 1693 (fig. 251). *Context:* Trench K; 4A; Between level 8.90 and 9.40; No information. *Type:* Long barrel/Circular; I.D.1.b. *Dimensions:* L 10.50, D 4.30 mm. *Material:* Carnelian. *Condition:* Complete. *Perforation:* Type II; PD 1.00 mm.

No. F3.ami, KM 1715 (fig. 252). *Context:* Trench P; 4A; 8.35; No information. *Type:* Long barrel/Circular; I.D.1.b. *Dimensions:* L 18.60, D 5.70 mm. *Material:* Agate. *Condition:* Complete. *Perforation:* Blank.

No. F3.220, KM 1683 (fig. 253). *Context:* Trench RM; Unknown; Found in sieve. *Type:* Long barrel/Circular; I.D.1.b. *Dimensions:* L 22.00, D 6.60 mm. *Material:* Lapis Lazuli. *Condition:* Complete. *Perforation:* Type II; PD 1.80-2.00 mm.

No. F3.caa, KM 1693 (fig. 254). *Context:* Trench X; 3B/4B; level 8.14; No information. *Type:* Long barrel/Circular; I.D.1.b. *Dimensions:* L 17.20, D 8.50 mm. *Material:* Agate. *Condition:* Complete. *Perforation:* Type II; PD 1.90 mm.

No. F3.ss, KM 1669 (fig. 255). *Context:* Trench X; 3B/4B; level 8.14; 55.00N/4.90E. *Type:* Long barrel/Circular; I.D.1.b. *Dimensions:* L 7.50, D 7.80 mm. *Material:* Carnelian. *Condition:* Fragmented. *Perforation:* Type II; PD 2.00 mm.

No. F3.sh, KM 1693 (fig. 256). *Context:* Baulk between Trench Æ and Ø; Unknown; Found in sieve. *Type:* Long barrel/Circular; I.D.1.b. *Dimensions:* L 20.20, D 6.80 mm. *Material:* Agate. *Condition:* Complete. *Perforation:* Type II; PD 1.90 mm.

No. F3.sz, KM 1693 (fig. 257). *Context:* Baulk between Trench Æ and Ø; Unknown; Found in sieve. *Type:* Long barrel/Circular; I.D.1.b. *Dimensions:* L 11.90, D 6.00 mm. *Material:* Agate. *Condition:* Complete. *Perforation:* Type II; PD 2.50-2.70 mm.

No. F3.avå, KM 1685 (fig. 258). *Context:* Trench AB; 4B; level 7.95; No information. *Type:* Long barrel/Circular; I.D.1.b. *Dimensions:* L 9.40, D 6.20 mm. *Material:* Carnelian. *Condition:* Complete. *Perforation:* Type II; PD 1.50 mm.

No. F3.xu.1, KM 1693 (fig. 259). *Context:* Trench AB; Unknown; Found in sieve. *Type:* Long barrel/Circular; I.D.1.b. *Dimensions:* L 24.50, D 7.20 mm. *Material:* Agate. *Condition:* Complete. *Perforation:* Type II; PD 2.50 mm.

No. F3.æn.5, KM 1693 (fig. 260). *Context:* Baulk between Trench AB and AF; Unknown; Found in sieve. *Type:* Long barrel/Circular; I.D.1.b. *Dimensions:* L 12.90, D 5.50 mm. *Material:* Agate. *Condition:* Complete. *Perforation:* Type II; PD 1.80 mm.

No. F3.æz.2, KM 1685 (fig. 261). *Context:* Trench AD; Unknown; Found in sieve. *Type:* Long barrel/Circular; I.D.1.b. *Dimensions:* L 8.70, D 6.10 mm. *Material:* Carnelian. *Condition:* Complete. *Perforation:* Type II; PD 2.30 mm.

No. F3.øk.1, KM 1693 (fig. 262). *Context:* Trench AE; 3A; Found in sieve. *Type:* Long barrel/Circular; I.D.1.b. *Dimensions:* L 16.50, D 13.80 mm. *Material:* Jasper. *Condition:* Fragmented. *Perforation:* Type III; PD 2.70-3.20 mm.

No. F3.øw.1, KM 1693 (fig. 263). *Context:* Trench AE; 3A; Found in sieve. *Type:* Long barrel/Circular; I.D.1.b. *Dimensions:* L 18.90, D 9.50 mm. *Material:* Jasper. *Condition:* Complete. *Perforation:* Type II; PD 2.50 mm.

No. F3.ås.3, KM 1693 (fig. 264). *Context:* Trench AE; 3A; Found in sieve. *Type:* Long barrel/Circular; I.D.1.b. *Dimensions:* L 11.40, D 5.60 mm. *Material:* Jasper. *Condition:* Complete. *Perforation:* Type II; PD 2.10-2.20 mm.

No. F3.åz, KM 1685 (fig. 265). *Context:* Trench AI; Unknown; Found in sieve. *Type:* Long barrel/Circular; I.D.1.b. *Dimensions:* L 10.40, D 7.10 mm. *Material:* Carnelian. *Condition:* Complete. *Perforation:* Type II; PD 1.60-2.40 mm.

No. F3.aye.1, KM 1693 (fig. 266). *Context:* Trench AO; 4A/4B; level 7.53; No information. *Type:* Long barrel/Circular; I.D.1.b. *Dimensions:* L 28.70, D 10.80 mm. *Material:* Jasper. *Condition:* Complete. *Perforation:* Type II; PD 2.50-2.80 mm.

No. F3.azp, KM 1693 (fig. 267). *Context:* Trench AO; 4A/4B; Between level 6.87 and 6.63; No information. *Type:* Long barrel/Circular; I.D.1.b. *Dimensions:* L 20.90, D 7.30 mm. *Material:* Carnelian. *Condition:* Complete. *Perforation:* Type II; PD 2.30 mm.

No. F3.bif.2, KM 1693 (fig. 268). *Context:* Trench AV; Unknown; Found in sieve. *Type:* Long barrel/Circular; I.D.1.b. *Dimensions:* L 19.10, D 9.20 mm. *Material:* Calcite. *Condition:* Fragmented. *Perforation:* Type II; PD 1.80-2.00 mm.

No. F3.bfb.2, KM 1685 (fig. 269). *Context:* No provenience; Unknown; No information. *Type:* Long barrel/Circular; I.D.1.b. *Dimensions:* L 10.30, D 6.80 mm. *Material:* Agate. *Condition:* Complete. *Perforation:* Type II; PD 2.20-2.50 mm.

No. F3.li, KM 1693 (fig. 270). *Context:* No provenience; Unknown; No information. *Type:* Long barrel/Circular; I.D.1.b. *Dimensions:* L 19.00, D 7.10 mm. *Material:* Agate. *Condition:* Complete. *Perforation:* Type II; PD 2.30 mm.

No. F3.without no.2, KM 1693 (fig. 271). *Context:* No provenience; Unknown; No information. *Type:* Long barrel/Circular; I.D.1.b. *Dimensions:* L 18.10, D 8.20 mm. *Material:* Carnelian. *Condition:* Complete. *Perforation:* Type II; PD 2.30 mm.

No. F3.anm, KM 1693 (fig. 272). *Context:* Trench K; Unknown; Found in sieve. *Type:* Long barrel/Circular; I.D.1.b. *Dimensions:* L 18.60, D 7.60 mm. *Material:* Jasper. *Condition:* Complete. *Perforation:* Type II; PD 2.00 mm.

No. F6.127, KM 1696 (fig. 273). *Context:* Trench A1; 2-4A; level -0.62; 6.20S/3.00W. *Type:* Long barrel/Circular; I.D.1.b. *Dimensions:* L 14.90, D 12.20 mm. *Material:* Agate. *Condition:* Complete. *Perforation:* Type II; PD 2.50 mm.

No. F6.126, KM 1695 (fig. 274). *Context:* Trench A2; 2-4A; level -0.61; 14.60S/3.00W. *Type:* Long barrel/Circular; I.D.1.b. *Dimensions:* L 15.90, D 10.00 mm. *Material:* Agate. *Condition:* Complete. *Perforation:* Type II; PD 1.80-2.00 mm.

No. F6.352, KM 1691 (fig. 275). *Context:* Trench B2; 2-4A; level 0.85; 17.00S/6.10W. *Type:* Long barrel/Circular; I.D.1.b. *Dimensions:* L 6.60, D 3.90 mm. *Material:* Lapis Lazuli. *Condition:* Fragmented. *Perforation:* Type II; PD 1.50 mm.

No. F6.351, KM 1691 (fig. 276). *Context:* Trench C3; 2-4A; level -1.50; 23.00S/1.60E. *Type:* Long barrel/Circular; I.D.1.b. *Dimensions:* L 7.50, D 5.30 mm. *Material:* Carnelian. *Condition:* Complete. *Perforation:* Type II; PD 1.80 mm.

No. F6.389, KM 1691 (fig. 277). *Context:* Trench D1; 2-4A; level 0.61; 1.00-10.00N/1.00 4.00W. *Type:* Long barrel/Circular; I.D.1.b. *Dimensions:* L 8.20, D 7.00 mm. *Material:* Carnelian. *Condition:* Complete. *Perforation:* Type II; PD 2.00 mm.

No. F6.431.3, KM 1682 (fig. 278). *Context:* Trench D1; 2-4A; level 0.16; 4.00-5.50N/2.00-3.00W. *Type:* Long barrel/Circular; I.D.1.b. *Dimensions:* L 22.20, D 10.00 mm. *Material:* Agate. *Condition:* Complete. *Perforation:* Type II; PD 2.30-2.50 mm.

No. F6.431.4, KM 1682 (fig. 279). *Context:* Trench D1; 2-4A; level 0.16; 4.00-5.50N/2.00-3.00W. *Type:* Long barrel/Circular; I.D.1.b. *Dimensions:* L 15.00, D 6.10 mm. *Material:* Carnelian. *Condition:* Fragmented. *Perforation:* Type III; PD 2.00 mm.

No. F6.447.2, KM 1682 (fig. 280). *Context:* Trench D1; 2-4A; level -0.26; 4.00-5.50N/2.00-3.00W. *Type:* Long barrel/Circular; I.D.1.b. *Dimensions:* L 28.00, D 9.50 mm. *Material:* Jasper. *Condition:* Fragmented. *Perforation:* Type II; PD 2.20 mm.

No. F6.557, KM 1680 (fig. 281). *Context:* Trench D1; Unknown; No information. *Type:* Long barrel/Circular; I.D.1.b. *Dimensions:* L 20.20, D 7.50 mm. *Material:* Glass. *Condition:* Fragmented. *Perforation:* Type IV; PD 2.90 mm.

No. F6.957, KM 1695 (fig. 282). *Context:* Trench D1; Unknown; Found in sieve. *Type:* Long barrel/Circular; I.D.1.b. *Dimensions:* L 11.10, D 6.10 mm. *Material:* Carnelian. *Condition:* Complete. *Perforation:* Type II; PD 1.90 mm.

No. F6.961, KM 1695 (fig. 283). *Context:* Trench D1; 1; level -1.61; 2.00N/0.50W. *Type:* Long barrel/Circular; I.D.1.b. *Dimensions:* L 12.00, D 5.50 mm. *Material:* Carnelian. *Condition:* Complete. *Perforation:* Type II; PD 2.30 mm.

No. F6.362.9, KM 1678 (fig. 284). *Context:* Trench D2; 2-4A; level -0.59; 14.00-15.00N/3.50-4.00W. *Type:* Long barrel/Circular; I.D.1.b. *Dimensions:* L 28.00, D 12.70 mm. *Material:* Glass. *Condition:* Fragmented. *Perforation:* Type IV; PD 1.80 mm.

No. F6.362.10, KM 1560 (fig. 285). *Context:* Trench D2; 2-4A; level -0.59; 14.00-15.00N/3.50-4.00W. *Type:* Long barrel/Circular; I.D.1.b. *Dimensions:* L 30.40, D 8.90 mm. *Material:* Glass. *Condition:* Complete. *Perforation:* Type IV; PD 2.10 mm.

No. F6.400.2, KM 1682 (fig. 286). *Context:* Trench D2; 2-4A; level -1.10; 19.00N/3.00W. *Type:* Long barrel/Circular; I.D.1.b. *Dimensions:* L 28.10, D 13.70 mm. *Material:* Hematite. *Condition:* Complete. *Perforation:* Type II; PD 2.50-2.70 mm.

No. F6.406.3, KM 1691 (fig. 287). *Context:* Trench D2; 2-4A; level -1.08; 13.00-15.00N/2.50-4.00W. *Type:* Long barrel/Circular; I.D.1.b. *Dimensions:* L 9.00, D 7.20 mm. *Material:* Carnelian. *Condition:* Complete. *Perforation:* Type III; PD 2.10-2.30 mm.

No. F6.406.4, KM 1682 (fig. 288). *Context:* Trench D2; 2-4A; level -1.08; 13.00-15.00N/2.50-4.00W. *Type:* Long barrel/Circular; I.D.1.b. *Dimensions:* L 24.20, D 12.00 mm. *Material:* Glass. *Condition:* Complete. *Perforation:* Type IV; PD 2.60-3.00 mm.

No. F6.406.5, KM 1504 (fig. 289). *Context:* Trench D2; 2-4A; level -1.08; 13.00-15.00N/2.50-4.00W. *Type:* Long barrel/Circular; I.D.1.b. *Dimensions:* L 24.40, D 11.50 mm. *Material:* Glass. *Condition:* Fragmented. *Perforation:* Type III; PD 2.70 mm.

No. F6.406.6, KM 1682 (fig. 290). *Context:* Trench D2; 2 4A; level -1.08; 13.00-15.00N/2.50-4.00W. *Type:* Long barrel/Circular; I.D.1.b. *Dimensions:* L 24.70, D 12.70 mm. *Material:* Glass. *Condition:* Fragmented. *Perforation:* Type IV; PD 2.40 mm.

No. F6.408.1, KM 1682 (fig. 291). *Context:* Trench D2; 2-4A; level -1.03; 18.40N/2.20W. *Type:* Long barrel/Circular; I.D.1.b. *Dimensions:* L 23.00, D 9.80 mm. *Material:* Glass. *Condition:* Fragmented. *Perforation:* Type IV; PD 2.00 mm.

No. F6.417.6, KM 1682 (fig. 292). *Context:* Trench D2; 2-4A; Between level 0.46 and -1.08; 13.00-15.00N/1.25-4.00W. *Type:* Long barrel/Circular; I.D.1.b. *Dimensions:* L 15.50, D 5.40 mm. *Material:* Agate. *Condition:* Complete. *Perforation:* Type II; PD 2.20 mm.

No. F6.417.5, KM 1682 (fig. 293). *Context:* Trench D2; 2-4A; Between level 0.46 and -1.08; 13.00-15.00N/1.25-4.00W. *Type:* Long barrel/Circular; I.D.1.b. *Dimensions:* L 8.60, D 6.30 mm. *Material:* Glass. *Condition:* Fragmented. *Perforation:* Type III; PD 2.10 mm.

No. F6.444.2, KM 1682 (fig. 294). *Context:* Trench D2; 2-4A; level -1.31; 16.00N/2.00W. *Type:* Long barrel/Circular; I.D.1.b. *Dimensions:* L 22.50, D 8.00 mm. *Material:* Glass. *Condition:* Fragmented. *Perforation:* Type IV; PD 2.30 mm.

No. F6.464.1, KM 1682 (fig. 295). *Context:* Trench D2; Unknown; found in hole in floor at level -1.86; 18.00N/2.50W; *Type:* Long barrel/Circular; I.D.1.b. *Dimensions:* L 23.30, D 12.20 mm. *Material:* Glass. *Condition:* Fragmented. *Perforation:* Type IV; PD 2.80 mm.

No. F6.464.2, KM 1711 (fig. 296). *Context:* Trench D2; Unknown; found in hole in floor at level -1.86; 18.00N/2.50W; *Type:* Long barrel/Circular; I.D.1.b. *Dimensions:* L 36.40, D 6.90 mm. *Material:* Glass. *Condition:* Fragmented. *Perforation:* Type IV; PD 0.90 mm.

No. F6.624, KM 1682 (fig. 297). *Context:* Trench D2; 1; level -2.03; 15.00N/3.00W. *Type:* Long barrel/Circular; I.D.1.b. *Dimensions:* L 11.70, D 6.10 mm. *Material:* Agate. *Condition:* Complete. *Perforation:* Type II; PD 2.10-2.20 mm.

No. F6.630, KM 1682 (fig. 298). *Context:* Trench D2; 1; level -1.88; 17.00N/3.50W. *Type:* Long barrel/Circular; I.D.1.b. *Dimensions:* L 16.00, D 4.90 mm. *Material:* Agate. *Condition:* Complete. *Perforation:* Type II; PD 2.10 mm.

No. F6.640, KM 1680 (fig. 299). *Context:* Trench D2; 2-4A; level -1.46; 17.00N/1.00W. *Type:* Long barrel/Circular; I.D.1.b. *Dimensions:* L 25.00, D 6.50 mm. *Material:* Glass. *Condition:* Fragmented. *Perforation:* Type IV; PD 3.20 mm.

No. F6.641, KM 1682 (fig. 300). *Context:* Trench D2; 2-4A; level -1.06; 16.50N/3.50W. *Type:* Long barrel/Circular; I.D.1.b. *Dimensions:* L 13.70, D 6.60 mm. *Material:* Agate. *Condition:* Complete. *Perforation:* Type II; PD 2.00-2.50 mm.

No. F6.646, KM 1695 (fig. 301). *Context:* Trench D2; Unknown; 11.00-17.00N/1.00-4.00W; Found in sieve. *Type:* Long barrel/Circular; I.D.1.b. *Dimensions:* L 11.80, D 5.00 mm. *Material:* Agate. *Condition:* Complete. *Perforation:* Type II; PD 1.80-1.90 mm.

No. F6.908, KM 1564 (fig. 302). *Context:* Trench D2; Unknown; 15.50-16.00N/3.00-4.00W; Found in sieve. *Type:* Long barrel/Circular; I.D.1.b. *Dimensions:* L 32.80, D 8.40 mm. *Material:* Glass. *Condition:* Fragmented. *Perforation:* Type IV; PD 3.00 mm.

No. F6.537.2, KM 1691 (fig. 303). *Context:* Trench D3; 2-4A; level -0.58; 21.00-24.00N/1.00-2.00W. *Type:* Long barrel/Circular; I.D.1.b. *Dimensions:* L 12.00, D 8.00 mm. *Material:* Carnelian. *Condition:* Complete. *Perforation:* Type II; PD 2.20-2.50 mm.

No. F6.554, KM 1709 (fig. 304). *Context:* Trench D3; 2-4A; level -0.69; No information. *Type:* Long barrel/Circular; I.D.1.b. *Dimensions:* L 24.00, D 10.50 mm. *Material:* Glass. *Condition:* Complete. *Perforation:* Type IV; PD 2.50 mm.

No. F6.493, KM 1701 (fig. 305). *Context:* Trench E2; 2-4A; level -1.08; 13.50-15.00N/1.50-3.00E. *Type:* Long barrel/Circular; I.D.1.b. *Dimensions:* L 27.20, D 8.40 mm. *Material:* Glass. *Condition:* Fragmented. *Perforation:* Type III; PD 3.60 mm.

No. F6.898, KM 1696 (fig. 306). *Context:* Trench E2; Unknown; Found in sieve. *Type:* Long barrel/Circular; I.D.1.b. *Dimensions:* L 16.50, D 6.90 mm. *Material:* Jasper. *Condition:* Complete. *Perforation:* Type II; PD 1.90 mm.

No. F6.583, KM 1558 (fig. 307). *Context:* Baulk between Trench D2 and SN11-20; Unknown; level 0.94; 19.00-20.00N/0.00-1.00W. *Type:* Long barrel/Circular; I.D.1.b. *Dimensions:* L 25.20, D 8.60 mm. *Material:* Glass. *Condition:* Fragmented. *Perforation:* Type IV; PD 2.50 mm.

No. F6.590.5, KM 1714 (fig. 308). *Context:* Baulk between Trench D2 and SN11-20; 2-4A; level -1.28; 14.50-16.00N/0.00-1.00W. *Type:* Long barrel/Circular; I.D.1.b. *Dimensions:* L 34.40, D 7.00 mm. *Material:* Glass. *Condition:* Fragmented. *Perforation:* Type IV; PD 1.50 mm.

No. F6.608.3, KM 1691 (fig. 309). *Context:* Trench SN11-20; 1; level -1.75; 13.00-14.00N/0.00-1.00E. *Type:* Long barrel/Circular; I.D.1.b. *Dimensions:* L 8.20, D 4.50 mm. *Material:* Carnelian. *Condition:* Complete. *Perforation:* Type II; PD 1.60 mm.

No. F6.608.4, KM 1691 (fig. 310). *Context:* Trench SN11-20; 1; level -1.75; 13.00-14.00N/0.00-1.00E. *Type:* Long barrel/Circular; I.D.1.b. *Dimensions:* L 13.10, D 5.40 mm. *Material:* Carnelian. *Condition:* Complete. *Perforation:* Type II; PD 2.20 mm.

No. F6.991, KM 1695 (fig. 311). *Context:* Trench F1; 2-4A; No deeper than level -0.71; Found in sieve. *Type:* Long barrel/Circular; I.D.1.b. *Dimensions:* L 20.00, D 7.00 mm. *Material:* Glass. *Condition:* Fragmented. *Perforation:* Type IV; PD 2.30 mm.

No. F6.991A, KM 1695 (fig. 312). *Context:* Trench F1; 2-4A; Found in sieve above level -0.71. *Type:* Long barrel/Circular; I.D.1.b. *Dimensions:* L 19.80, D 7.00 mm. *Material:* Jasper. *Condition:* Complete. *Perforation:* Type II; PD 2.40 mm.

No. F6.991B, KM 1691 (fig. 313). *Context:* Trench F1; 2-4A; Found in sieve above level -0.71. *Type:* Long barrel/Circular; I.D.1.b. *Dimensions:* L 7.90, D 6.30 mm. *Material:* Carnelian. *Condition:* Complete. *Perforation:* Type II; PD 1.90 mm.

No. F6.972, KM 1695 (fig. 314). *Context:* Trench F1; Unknown; Found in sieve. *Type:* Long barrel/Circular; I.D.1.b. *Dimensions:* L 30.20, D 9.30 mm. *Material:* Jasper. *Condition:* Fragmented. *Perforation:* Type II; PD 2.90 mm.

No. F6.996, KM 1667 (fig. 315). *Context:* Trench F1; 2-4A; level -0.85; 2.00N/6.00W. *Type:* Long barrel/Circular; I.D.1.b. *Dimensions:* L 25.10, D 7.50 mm. *Material:* Agate. *Condition:* Fragmented. *Perforation:* Semi-drilled. PD 1.50 mm.

No. F6.1001A, KM 1695 (fig. 316). *Context:* Trench F1; Unknown; Found in sieve. *Type:* Long barrel/Circular; I.D.1.b. *Dimensions:* L 24.90, D 10.50 mm. *Material:* Calcite. *Condition:* Fragmented. *Perforation:* Type II; PD 3.50 mm.

No. F6.1004, KM 1695 (fig. 317). *Context:* Trench F1; Unknown; Found in sieve. *Type:* Long barrel/Circular; I.D.1.b. *Dimensions:* L 15.00, D 6.90 mm. *Material:* Jasper. *Condition:* Complete. *Perforation:* Type II; PD 2.30 mm.

No. F6.639.1, KM 1691 (fig. 318). *Context:* Trench F2; Unknown; Between level -1.72 and -0.98; Found in sieve. *Type:* Long barrel/Circular; I.D.1.b. *Dimensions:* L 9.10, D 8.10 mm. *Material:* Carnelian. *Condition:* Complete. *Perforation:* Type II; PD 2.40-2.60 mm.

No. F6.666.2, KM 1505 (fig. 319). *Context:* Trench F2; 2-4A; level -0.78; 13.00N/5.00W. *Type:* Long barrel/Circular; I.D.1.b. *Dimensions:* L 29.40, D 8.30 mm. *Material:* Glass. *Condition:* Fragmented. *Perforation:* Type IV; PD 1.50 mm.

No. F6.666.3, KM 1505 (fig. 320). *Context:* Trench F2; 2-4A; level -0.78; 13.00N/5.00W. *Type:* Long barrel/Circular; I.D.1.b. *Dimensions:* L 41.60, D 12.10 mm. *Material:* Glass. *Condition:* Fragmented. *Perforation:* Type IV; PD 2.40 mm.

No. F6.677, KM 1682 (fig. 321). *Context:* Trench F2; 2-4A; level -1.09; 12.00N/6.00W. *Type:* Long barrel/Circular; I.D.1.b. *Dimensions:* L 15.20, D 5.20 mm. *Material:* Jasper. *Condition:* Complete. *Perforation:* Type II; PD 2.00 mm.

No. F6.689, KM 1691 (fig. 322). *Context:* Trench F2; Unknown; Found in sieve. *Type:* Long barrel/Circular; I.D.1.b. *Dimensions:* L 7.90, D 4.50 mm. *Material:* Jasper. *Condition:* Complete. *Perforation:* Type II; PD mm.

No. F6.933, KM 1691 (fig. 323). *Context:* Trench F2; Unknown; Found in sieve. *Type:* Long barrel/Circular; I.D.1.b. *Dimensions:* L 14.90, D 12.90 mm. *Material:* Agate. *Condition:* Complete. *Perforation:* Type II; PD 2.80 mm.

No. F6.935.2, KM 1691 (fig. 324). *Context:* Trench F2; Unknown; Found in sieve. *Type:* Long barrel/Circular; I.D.1.b. *Dimensions:* L 7.60, D 6.10 mm. *Material:* Carnelian. *Condition:* Complete. *Perforation:* Type II; PD 1.60 mm.

No. F6.657, KM 1682 (fig. 325). *Context:* Baulk between Trench D2 and F2; 2-4A; level -0.71; 15.00-16.00N/4.00-4.50W. *Type:* Long barrel/Circular; I.D.1.b. *Dimensions:* L 15.00, D 8.20 mm. *Material:* Jasper. *Condition:* Complete. *Perforation:* Type II; PD 2.70-2.80 mm.

No. F6.800.3, KM 1682 (fig. 326). *Context:* Trench M2; 2-4A; Found in sieve above level -1.07. *Type:* Long barrel/Circular; I.D.1.b. *Dimensions:* L 31.60, D 8.70 mm. *Material:* Porphyry. *Condition:* Complete. *Perforation:* Type II; PD 2.90 mm.

No. F6.800.2, KM 1705 (fig. 327). *Context:* Trench M2; 2-4A; Found in sieve above level -1.07. *Type:* Long barrel/Circular; I.D.1.b. *Dimensions:* L 21.00, D 8.50 mm. *Material:* Glass. *Condition:* Fragmented. *Perforation:* Type IV; PD 2.70 mm.

No. F6.827.4, KM 1691 (fig. 328). *Context:* Trench M2; Unknown; Found in sieve. *Type:* Long barrel/Circular; I.D.1.b. *Dimensions:* L 9.80, D 6.80 mm. *Material:* Agate. *Condition:* Complete. *Perforation:* Type II; PD 2.40 mm.

No. F6.827.2, KM 1691 (fig. 329). *Context:* Trench M2; Unknown; Found in sieve. *Type:* Long barrel/Circular; I.D.1.b. *Dimensions:* L 9.20, D 4.30 mm. *Material:* Carnelian. *Condition:* Complete. *Perforation:* Type II; PD 1.90 mm.

No. F6.827.1, KM 1682 (fig. 330). *Context:* Trench M2; Unknown; Found in sieve. *Type:* Long barrel/Circular; I.D.1.b. *Dimensions:* L 13.20, D 6.10 mm. *Material:* Carnelian. *Condition:* Complete. *Perforation:* Type II; PD 2.00 mm.

No. F6.851.2, KM 1691 (fig. 331). *Context:* Trench M2; Unknown; Found in sieve. *Type:* Long barrel/Circular; I.D.1.b. *Dimensions:* L 8.00, D 6.30 mm. *Material:* Carnelian. *Condition:* Complete. *Perforation:* Type II; PD 2.00-2.40 mm.

No. F6.851.1, KM 1682 (fig. 332). *Context:* Trench M2; Unknown; Found in sieve. *Type:* Long barrel/Circular; I.D.1.b. *Dimensions:* L 8.20, D 5.30 mm. *Material:* Carnelian. *Condition:* Fragmented. *Perforation:* Type II; PD 1.90 mm.

No. F6.875.2, KM 1691 (fig. 333). *Context:* Trench M2; Unknown; Found in sieve. *Type:* Long barrel/Circular; I.D.1.b. *Dimensions:* L 4.60, D 3.80 mm. *Material:* Carnelian. *Condition:* Complete. *Perforation:* Type II; PD 1.20 mm.

No. F6.880.5, KM 1691 (fig. 334). *Context:* Trench M2; 2-4A; Found in sieve above level -1.07. *Type:* Long barrel/Circular; I.D.1.b. *Dimensions:* L 8.20, D 7.40 mm. *Material:* Carnelian. *Condition:* Complete. *Perforation:* Type III; PD 2.20-2.90 mm.

No. F6.939, KM 1713 (fig. 335). *Context:* Trench M2; Unknown; Found in sieve. *Type:* Long barrel/Circular; I.D.1.b. *Dimensions:* L 19.70, D 8.10 mm. *Material:* Glass. *Condition:* Fragmented. *Perforation:* Type IV; PD 2.70 mm.

No. F6.116, KM 1695 (fig. 336). *Context:* Trench SN 1-10; 2-4A; level 0.77; 6.60N/0.80E. *Type:* Long barrel/Circular; I.D.1.b. *Dimensions:* L 17.20, D 9.70 mm. *Material:* Chlorite (type 3). *Condition:* Complete. *Perforation:* Type II; PD 2.70 mm.

No. F6.235, KM 1695 (fig. 337). *Context:* Trench SN 1-10; 2-4A; level -0.54; 1.00-10.00N/0.00-1.50E. *Type:* Long barrel/Circular; I.D.1.b. *Dimensions:* L 10.30, D 6.40 mm. *Material:* Agate. *Condition:* Complete. *Perforation:* Type II; PD 2.20 mm.

No. F6.221, KM 1695 (fig. 338). *Context:* Trench SN 11-20; 2-4A; level -0.60; 14.00-17.00N/0.00-0.50E. *Type:* Long barrel/Circular; I.D.1.b. *Dimensions:* L 22.00, D 9.10 mm. *Material:* Jasper. *Condition:* Complete. *Perforation:* Type II; PD 2.70 mm.

No. F6.280, KM 1557 (fig. 339). *Context:* Trench SN 11-20; 2-4A; level -0.99; 12.20N/1.00E. *Type:* Long barrel/Circular; I.D.1.b. *Dimensions:* L 40.00, D 7.00 mm. *Material:* Glass. *Condition:* Fragmented. *Perforation:* Type IV; PD 1.90 mm.

No. F6.945.12, KM 1695 (fig. 340). *Context:* No provenience; Unknown; Found in sieve. *Type:* Long barrel/Circular; I.D.1.b. *Dimensions:* L 7.40, D 4.00 mm. *Material:* Carnelian. *Condition:* Complete. *Perforation:* Type II; PD 1.60 mm.

No. F6.945.11, KM 1691 (fig. 341). *Context:* No provenience; Unknown; Found in sieve. *Type:* Long barrel/Circular; I.D.1.b. *Dimensions:* L 7.60, D 6.30 mm. *Material:* Carnelian. *Condition:* Complete. *Perforation:* Type II; PD 1.70 mm.

No. F6.1119, KM 1695 (fig. 342). *Context:* No provenience; Unknown; Found in sieve. *Type:* Long barrel/Circular; I.D.1.b. *Dimensions:* L 18.40, D 9.00 mm. *Material:* Chlorite (type 2). *Condition:* Complete. *Perforation:* Type II; PD 2.00 mm.

No. F6.without no.26, KM 1696 (fig. 343). *Context:* No provenience; Unknown; No information. *Type:* Long barrel/Circular; I.D.1.b. *Dimensions:* L 10.60, D 5.60 mm. *Material:* Agate. *Condition:* Complete. *Perforation:* Type II; PD 2.20 mm.

No. F6.without no.34, KM 1695 (fig. 344). *Context:* No provenience; Unknown; No information. *Type:* Long barrel/Circular; I.D.1.b. *Dimensions:* L 11.20, D 5.10 mm. *Material:* Agate. *Condition:* Complete. *Perforation:* Type II; PD 2.10 mm.

No. F6.without no.28, KM 1682 (fig. 345). *Context:* No provenience; Unknown; No information. *Type:* Long barrel/Circular; I.D.1.b. *Dimensions:* L 17.60, D 7.90 mm. *Material:* Agate. *Condition:* Complete. *Perforation:* Type II; PD 2.60 mm.

No. F6.without no.29, KM 1682 (fig. 346). *Context:* No provenience; Unknown; No information. *Type:* Long barrel/Circular; I.D.1.b. *Dimensions:* L 27.50, D 8.70 mm. *Material:* Agate. *Condition:* Complete. *Perforation:* Type II; PD 2.10 mm.

No. F6.without no.31, KM 1696 (fig. 347). *Context:* No provenience; Unknown; No information. *Type:* Long barrel/Circular; I.D.1.b. *Dimensions:* L 7.60, D 4.50 mm. *Material:* Carnelian. *Condition:* Complete. *Perforation:* Type III; PD 1.30-2.10 mm.

No. F6.without no.32, KM 1687 (fig. 348). *Context:* No provenience; Unknown; No information. *Type:* Long barrel/Circular; I.D.1.b. *Dimensions:* L 8.70, D 4.90 mm. *Material:* Carnelian. *Condition:* Complete. *Perforation:* Type II; PD 1.90 mm.

No. F6.without no.33, KM 1687 (fig. 349). *Context:* No provenience; Unknown; No information. *Type:* Long barrel/Circular; I.D.1.b. *Dimensions:* L 8.80, D 5.00 mm. *Material:* Carnelian. *Condition:* Complete. *Perforation:* Type II; PD 1.60 mm.

No. F6.without no.35, KM 1695 (fig. 350). *Context:* No provenience; Unknown; No information. *Type:* Long barrel/Circular; I.D.1.b. *Dimensions:* L 11.20, D 6.50 mm. *Material:* Jasper. *Condition:* Fragmented. *Perforation:* Type IV; PD 2.00 mm.

No. F6.without no.27, KM 1695 (fig. 351). *Context:* No provenience; Unknown; No information. *Type:* Long barrel/Circular; I.D.1.b. *Dimensions:* L 12.60, D 6.60 mm. *Material:* Jasper. *Condition:* Complete. *Perforation:* Type II; PD 2.30 mm.

No. F6.without no.30, KM 1682 (fig. 352). *Context:* No provenience; Unknown; No information. *Type:* Long barrel/Circular; I.D.1.b. *Dimensions:* L 17.00, D 9.50 mm. *Material:* Glass. *Condition:* Fragmented. *Perforation:* Type IV; PD 2.00 mm.

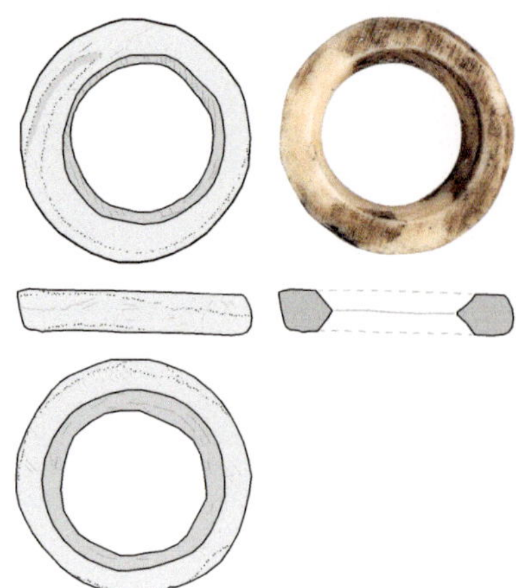

Fig. 217.

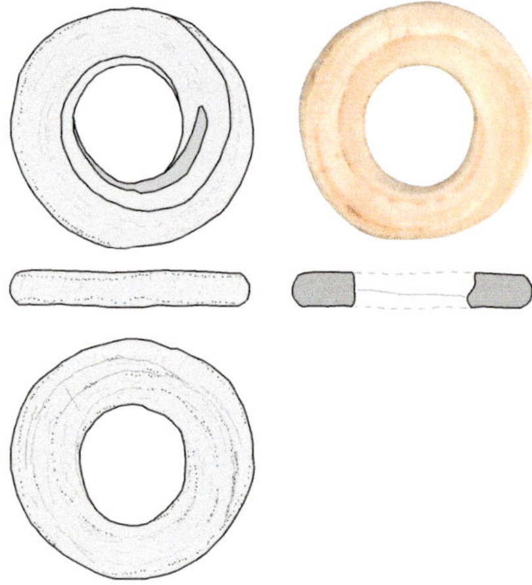

Fig. 218.

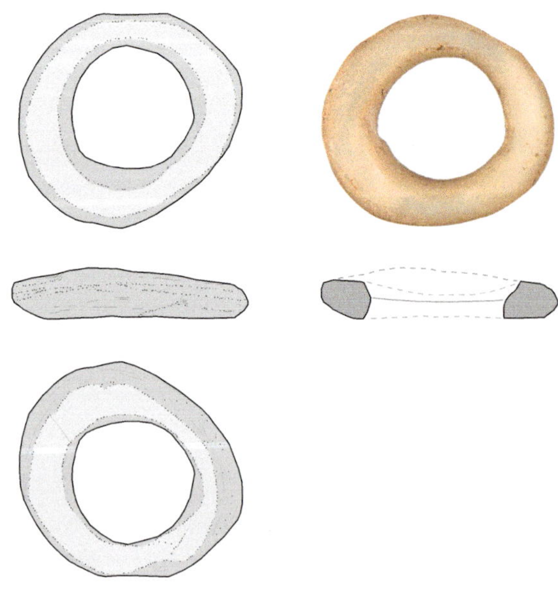

Fig. 219.

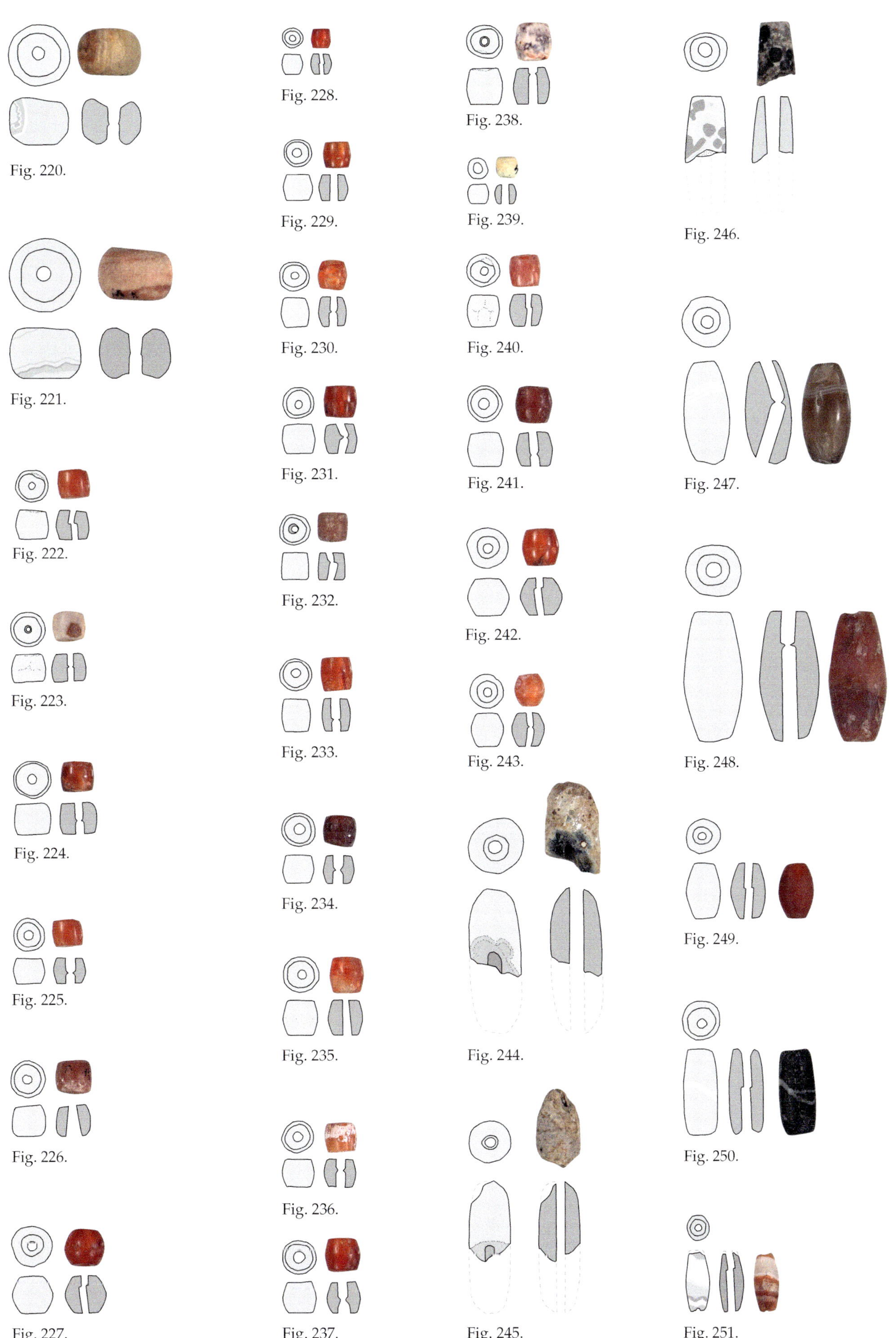

Fig. 220.

Fig. 221.

Fig. 222.

Fig. 223.

Fig. 224.

Fig. 225.

Fig. 226.

Fig. 227.

Fig. 228.

Fig. 229.

Fig. 230.

Fig. 231.

Fig. 232.

Fig. 233.

Fig. 234.

Fig. 235.

Fig. 236.

Fig. 237.

Fig. 238.

Fig. 239.

Fig. 240.

Fig. 241.

Fig. 242.

Fig. 243.

Fig. 244.

Fig. 245.

Fig. 246.

Fig. 247.

Fig. 248.

Fig. 249.

Fig. 250.

Fig. 251.

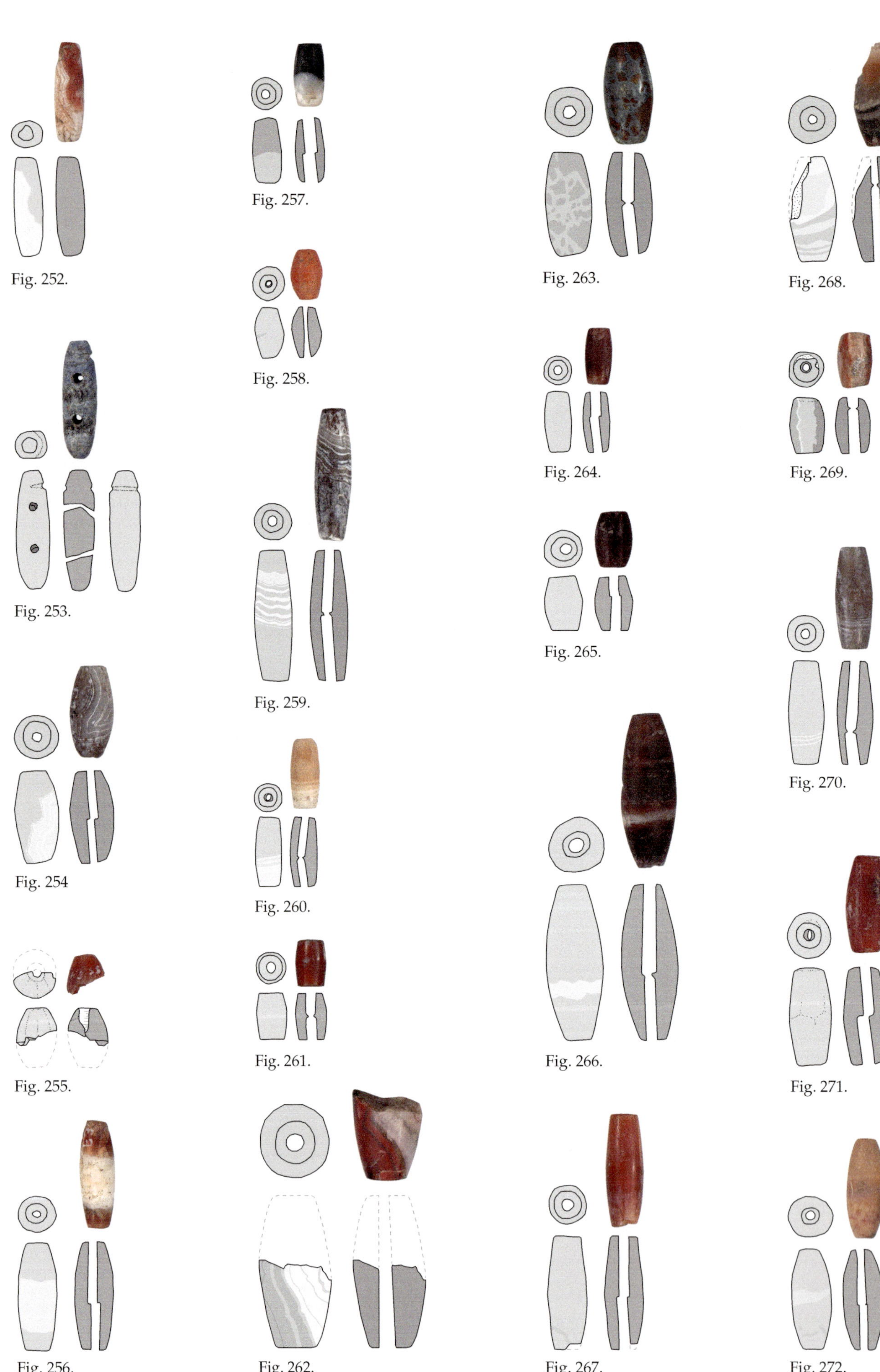
Fig. 252.
Fig. 253.
Fig. 254
Fig. 255.
Fig. 256.
Fig. 257.
Fig. 258.
Fig. 259.
Fig. 260.
Fig. 261.
Fig. 262.
Fig. 263.
Fig. 264.
Fig. 265.
Fig. 266.
Fig. 267.
Fig. 268.
Fig. 269.
Fig. 270.
Fig. 271.
Fig. 272.

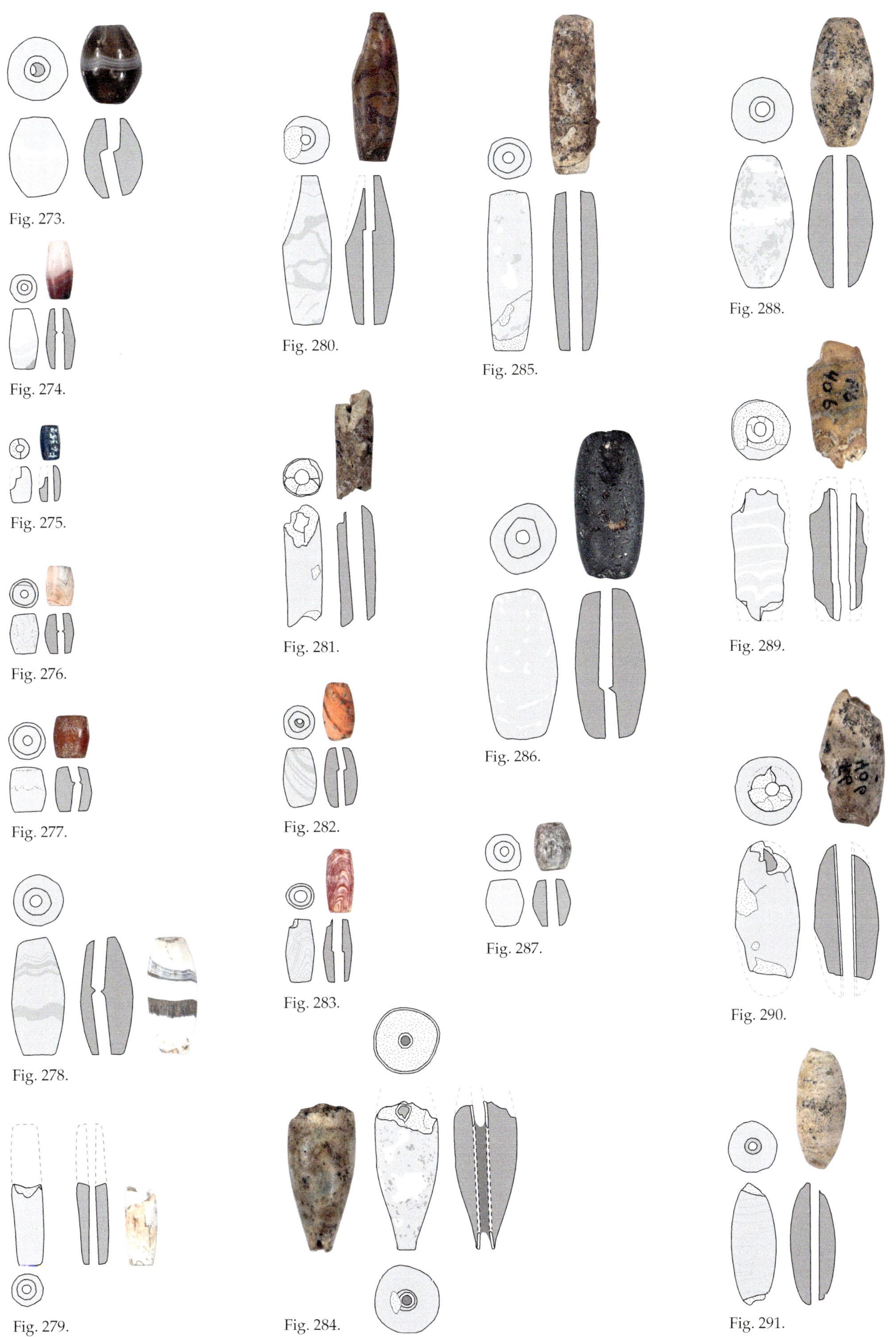

Fig. 273.

Fig. 274.

Fig. 275.

Fig. 276.

Fig. 277.

Fig. 278.

Fig. 279.

Fig. 280.

Fig. 281.

Fig. 282.

Fig. 283.

Fig. 284.

Fig. 285.

Fig. 286.

Fig. 287.

Fig. 288.

Fig. 289.

Fig. 290.

Fig. 291.

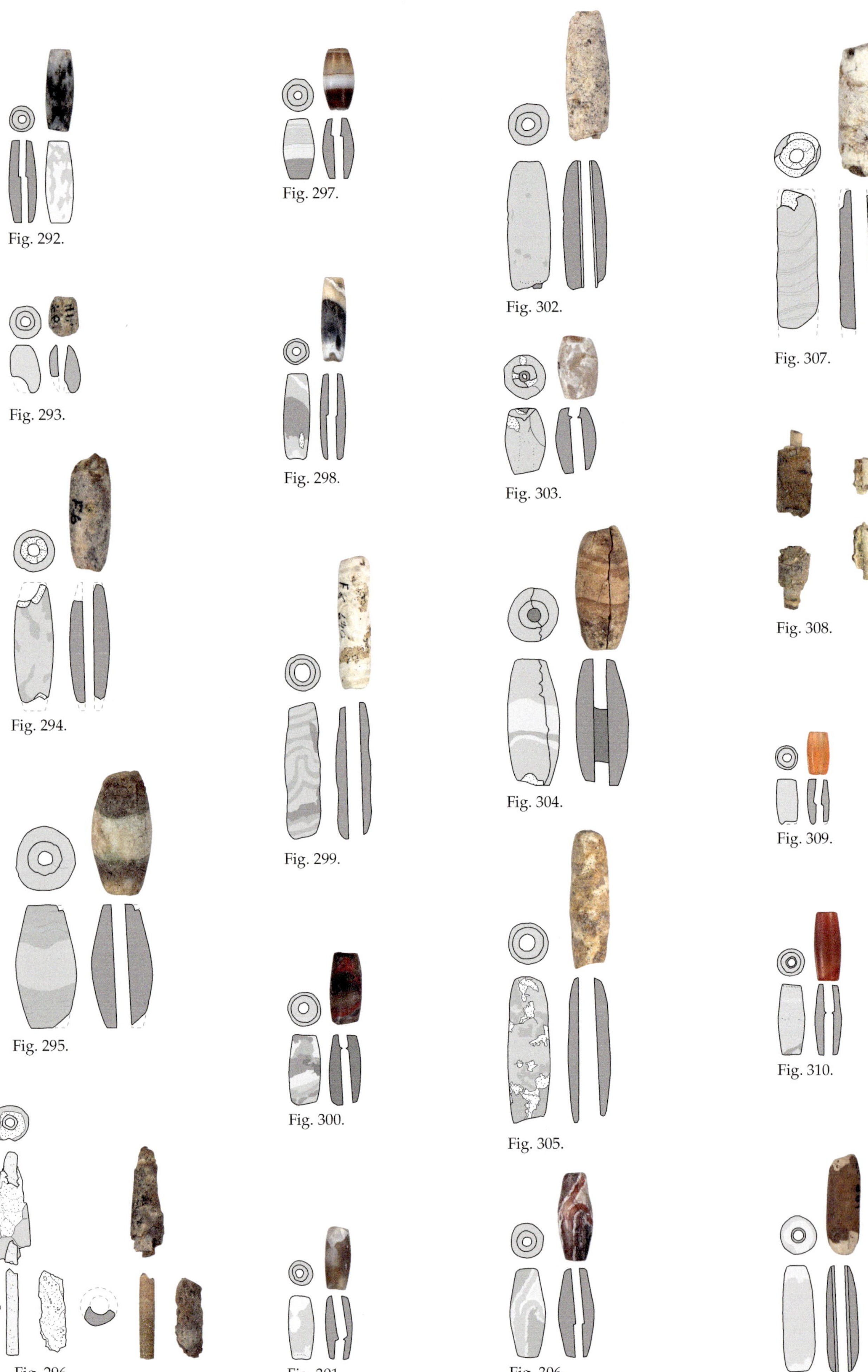
Fig. 292.
Fig. 293.
Fig. 294.
Fig. 295.
Fig. 296.
Fig. 297.
Fig. 298.
Fig. 299.
Fig. 300.
Fig. 301.
Fig. 302.
Fig. 303.
Fig. 304.
Fig. 305.
Fig. 306.
Fig. 307.
Fig. 308.
Fig. 309.
Fig. 310.
Fig. 311.

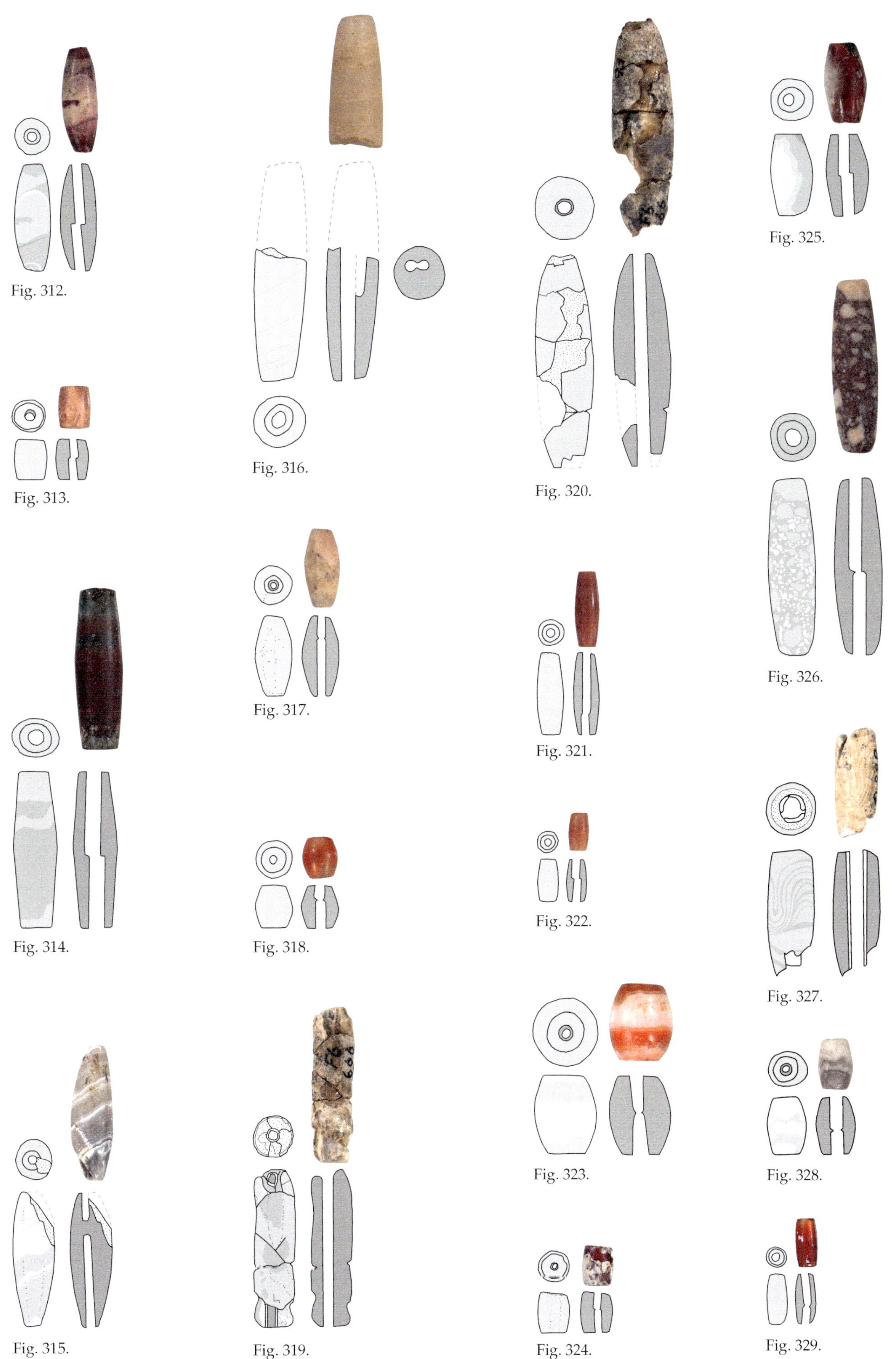

Fig. 312.

Fig. 313.

Fig. 314.

Fig. 315.

Fig. 316.

Fig. 317.

Fig. 318.

Fig. 319.

Fig. 320.

Fig. 321.

Fig. 322.

Fig. 323.

Fig. 324.

Fig. 325.

Fig. 326.

Fig. 327.

Fig. 328.

Fig. 329.

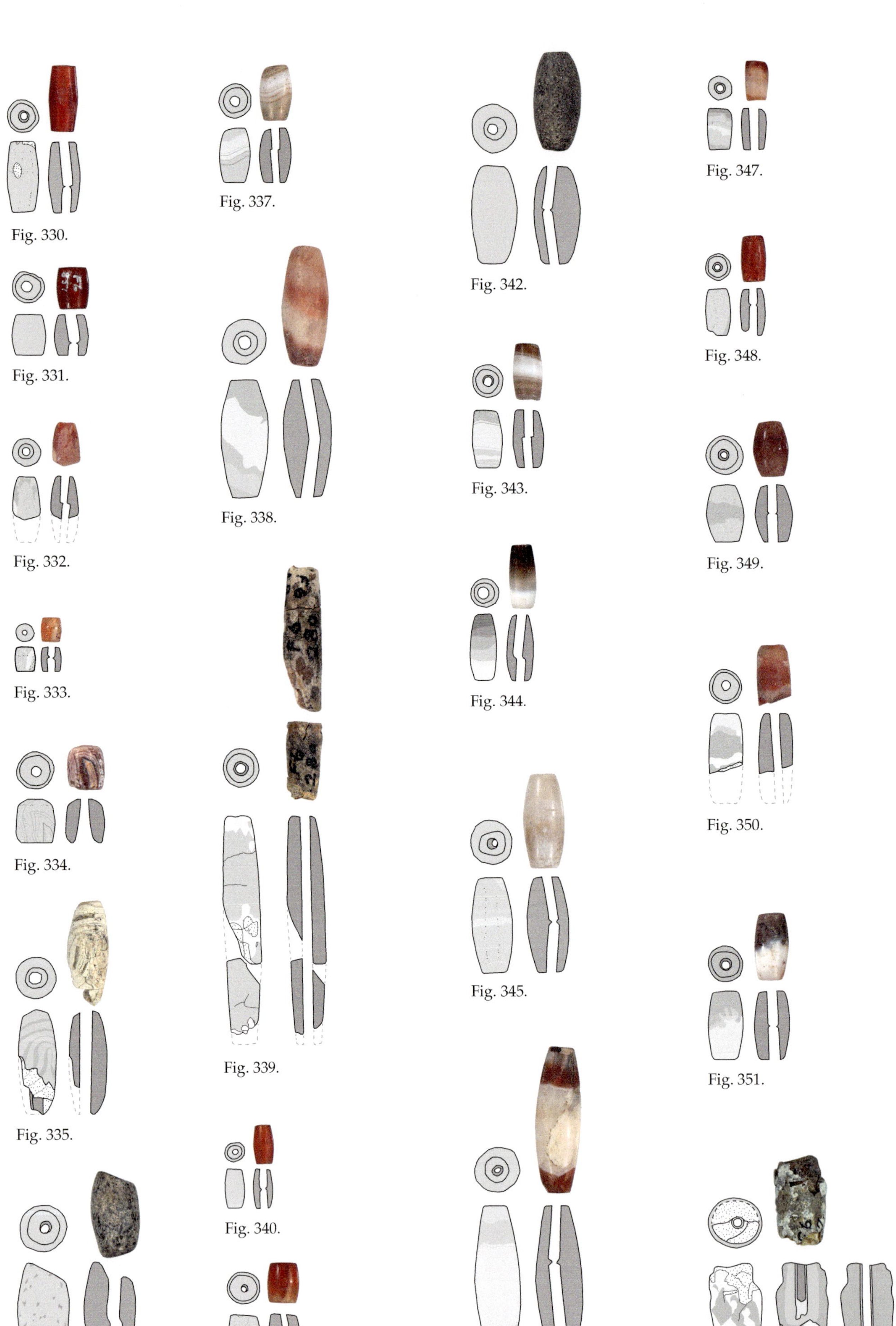
Fig. 330.
Fig. 331.
Fig. 332.
Fig. 333.
Fig. 334.
Fig. 335.
Fig. 336.
Fig. 337.
Fig. 338.
Fig. 339.
Fig. 340.
Fig. 341.
Fig. 342.
Fig. 343.
Fig. 344.
Fig. 345.
Fig. 346.
Fig. 347.
Fig. 348.
Fig. 349.
Fig. 350.
Fig. 351.
Fig. 352.

Barrels with elliptical cross section (figs. 353-356)

II.D.1.b. Long barrels with elliptical cross section

No. F3.æn.8, KM 1692 (fig. 353). *Context:* Baulk between Trench AB and AF; Unknown; Found in sieve. *Type:* Long barrel/Elliptical; II.D.1.b. *Dimensions:* L 22.30, W 13.20, H 9.10 mm. *Material:* Milky quartz. *Condition:* Complete. *Perforation:* Type II; PD 2.20-2.80 mm.

No. F3.få.3, KM 1693 (fig. 354). *Context:* Trench J; Unknown; No information. *Type:* Long barrel/Elliptical; II.D.1.b. *Dimensions:* L 14.40, D 9.60, H 7.50 mm. *Material:* Quartz. *Condition:* Complete. *Perforation:* Type II; PD 1.90 mm.

No. F6.512, KM 1697 (fig. 355). *Context:* Trench D1; 2-4A; level -1.08; 3.00-5.00N/2.00-4.00W. *Type:* Long barrel/Elliptical; II.D.1.b. *Dimensions:* L 26.50, W 22.50, H 14.70 mm. *Material:* Limestone. *Condition:* Complete. *Perforation:* Type II; PD 3.70 mm.

No. F6.799, KM 1688 (fig. 356). *Context:* Trench M2; 2-4A; found in sieve above level -1.07. *Type:* Long barrel/Elliptical; II.D.1.b. *Dimensions:* L 9.70, W 8.00, H 5.50 mm. *Material:* Agate. *Condition:* Complete. *Perforation:* Type II; PD 3.10 mm.

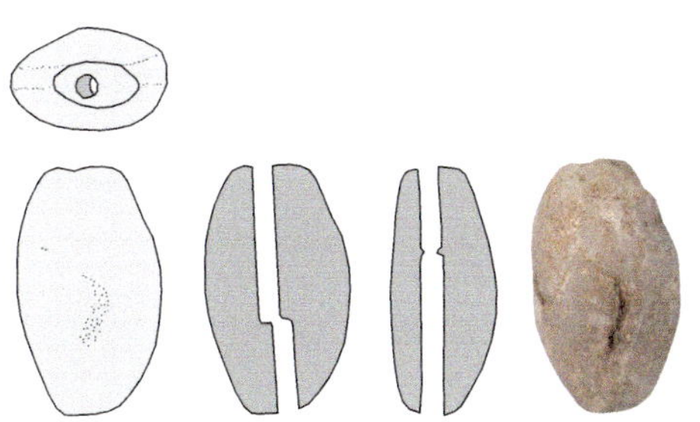

Fig. 353.

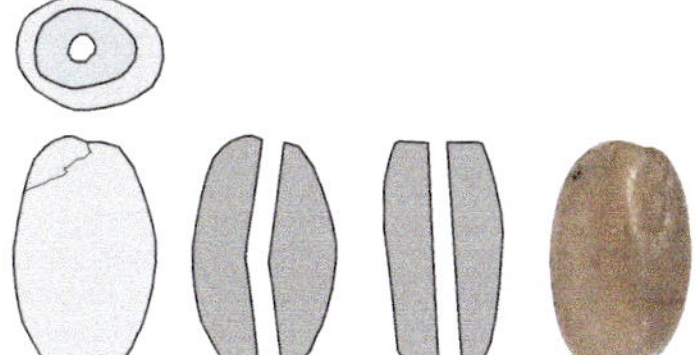

Fig. 354.

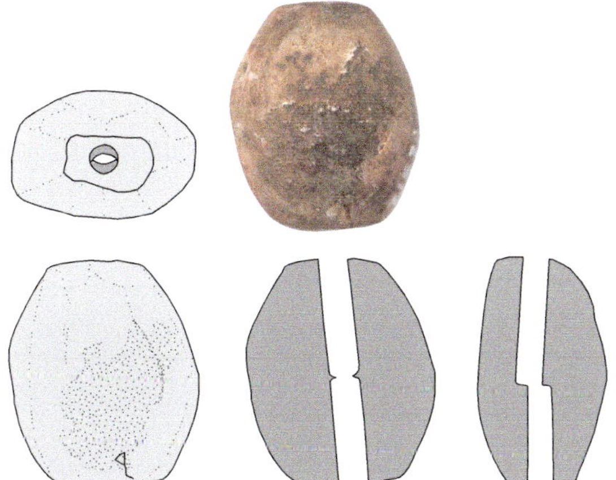

Fig. 355.

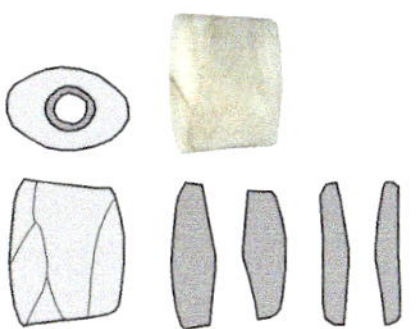

Fig. 356.

Barrels with lenticular cross section (figs. 357-379)

IV.B.1.b. Short barrels with lenticular cross section (fig. 357)

No. F6.864, KM 1688 (fig. 357). *Context:* Trench M2; 1; level -1.98; 19.00-20.00N/9.00-10.00W. *Type:* Short barrel/Lenticular; IV.B.1.b. *Dimensions:* L 5.30, W 7.00, H 3.80 mm. *Material:* Agate. *Condition:* Complete. *Perforation:* Type II; PD 1.10 mm.

IV.C.1.b. Standard barrels with lenticular cross section (figs. 358-361)

No. F6.409, KM 1688 (fig. 358). *Context:* Trench D2; 2-4A; 2-4A; level -0.99; 16.00N/4.00W. *Type:* Standard barrel/Lenticular; IV.C.1.b. *Dimensions:* L 8.80, W 8.70, H 3.80 mm. *Material:* Agate. *Condition:* Complete. *Perforation:* Type II; PD 0.50-2.00 mm.

No. F6.485.1, KM 1688 (fig. 359). *Context:* Trench D2; 1; level -1.71; 14.00-16.00N/2.00-3.00W. *Type:* Standard barrel/Lenticular; IV.C.1.b. *Dimensions:* L 12.40, W 12.70, H 10.00 mm. *Material:* Shell (unidentified). *Condition:* Complete. *Perforation:* Type II; PD 1.25-1.60 mm.

No. F6.590.7, KM 1688 (fig. 360). *Context:* Baulk between D2 and E2; 2-4A; level -1.28; 14.50-16.00N/0.00-1.00W. *Type:* Standard barrel/Lenticular; IV.C.1.b. *Dimensions:* L 12.40, W 13.70, H 5.30 mm. *Material:* Agate. *Condition:* Complete. *Perforation:* Type III; PD 1.20-2.00 mm.

No. F6.665, KM 1718 (fig. 361). *Context:* Trench F2; 2-4A; level -0.26; 17.00N/5.00W. *Type:* Standard barrel/Elliptical; IV.C.1.b. *Dimensions:* L 11.00, W 6.00 (pres.), H 4.50 mm. *Material:* Agate. *Condition:* Fragmented. *Perforation:* Type II; PD 1.50-1.70 mm (est.).

IV.D.1.b. Long barrels with lenticular cross section (figs. 362-379)

No. F3.kc, KM 1684 (fig. 362). *Context:* Trench I; 3A/3B; level 6.55; No information. *Type:* Long barrel/Lenticular; IV.D.1.b. *Dimensions:* L 21.80, W 17.00, H 7.60 mm. *Material:* Agate. *Condition:* Complete. *Perforation:* Type II; PD 2.50 mm.

No. F3.249, KM 1676 (fig. 363). *Context:* Trench RM; Unknown; level 8.45; 58.00N/1.00W. *Type:* Long barrel/Lenticular; IV.D.1.b. *Dimensions:* L 14.65 (pres.), W 14.70, H 4.70 mm. *Material:* Carnelian. *Condition:* Fragmented. *Perforation:* Type II; PD 2.00-2.40 mm.

No. F3.265.1, KM 1692 (fig. 364). *Context:* Trench RM; Unknown; Found in sieve. *Type:* Long barrel/Lenticular; IV.D.1.b. *Dimensions:* L 39.50, W 23.30, H 11.30 mm. *Material:* Agate. *Condition:* Fragmented. *Perforation:* Type II; PD 2.20-2.50 mm.

No. F3.306, KM 1692 (fig. 365). *Context:* Trench RM; Unknown; Found in sieve; 40.00-58.00N/0.00-5.00W. *Type:* Long barrel/Lenticular; IV.D.1.b. *Dimensions:* L 23.00, D 18.00, H 8.00 mm. *Material:* Carnelian. *Condition:* Fragmented. *Perforation:* Type II; PD 2.20-2.40 mm.

No. F3.sy, KM 1692 (fig. 366). *Context:* Trench X; 3B/4B; level 8.06; 55.90N/6.40E. *Type:* Long barrel/Lenticular; IV.D.1.b. *Dimensions:* L 17.80, W 14.70, H 8.40 mm. *Material:* Agate. *Condition:* Complete. *Perforation:* Type II; PD 1.55 mm.

No. F3.ayx, KM 1692 (fig. 367). *Context:* Trench AO; 4A/4B; level 6.97; 61.50N/3.00W. *Type:* Long barrel/Lenticular; IV.D.1.b. *Dimensions:* L 22.00, D 25.00, H 14.00 mm. *Material:* Agate. *Condition:* Fragmented. *Perforation:* Type II; PD 3.50-3.90 mm.

No. F3.azd, KM 1692 (fig. 368). *Context:* Trench AO; 4A/4B; level 6.62; 59.50N/2.50W. *Type:* Long barrel/Lenticular; IV.D.1.b. *Dimensions:* L 31.60, W 2.00, H 11.60 mm. *Material:* Quartz. *Condition:* Complete. *Perforation:* Type II; PD 1.70-2.90 mm.

No. F3.aot, KM 1684 (fig. 369). *Context:* No provenience; Unknown; Found in sieve. *Type:* Long barrel/Lenticular; IV.D.1.b. *Dimensions:* L 15.40, W 7.30, H 4.00 mm. *Material:* Carnelian. *Condition:* Complete. *Perforation:* Type II; PD 1.10 mm.

No. F6.447.3, KM 1688 (fig. 370). *Context:* Trench D1; 2-4A; level -0.26; 4.00-5.00N/2.00-3.00W. *Type:* Long barrel/ Lenticular; IV.D.1.b. *Dimensions:* L 29.00, W 18.00, H 8.00 mm. *Material:* Fossilized coral. *Condition:* Complete. *Perforation:* Type III; PD 1.60-2.30 mm.

No. F6.955, KM 1699 (fig. 371). *Context:* Trench D1; 2-4A; level -0.99; 0.00-10.00N/0.00-1.00W. *Type:* Long barrel/Lenticular; IV.D.1.b. *Dimensions:* L 19.00, W 15.50, H 9.00 mm. *Material:* Agate. *Condition:* Fragmented. *Perforation:* Type III; PD 2.00 mm.

No. F6.485.2, KM 1688 (fig. 372). *Context:* Trench D2; 1; level -1.71; 14.00-16.00N/2.00-3.00W. *Type:* Long barrel/Lenticular; IV.D.1.b. *Dimensions:* L 14.00, W 6.50, H 3.50 mm. *Material:* Agate. *Condition:* Complete. *Perforation:* Type II; PD 1.50 mm.

No. F6.448, KM 1688 (fig. 373). *Context:* Trench E2; 2-4A; level -0.51; 14.00N/2.00E. *Type:* Long barrel/Lenticular; IV.D.1.b. *Dimensions:* L 19.60, W 14.10, H 8.90 mm. *Material:* Carnelian. *Condition:* Complete. *Perforation:* Type II; PD 1.50 mm.

No. F6.590.8, KM 1688 (fig. 374). *Context:* Baulk between D2 and E2; 2-4A; level -1.28; 14.50-16.00N/0.00-1.00W. *Type:* Long barrel/Lenticular; IV.D.1.b. *Dimensions:* L 14.20, D 12.00, H 6.00 mm. *Material:* Agate. *Condition:* Complete. *Perforation:* Type III; PD 1.20-2.00 mm.

No. F6.1118, KM 1697 (fig. 375). *Context:* Trench F1; Unknown; Found in sieve. *Type:* Long barrel/Lenticular; IV.D.1.b. *Dimensions:* L 24.90, W 20.00, H 10.70 mm. *Material:* Unidentified stone (light brown stone). *Condition:* Complete. *Perforation:* Type II; PD 2.10-2.50 mm.

No. F6.1187A, KM 1688 (fig. 376). *Context:* No provenience; 2-4A; level -1.98; No information. *Type:* Long barrel/ Lenticular; IV.D.1.b. *Dimensions:* L 20.15, W 10.60, H 6.65 mm. *Material:* Carnelian. *Condition:* Fragmented. *Perforation:* Type III; PD 2.50 mm.

No. F6.944.7, KM 1699 (fig. 377). *Context:* No provenience; Unknown; Found in sieve. *Type:* Long barrel/Lenticular; IV.D.1.b. *Dimensions:* L 29.00, D 16.00, H 8.00 mm. *Material:* Porphyry. *Condition:* Complete. *Perforation:* Type II; PD 2.20-2.40 mm.

No. F6.945.15, KM 1699 (fig. 378). *Context:* No provenience; Unknown; Found in sieve. *Type:* Long barrel/Lenticular; IV.D.1.b. *Dimensions:* L 11.00, W 14.00, H 7.00 mm. *Material:* Agate. *Condition:* Fragmented. *Perforation:* Type II; PD 1.60-1.80 mm.

No. F6.without no.45, KM 1696 (fig. 379). *Context:* No provenience; Unknown; No information. *Type:* Long barrel/ Lenticular; IV.D.1.b. *Dimensions:* L 21.60, W 13.60, H 12.10 mm. *Material:* Jasper. *Condition:* Complete. *Perforation:* Type II; PD 1.60-2.30 mm.

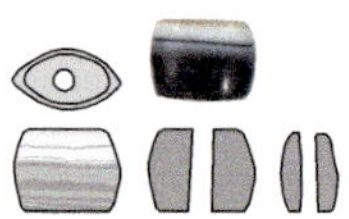

Fig. 357.

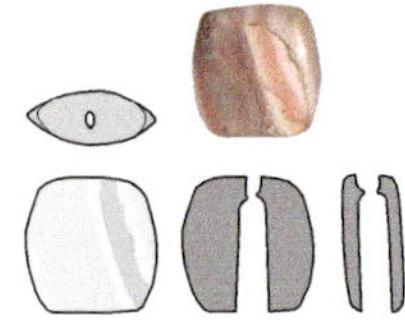

Fig. 358.

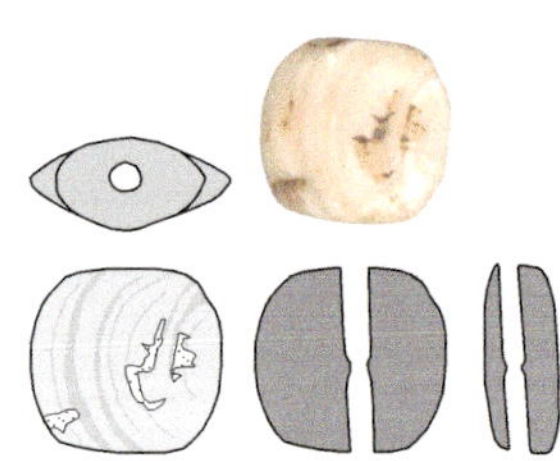

Fig. 359.

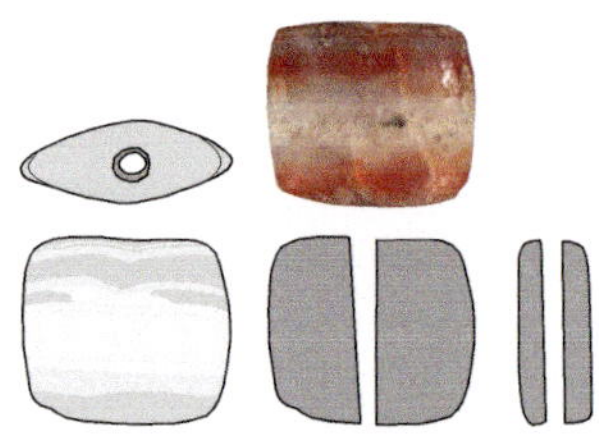

Fig. 360.

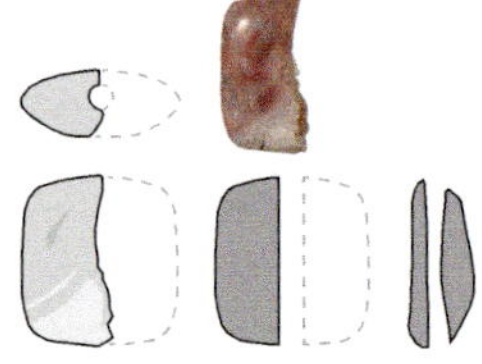

Fig. 361.

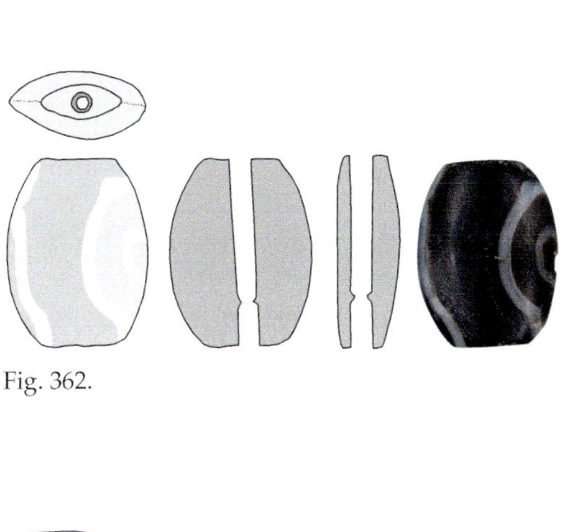
Fig. 362.

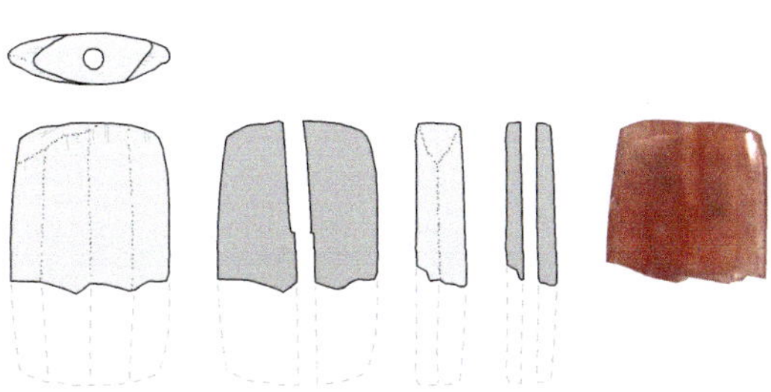
Fig. 363.

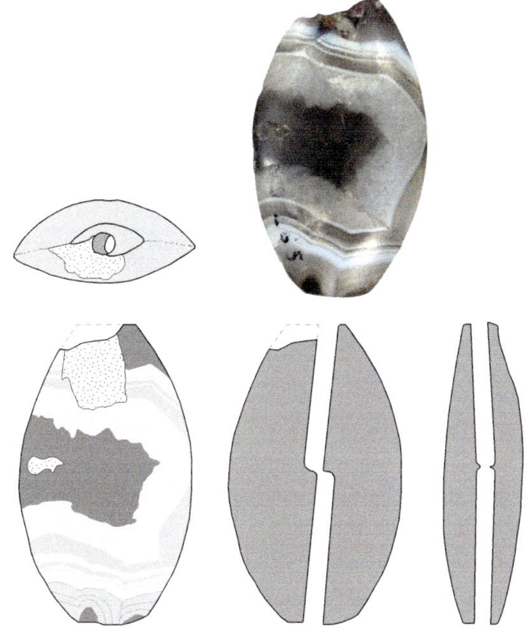
Fig. 364.

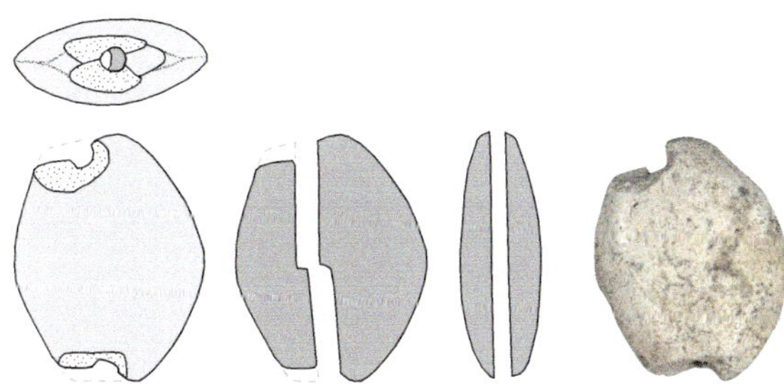
Fig. 365.

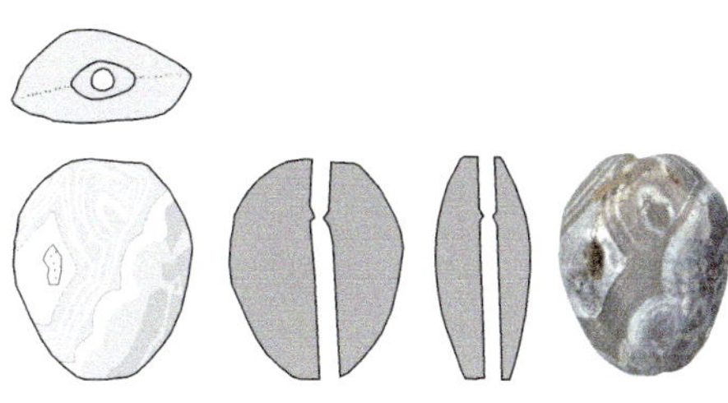
Fig. 366

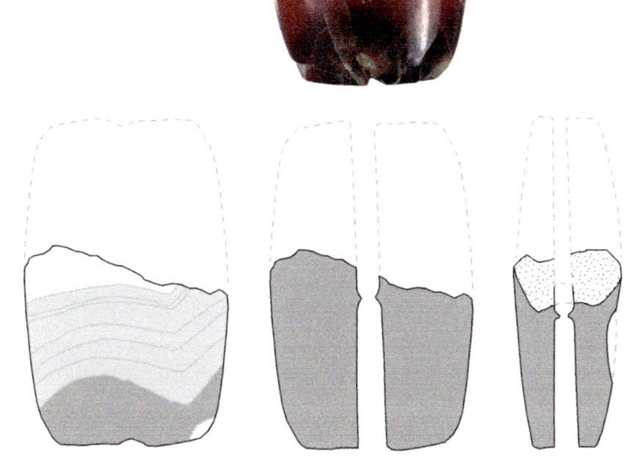
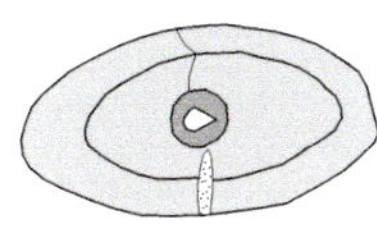
Fig. 367

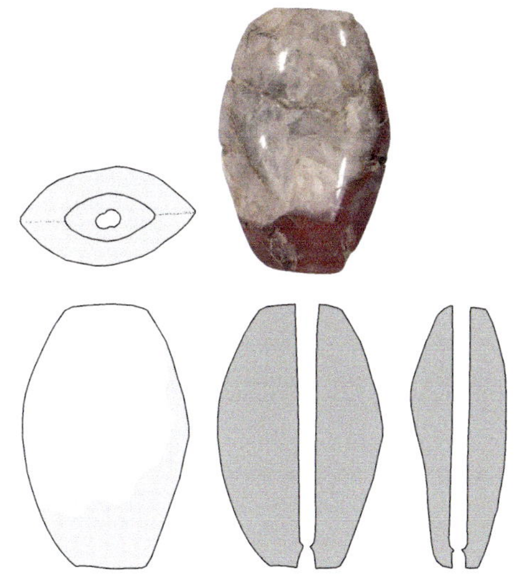
Fig. 368.

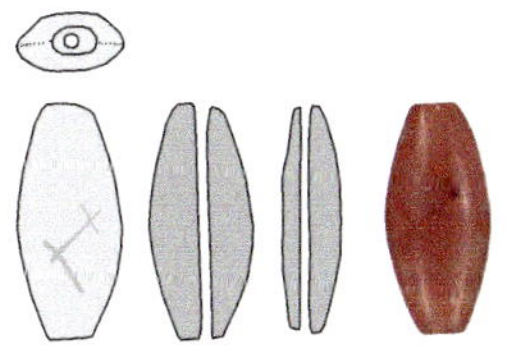
Fig. 369.

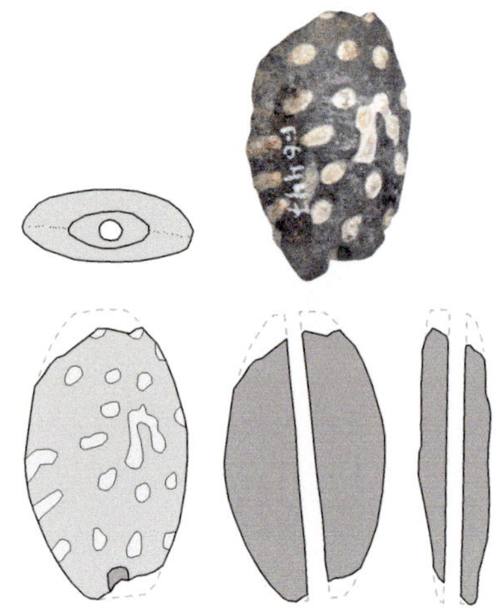

Fig. 370.

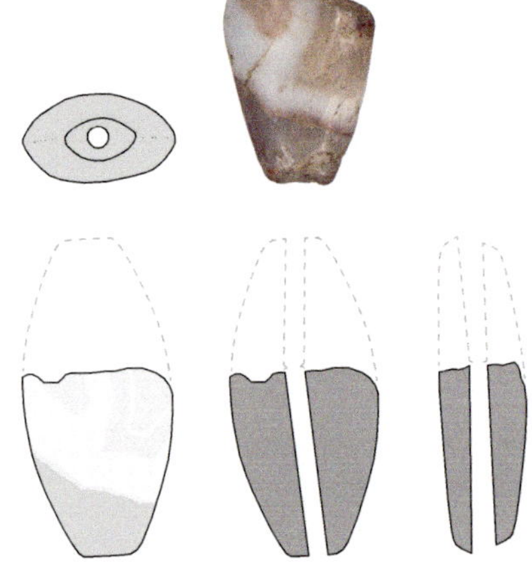

Fig. 371.

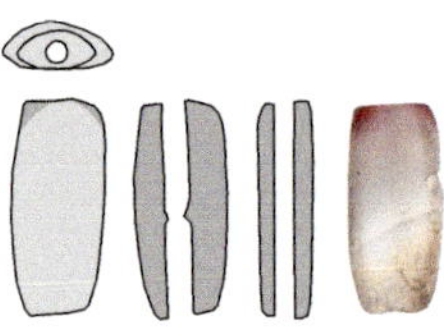

Fig. 372.

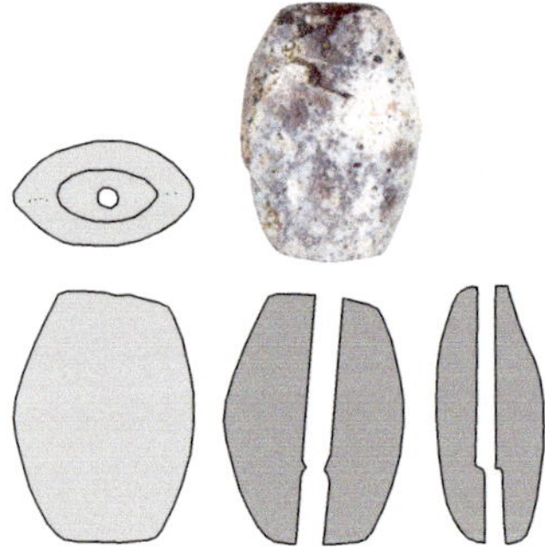

Fig. 373.

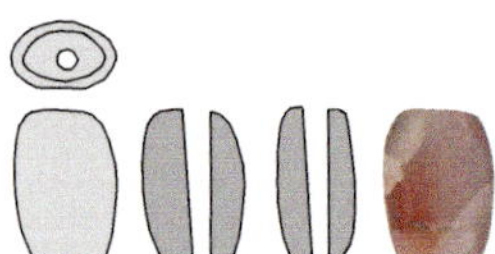

Fig. 374.

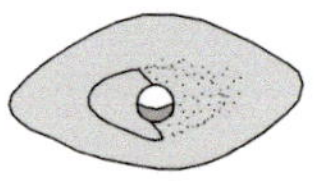

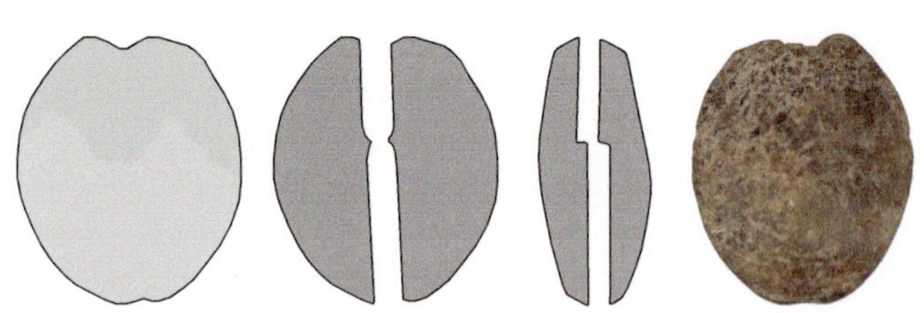

Fig. 375.

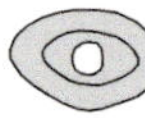

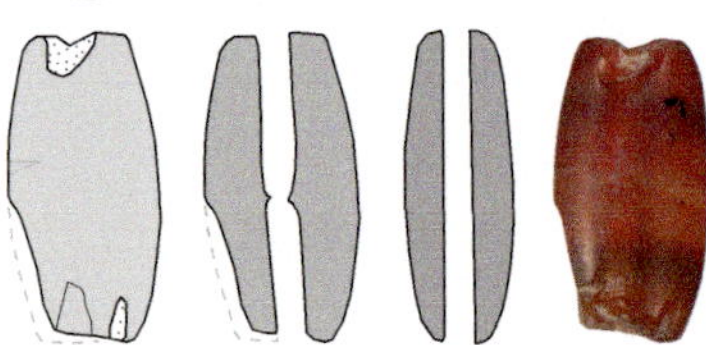

Fig. 376.

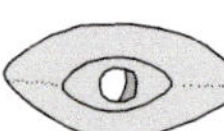

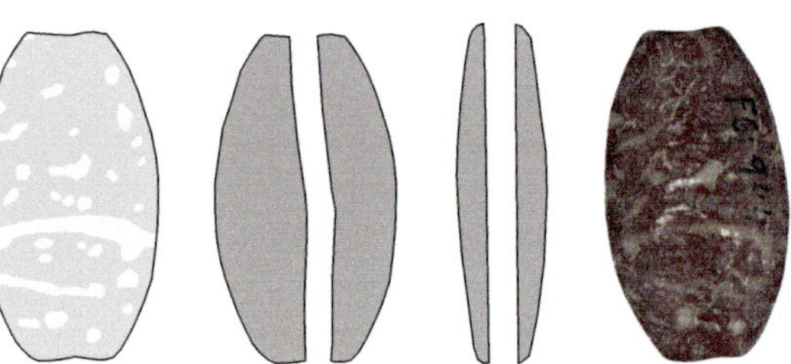

Fig. 377.

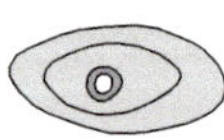

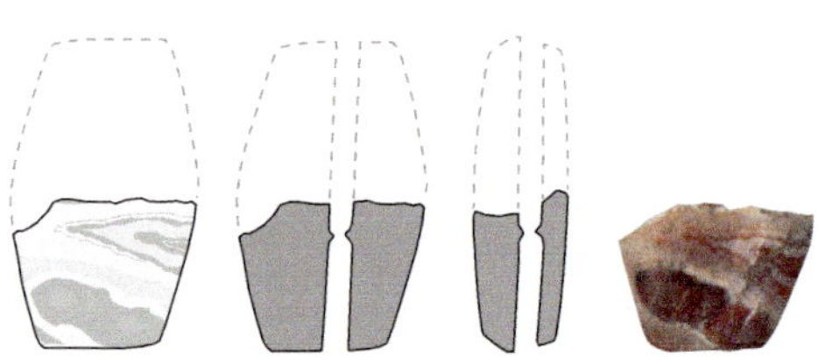

Fig. 378.

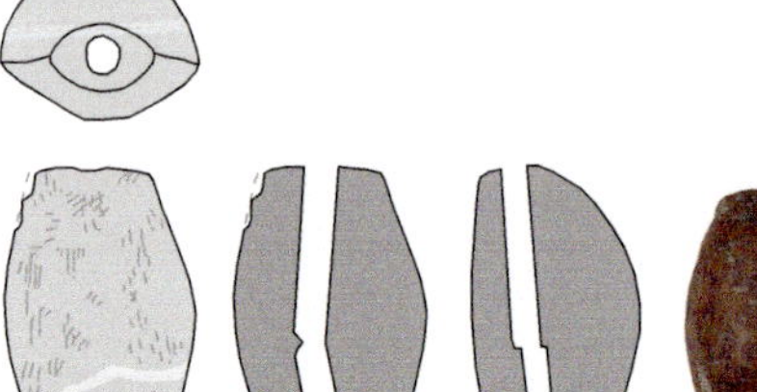

Fig. 379.

Barrels with plano-convex cross section (figs. 380-382)

V.B.1.b. Short barrels with plano-convex cross section (fig. 380)

No. F6.417.8, KM 1688 (fig. 380). *Context:* Trench D2; 2-4A; Between level -0.46 and -1.08; 13.00-15.00N/1.25-4.00W. *Type:* Short barrel/Plano-convex; V.B.1.b. *Dimensions:* L 20.00, W 24.00, H 9.00 mm. *Material:* Glass. *Condition:* Complete. *Perforation:* Type III; PD 2.60-3.70 mm.

V.C.1.b. Standard barrels with plano-convex cross section (figs. 381-382)

No. F6.396.2, KM 1562 (fig. 381). *Context:* Trench D2; 2-4A; level -0.96; 14.00-15.00/3.50-4.00W. *Type:* Standard barrel/Plano-convex; V.C.1.b. *Dimensions:* L 20.00, W 26.00, H 7.50 mm. *Material:* Glass. *Condition:* Fragmented. *Perforation:* Type IV; PD 2.00 mm.

No. F6.444.1, KM 1710 (fig. 382). *Context:* Trench D2; 2-4A; level -1.31; 16.00N/2.00W. *Type:* Standard barrel/Plano-convex; V.C.1.b. *Dimensions:* L 20.00, W 23.00, H 9.00 mm. *Material:* Glass. *Condition:* Fragmented. *Perforation:* Type IV; PD 1.50 mm.

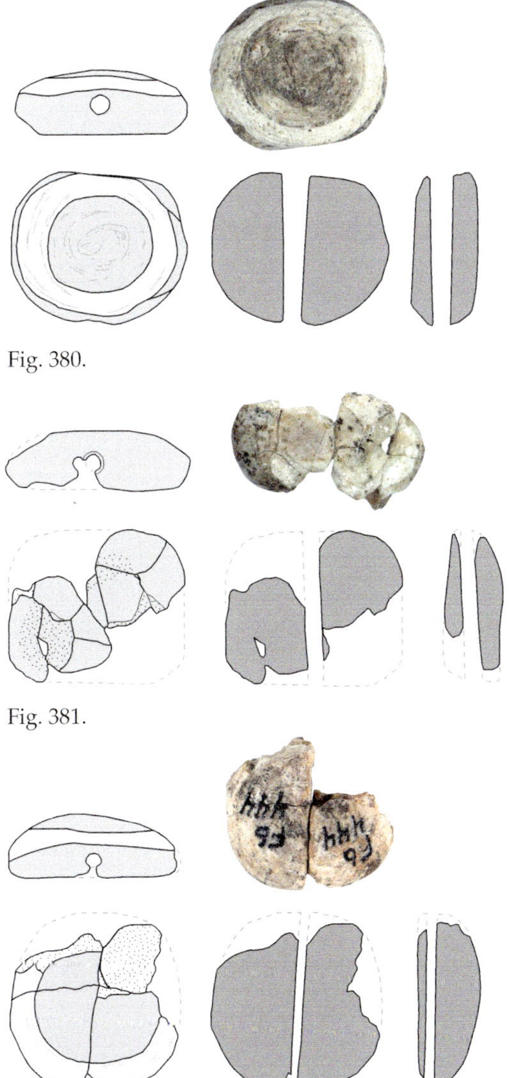

Fig. 380.

Fig. 381.

Fig. 382.

Barrels with semi-circular cross section (figs. 383-399)

VI.C.1.b. Standard barrels with semi-circular cross section (fig. 383)

No. F6.without no.44, KM 1486 (fig. 383). *Context:* No provenience; Unknown; No information. *Type:* Standard Barrel/Semi-circular; VI.C.1.b. *Dimensions:* L 21.80, W 19.50, H 10.50 mm. *Material:* Jasper. *Condition:* Complete. *Perforation:* Type III; PD 2.40-3.50 mm.

VI.D.1.b. Long barrels with semi-circular cross section (figs. 384-399)

No. F3.få.1, KM 1684 (fig. 384). *Context:* Trench J; 4B; level 7.28, No information. *Type:* Long barrel/Semi-circular; VI.D.1.b. *Dimensions:* L 35.00, W 27.20, H 12.60 mm. *Material:* Calcite. *Condition:* Fragmented. *Perforation:* Type II; PD 3.70 mm.

No. F3.pt, KM 1692 (fig. 385). *Context:* Trench X; 3B/4B; level 8.33; 51.00N/6.00E. *Type:* Long barrel/Semi-circular; VI.D.1.b. *Dimensions:* L 23.00, W 14.20, H 9.40 mm. *Material:* Rose quartz. *Condition:* Complete. *Perforation:* Type II; PD 2.80 mm.

No. F3.td.1, KM 1692 (fig. 386). *Context:* Trench Æ; Unknown; Found in sieve. *Type:* Long barrel/Semi-circular; VI.D.1.b. *Dimensions:* L 26.30, W 15.80, H 10.50 mm. *Material:* Milky quartz. *Condition:* Complete. *Perforation:* Type II; PD 2.80 mm.

No. F3.sq.2, KM 1692 (fig. 387). *Context:* Trench AB; Unknown; Found in sieve. *Type:* Long barrel/Semi-circular; VI.D.1.b. *Dimensions:* L 26.10, W 14.20, H 8.00 mm. *Material:* Limestone. *Condition:* Fragmented. *Perforation:* Type II; PD 3.00 mm.

No. F3.axa, KM 1692 (fig. 388). *Context:* Trench AN; 4B; level 7.45; No information. *Type:* Long barrel/Semi-circular; VI.D.1.b. *Dimensions:* L 25.60, W 17.10, H 11.40 mm. *Material:* Milky quartz. *Condition:* Complete. *Perforation:* Type II; PD 2.50 mm.

No. F3.bjm, KM 1692 (fig. 389). *Context:* Trench AM; Unknown; Found in sieve. *Type:* Long barrel/Semi-circular; VI.D.1.b. *Dimensions:* L 27.70, W 16.00, H 6.70 mm. *Material:* Agate. *Condition:* Complete. *Perforation:* Type II; PD 2.40 mm.

No. F3.bco, KM 1692 (fig. 390). *Context:* Trench AO; Unknown; Found in sieve. *Type:* Long barrel/Semi-circular; VI.D.1.b. *Dimensions:* L 25.40, W 16.50, H 13.10 mm. *Material:* Milky quartz. *Condition:* Complete. *Perforation:* Type II; PD 2.70 mm.

No. F3.bif.1, KM 1692 (fig. 391). *Context:* Trench AV; Unknown; Found in sieve. *Type:* Long barrel/Semi-circular; VI.D.1.b. *Dimensions:* L 34.00, W 21.10, H 13.20 mm. *Material:* Limestone. *Condition:* Complete. *Perforation:* Type II; PD 2.90-3.50 mm.

No. F3.kg, KM 1684 (fig. 392). *Context:* No provenience; Unknown; Found in sieve. *Type:* Long barrel/Semi-circular; VI.D.1.b. *Dimensions:* L 24.00, W 15.30, H 10.70 mm. *Material:* Milky quartz. *Condition:* Complete. *Perforation:* Type II; PD 2.20 mm.

No. F3.yl.2, KM 1673 (fig. 393). *Context:* No provenience; Unknown; No information. *Type:* Long barrel/Semi-circular; VI.D.1.b. *Dimensions:* L 18.60, W 13.80, H 7.90 mm. *Material:* Agate. *Condition:* Complete. *Perforation:* Type II; PD 2.10 mm.

No. F6.501, KM 1667 (fig. 394). *Context:* Trench D1; 2-4A; level -0.79; 4.00N/2.00W. *Type:* Long barrel/Semi-circular; VI.D.1.b. *Dimensions:* L 23.70, W 15.90, H 10.90 mm. *Material:* Jasper. *Condition:* Complete. *Perforation:* Type II; PD 2.70-2.90 mm.

No. F6.990, KM 1699 (fig. 395). *Context:* Trench F1; 2-4A; Found in sieve no deeper than level -0.85. *Type:* Long barrel/Semi-circular; VI.D.1.b. *Dimensions:* L 24.40, W 15.50, H 10.00 mm. *Material:* Milky quartz. *Condition:* Complete. *Perforation:* Type II; PD 3.00 mm.

No. F6.1233, KM 1697 (fig. 396). *Context:* No provenience; Unknown; Found in sieve. *Type:* Long barrel/Semi-circular; VI.D.1.b. *Dimensions:* L 21.50, W 15.10, H 9.30 mm. *Material:* Unidentified stone (black stone). *Condition:* Complete. *Perforation:* Type II; PD 2.80-2.90 mm.

No. F6.without no.46, KM 1696 (fig. 397). *Context:* No provenience; Unknown; No information. *Type:* Long barrel/Semi-circular; VI.D.1.b. *Dimensions:* L 26.20, W 16.20, H 10.60 mm. *Material:* Quartz. *Condition:* Complete. *Perforation:* Type II; PD 2.60-2.70 mm.

No. F6.without no.47, KM 1697 (fig. 398). *Context:* No provenience; Unknown; No information. *Type:* Long barrel/Semi-circular; VI.D.1.b. *Dimensions:* L 25.50, W 14.10, H 9.60 xxx mm. *Material:* Jasper. *Condition:* Complete. *Perforation:* Type II; PD 3.00 mm.

No. F6.without no.48, KM 1696 (fig. 399). *Context:* No provenience; Unknown; No information. *Type:* Long barrel/Semi-circular; VI.D.1.b. *Dimensions:* L 20.00, W 13.60, H 7.80 mm. *Material:* Jasper. *Condition:* Fragmented. *Perforation:* Type II; PD 2.20-2.40 mm.

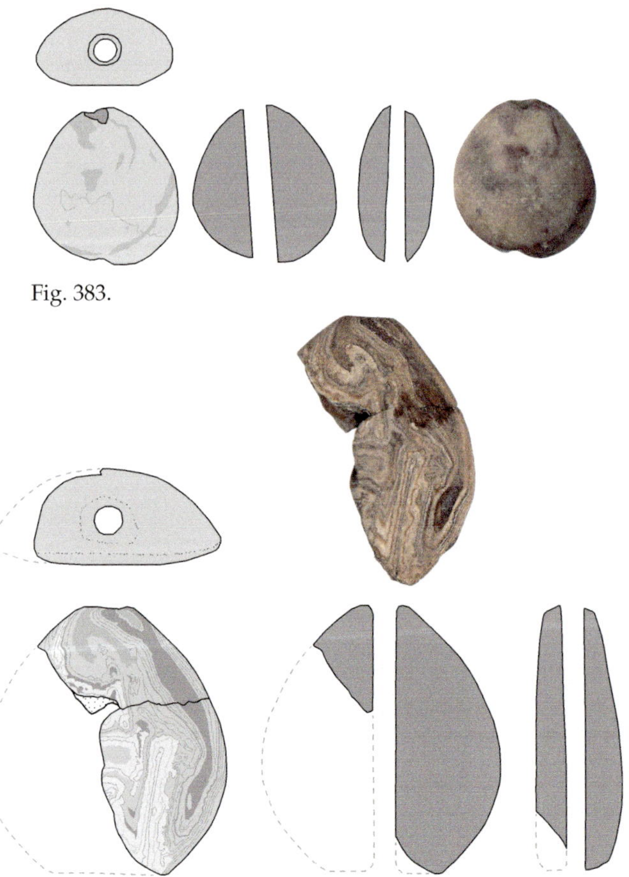

Fig. 383.

Fig. 384.

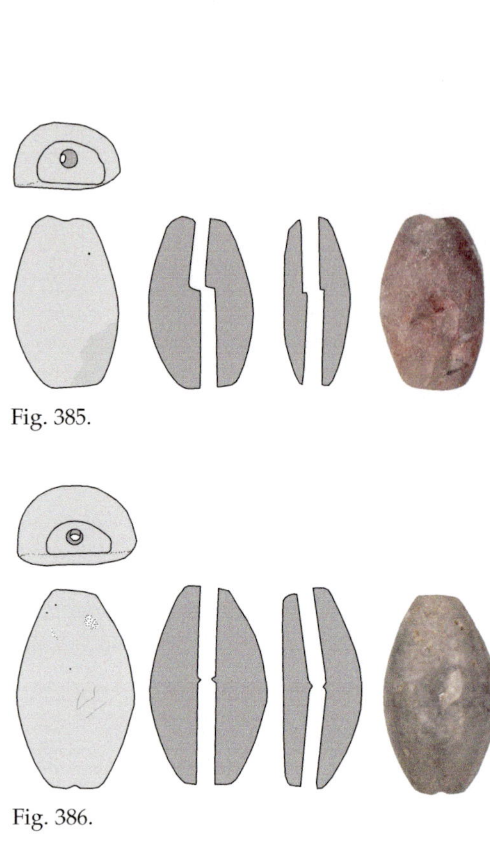

Fig. 385.

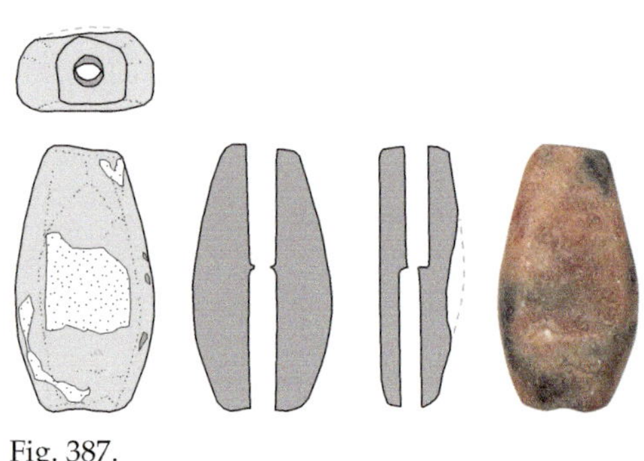

Fig. 386.

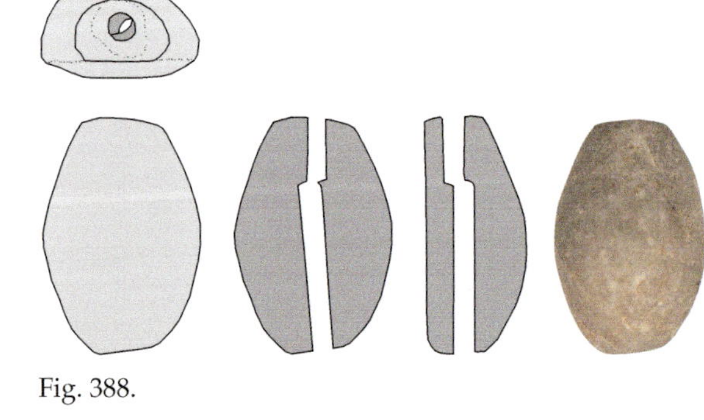

Fig. 387.

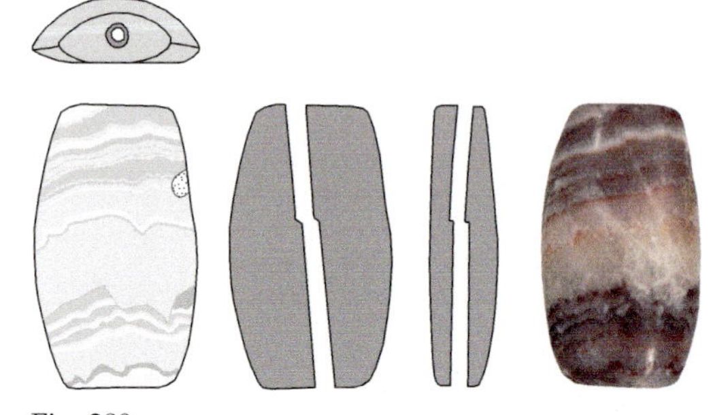

Fig. 388.

Fig. 389.

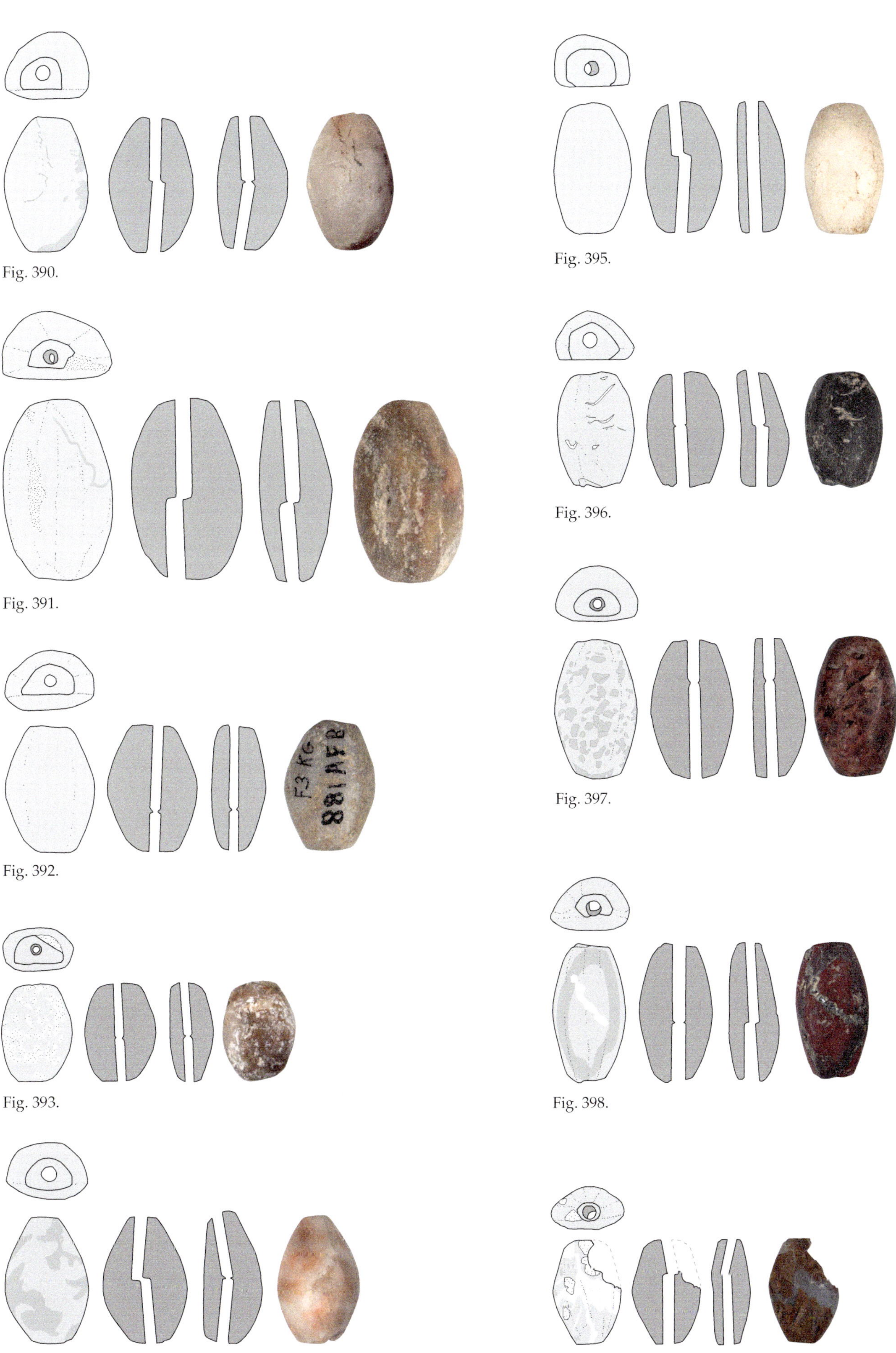

Fig. 390.

Fig. 391.

Fig. 392.

Fig. 393.

Fig. 394.

Fig. 395.

Fig. 396.

Fig. 397.

Fig. 398.

Fig. 399.

Barrels with circle and flat cross section (figs. 400-428)

VII.C.1.b. Standard barrels with circle and flat cross section (fig. 400)

No. F6.without no.49, KM 1695 (fig. 400). *Context:* No provenience; Unknown; No information. *Type:* Standard barrel/Circle and flat; VII.C.1.b. *Dimensions:* L 8.50, W 7.70, H 6.90 mm. *Material:* Jasper. *Condition:* Fragmented. *Perforation:* Type II; PD 2.60 mm.

VII.D.1.b. Long barrels with circle and flat cross section (figs. 401-428)

No. F3.aak, KM 1684 (fig. 401). *Context:* Trench C; Unknown; No information. *Type:* Long barrel/Circle and flat; VII.D.1.b. *Dimensions:* L 25.50, W 19.60, H 12.80 mm. *Material:* Limestone. *Condition:* Complete. *Perforation:* Type II; PD 2.70 mm.

No. F3.hl, KM 1684 (fig. 402). *Context:* Trench E; 2; level 5.95; 34.15N/7.20E. *Type:* Long barrel/Circle and flat; VII.D.1.b. *Dimensions:* L 20.40, W 15.10, H 10.70 mm. *Material:* Jasper. *Condition:* Complete. *Perforation:* Type II; PD 2.50 mm.

No. F3.ps, KM 1692 (fig. 403). *Context:* Trench X; 3B/4B; level 8.33; 51.00N/6.00E. *Type:* Long barrel/Circle and flat; VII.D.1.b. *Dimensions:* L 26.00, W 16.40, H 13.70 mm. *Material:* Jasper. *Condition:* Complete. *Perforation:* Type II; PD 2.90 mm.

No. F3.pu, KM 1692 (fig. 404). *Context:* Baulk between Trench N and X; 3B/4B; level 8.41; 50.30N/5.25E. *Type:* Long barrel/Circle and flat; VII.D.1.b. *Dimensions:* L 22.00, W 17.10, H 12.30 mm. *Material:* Agate. *Condition:* Complete. *Perforation:* Type II; PD 2.70 mm.

No. F3.rx, KM 1692 (fig. 405). *Context:* Baulk between Trench N and X; Unknown; level 7.76; 49.50N/4.00W. *Type:* Long barrel/Circle and flat; VII.D.1.b. *Dimensions:* L 25.00, W 16.40, H 11.70 mm. *Material:* Jasper. *Condition:* Complete. *Perforation:* Type II; PD 3.00 mm.

No. F3.qæ.2, KM 1684 (fig. 406). *Context:* Trench Z; Unknown; Found in sieve. *Type:* Long barrel/Circle and flat; VII.D.1.b. *Dimensions:* L 16.70, W 14.60, H 9.80 mm. *Material:* Faience. *Condition:* Complete. *Perforation:* Type IV; PD 4.00 mm.

No. F3.rz, KM 1692 (fig. 407). *Context:* Trench Æ; Unknown; No information. *Type:* Long barrel/Circle and flat; VII.D.1.b. *Dimensions:* L 16.50, W 14.00, H 14.50 mm. *Material:* Agate. *Condition:* Complete. *Perforation:* Type II; PD 2.10-2.50 mm.

No. F3.zb, KM 1692 (fig. 408). *Context:* Trench Ø; Unknown; level 7.25; 54.00N/12.50E. *Type:* Long barrel/Circle and flat; VII.D.1.b. *Dimensions:* L 15.70, W 9.30, H 7.30 mm. *Material:* Chlorite (type 3). *Condition:* Complete. *Perforation:* Type II; PD 3.00-3.50 mm.

No. F3.øk.2, KM 1692 (fig. 409). *Context:* Trench AE; 3A; Found in sieve. *Type:* Long barrel/Circle and flat; VII.D.1.b. *Dimensions:* L 18.90, W 12.90, H 9.40 mm. *Material:* Agate. *Condition:* Complete. *Perforation:* Type II; PD 2.20-2.50 mm.

No. F3.ås.2, KM 1684 (fig. 410). *Context:* Trench AE; 3A; Found in sieve. *Type:* Long barrel/Circle and flat; VII.D.1.b. *Dimensions:* L 18.80, W 9.80, H 8.80 mm. *Material:* Agate. *Condition:* Complete. *Perforation:* Type II; PD 2.30 mm.

No. F3.bgc, KM 1692 (fig. 411). *Context:* Trench AO; 4A/4B; level 7.41; 59.00N/6.00W. *Type:* Long barrel/Circle and flat; VII.D.1.b. *Dimensions:* L 20.00, W 14.80, H 11.30 mm. *Material:* Agate. *Condition:* Complete. *Perforation:* Type II; PD 2.50 mm.

No. F3.bgu, KM 1692 (fig. 412). *Context:* Trench AO; Unknown; Found in sieve. *Type:* Long barrel/Circle and flat; VII.D.1.b. *Dimensions:* L 21.10, W 13.00, H 10.10 mm. *Material:* Agate. *Condition:* Complete. *Perforation:* Type II; PD 2.20-2.30 mm.

No. F3.bdc, KM 1692 (fig. 413). *Context:* Trench AT; 4A/4B; level 8.09; No information. *Type:* Long barrel/Circle and flat; VII.D.1.b. *Dimensions:* L 31.10, W 19.00, H 12.30 mm. *Material:* Limestone. *Condition:* Complete. *Perforation:* Type II; PD 4.30 mm.

No. F3.ng, KM 1692 (fig. 414). *Context:* No provenience; Unknown; No information. *Type:* Long barrel/Circle and flat; VII.D.1.b. *Dimensions:* L 22.60, W 16.00, H 10.60 mm. *Material:* Limestone. *Condition:* Complete. *Perforation:* Type II; PD 2.10-2.50 mm.

No. F6.523, KM 1697 (fig. 415). *Context:* Trench A1; 1; level -1.61; 0.10-0.50S/3.00-4.00W. *Type:* Long barrel/Circle and flat; VII.D.1.b. *Dimensions:* L 26.80, W 13.30, H 13.40 mm. *Material:* Jasper. *Condition:* Complete. *Perforation:* Type II; PD 2.60 mm.

No. F6.88.4, KM 1697 (fig. 416). *Context:* Trench A3; 2-4A; level 0.08; 20.00-20.55S/1.00-4.00W. *Type:* Long barrel/Circle and flat; VII.D.1.b. *Dimensions:* L 27.50, W 16.50, H 15.00 mm. *Material:* Milky quartz. *Condition:* Complete. *Perforation:* Type II; PD 3.00 mm.

No. F6.88.5, KM 1697 (fig. 417). *Context:* Trench A3; 2-4A; level 0.08; 20.00-20.55S/1.00-4.00W. *Type:* Long barrel/Circle and flat; VII.D.1.b. *Dimensions:* L 25.20, W 18.60, H 13.20 mm. *Material:* Limestone. *Condition:* Complete. *Perforation:* Type II; PD 3.00 mm.

No. F6.107, KM 1697 (fig. 418). *Context:* Trench A3; 2-4A; level -0.18; No information. *Type:* Long barrel/Circle and flat; VII.D.1.b. *Dimensions:* L 35.70, W 22.00, H 18.10 mm. *Material:* Limestone. *Condition:* Complete. *Perforation:* Type II; PD 3.70-4.00 mm.

No. F6.154, KM 1697 (fig. 419). *Context:* Trench A3; 2-4A; level -1.26; 27.20S/1.00-4.00W. *Type:* Long barrel/Circle and flat; VII.D.1.b. *Dimensions:* L 18.20, W 14.70, H 10.70 mm. *Material:* Agate. *Condition:* Complete. *Perforation:* Type II; PD 1.80 mm.

No. F6.952, KM 1699 (fig. 420). *Context:* Baulk between trench D1 and SN 1-10; 2-4A; level -0.99; 0.00-10.00N/0.00-1.00W. *Type:* Long barrel/Circle and flat; VII.D.1.b. *Dimensions:* L 25.60, W 17.00, H 11.50 mm. *Material:* Milky quartz. *Condition:* Complete. *Perforation:* Type II; PD 2.70 mm.

No. F6.975, KM 1699 (fig. 421). *Context:* Trench D1; Unknown; Found in sieve. *Type:* Long barrel/Circle and flat; VII.D.1.b. *Dimensions:* L 23.50, W 15.30, H 12.50 mm. *Material:* Unidentified stone (grey stone). *Condition:* Complete. *Perforation:* Type II; PD 2.70-2.80 mm.

No. F6.964B, KM 1699 (fig. 422). *Context:* Trench F1; 2-4A; Found in sieve above level 0.00. *Type:* Long barrel/Circle and flat; VII.D.1.b. *Dimensions:* L 16.60, W 10.50, H 6.40 mm. *Material:* Agate. *Condition:* Complete. *Perforation:* Type II; PD 2.00 mm.

No. F6.978, KM 1699 (fig. 423). *Context:* Trench F1; 2-4A; level -0.72, No information. *Type:* Long barrel/Circle and flat; VII.D.1.b. *Dimensions:* L 17.30, W 12.20, H 8.80 mm. *Material:* Jasper. *Condition:* Complete. *Perforation:* Type II; PD 1.10-2.10 mm.

No. F6.1044, KM 1699 (fig. 424). *Context:* Baulk between Trench N1 and N2; Unknown; Found in sieve. *Type:* Long barrel/Circle and flat; VII.D.1.b. *Dimensions:* L 25.20, W 12.90, H 14.10 mm. *Material:* Limestone. *Condition:* Complete. *Perforation:* Type II; PD 2.50-3.40 mm.

No. F6.1004A, KM 1699 (fig. 425). *Context:* Trench N2; Unknown; Found in sieve. *Type:* Long barrel/Circle and flat; VII.D.1.b. *Dimensions:* L 14.30, W 8.70, H 6.00 mm. *Material:* Agate. *Condition:* Complete. *Perforation:* Type II; PD 2.10-2.20 mm.

No. F6.without no.50, KM 1696 (fig. 426). *Context:* No provenience; Unknown; No information. *Type:* Long barrel/Circle and flat; VII.D.1.b. *Dimensions:* L 7.90, W 5.80, H 5.10 mm. *Material:* Lapis Lazuli. *Condition:* Complete. *Perforation:* Type II; PD 2.00 mm.

No. F6.without no.51, KM 1494 (fig. 427). *Context:* No provenience; Unknown; No information. *Type:* Long barrel/Circle and flat; VII.D.1.b. *Dimensions:* L 28.00, W 22.50, H 14.70 mm. *Material:* Limestone. *Condition:* Complete. *Perforation:* Type II; PD 2.60 mm.

No. F6.without no.52, KM 1696 (fig. 428). *Context:* No provenience; Unknown; No information. *Type:* Long barrel/Circle and flat; VII.D.1.b. *Dimensions:* L 36.70, W 18.90, H 10.80 mm. *Material:* Jasper. *Condition:* Complete. *Perforation:* Type II; PD 3.00 mm.

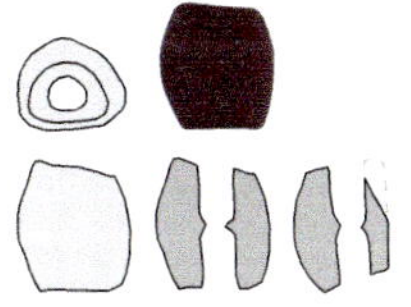

Fig. 400.

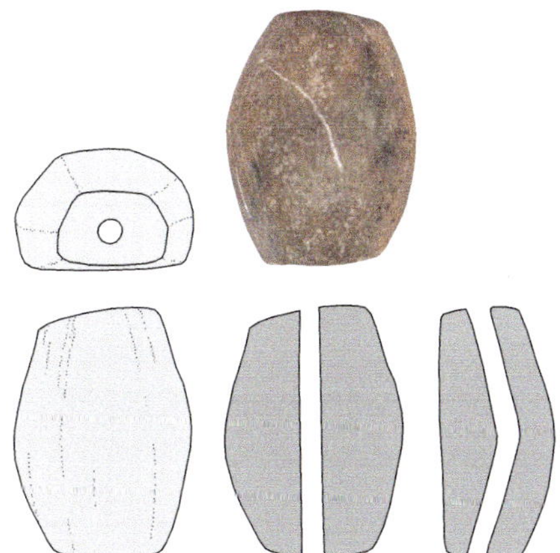

Fig. 401.

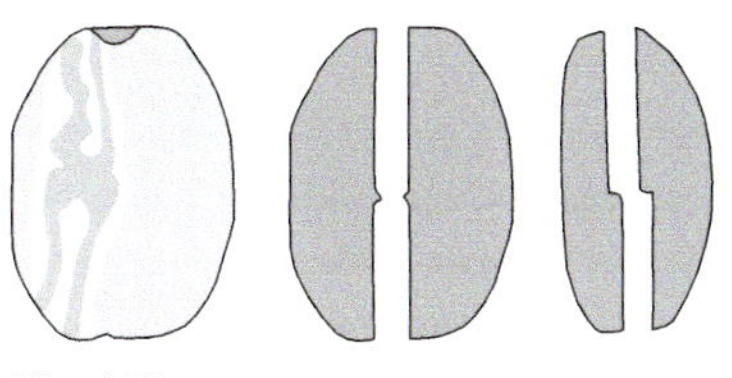

Fig. 402.

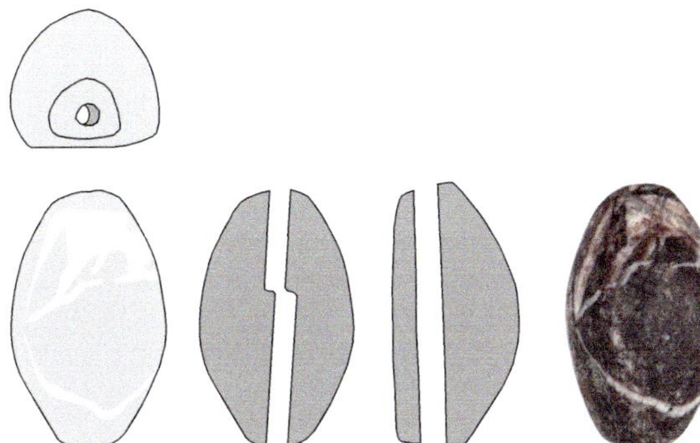

Fig. 403.

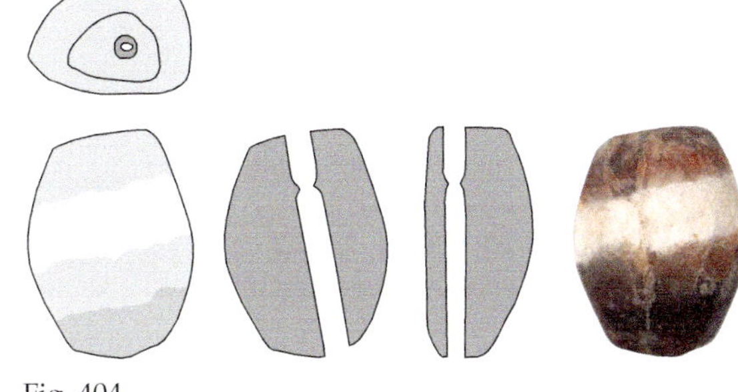

Fig. 404.

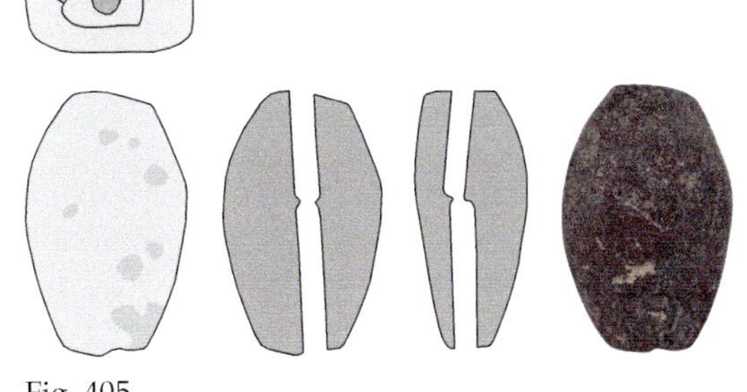

Fig. 405.

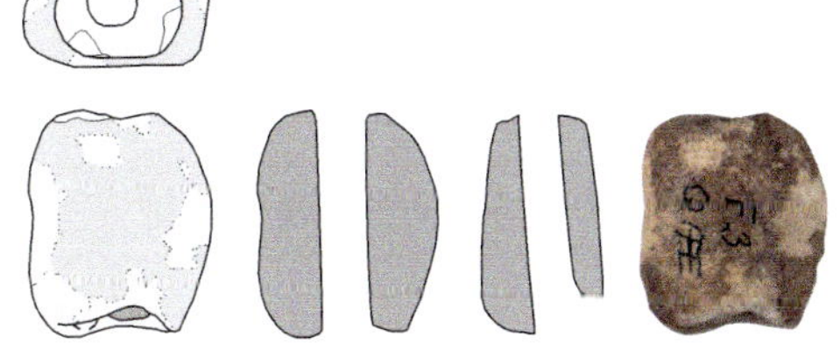

Fig. 406.

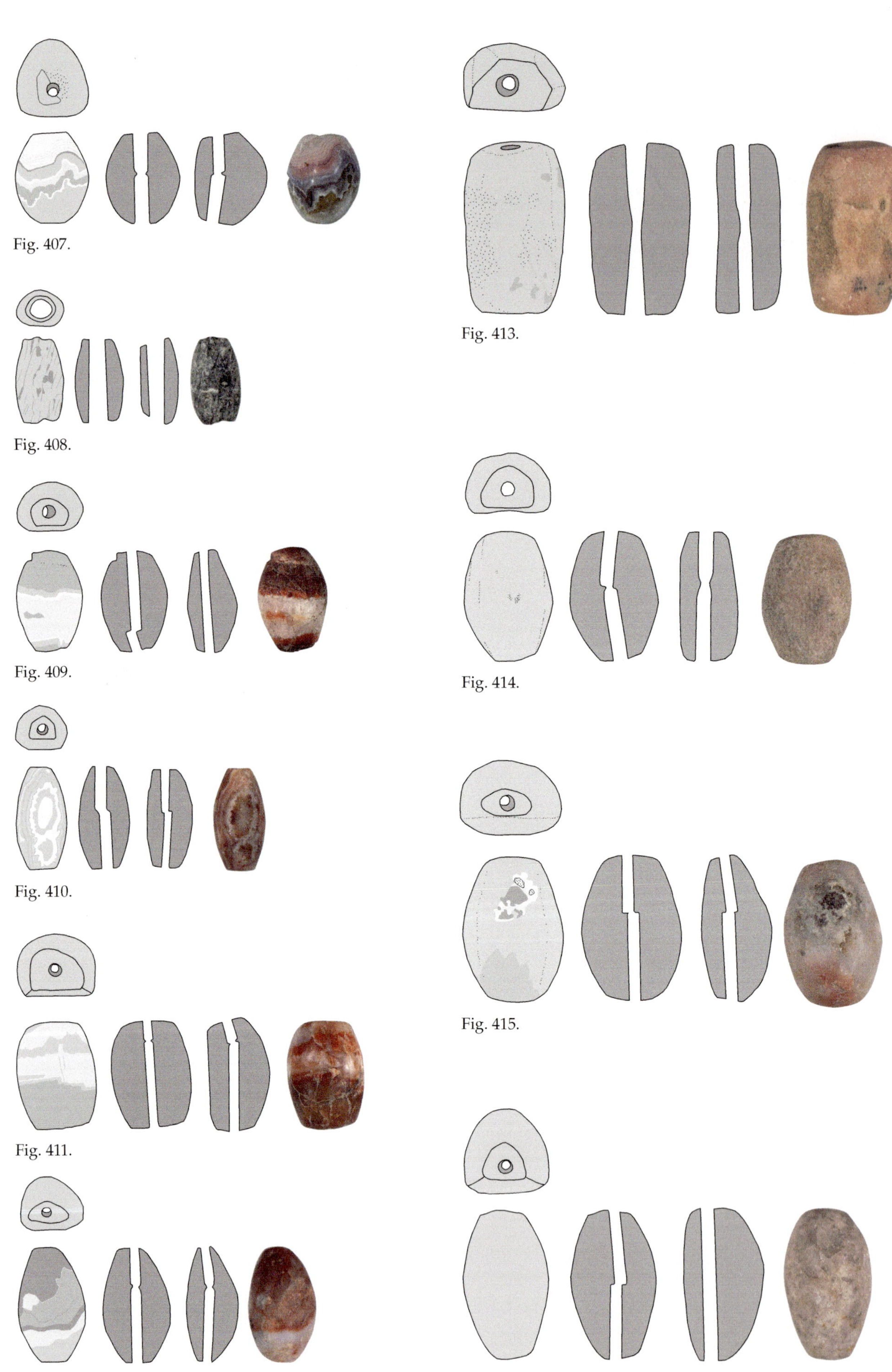

Fig. 407.

Fig. 408.

Fig. 409.

Fig. 410.

Fig. 411.

Fig. 412.

Fig. 413.

Fig. 414.

Fig. 415.

Fig. 416.

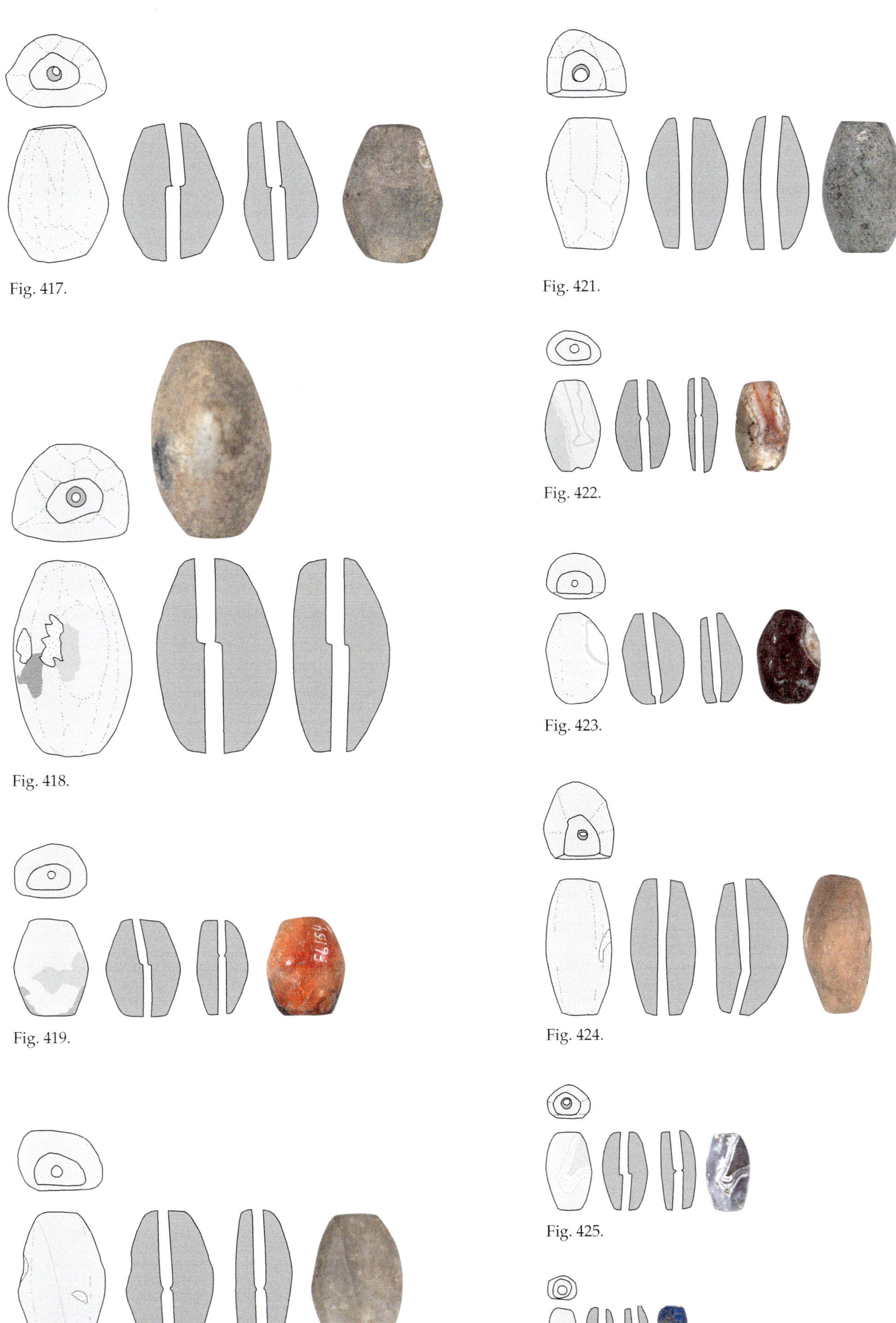

Fig. 417.

Fig. 418.

Fig. 419.

Fig. 420.

Fig. 421.

Fig. 422.

Fig. 423.

Fig. 424.

Fig. 425.

Fig. 426.

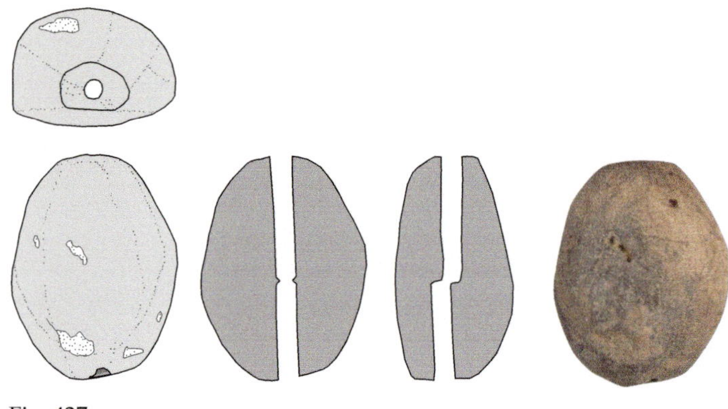

Fig. 427.

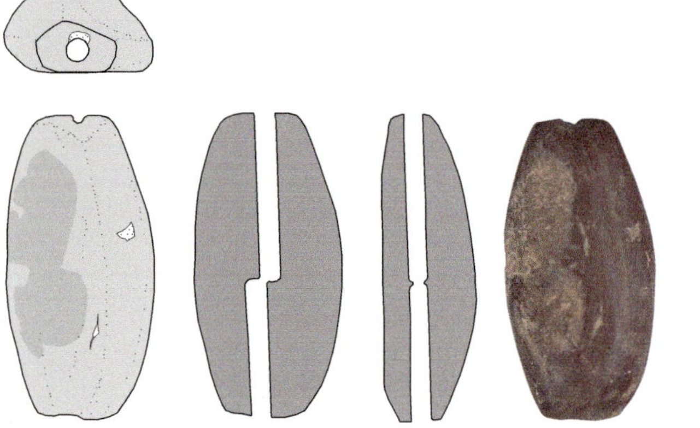

Fig. 428.

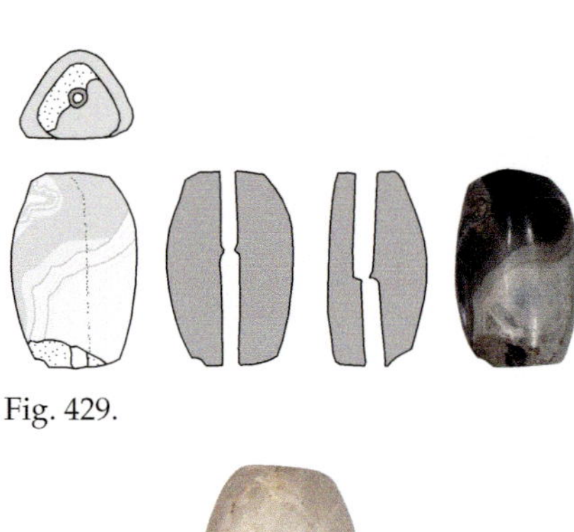

Fig. 429.

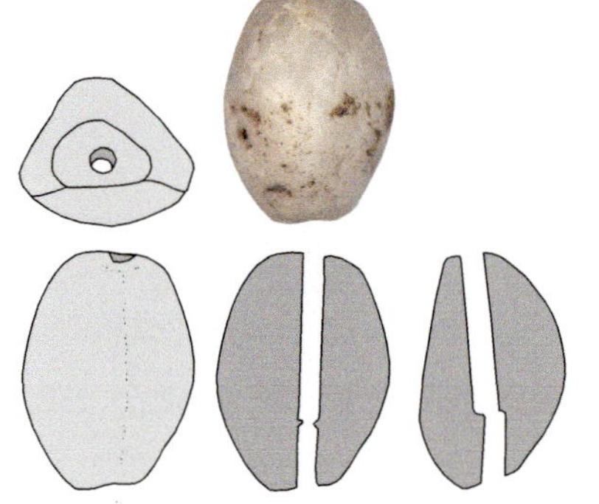

Fig. 430.

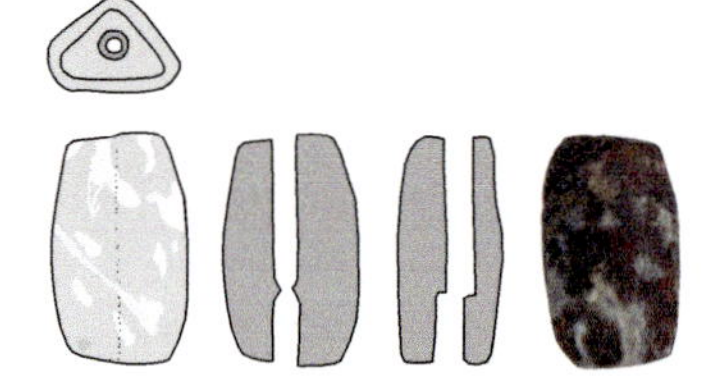

Fig. 431.

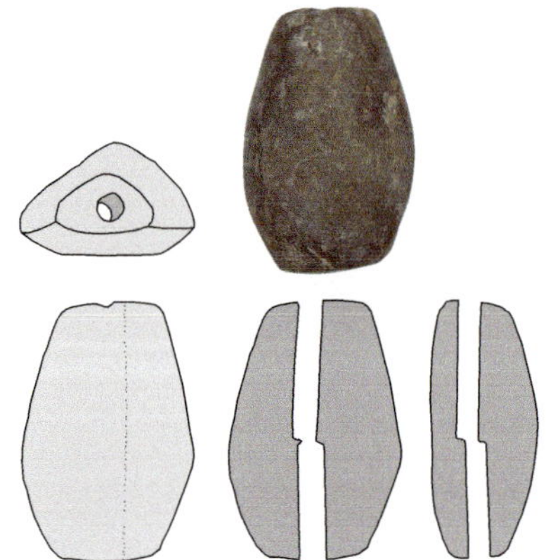

Fig. 432.

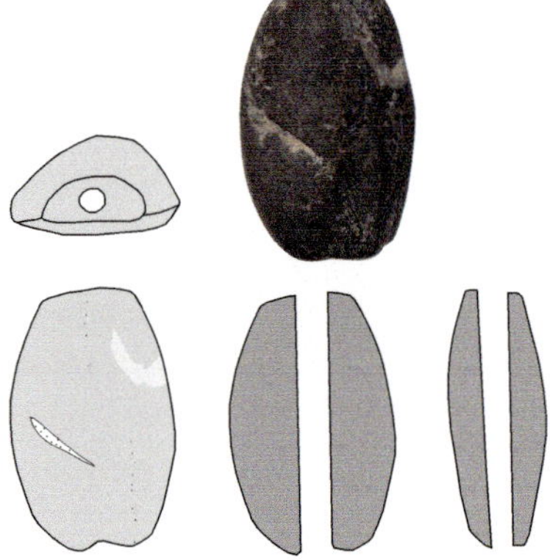

Fig. 433.

Barrels with triangular cross section (figs. 429-433)

VIII.D.1.b. Long barrels with triangular cross section

No. F3.acz, KM 1684 (fig. 429). *Context:* Trench D; 4A; Between level 7.37 and 7.67; No information. *Type:* Long barrel/Triangular; VIII.D.1.b. *Dimensions:* L 18.00, W 12.00, H 8.00 mm. *Material:* Agate. *Condition:* Complete. *Perforation:* Type II; PD 1.50-1.70 mm.

No. F3.ayq, KM 1692 (fig. 430). *Context:* Trench AQ; 4A/4B; level 8.72; No information. *Type:* Long barrel/Triangular; VIII.D.1.b. *Dimensions:* L 20.70, W 15.40, H 12.90 mm. *Material:* Milky quartz. *Condition:* Complete. *Perforation:* Type II; PD 2.50-2.80 mm.

No. F3.vj, KM 1692 (fig. 431). *Context:* Trench AA; 4B; level 7.06; No information. *Type:* Long barrel/Triangular; VIII.D.1.b. *Dimensions:* L 15.50, W 9.50, H 7.00 mm. *Material:* Jasper. *Condition:* Complete. *Perforation:* Type II; PD 1.60-2.20 mm.

No. F3.130, KM 1692 (fig. 432). *Context:* Trench RM; Unknown; Found in sieve; 0.00-15.00N/0.00-5.00W. *Type:* Long barrel/Triangular; VIII.D.1.b. *Dimensions:* L 25.00, W 16.50, H 10.50 mm. *Material:* Quartz. *Condition:* Complete. *Perforation:* Type II; PD 2.70 mm.

No. F6.954, KM 1699 (fig. 433). *Context:* Trench F1; 2-4A; Found in sieve. *Type:* Long barrel/Triangular; VIII.D.1.b. *Dimensions:* L 22.90, W 14.50, H 8.30 mm. *Material:* Unidentified stone (black stone with white vein). *Condition:* Complete. *Perforation:* Type II; PD 1.50 mm.

Barrels with rectangular cross section (figs. 434-437)

X.C.1.b. Standard barrels with rectangular cross section (fig. 434)

No. F6.1001B, KM 1508 (fig. 434). *Context:* Trench F1; Unknown; Found in sieve. *Type:* Standard barrel/ Rectangular; X.C.1.b. *Dimensions:* L 18.60, W 17.60, H 4.90 mm. *Material:* Agate. *Condition:* Complete. *Perforation:* Blank.

X.D.1.b. Long barrels with rectangular cross section (figs. 435-437)

No. F3.axc, KM 1679 (fig. 435). *Context:* Trench AN; 4B; level 7.55; 74.00N/7.00E. *Type:* Long barrel/Rectangular; X.D.1.b. *Dimensions:* L 17.00, W 10.00, H 5.00 mm. *Material:* Chrysoprase. *Condition:* Complete. *Perforation:* Type II; PD 1.60-1.90 mm.

No. F3.bfb.1, KM 1683 (fig. 436). *Context:* No provenience; Unknown; Found in sieve. *Type:* Long barrel/Rectangular; X.D.1.b. *Dimensions:* L 20.00 (pres.), W 10.00, H 8.00 mm. *Material:* Calcite. *Condition:* Fragmented. *Perforation:* Type II; PD 2.00-2.60 mm.

No. F6.without no.53, KM 1695 (fig. 437). *Context:* No provenience; Unknown; No information. *Type:* Long barrel/ Rectangular; X.D.1.b. *Dimensions:* L 22.50, W 13.20, H 6.30 mm. *Material:* Agate. *Condition:* Complete. *Perforation:* Type II; PD 2.10-2.60 mm.

Fig. 434.

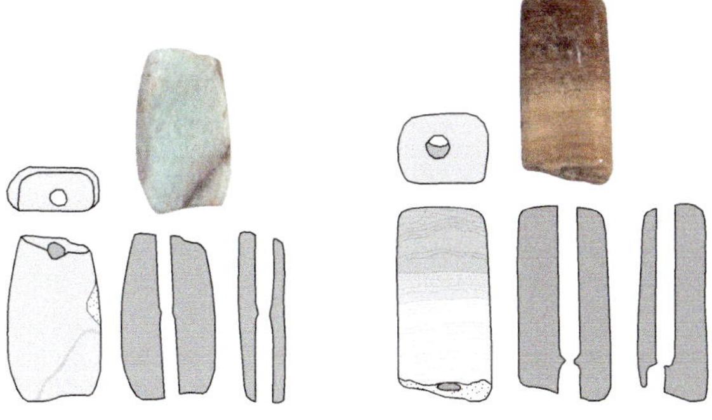

Fig. 435. Fig. 436.

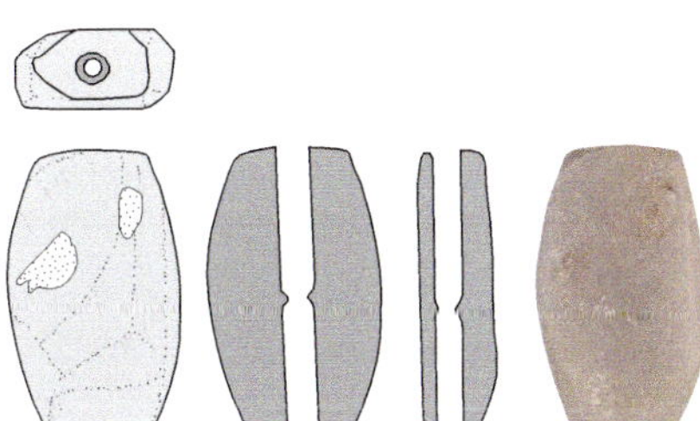

Fig. 437.

Barrels with hexagonal cross section (figs. 438-443)

XIII.D.1.b. Long barrels with hexagonal cross section (figs. 438-443)

No. F3.få.2, KM 1487 (fig. 438). *Context:* Trench J; 4B; level 7.28; No information. *Type:* Long barrel/Hexagonal; XIII.D.1.b. *Dimensions:* L 21.70, W 9.00, H 8.70 mm. *Material:* Calcite (stone type 10). *Condition:* Complete. *Perforation:* Blank.

No. F3.zø.3, KM 1690 (fig. 439). *Context:* Trench AB; Unknown; Found in sieve. *Type:* Long barrel/Hexagonal; XIII.D.1.b. *Dimensions:* L 16.10, W 9.00, H 8.40 mm. *Material:* Chlorite (stone type 3). *Condition:* Complete. *Perforation:* Type II; PD 2.90 mm.

No. F3.æz.1, KM 1669 (fig. 440). *Context:* Trench AD; Unknown; Found in sieve. *Type:* Long barrel/Hexagonal; XIII.D.1.b. *Dimensions:* L 16.25, W 13.40, H 6.40 mm. *Material:* Carnelian. *Condition:* Complete. *Perforation:* Type II; PD 2.25-2.90 mm.

No. F3.awl, KM 1670 (fig. 441). *Context:* Trench AO; 4A/4B; level 9.30-9.14; No information. *Type:* Long barrel/Hexagonal; XIII.D.1.b. *Dimensions:* L 32.00, W 20.50, H 19.90 mm. *Material:* Carnelian. *Condition:* Fragmented. *Perforation:* Unidentified; PD 1.90 mm.

No. F6.262, KM 1669 (fig. 442). *Context:* Trench B2; 2-4A; level -0.11; 10.00-19.00N/5.00-8.00W. *Type:* Long barrel/Hexagonal; XIII.D.1.b. *Dimensions:* L 14.80, W 6.75, H 7.75 mm. *Material:* Carnelian. *Condition:* Fragmented. *Perforation:* Type III; PD 1.20-2.95 mm.

No. F6.447.4, KM 1689 (fig. 443). *Context:* Trench D1; 2-4A; level -0.26; 4.00-5.00N/2.00-3.00W. *Type:* Long barrel/ Hexagonal; XIII.D.1.b. *Dimensions:* L 21.00, W 13.00, H 7.50 mm. *Material:* Carnelian. *Condition:* Complete. *Perforation:* Type II; PD 1.80-2.30 mm.

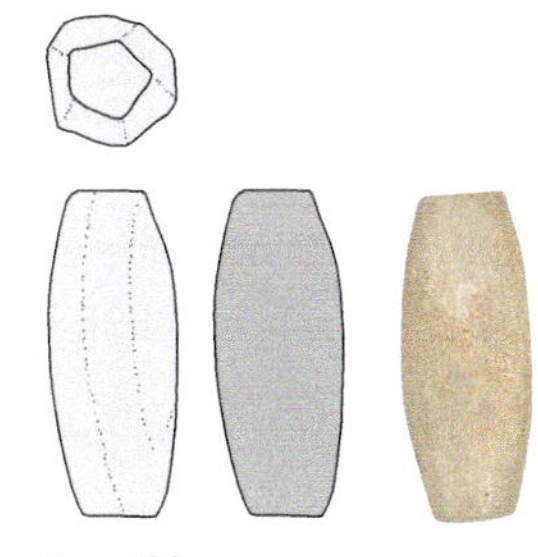

Fig. 438.

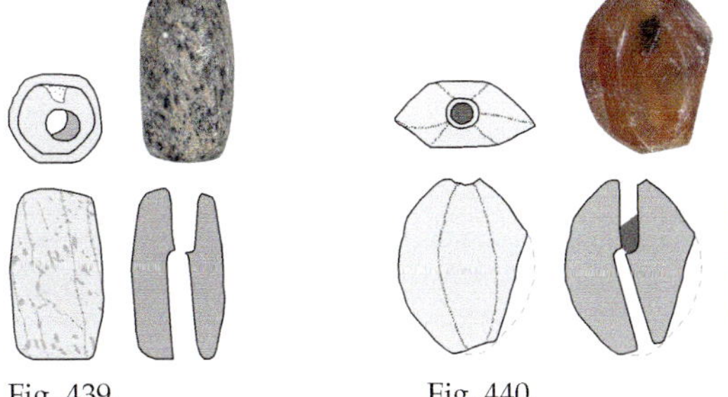

Fig. 439. Fig. 440.

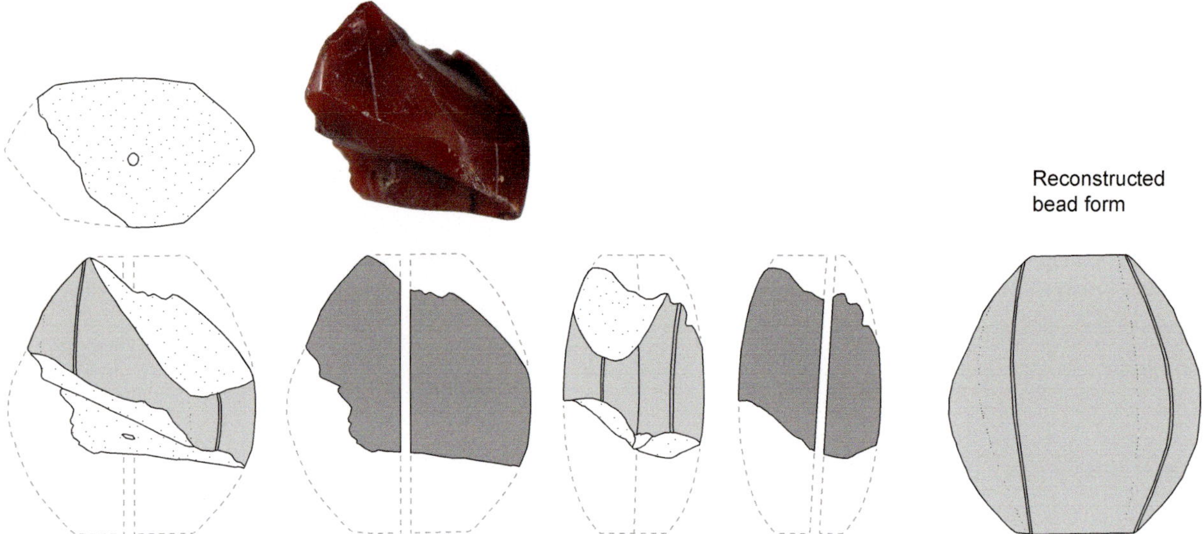

Fig. 441.

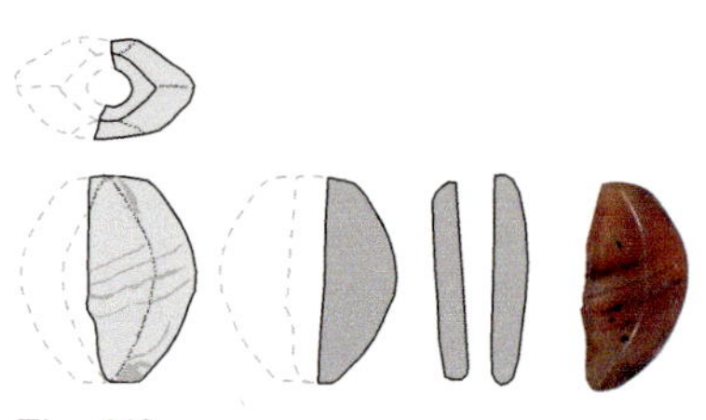

Fig. 442.

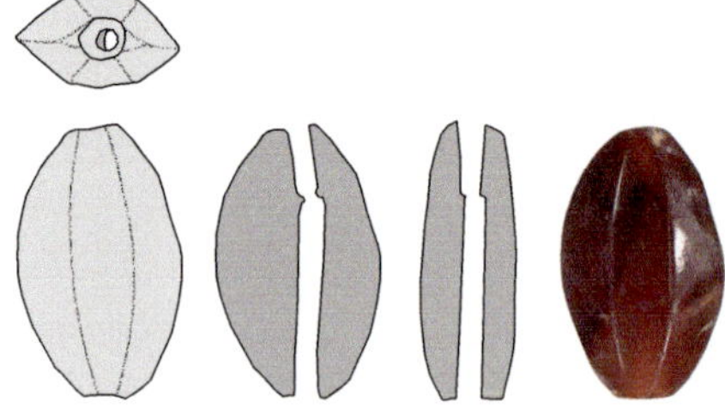

Fig. 443.

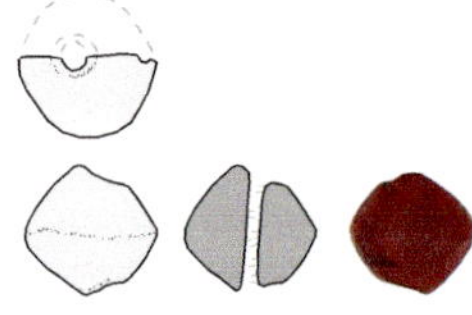

Fig. 444.

Convex bicones with circular cross section (fig. 444)

I.C.1.e. Standard convex bicones with circular cross section

No. F3.without no.1, KM 1669 (fig. 444). *Context:* No provenience; Unknown; No information. *Type:* Standard convex bicone/Circular; I.C.1.e. *Dimensions:* L 8.00, W 8.70 mm. *Material:* Carnelian. *Condition:* Fragmented. *Perforation:* Type III; PD 1.10-1.30 mm.

Truncated convex bicones with circular cross section (figs. 445-459)

I.B.1.f. Short truncated convex bicones with circular cross section

No. F3.152, KM 1683 (fig. 445). *Context:* Trench RM; Unknown; Found in sieve; 34.00-38.00N/0.00-5.00W. *Type:* Short truncated convex bicone/Circular; I.B.1.f. *Dimensions:* L 6.30, D 12.40-13.00, ED 5.50-6.00 mm. *Material:* Carnelian. *Condition:* Complete. *Perforation:* Type II; PD 2.00 mm.

No. F3.pm.1, KM 1495 (fig. 446). *Context:* Trench Y; 4B; Between level 9.38 and 8.85; No information. *Type:* Short truncated convex bicone/Circular; I.B.1.f. *Dimensions:* L 9.00, D 18.00 mm. *Material:* Faience. *Condition:* Complete. *Perforation:* Type IV; PD 4.00 mm.

No. F3.pm.2, KM 1495 (fig. 447). *Context:* Trench Y; 4B; Between level 9.38 and 8.85; No information. *Type:* Short truncated convex bicone/Circular; I.B.1.f. *Dimensions:* L 9.00, D 18.50 mm. *Material:* Faience. *Condition:* Complete. *Perforation:* Type IV; PD 3.50-3.90 mm.

No. F3.sb, KM 1683 (fig. 448). *Context:* Trench Y; 4B; level 7.64; 70.40N/2.40W. *Type:* Short truncated convex bicone/Circular; I.B.1.f. *Dimensions:* L 3.60, D 7.50-8.00 mm. *Material:* Carnelian. *Condition:* Complete. *Perforation:* Type I.1; PD 3.50-4.00 mm.

No. F3.xu.3, KM 1675 (fig. 449). *Context:* Trench AB; Unknown; Found in sieve. *Type:* Short truncated convex bicone/Circular; I.B.1.f. *Dimensions:* L 10.60, D 15.00 mm. *Material:* Faience. *Condition:* Complete. *Perforation:* Type IV; PD 3.20 mm.

No. F3.xf, KM 1683 (fig. 450). *Context:* Baulk between Trench AD and AE; Unknown; 7.10; No information. *Type:* Short truncated convex bicone/Circular; I.B.1.f. *Dimensions:* L 3.40, D 5.50, ED 3.00 mm. *Material:* Carnelian. *Condition:* Complete. *Perforation:* Type II; PD 1.00 mm.

No. F3.awj, KM 1675 (fig. 451). *Context:* Trench AN; 4B; level 8.64; 72.60N/7.10E. *Type:* Short truncated convex bicone/Circular; I.B.1.f. *Dimensions:* L 9.00, D 17.20 mm. *Material:* Faience. *Condition:* Complete. *Perforation:* Type IV; PD 3.00 mm.

No. F3.ase, KM 1675 (fig. 452). *Context:* No provenience; Unknown; Found in sieve. *Type:* Short truncated convex bicone/Circular; I.B.1.f. *Dimensions:* L 10.00, D 18.00 mm. *Material:* Faience. *Condition:* Complete. *Perforation:* Type IV; PD 3.20 mm.

No. F3.atn.1, KM 1675 (fig. 453). *Context:* No provenience; Unknown; No information. *Type:* Short truncated convex bicone/Circular; I.B.1.f. *Dimensions:* L 9.50, D 18.00 mm. *Material:* Faience. *Condition:* Complete. *Perforation:* Type IV; PD 3.20 mm.

No. F6.222, KM 1689 (fig. 454). *Context:* Trench C1; 2-4A; level -0.17; 1.50S/2.50E. *Type:* Short truncated convex bicone/ Circular; I.B.1.f. *Dimensions:* L 3.30, D 6.80-7.00 mm. *Material:* Carnelian. *Condition:* Complete. *Perforation:* Type II; PD 3.40 mm.

No. F6.522, KM 1509 (fig. 455). *Context:* Trench D3; 2-4A; level -0.12; 21.00-24.00N/1.00-2.00W. *Type:* Short truncated convex bicone/Circular; I.B.1.f. *Dimensions:* L 10.00, D 16.00 mm. *Material:* Faience. *Condition:* Complete. *Perforation:* Type III; PD 3.80-4.20 mm.

No. F6.1229, KM 1509 (fig. 456). *Context:* Trench M1; 1; level -1.70; 2.00-3.00N/8.00-9.00W. *Type:* Short truncated convex bicone/Circular; I.B.1.f. *Dimensions:* L 8.00, D 17.00 mm. *Material:* Faience. *Condition:* Complete. *Perforation:* Type IV; PD 2.40-3.20 mm.

No. F6.1241.2, KM 1509 (fig. 457). *Context:* No provenience; Unknown; Found in sieve. *Type:* Short truncated convex bicone/Circular; I.B.1.f. *Dimensions:* L 9.70, D 18.50 mm. *Material:* Faience. *Condition:* Complete. *Perforation:* Type IV; PD 3.10 mm.

No. F6.without no.17, KM 1687 (fig. 458). Context: No provenience; Unknown; No information. Type: Short truncated convex bicone/Circular; I.B.1.f. Dimensions: L 5.10, D 6.10 mm. Material: Carnelian. Condition: Complete. Perforation: Type II; PD 1.60 mm.

No. F6.without no.18, KM 1687 (fig. 459). *Context:* No provenience; Unknown; No information. *Type:* Short truncated convex bicone/Circular; I.B.1.f. *Dimensions:* L 2.40, D 4.70 mm. *Material:* Carnelian. *Condition:* Complete. *Perforation:* Type I.1; PD 1.00-1.70 mm.

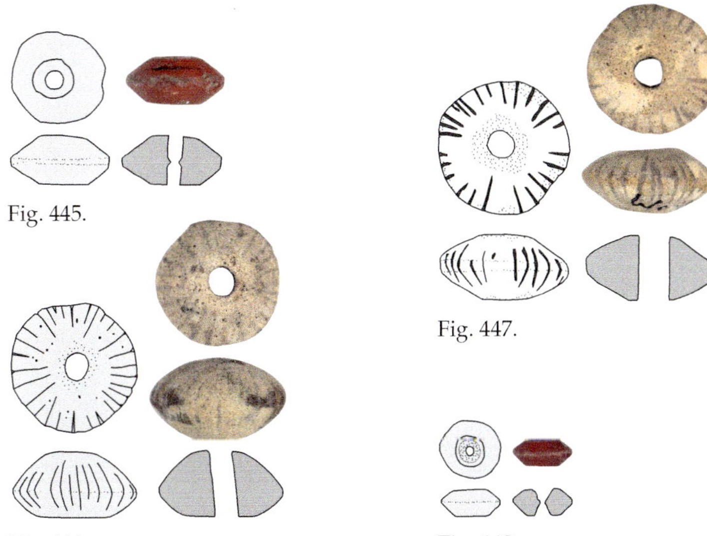

Fig. 445.

Fig. 446.

Fig. 447.

Fig. 448.

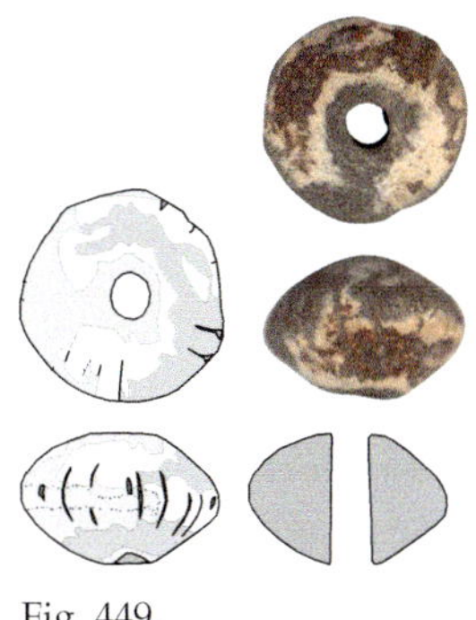

Fig. 449.

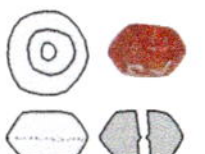

Fig. 450.

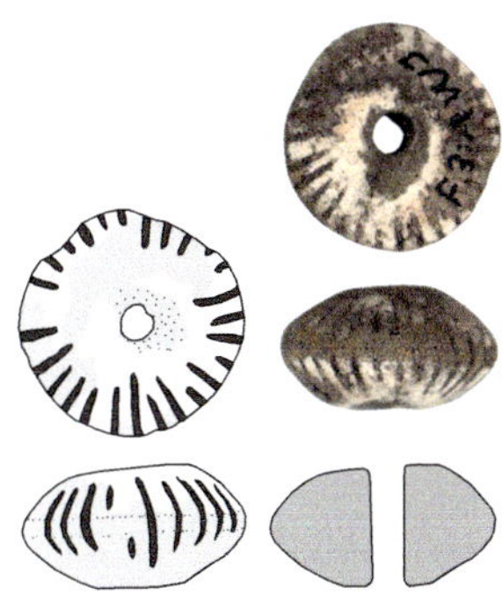

Fig. 451.

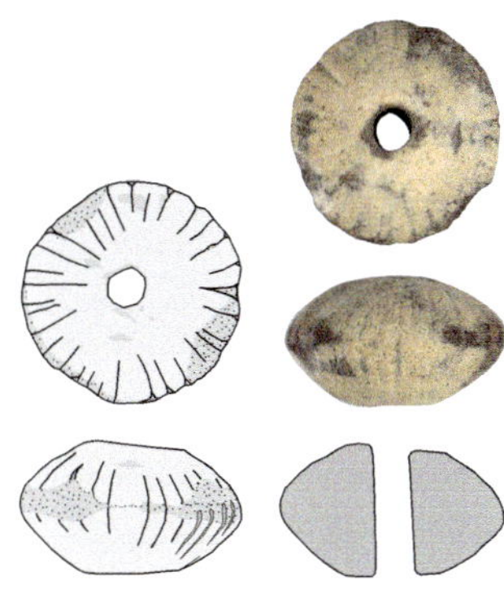

Fig. 452.

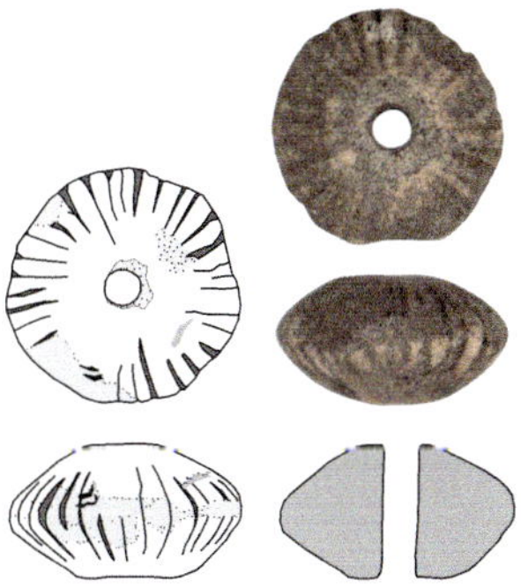

Fig. 453.

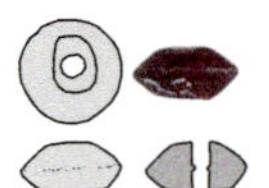
Fig. 454.

Fig. 455.

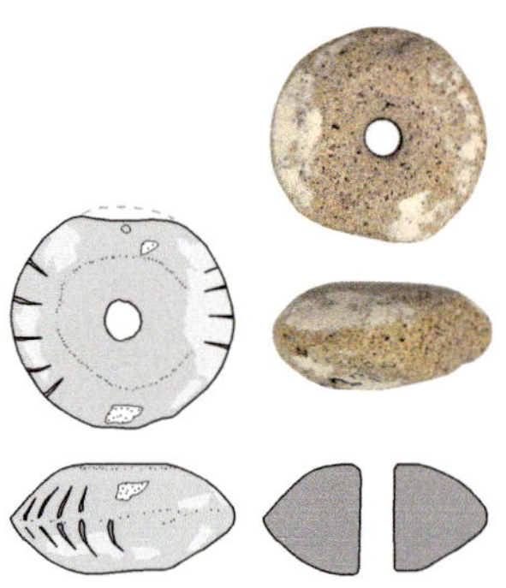
Fig. 456.

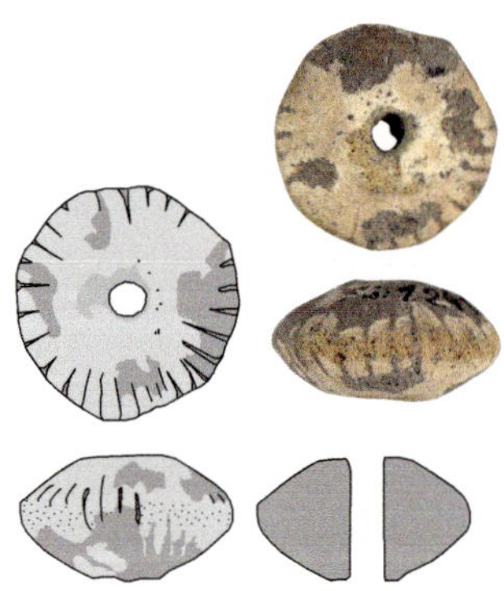
Fig. 457.

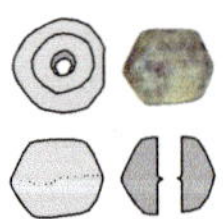
Fig. 458.

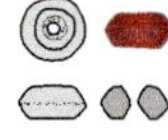
Fig. 459.

Truncated convex bicones with lenticular cross section (figs. 460-463)

IV.C.1.f. Standard truncated convex bicones with lenticular cross section (figs. 460-461)

No. F6.88.3, KM 1688 (fig. 460). *Context:* Trench A3; 2-4A; level 0.08; 20.00-20.55S/1.00-4.00W. *Type:* Standard truncated convex bicone/Lenticular; IV.C.1.f. *Dimensions:* L 25.00, W 25.00, H 7.00 mm. *Material:* Lapis Lazuli. *Condition:* Complete. *Perforation:* Type II; PD 3.20 mm.

No. F6.940, KM 1723 (fig. 461). *Context:* Trench F2; Unknown; Found in sieve. *Type:* Standard truncated convex bicone/Lenticular; IV.C.1.f. *Dimensions:* L 8.60, W 8.60, H 3.70 mm. *Material:* Turquoise. *Condition:* Complete. *Perforation:* Unidentified.; PD 0.60-0.80 mm.

IV.D.1.f. Long truncated convex bicones with lenticular cross section (figs. 462-463)

No. F3.ån.1, KM 1683 (fig. 462). *Context:* Trench AF; Unknown; Found in sieve. *Type:* Standard truncated convex bicone/Lenticular; IV.D.1.f. *Dimensions:* L 16.50, W 14.50, H 7.20 mm. *Material:* Agate. *Condition:* Complete. *Perforation:* Type II; PD 2.00 mm.

No. F6.678.3, KM 1688 (fig. 463). *Context:* Trench F2; Unknown; Found in sieve. *Type:* Standard truncated convex bicone/Lenticular; IV.D.1.f. *Dimensions:* L 10.45, W 12.45, H 5.00 mm. *Material:* Agate. *Condition:* Complete. *Perforation:* Type II; PD 0.90-1.20 mm.

Bicones with circular cross section (figs. 464-468)

I.D.2.e. Long bicones with circular cross section

No. F3.tk, KM 1685 (fig. 464). *Context:* Baulk between Trench RM and S; Unknown; 26.00N/5.50W. *Type:* Long bicone/Circular; I.D.2.e. *Dimensions:* L 14.10, D 7.10 mm. *Material:* Carnelian. *Condition:* Complete. *Perforation:* Type II; PD 1.90 mm.

No. F3.æl, KM 1693 (fig. 465). *Context:* Trench AA; 4B; level 8.18; 66.65N/5.20E. *Type:* Long bicone/Circular; I.D.2.e. *Dimensions:* L 18.20, D 11.20 mm. *Material:* Carnelian. *Condition:* Complete. *Perforation:* Type II; PD 2.70 mm.

No. F3.øp, KM 1693 (fig. 466). *Context:* Trench AE; 3A; Found in sieve. *Type:* Long bicone/Circular; I.D.2.e. *Dimensions:* L 19.80, D 11.00 mm. *Material:* Agate. *Condition:* Complete. *Perforation:* Type II; PD 2.30-2.40 mm.

No. F3.without no.4, KM 1669 (fig. 467). *Context:* No provenience; Unknown; No information. *Type:* Long bicone/Circular; I.D.2.e. *Dimensions:* L 10.80, D 6.60 mm. *Material:* Carnelian. *Condition:* Complete. *Perforation:* Type II; PD 1.30 mm.

No. F6.1036, KM 1691 (fig. 468). *Context:* Trench N1; Unknown; Found in sieve. *Type:* Long bicone/Circular; I.D.2.e. *Dimensions:* L 12.00, D 6.80 mm. *Material:* Carnelian. *Condition:* Complete. *Perforation:* Type II; PD 2.00 mm.

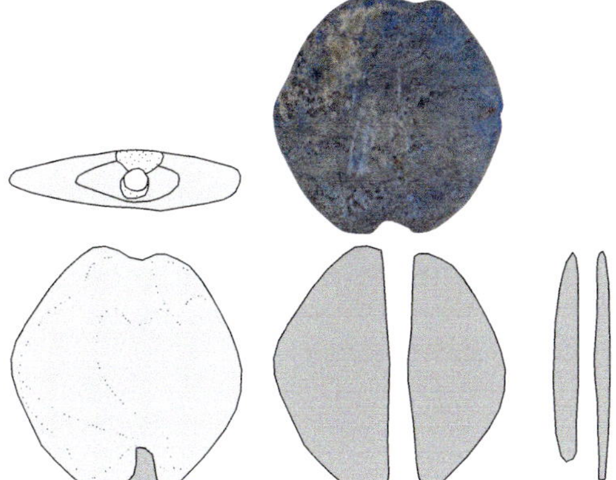

Fig. 460.

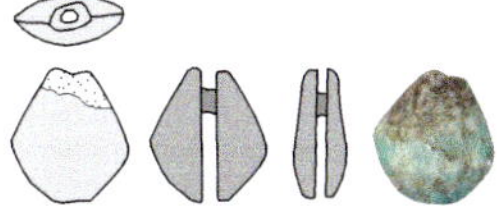

Fig. 461.

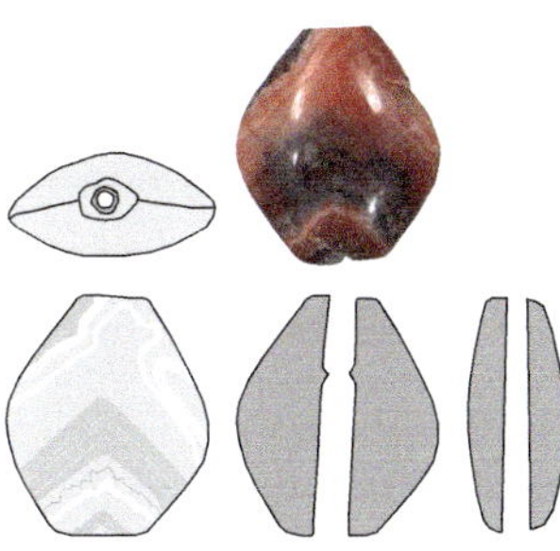

Fig. 462.

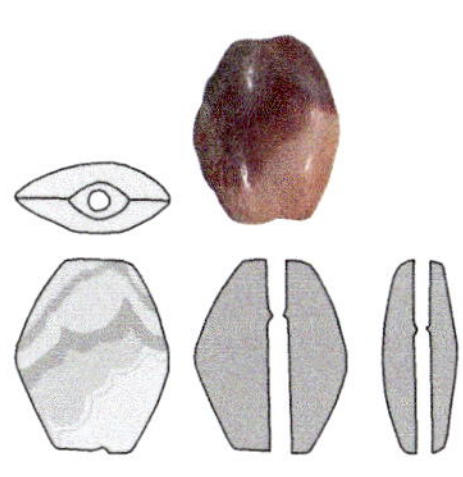

Fig. 463.

Fig. 464.

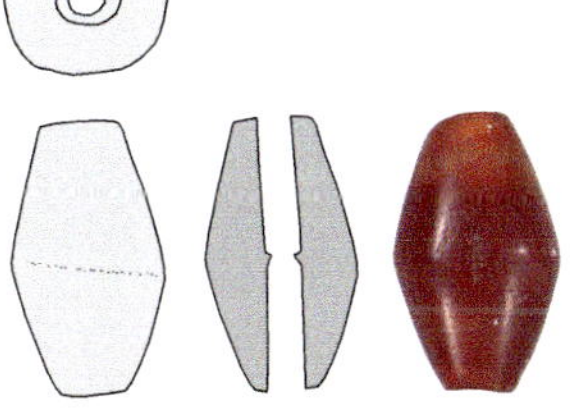

Fig. 465.

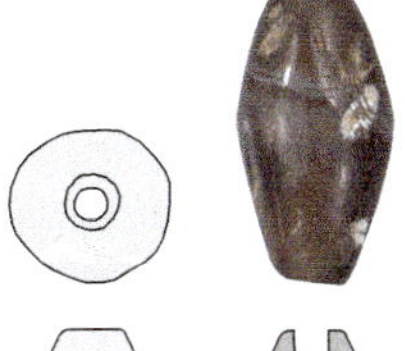

Fig. 466.

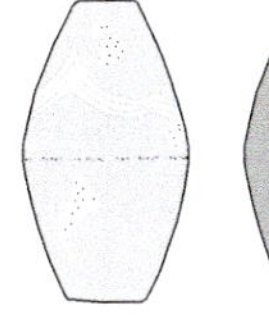

Fig. 467.

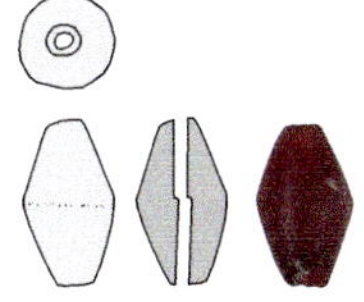

Fig. 468.

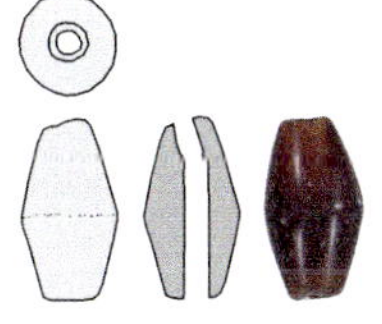

Truncated bicones with circular cross section (figs. 469-527)

I.B.2.f. Short truncated bicones with circular cross section (figs. 469-473)

No. F3.yh, KM 1683 (fig. 469). *Context:* Trench AD; 3A; level 6.24; No information. *Type:* Short truncated bicone/Circular; I.B.2.f. *Dimensions:* L 8.00, D 13.50 mm. *Material:* Bone. *Condition:* Complete. *Perforation:* Type IV; PD 7.50 mm.

No. F6.178.1, KM 1691 (fig. 470). *Context:* Trench A1; 2-4A; Between level -1.23 and -1.02; 0.00-1.00S/1.00-4.00W. *Type:* Short truncated bicone/Circular; I.B.2.f. *Dimensions:* L 5.70, D 6.60 mm. *Material:* Carnelian. *Condition:* Complete. *Perforation:* Type II; PD 1.80 mm.

No. F6.178.2, KM 1691 (fig. 471). *Context:* Trench A1; 2-4A; Between level -1.23 and -1.02; 0.00-1.00S/1.00-4.00W. *Type:* Short truncated bicone/Circular; I.B.2.f. *Dimensions:* L 5.50, D 7.10 mm. *Material:* Carnelian. *Condition:* Complete. *Perforation:* Type II; PD 1.90 mm.

No. F6.639.3, KM 1694 (fig. 472). *Context:* Trench F2; Unknown; Between level -1.72 and -0.98; Found in sieve. *Type:* Short truncated bicone/Circular; I.B.2.f. *Dimensions:* L 4.70, D 6.20 mm. *Material:* Carnelian. *Condition:* Complete. *Perforation:* Type II; PD 1.80 mm.

No. F6.1234, KM 1687 (fig. 473). *Context:* No provenience; Unknown; Found in sieve. *Type:* Short truncated bicone/Circular; I.B.2.f. *Dimensions:* L 5.70, D 6.40 mm. *Material:* Carnelian. *Condition:* Complete. *Perforation:* Type II; PD 1.70-2.10 mm.

I.C.2.f. Standard truncated bicones with circular cross section (figs. 474-499)

No. F3.ak, KM 1669 (fig. 474). *Context:* Trench A; 3A; Found in sieve above level 7.80. *Type:* Standard truncated bicone/Circular; I.C.2.f. *Dimensions:* L 7.10, D 7.80 mm. *Material:* Carnelian. *Condition:* Complete. *Perforation:* Type II; PD 2.40 mm. Remains of copper rod in perforation.

No. F3.gb, KM 1685 (fig. 475). *Context:* Trench M; 3B; level 8.00; No information. *Type:* Standard truncated bicone/Circular; I.C.2.f. *Dimensions:* L 5.10, D 4.60 mm. *Material:* Carnelian. *Condition:* Complete. *Perforation:* Type II; PD 1.30-1.40 mm.

No. F6.73, KM 1691 (fig. 476). *Context:* Trench A2; Unknown; Found in sieve; 12.10S/3.55W. *Type:* Standard truncated bicone/Circular; I.C.2.f. *Dimensions:* L 6.60, D 6.00 mm. *Material:* Carnelian. *Condition:* Complete. *Perforation:* Type II; PD 1.50-1.60 mm.

No. F6.445, KM 1691 (fig. 477). *Context:* Baulk between Trench A2 and A3; 2-4A; level 1.38; 19.00-20.00S/1.00-2.00W. *Type:* Standard truncated bicone/Circular; I.C.2.f. *Dimensions:* L 5.00, D 4.60 mm. *Material:* Carnelian. *Condition:* Complete. *Perforation:* Type II; PD 1.30 mm.

No. F6.234, KM 1691 (fig. 478). *Context:* Trench B2; 2-4A; level -0.26; 17.50S/6.00W. *Type:* Standard truncated bicone/Circular; I.C.2.f. *Dimensions:* L 6.30, D 6.00 mm. *Material:* Carnelian. *Condition:* Complete. *Perforation:* Type II; PD 2.20-2.30 mm.

No. F6.566, KM 1691 (fig. 479). *Context:* Trench D3; 2-4A; level -0.96; 21.00-23.00N/1.00-4.00W. *Type:* Standard truncated bicone/Circular; I.C.2.f. *Dimensions:* L 5.40, D 4.90 mm. *Material:* Carnelian. *Condition:* Complete. *Perforation:* Type II; PD 1.50 mm.

No. F6.953.1, KM 1691 (fig. 480). *Context:* Trench F1; 2-4A; level -0.99; No information. *Type:* Standard truncated bicone/Circular; I.C.2.f. *Dimensions:* L 6.40, D 6.70 mm. *Material:* Carnelian. *Condition:* Complete. *Perforation:* Type II; PD 1.90 mm.

No. F6.964A, KM 1691 (fig. 481). *Context:* Trench F1; 2-4A; Found in sieve above level 0.00. *Type:* Standard truncated bicone/Circular; I.C.2.f. *Dimensions:* L 6.70, D 6.40 mm. *Material:* Carnelian. *Condition:* Complete. *Perforation:* Type II; PD 1.60 mm.

No. F6.1037, KM 1691 (fig. 482). *Context:* Trench F1; Unknown; Found in sieve. *Type:* Standard truncated bicone/Circular; I.C.2.f. *Dimensions:* L 7.70, D 7.00 mm. *Material:* Carnelian. *Condition:* Complete. *Perforation:* Type II; PD 1.70 mm.

No. F6.707, KM 1691 (fig. 483). *Context:* Trench F2; Unknown; level -1.16; 18.50N/7.50W. *Type:* Standard truncated bicone/Circular; I.C.2.f. *Dimensions:* L 6.10, D 5.60 mm. *Material:* Carnelian. *Condition:* Complete. *Perforation:* Type II; PD 1.70 mm.

No. F6.936.3, KM 1631 (fig. 484). *Context:* Trench F2; Unknown; Found in sieve. *Type:* Standard truncated bicone/Circular; I.C.2.f. *Dimensions:* L 5.00, D 4.60 mm. *Material:* Carnelian. *Condition:* Complete. *Perforation:* Type II; PD 1.50 mm.

No. F6.936.4, KM 1631 (fig. 485). *Context:* Trench F2; Unknown; Found in sieve. *Type:* Standard truncated bicone/Circular; I.C.2.f. *Dimensions:* L 5.30, D 5.30 mm. *Material:* Carnelian. *Condition:* Complete. *Perforation:* Type II; PD 1.50 mm.

No. F6.829, KM 1691 (fig. 486). *Context:* Trench M2; 1; level -1.63; No information. *Type:* Standard truncated bicone/Circular; I.C.2.f. *Dimensions:* L 6.30, D 6.60 mm. *Material:* Carnelian. *Condition:* Complete. *Perforation:* Type II; PD 1.80-2.10 mm.

No. F6.846, KM 1691 (fig. 487). *Context:* Trench M2; 2-4A; level -1.44; 12.60N/11.10W. *Type:* Standard truncated bicone/Circular; I.C.2.f. *Dimensions:* L 6.50, D 6.50 mm. *Material:* Carnelian. *Condition:* Complete. *Perforation:* Type II; PD 1.80 mm.

No. F6.847.3, KM 1691 (fig. 488). *Context:* Trench M2; 2-4A; Found in sieve above level -1.34. *Type:* Standard truncated bicone/Circular; I.C.2.f. *Dimensions:* L 6.40, D 7.00 mm. *Material:* Carnelian. *Condition:* Complete. *Perforation:* Type II; PD 2.10-2.20 mm.

No. F6.847.4, KM 1691 (fig. 489). *Context:* Trench M2; 2-4A; Found in sieve above level -1.34. *Type:* Standard truncated bicone/Circular; I.C.2.f. *Dimensions:* L 5.70, D 5.50 mm. *Material:* Carnelian. *Condition:* Complete. *Perforation:* Type II; PD 1.70 mm.

No. F6.851.4, KM 1691 (fig. 490). *Context:* Trench M2; Unknown; Found in sieve. *Type:* Standard truncated bicone/Circular; I.C.2.f. *Dimensions:* L 5.30, D 5.00 mm. *Material:* Carnelian. *Condition:* Complete. *Perforation:* Type II; PD 1.20 mm.

No. F6.894, KM 1691 (fig. 491). *Context:* No provenience; Unknown; No information. *Type:* Standard truncated bicone/Circular; I.C.2.f. *Dimensions:* L 6.80, D 6.20 mm. *Material:* Carnelian. *Condition:* Complete. *Perforation:* Type II; PD 1.90-2.20 mm.

No. F6.944.6, KM 1691 (fig. 492). *Context:* No provenience; Unknown; Found in sieve. *Type:* Standard truncated bicone/Circular; I.C.2.f. *Dimensions:* L 6.50, D 6.40 mm. *Material:* Carnelian. *Condition:* Complete. *Perforation:* Type II; PD 1.90 mm.

No. F6.945.10, KM 1691 (fig. 493). *Context:* No provenience; Unknown; Found in sieve. *Type:* Standard truncated bicone/Circular; I.C.2.f. *Dimensions:* L 5.10, D 4.70 mm. *Material:* Carnelian. *Condition:* Complete. *Perforation:* Type II; PD 1.50 mm.

No. F6.1165, KM 1691 (fig. 494). *Context:* No provenience; Unknown; Found in sieve. *Type:* Standard truncated bicone/Circular; I.C.2.f. *Dimensions:* L 6.30, D 6.40 mm. *Material:* Carnelian. *Condition:* Complete. *Perforation:* Type II; PD 2.30 mm.

No. F6.1245, KM 1691 (fig. 495). *Context:* No provenience; Unknown; No information. *Type:* Standard truncated bicone/Circular; I.C.2.f. *Dimensions:* L 6.00, D 5.80 mm. *Material:* Carnelian. *Condition:* Complete. *Perforation:* Type II; PD 1.70 mm.

No. F6.without no.21, KM 1687 (fig. 496). *Context:* No provenience; Unknown; No information. *Type:* Standard truncated bicone/Circular; I.C.2.f. *Dimensions:* L 5.30, D 5.10 mm. *Material:* Carnelian. *Condition:* Complete. *Perforation:* Type II; PD 1.50 mm.

No. F6.without no.22, KM 1687 (fig. 497). *Context:* No provenience; Unknown; No information. *Type:* Standard truncated bicone/Circular; I.C.2.f. *Dimensions:* L 5.90, D 5.30 mm. *Material:* Carnelian. *Condition:* Complete. *Perforation:* Type II; PD 1.50 mm.

No. F6.without no.23, KM 1691 (fig. 498). *Context:* No provenience; Unknown; No information. *Type:* Standard truncated bicone/Circular; I.C.2.f. *Dimensions:* L 5.60, D 5.80 mm. *Material:* Carnelian. *Condition:* Complete. *Perforation:* Type II; PD 1.50 mm.

No. F6.without no.24, KM 1687 (fig. 499). *Context:* No provenience; Unknown; No information. *Type:* Standard truncated bicone/Circular; I.C.2.f. *Dimensions:* L 7.60, D 8.00 mm. *Material:* Carnelian. *Condition:* Complete. *Perforation:* Type II; PD 2.60 mm.

I.D.2.f. Long truncated bicones with circular cross section (figs. 500-527)

No. F3.gc, KM 1693 (fig. 500). *Context:* Trench F; Unknown; Found in sieve. *Type:* Long truncated bicone/Circular; I.D.2.f. *Dimensions:* L 12.80, D 5.70 mm. *Material:* Carnelian. *Condition:* Complete. *Perforation:* Type II; PD 2.30 mm.

No. F3.265.2, KM 1690 (fig. 501). *Context:* Trench RM; Unknown; Found in sieve. *Type:* Long truncated bicone/Circular; I.D.2.f. *Dimensions:* L 23.50, D 8.30 mm. *Material:* Carnelian. *Condition:* Fragmented. *Perforation:* Type II; PD 3.40 mm.

No. F3.vo, KM 1693 (fig. 502). *Context:* Trench Ø; Unknown; Found in sieve. *Type:* Long truncated bicone/Circular; I.D.2.f. *Dimensions:* L 16.30, D 7.70 mm. *Material:* Agate. *Condition:* Complete. *Perforation:* Type II; PD 2.60 mm.

No. F3.sæ, KM 1685 (fig. 503). *Context:* Trench AA; 4B; level 8.68; 71.50N/7.90E. *Type:* Long truncated bicone/Circular; I.D.2.f. *Dimensions:* L 9.90, D 7.50 mm. *Material:* Carnelian. *Condition:* Complete. *Perforation:* Type II; PD 1.90 mm.

No. F3.øw.2, KM 1693 (fig. 504). *Context:* Trench AE; 3A; Found in sieve. *Type:* Long truncated bicone/Circular; I.D.2.f. *Dimensions:* L 14.20, D 6.60 mm. *Material:* Carnelian. *Condition:* Complete. *Perforation:* Type III; PD 1.90-2.50 mm.

No. F3.axy, KM 1693 (fig. 505). *Context:* Trench AN; 4B; level 7.09; No information. *Type:* Long truncated bicone/Circular; I.D.2.f. *Dimensions:* L 16.40, D 7.30 mm. *Material:* Carnelian. *Condition:* Complete. *Perforation:* Type II; PD 2.20-2.40 mm.

No. F3.aye.2, KM 1693 (fig. 506). *Context:* Trench AO; 4A/4B; level 7.53; No information. *Type:* Long truncated bicone/Circular; I.D.2.f. *Dimensions:* L 22.60, D 7.70 mm. *Material:* Carnelian. *Condition:* Fragmented. *Perforation:* Type II; PD 3.00 mm.

No. F3.bet, KM 1685 (fig. 507). *Context:* Trench AR; Unknown; level 7.02; No information. *Type:* Long truncated bicone/Circular; I.D.2.f. *Dimensions:* L 9.50, D 7.30 mm. *Material:* Amethyst. *Condition:* Complete. *Perforation:* Type II; PD 1.50-1.60 mm.

No. F3.without no.5, KM 1685 (fig. 508). *Context:* No provenience; Unknown; No information. *Type:* Long truncated bicone/Circular; I.D.2.f. *Dimensions:* L 10.00, D 6.60 mm. *Material:* Carnelian. *Condition:* Complete. *Perforation:* Type II; PD 1.60 mm.

No. F6.321, KM 1691 (fig. 509). *Context:* Trench C3; 2-4A; level -1.45; 27.20S/2.15E. *Type:* Long truncated bicone/Circular; I.D.2.f. *Dimensions:* L 11.30, D 6.40 mm. *Material:* Carnelian. *Condition:* Complete. *Perforation:* Type II; PD 2.30 mm.

No. F6.362.11, KM 1695 (fig. 510). *Context:* Trench D2; 2-4A; level -0.59; 14.00-15.00N/3.50-4.00W. *Type:* Long truncated bicone/Circular; I.D.2.f. *Dimensions:* L 14.10, D 8.30 mm. *Material:* Agate. *Condition:* Complete. *Perforation:* Type II; PD 2.10 mm.

No. F6.417.7, KM 1691 (fig. 511). *Context:* Trench D2; 2-4A; Between level -0.46 and -1.08; 13.00-15.00N/1.25-4.00W. *Type:* Long truncated bicone/Circular; I.D.2.f. *Dimensions:* L 7.10, D 5.80 mm. *Material:* Carnelian. *Condition:* Complete. *Perforation:* Type II; PD 1.80 mm.

No. F6.625, KM 1691 (fig. 512). *Context:* Trench D2; 1; level -2.10; 13.00-14.00N/1.00-3.00W. *Type:* Long truncated bicone/Circular; I.D.2.f. *Dimensions:* L 15.30, D 6.60 mm. *Material:* Carnelian. *Condition:* Complete. *Perforation:* Type II; PD 2.50-2.70 mm.

No. F6.935.1, KM 1691 (fig. 513). *Context:* Trench F2; Unknown; Found in sieve. *Type:* Long truncated bicone/Circular; I.D.2.f. *Dimensions:* L 5.90, D 4.90 mm. *Material:* Carnelian. *Condition:* Complete. *Perforation:* Type II; PD 1.60 mm.

No. F6.936.1, KM 1631 (fig. 514). *Context:* Trench F2; Unknown; Found in sieve. *Type:* Long truncated bicone/Circular; I.D.2.f. *Dimensions:* L 14.00, D 6.20 mm. *Material:* Carnelian. *Condition:* Complete. *Perforation:* Type II; PD 2.30-2.40 mm.

No. F6.825, KM 1681 (fig. 515). *Context:* Trench M2; Unknown; Found in sieve. *Type:* Long truncated bicone/Circular; I.D.2.f. *Dimensions:* L 8.50, D 6.30 mm. *Material:* Carnelian. *Condition:* Complete. *Perforation:* Type II; PD 1.80 mm.

No. F6.827.3, KM 1691 (fig. 516). *Context:* Trench M2; Unknown; Found in sieve. *Type:* Long truncated bicone/Circular; I.D.2.f. *Dimensions:* L 5.50, D 4.70 mm. *Material:* Carnelian. *Condition:* Complete. *Perforation:* Type II; PD 1.70 mm.

No. F6.847.1, KM 1682 (fig. 517). *Context:* Trench M2; 2-4A; Found in sieve above level -1.34. *Type:* Long truncated bicone/Circular; I.D.2.f. *Dimensions:* L 14.25, D 7.65 mm. *Material:* Carnelian. *Condition:* Complete. *Perforation:* Type 2.65-2.75; PD II mm.

No. F6.847.2, KM 1691 (fig. 518). *Context:* Trench M2; 2-4A; Found in sieve above level -1.34. *Type:* Long truncated bicone/Circular; I.D.2.f. *Dimensions:* L 6.20, D 4.60 mm. *Material:* Carnelian. *Condition:* Complete. *Perforation:* Type II; PD 1.30-1.40 mm.

No. F6.854.2, KM 1682 (fig. 519). *Context:* Trench M2; 1; level -1.98; 18.00-20.00N/9.00-11.00W. *Type:* Long truncated bicone/Circular; I.D.2.f. *Dimensions:* L 12.50, D 5.50 mm. *Material:* Carnelian. *Condition:* Complete. *Perforation:* Type II; PD 1.90 mm.

No. F6.875.1, KM 1691 (fig. 520). *Context:* Trench M2; Unknown; Found in sieve. *Type:* Long truncated bicone/Circular; I.D.2.f. *Dimensions:* L 5.60, D 4.80 mm. *Material:* Carnelian. *Condition:* Complete. *Perforation:* Type II; PD 1.50 mm.

No. F6.880.6, KM 1691 (fig. 521). *Context:* Trench M2; 2-4A; Found in sieve above level -1.07. *Type:* Long truncated bicone/Circular; I.D.2.f. *Dimensions:* L 9.90, D 6.30 mm. *Material:* Agate. *Condition:* Complete. *Perforation:* Type II; PD 2.20-2.40 mm.

No. F6.945.13, KM 1695 (fig. 522). *Context:* No provenience; Unknown; Found in sieve. *Type:* Long truncated bicone/Circular; I.D.2.f. *Dimensions:* L 12.50, D 5.30 mm. *Material:* Carnelian. *Condition:* Complete. *Perforation:* Type II; PD 2.00 mm.

No. F6.1243, KM 1691 (fig. 523). *Context:* No provenience; Unknown; No information. *Type:* Long truncated bicone/Circular; I.D.2.f. *Dimensions:* L 10.00, D 7.10 mm. *Material:* Carnelian. *Condition:* Complete. *Perforation:* Type II; PD 1.90-2.00 mm.

No. F6.without no.40, KM 1687 (fig. 524). *Context:* No provenience; Unknown; No information. *Type:* Long truncated bicone/Circular; I.D.2.f. *Dimensions:* L 5.70, D 5.10 mm. *Material:* Carnelian. *Condition:* Complete. *Perforation:* Type II; PD 1.50 mm.

No. F6.without no.41, KM 1687 (fig. 525). *Context:* No provenience; Unknown; No information. *Type:* Long truncated bicone/Circular; I.D.2.f. *Dimensions:* L 10.30, D 6.90 mm. *Material:* Carnelian. *Condition:* Complete. *Perforation:* Type II; PD 2.00 mm.

No. F6.without no.42, KM 1687 (fig. 526). *Context:* No provenience; Unknown; No information. *Type:* Long truncated bicone/Circular; I.D.2.f. *Dimensions:* L 9.80, D 6.70 mm. *Material:* Carnelian. *Condition:* Complete. *Perforation:* Type III; PD 1.60-2.00 mm.

No. F6.without no.43, KM 1695 (fig. 527). *Context:* No provenience; Unknown; No information. *Type:* Long truncated bicone/Circular; I.D.2.f. *Dimensions:* L 13.30, D 5.70 mm. *Material:* Carnelian. *Condition:* Complete. *Perforation:* Type II; PD 1.70 mm.

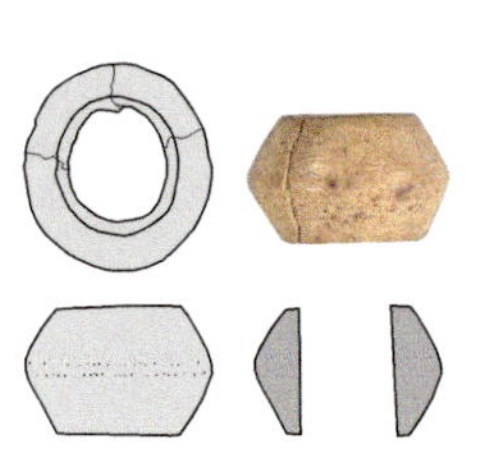

Fig. 469.

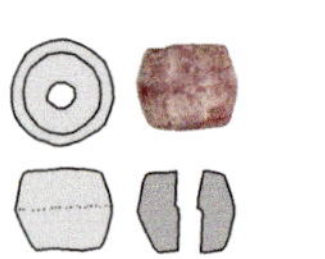

Fig. 470.

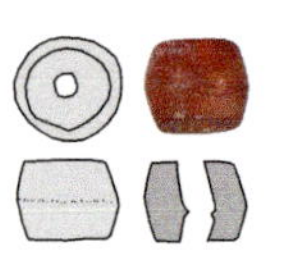

Fig. 471.

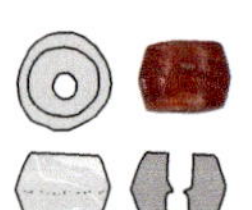

Fig. 472.

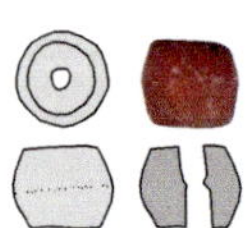

Fig. 473.

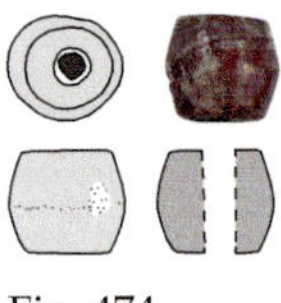

Fig. 474.

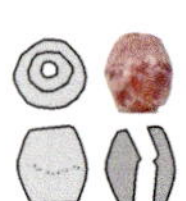

Fig. 475.

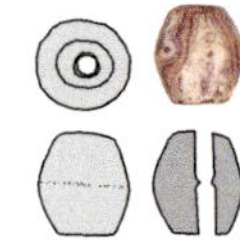

Fig. 476.

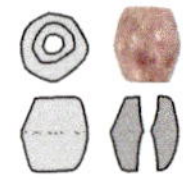

Fig. 477.

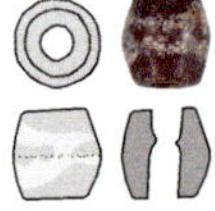

Fig. 478.

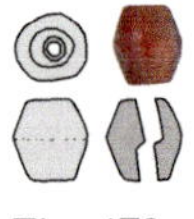

Fig. 479.

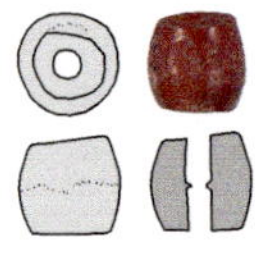

Fig. 480.

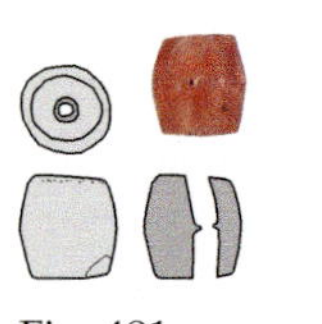

Fig. 481.

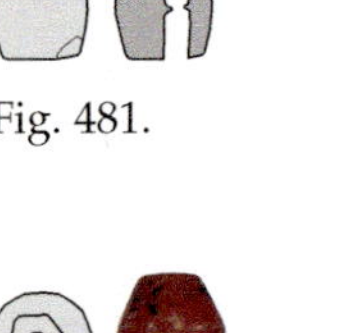

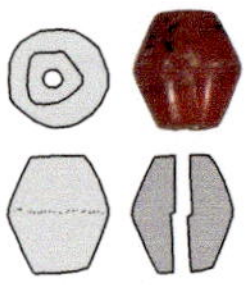

Fig. 482.

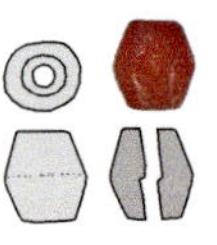

Fig. 483.

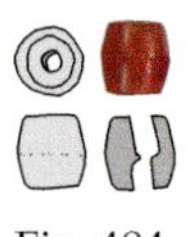

Fig. 484.

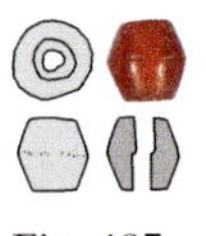

Fig. 485.

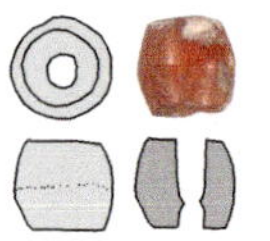

Fig. 486.

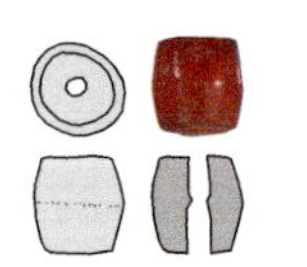

Fig. 487.

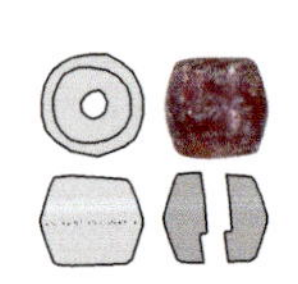

Fig. 488.

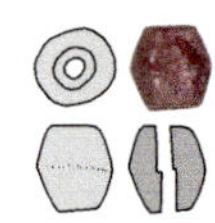

Fig. 489.

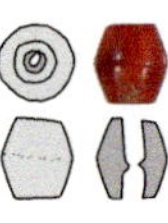

Fig. 490.

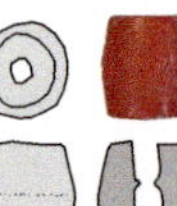

Fig. 491.

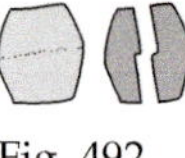

Fig. 492.

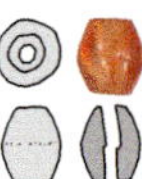

Fig. 493.

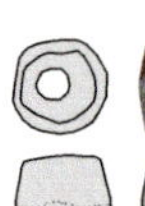

Fig. 494.

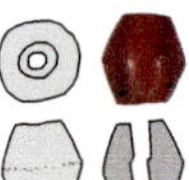

Fig. 495.

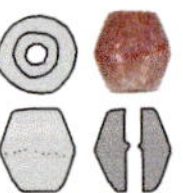

Fig. 496.

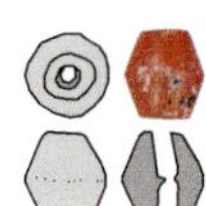

Fig. 497.

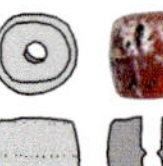

Fig. 498.

Fig. 499.

Fig. 500.

Fig. 501.

Fig. 502.

Fig. 503.

Fig. 504.

Fig. 505.

Fig. 506.

Fig. 507.

Fig. 508.

Fig. 509.

Fig. 510.

Fig. 511.

Fig. 512.

Fig. 513.

Fig. 514.

Fig. 515.

Fig. 516.

Fig. 517.

Fig. 518.

Fig. 519.

Fig. 520.

Fig. 521.

Fig. 522.

Fig. 523.

Fig. 524.

Fig. 525.

Fig. 526.

Fig. 527.

Cylinders with circular cross section (figs. 528-563)

I.B.2.b. Short cylinder with circular cross section (figs. 528-533)

No. F3.td.2, KM 1690 (fig. 528). *Context:* Trench Æ; Unknown; Found in sieve. *Type:* Short cylinder/Circular; I.B.2.b. *Dimensions:* L 6.80, D 10.90 mm. *Material:* Hematite. *Condition:* Complete. *Perforation:* Type II; PD 2.50 mm.

No. F3.yi, KM 1690 (fig. 529). *Context:* Trench AB; Unknown; Found in sieve. *Type:* Short cylinder/Circular; I.B.2.b. *Dimensions:* L 5.50, D 15.00 mm. *Material:* Carnelian. *Condition:* Complete. *Perforation:* Type I.1; PD 4.20 mm.

No. F6.88.1, KM 1680 (fig. 530). *Context:* Trench A3; 2-4A; level 0.08; 20.00-20.50N/1.00-4.00W. *Type:* Short cylinder/Circular; I.B.2.b. *Dimensions:* L 3.20-5.00, D 5.60 mm. *Material:* Lapis Lazuli. *Condition:* Complete. *Perforation:* Type III; PD 1.60-2.00 mm.

No. F6.537.1, KM 1680 (fig. 531). *Context:* Trench D3; 2-4A; level -0.58; 21.00-24.00N/1.00-2.00W. *Type:* Short cylinder/Circular; I.B.2.b. *Dimensions:* L 2.50, D 5.60 mm. *Material:* Carnelian. *Condition:* Complete. *Perforation:* Type II; PD 1.40 mm.

No. F6.458.1, KM 1688 (fig. 532). *Context:* Trench E2; 2-4A; level -0.35; 16.00-18.00N/1.50-3.00E. *Type:* Short cylinder/Circular; I.B.2.b. *Dimensions:* L 10.00, D 14.00 mm. *Material:* Smoky Quartz. *Condition:* Complete. *Perforation:* Type III; PD 3.00-3.50 mm.

No. F6.953.3, KM 1689 (fig. 533). *Context:* Trench F1; 2-4A; level -0.99; No information. *Type:* Short cylinder/Circular; I.B.2.b. *Dimensions:* L 7.60, D 11.60 mm. *Material:* Glass. *Condition:* Complete. *Perforation:* Type III; PD 2.70-3.20 mm.

I.C.2.b. Standard cylinders with circular cross section (fig. 534)

No. F3.qæ.1, KM 1707 (fig. 534). *Context:* Trench Z; Unknown; No information. *Type:* Standard cylinder/Circular; I.C.2.b. *Dimensions:* L 16.00, D 15.00 mm. *Material:* Ivory. *Condition:* Fragmented. *Perforation:* Type II; PD 3.80 mm.

I.D.2.b. Long cylinders with circular cross section (figs. 535-563)

No. F3.fh, KM 1690 (fig. 535). *Context:* Trench F; Unknown; Found in sieve. *Type:* Long cylinder/Circular; I.D.2.b. *Dimensions:* L 15.50, D 8.50 mm. *Material:* Carnelian. *Condition:* Complete. *Perforation:* Type II; PD 2.70 mm.

No. F3.qu, KM 1690 (fig. 536). *Context:* Baulk between Trench N and X; 3B/4B; level 8.56; 50.00N/7.50E. *Type:* Long cylinder/Circular; I.D.2.b. *Dimensions:* L 12.30, D 5.80 mm. *Material:* Jasper. *Condition:* Complete. *Perforation:* Type II; PD 2.50 mm.

No. F3.xn, KM 1690 (fig. 537). *Context:* Trench AB; Unknown; No information. *Type:* Long cylinder/Circular; I.D.2.b. *Dimensions:* L 13.30, D 5.90 mm. *Material:* Carnelian. *Condition:* Fragmented. *Perforation:* Type II; PD 1.60-1.90 mm.

No. F3.xu.2, KM 1690 (fig. 538). *Context:* Trench AB; Unknown; No information. *Type:* Long cylinder/Circular; I.D.2.b. *Dimensions:* L 8.10, D 6.50 mm. *Material:* Bone. *Condition:* Fragmented. *Perforation:* Type IV; PD 2.40-3.00 mm.

No. F3.ån.2, KM 1690 (fig. 539). *Context:* Trench AF; Unknown; Found in sieve. *Type:* Long cylinder/Circular; I.D.2.b. *Dimensions:* L 19.50, D 4.80 mm. *Material:* Carnelian. *Condition:* Complete. *Perforation:* Type II; PD 2.30 mm.

No. F3.yå.3, KM 1704 (fig. 540). *Context:* Trench AF; Unknown; Found in sieve. *Type:* Long cylinder/Circular; I.D.2.b. *Dimensions:* L 12.50, D 14.00 mm. *Material:* Glass. *Condition:* Fragmented. *Perforation:* Unidentified; PD 3.80 mm.

F3.æg, KM 1700 (fig. 541). *Context:* Baulk between Trench AB and AF; Unknown; Found in sieve. *Type:* Long cylinder/Circular; I.D.2.b. *Dimensions:* L 8.20, D 10.00 mm. *Material:* Glass. *Condition:* Fragmented. *Perforation:* Unidentified; PD 4.00 mm.

No. F3.ån.3, KM 1690 (fig. 542). *Context:* Trench AF; Unknown; Found in sieve. *Type:* Long cylinder/Circular; I.D.2.b. *Dimensions:* L 22.60, D 7.20 mm. *Material:* Rock crystal. *Condition:* Complete. *Perforation:* Type II; PD 2.00-3.00 mm.

No. F3.bae.2, KM 1690 (fig. 543). *Context:* Baulk between Trench AP and AQ; Unknown; Found in sieve. *Type:* Long cylinder/Circular; I.D.2.b. *Dimensions:* L 14.70, D 8.00 mm. *Material:* Carnelian. *Condition:* Complete. *Perforation:* Type I; PD 1.50-3.20 mm.

No. F3.pl, KM 1690 (fig. 544). *Context:* Trench Y; 4B; Found in sieve between level 8.85 and 9.38. *Type:* Long cylinder/Circular; I.D.2.b. *Dimensions:* L (pres.) 13.50, D (pres.) 14.90 mm. *Material:* Agate. *Condition:* Fragmented. *Perforation:* Unidentified; PD 2.90 mm.

No. F3.without no.3, KM 1720 (fig. 545). *Context:* No provenience; Unknown; Found in sieve. *Type:* Long cylinder/Circular; I.D.2.b. *Dimensions:* L 6.80, D 4.70 mm. *Material:* Lapis Lazuli. *Condition:* Fragmented. *Perforation:* Type II; PD 1.40 mm.

No. F6.88.2, KM 1680 (fig. 546). *Context:* Trench A3; 2-4A; level 0.08; 20.00-20.55S/1.00-4.00W. *Type:* Long cylinder/Circular; I.D.2.b. *Dimensions:* L 13.00, D 7.50 mm. *Material:* Agate. *Condition:* Complete. *Perforation:* Type II; PD 2.20-2.70 mm.

No. F6.379/541, KM 1680 (fig. 547). *Context:* Trench D1; 2-4A; level -1.20; 5.50-7.00N/1.05-3.00W. *Type:* Long cylinder/Circular; I.D.2.b. *Dimensions:* L 19.20, D 5.30 mm. *Material:* Carnelian. *Condition:* Complete. *Perforation:* Type II; PD 2.10 mm.

No. F6.353, KM 1719 (fig. 548). *Context:* Trench D2; 2-4A; level -0.13; 17.00N/3.75W. *Type:* Long cylinder/Circular; I.D.2.b. *Dimensions:* L 25.80, D 9.20 mm. *Material:* Glass. *Condition:* Complete. *Perforation:* Unidentified; PD 2.00 mm.

No. F6.396.1, KM 1562 (fig. 549). *Context:* Trench D2; 2-4A; level -0.96; 14.00-15.00N/3.50-4.00W. *Type:* Long cylinder/Circular; I.D.2.b. *Dimensions:* Not preserved. *Material:* Glass. *Condition:* Fragmented. *Perforation:* Type IV; PD 2.20-3.30 mm.

No. F6.500, KM 1563 (fig. 550). *Context:* Trench E2; 2-4A; level -0.95; 16.00-18.00N/1.50-3.00E. *Type:* Long cylinder/Circular; I.D.2.b. *Dimensions:* L 23.00, D 10.00 mm. *Material:* Glass. *Condition:* Fragmented. *Perforation:* Unidentified; PD 2.00-2.20 mm.

No. F6.590.6, KM 1680 (fig. 551). *Context:* Baulk between Trench D2 and E2; 2-4A; level -1.28; 14.50-16.00N/0.00-1.00W. *Type:* Long cylinder/Circular; I.D.2.b. *Dimensions:* L 4.50, D 4.00 mm. *Material:* Lapis Lazuli. *Condition:* Complete. *Perforation:* Type III; PD 1.00-1.70 mm.

No. F6.967, KM 1680 (fig. 552). *Context:* Trench F1; 2-4A; level -0.20; Found in sieve. *Type:* Long cylinder/Circular; I.D.2.b. *Dimensions:* L 18.60, D 4.70 mm. *Material:* Carnelian. *Condition:* Complete. *Perforation:* Type II; PD 2.10-2.20 mm.

No. F6.977, KM 1680 (fig. 553). *Context:* Trench F1; 2-4A; level -0.72; No information. *Type:* Long cylinder/Circular; I.D.2.b. *Dimensions:* L 17.50, D 9.00 mm. *Material:* Agate. *Condition:* Complete. *Perforation:* Type II; PD 2.60-3.20 mm.

No. F6.639.2, KM 1680 (fig. 554). *Context:* Trench F2; Unknown; Found in sieve between level -0.98 and -1.72. *Type:* Long cylinder/Circular; I.D.2.b. *Dimensions:* L 15.00, D 5.00 mm. *Material:* Lapis lazuli and gold. *Condition:* Fragmented. *Perforation:* Type II; PD 1.50-2.00 mm.

No. F6.656.2, KM 1680 (fig. 555). *Context:* Trench F2; 2-4A; level -0.71; 15.00-16.00N/4.50W. *Type:* Long cylinder/Circular; I.D.2.b. *Dimensions:* L 10.90, D 4.40 mm. *Material:* Carnelian. *Condition:* Complete. *Perforation:* Type II; PD 2.10-2.20 mm.

No. F6.666.1, KM 1505 (fig. 556). *Context:* Trench F2; 2-4A; level -0.78; 13.00N/5.00W. *Type:* Long cylinder/Circular; I.D.2.b. *Dimensions:* L 16.50 (pres.), D 8.50 (pres.) mm. *Material:* Glass. *Condition:* Fragmented. *Perforation:* Type IV; PD 2.00-2.10 mm.

No. F6.678.2, KM 1490 (fig. 557). *Context:* Trench F2; Unknown; Found in sieve. *Type:* Long cylinder/Circular; I.D.2.b. *Dimensions:* L 15.50, D 6.50 mm. *Material:* Faience. *Condition:* Complete. *Perforation:* Unidentified; PD 1.50 mm.

No. F6.800.4, KM 1705 (fig. 558). *Context:* Trench M2; 2-4A; Found in sieve above level -1.07. *Type:* Long cylinder/Circular; I.D.2.b. *Dimensions:* L 19.20, D 13.40 mm. *Material:* Glass. *Condition:* Fragmented. *Perforation:* Unidentified; PD 3.40 mm.

No. F6.800.5, KM 1705 (fig. 559). *Context:* Trench M2; 2-4A; Found in sieve above level -1.07. *Type:* Long cylinder/Circular; I.D.2.b. *Dimensions:* L 10.30, D 7.00 mm. *Material:* Unidentified organic material. *Condition:* Fragmented. *Perforation:* Unidentified; PD 1.80 mm.

No. F6.without no.36, KM 1696 (fig. 560). *Context:* No provenience; Unknown; No information. *Type:* Long cylinder/Circular; I.D.2.b. *Dimensions:* L 12.90, D 5.80 mm. *Material:* Lapis Lazuli. *Condition:* Complete. *Perforation:* Type III; PD 1.80-2.40 mm.

No. F6.without no.37, KM 1696 (fig. 561). *Context:* No provenience; Unknown; No information. *Type:* Long cylinder/Circular; I.D.2.b. *Dimensions:* L 20.00, D 8.60 mm. *Material:* Carnelian. *Condition:* Complete. *Perforation:* Type II; PD 3.00-3.20 mm.

No. F6.without no.38, KM 1696 (fig. 562). *Context:* No provenience; Unknown; No information. *Type:* Long cylinder/Circular; I.D.2.b. *Dimensions:* L 35.90, D 4.30 mm. *Material:* Carnelian. *Condition:* Complete. *Perforation:* Type II; PD 1.90 mm.

No. F6.without no.39, KM 1696 (fig. 563). *Context:* No provenience; Unknown; No information. *Type:* Long cylinder/Circular; I.D.2.b. *Dimensions:* L 19.90, D 4.50 mm. *Material:* Carnelian. *Condition:* Complete. *Perforation:* Type II; PD 2.00-2.10 mm.

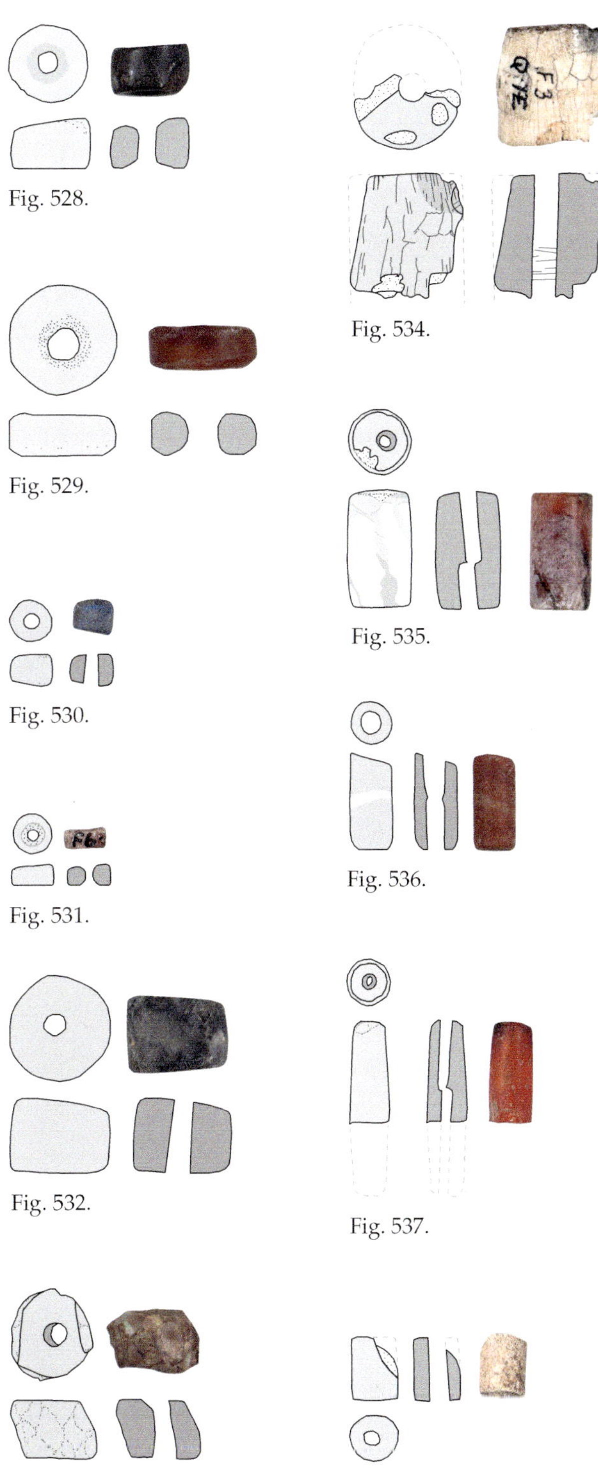

Fig. 528.

Fig. 529.

Fig. 530.

Fig. 531.

Fig. 532.

Fig. 533.

Fig. 534.

Fig. 535.

Fig. 536.

Fig. 537.

Fig. 538.

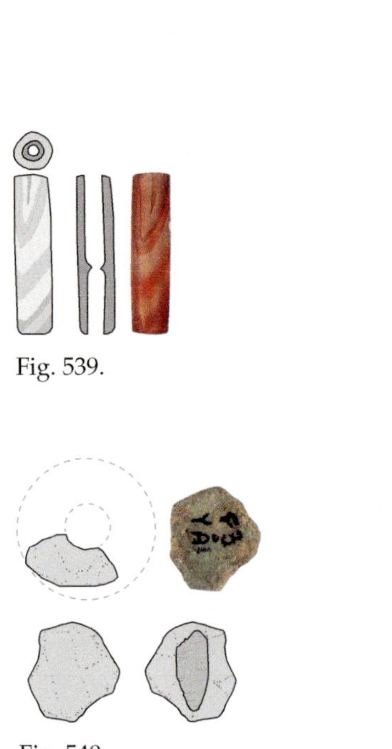

Fig. 539.

Fig. 540.

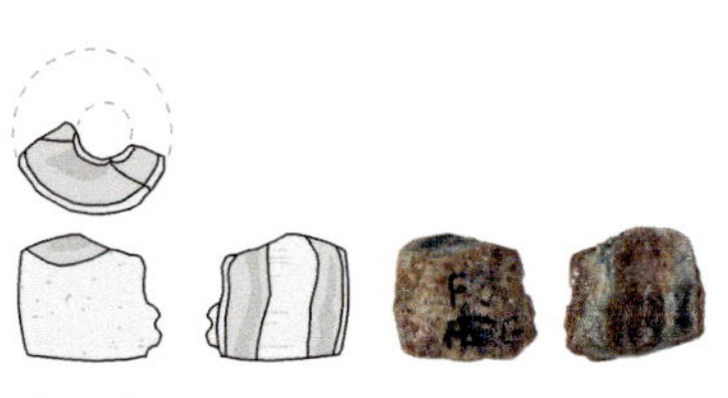

Fig. 541.

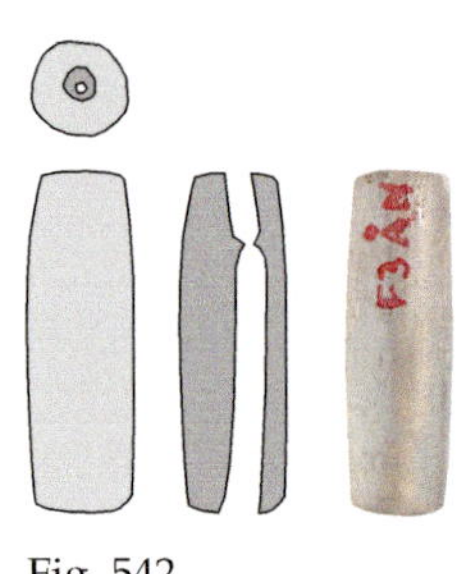

Fig. 542.

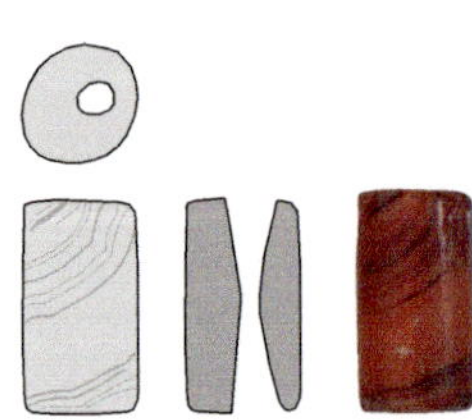

Fig. 543.

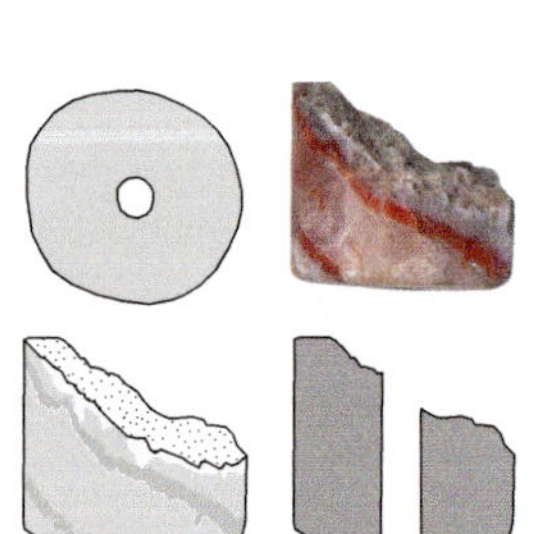

Fig. 544.

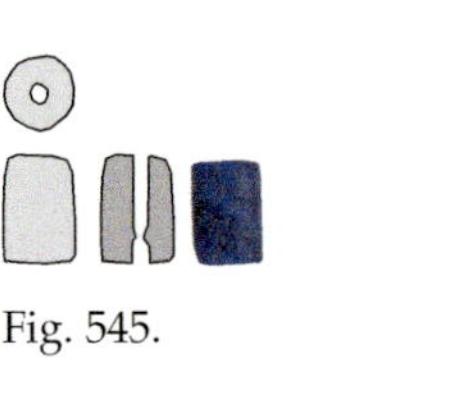

Fig. 545.

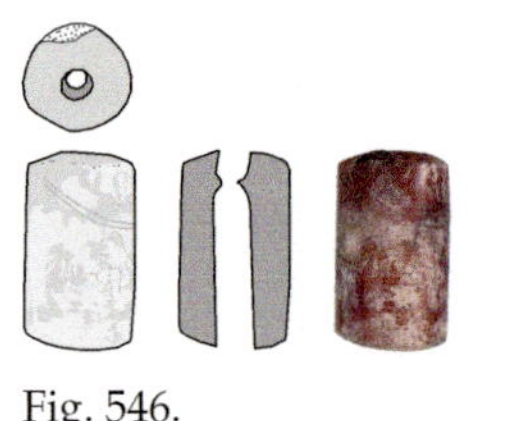

Fig. 546.

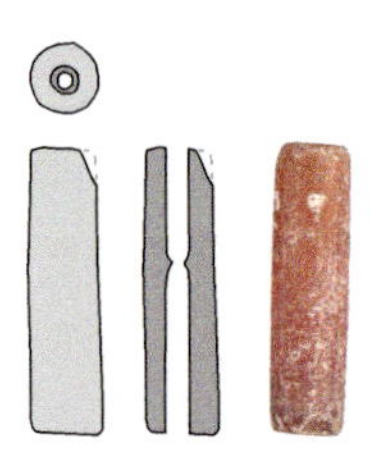

Fig. 547.

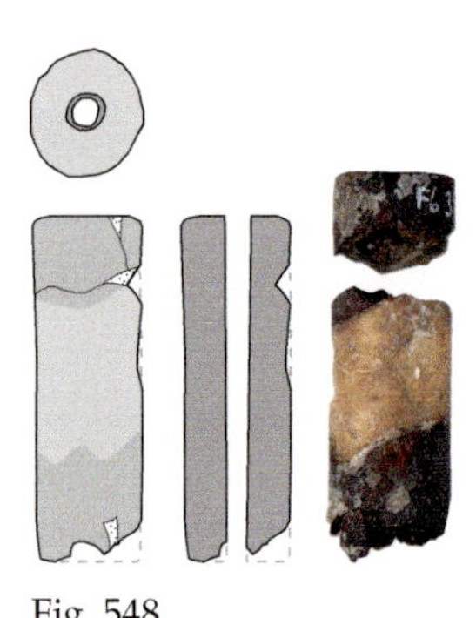

Fig. 548.

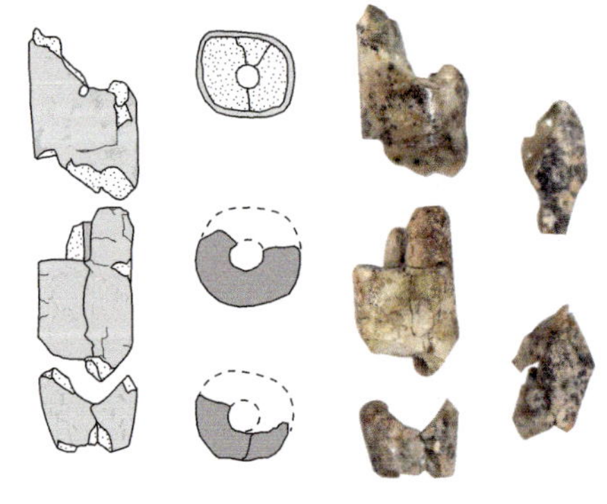

Fig. 549.

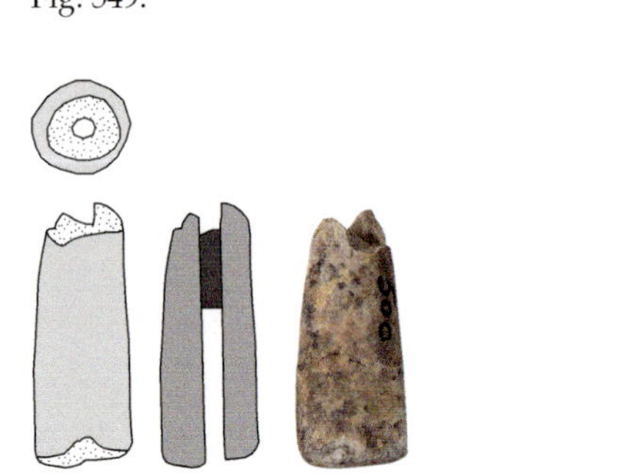

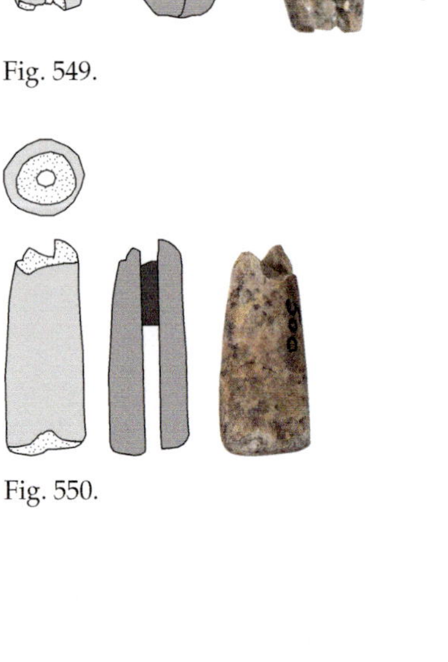

Fig. 550.

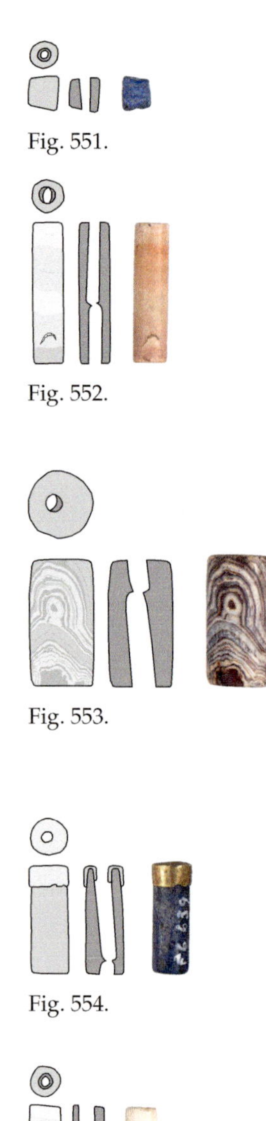

Fig. 551.

Fig. 552.

Fig. 553.

Fig. 554.

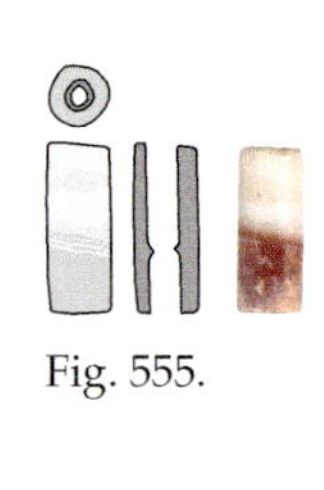

Fig. 555.

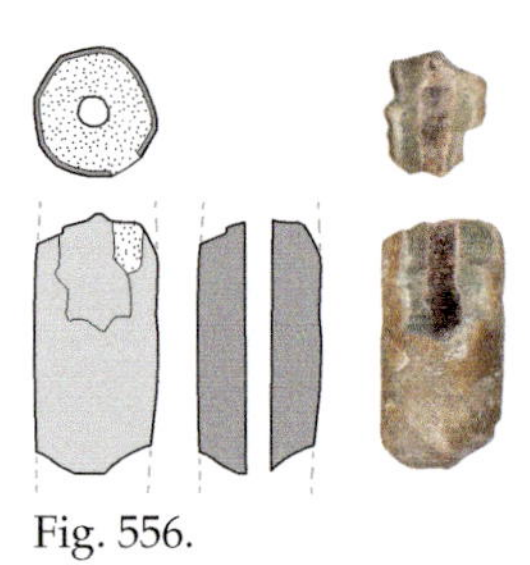

Fig. 556.

Fig. 557.

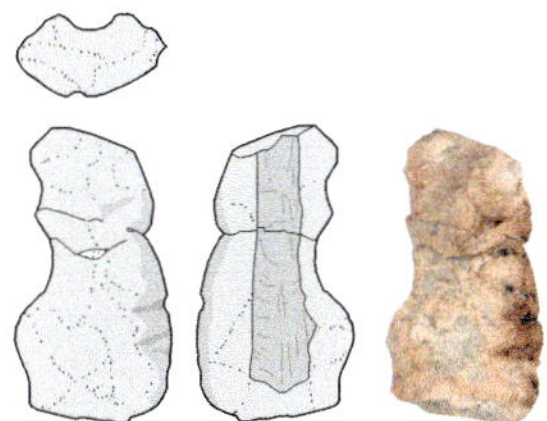

Fig. 558.

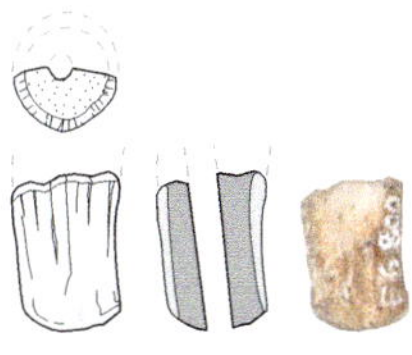

Fig. 559.

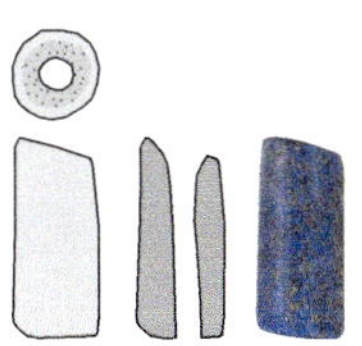

Fig. 560.

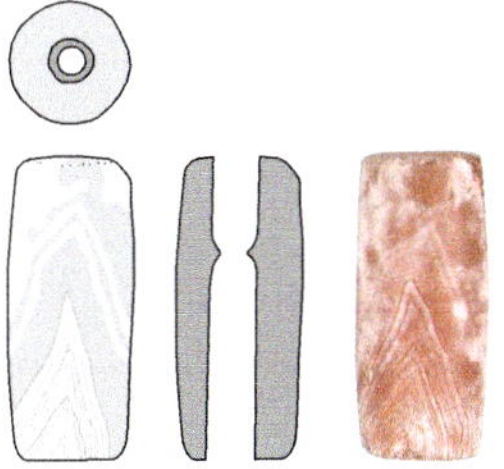

Fig. 561.

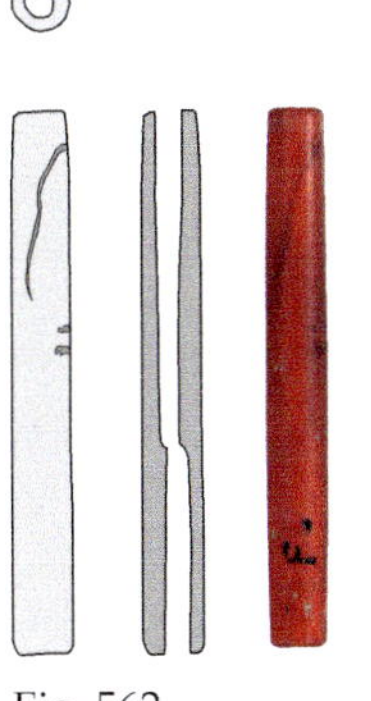

Fig. 562.

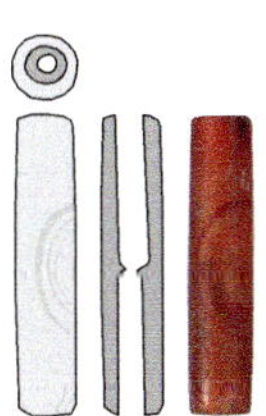

Fig. 563.

Unidentified cylinders with circular cross section (fragments) (figs. 564-566)

No. F6.362.13, KM 1561 (fig. 564). *Context:* Trench D2; 2-4A; level -0.59; 14.00-15.00N/3.50-4.00W. *Type:* Unidentified cylinder/Circular. *Dimensions:* L 7.30 (pres.), D 10.50 (pres.) mm. *Material:* Glass. *Condition:* Fragmented. *Perforation:* Unidentified; PD 2.50 mm.

No. F6.362.14, KM 1561 (no illustration). *Context:* Trench D2; 2-4A; level -0.59; 14.00-15.00N/3.50-4.00W. *Type:* Unidentified cylinder/Circular. *Dimensions:* Not preserved. *Material:* Glass. *Condition:* Fragmented. *Perforation:* Unidentified; PD 2.60 mm.

No. F6.417.11, KM 1559 (fig. 565). *Context:* Trench D2; 2-4A; Between level -0.46 and -1.08; 13.00-15.00N/1.25-4W. *Type:* Unidentified cylinder/Circular. *Dimensions:* L 8.20 (pres.), D 8.60 (est.) mm. *Material:* Glass. *Condition:* Fragmented. *Perforation:* Unidentified; PD 2.00 mm.

No. F6.458.3, KM 1722 (fig. 566). *Context:* Trench E2; 2-4A; level -0.35; 16.00-18.00N/1.50-3.00E. *Type:* Unidentified cylinder/Circular. *Dimensions:* L 12.20 (pres.), D 19.50 (est.) mm. *Material:* Glass. *Condition:* Fragmented. *Perforation:* Unidentified; PD 3.20 mm.

Fig. 564.

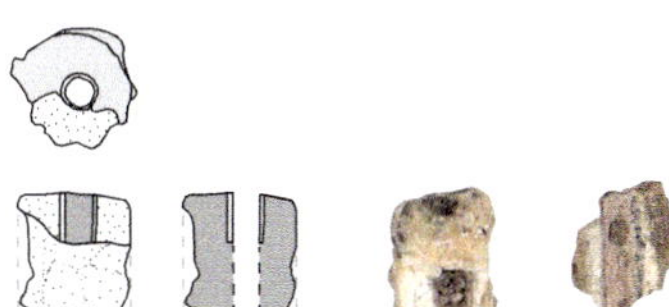

Fig. 565.

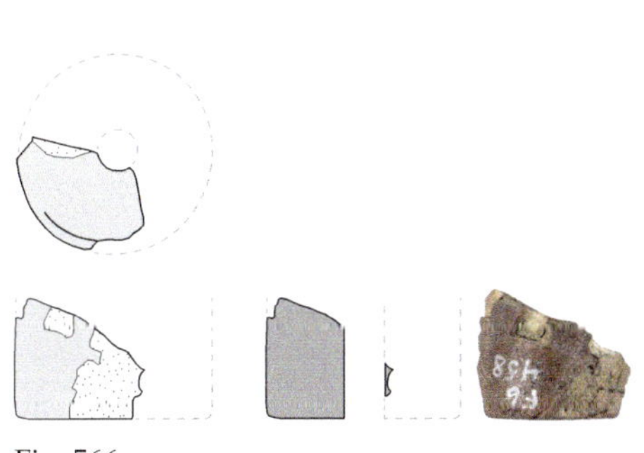

Fig. 566.

Cylinders with lenticular cross section (figs. 567-571)

IV.C.2.b. Standard cylinders with lenticular cross section (fig. 567)

No. F3.sq.1, KM 1670 (fig. 567). *Context:* Trench AB; Unknown; Found in sieve. *Type:* Standard cylinder/ Lenticular; IV.C.2.b. *Dimensions:* L 16.70, W 17.60, H 4.60 mm. *Material:* Agate. *Condition:* Complete. *Perforation:* Type III; PD 1.10-1.30 mm.

IV.D.2.b. Long cylinder with lenticular cross section (figs. 568-571)

No. F3.without no.6, KM 1696 (fig. 568). *Context:* No provenience; Unknown; No information. *Type:* Long cylinder/Lenticular; IV.D.2.b. *Dimensions:* L 16.90, W 12.50, H 6.00 mm. *Material:* Faience. *Condition:* Complete. *Perforation:* Unidentified; PD 2.10-2.80 mm.

No. F6.516, KM 1689 (fig. 569). *Context:* Trench D1; 2-4A; level -0.98; 1.50-2.00N/1.00-1.50W. *Type:* Long cylinder/Lenticular; IV.D.2.b. *Dimensions:* L 40.00, W 35.50, H 5.70 mm. *Material:* Lapis Lazuli. *Condition:* Fragmented. *Perforation:* Type II; PD 1.40-1.90 mm.

No. F6.619, KM 1696 (fig. 570). *Context:* Trench D2; 1; level -1.94; 14.50-15.00N/1.00-2.00W. *Type:* Long barrel/Lenticular; IV.D.2.b. *Dimensions:* L 18.00, W 15.00, H 5.30 mm. *Material:* Agate. *Condition:* Complete. *Perforation:* Type II; PD 1.60-1.90 mm.

No. F6.945.14, KM 1688 (fig. 571). *Context:* No provenience; Unknown; Found in sieve. *Type:* Long cylinder/Lenticular; IV.D.2.b. *Dimensions:* L 23.00, W 16.00, H 6.00 mm. *Material:* Agate. *Condition:* Complete. *Perforation:* Type II; PD 1.60-1.90 mm.

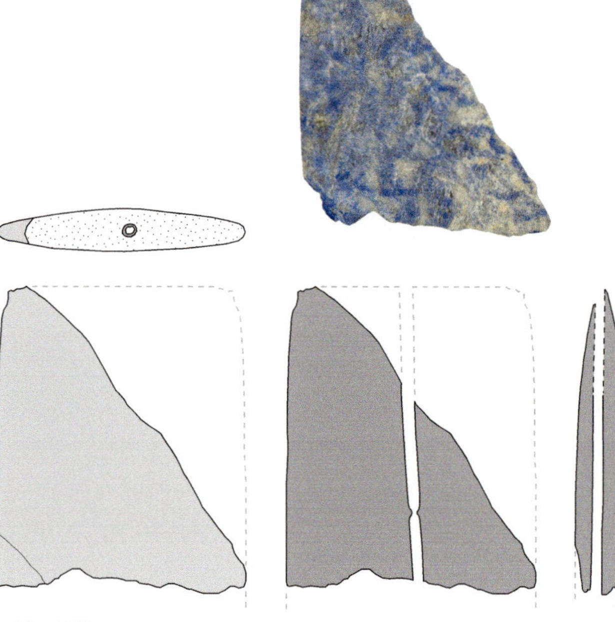

Fig. 569.

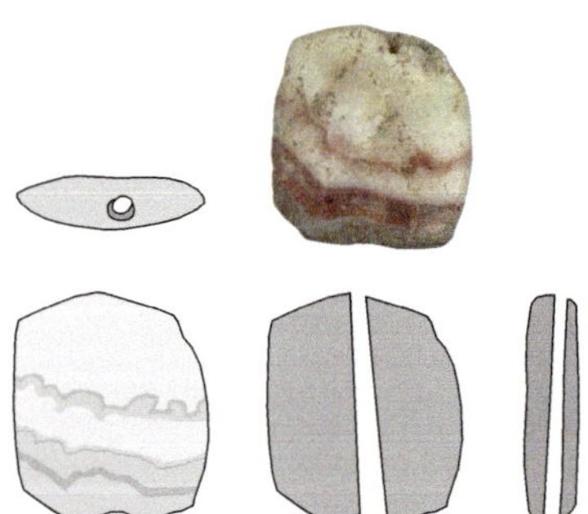

Fig. 567.

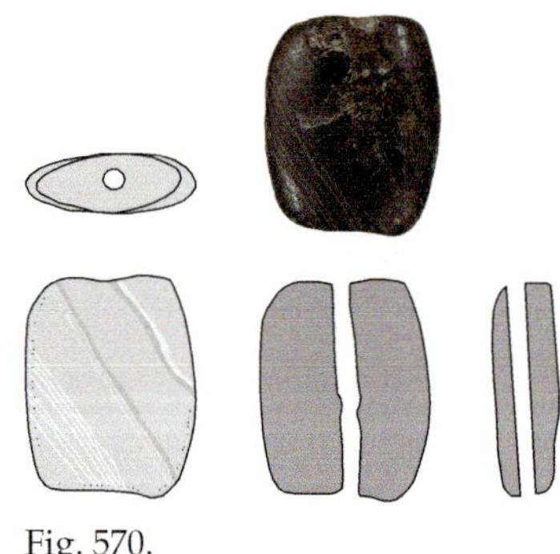

Fig. 570.

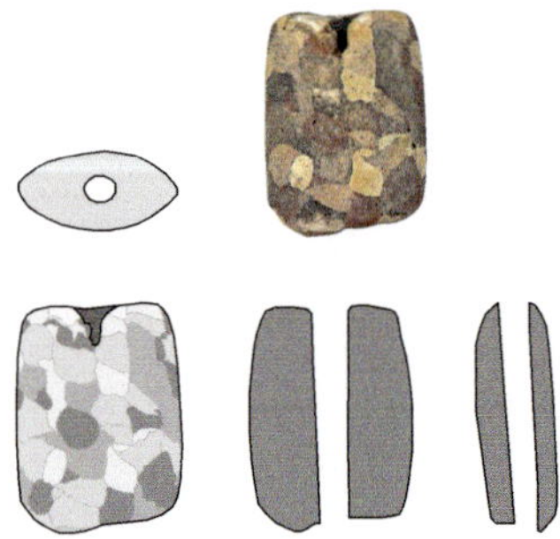

Fig. 568.

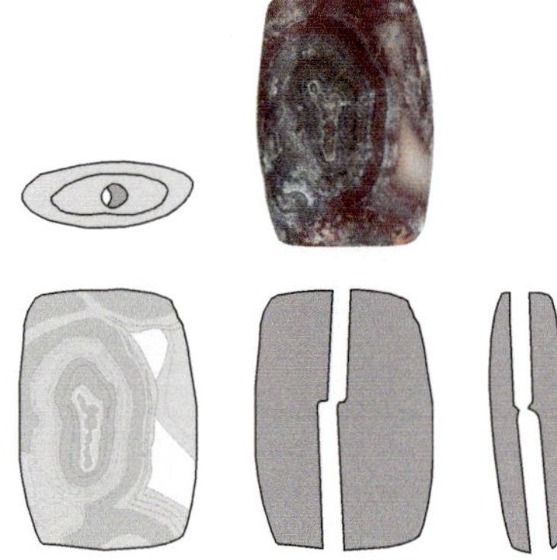

Fig. 571.

7.20. Varia (figs. 572-588)

Figurative (figs. 572-575)

No. F3.azx, KM 1676 (fig. 572). *Context:* Trench AP; 4A/4B; Found in sieve. *Type:* Varia (Eye-bead); XLVI.A.1.a. *Dimensions:* L 5.00, D 17.00-19.00 mm. *Material:* Agate. *Condition:* Complete. *Perforation:* Type II; PD 1.60-2.10 mm.

No. F6.712, KM 1688 (fig. 573). *Context:* Trench F2; Unknown; level -1.34; 19.50N/6.50W. *Type:* Varia (Eye-bead); XLVI.A.1.a. *Dimensions:* L 6.30, D 14.90 mm. *Material:* Agate. *Condition:* Complete. *Perforation:* Type II; PD 1.40-1.60 mm.

No. F3.æn.7, KM 1683 (fig. 574). *Context:* Baulk between Trench AB and AF; Unknown; Found in sieve. *Type:* Varia (vase-shape or stylized pomegranate); XXIX.A.15. *Dimensions:* L 7.10, D 5.80, ED 4.00-4.10 mm. *Material:* Turquoise. *Condition:* Complete. *Perforation:* Unidentified; PD 2.00 mm.

No. F3.yå.2, KM 1704 (fig. 575). *Context:* Trench AF; Unknown; Found in sieve. *Type:* Varia (unidentified animal-shape); XXXII-XXXV. *Dimensions:* L 12.50, W 6.00, H 6.00 mm. *Material:* Agate. *Condition:* Fragmented. *Perforation:* Type III; PD 1.50 mm.

Geometric (figs. 576-582)

No. F6.417.10, KM 1689 (fig. 576). *Context:* Trench D2; 2-4A; Between level -0.46 and -1.08; 13.00-15.00N/1.20-4.00W. *Type:* Varia; Short truncated bicone/Rectangular; X.B.2.f. *Dimensions:* L 4.30, W 7.90, H 2.90 mm. *Material:* Carnelian. *Condition:* Complete. *Perforation:* Type II; PD 0.90 mm.

No. F3.aiå, KM 1683 (fig. 577). *Context:* Trench K; 3A/4A; Between level 9.40 and 7.40; No information. *Type:* Varia; Short truncated bicone/Hexagonal; XIII.B.2.f. *Dimensions:* L 9.00, D 12.00 mm. *Material:* Carnelian. *Condition:* Complete. *Perforation:* Type III; PD 2.10-3.00 mm.

No. F6.362.12, KM 1677 (fig. 578). *Context:* Trench D2; 2-4A; level -0.59; 14.00-15.00N/3.50-4.00W. *Type:* Varia (collared melon bead); XXIII.A.3.a. *Dimensions:* L 5.00, D 5.00 mm. *Material:* Gold. *Condition:* Fragmented. *Perforation:* Unidentified; PD Unknown.

No. F6.947, KM 1556 (fig. 579). *Context:* No provenience; Unknown; Found in sieve. *Type:* Varia (collared ellipsoid); I.D.1.a. *Dimensions:* L 24.00, D 19.00. *Material:* Clay. *Condition:* Fragmented. *Perforation:* Unidentified; PD Unknown mm.

No. F3.aug, KM 1683 (fig. 580). *Context:* No provenience; Unknown; Found in sieve. *Type:* Varia (Long barrel with elliptical cross section decorated with incised horizontal and vertical lines crisscrossing); II.D.1.b. *Dimensions:* L 16.50, D 11.00 mm. *Material:* Clay. *Condition:* Complete. *Perforation:* Unidentified; PD 1.60-2.60 mm.

No. F6.without no.54, KM 1687 (fig. 581). *Context:* No provenience; Unknown; No information. *Type:* Varia (s-shape with rectangular cross section). *Dimensions:* L 13.00, W 5.80-6.00, H 5.00 mm. *Material:* Carnelian. *Condition:* Complete. *Perforation:* Type II; PD 1.50-2.00 mm.

No. F6.without no.55, KM 1687 (fig. 582). *Context:* No provenience; Unknown; No information. *Type:* Varia (Cornerless cube); XIX.1.a. *Dimensions:* L 8.80, W 7.90, H 8.20, ED 7.00 mm. *Material:* Carnelian. *Condition:* Complete. *Perforation:* Type II; PD 1.90-2.10 mm.

Pendants (figs. 583-588)

No. F3.262, KM 1683 (fig. 583). *Context:* Trench RM; Unknown; Found in sieve. *Type:* Varia ("plate" pendant). *Dimensions:* L 24.00, W 13.00, H 2.00 mm. *Material:* Shell (spiny oyster shell). *Condition:* Complete. *Perforation:* Type III; PD 1.90-2.70 mm.

No. F3.rn, KM 1683 (fig. 584). *Context:* Trench Y; 4B; level 7.06; 64.70N/0.10E. *Type:* Varia (drop pendant); XXII.B.2.b. *Dimensions:* L 18.50, W 8.00, H 8.30 mm. *Material:* Carnelian. *Condition:* Complete. *Perforation:* Type II; PD 1.50-2.70 mm.

No. F3.bae.1, KM 1683 (fig. 585). *Context:* Baulk between Trench AP and AQ; 4A/4B; Found in sieve. *Type:* Varia (drop pendant); XXII.B.2.b. *Dimensions:* L 13.30, W 9.50, H 5.90 mm. *Material:* Jasper. *Condition:* Complete. *Perforation:* Type II; PD 3.50-4.00 mm.

No. F3.asl, KM 1683 (fig. 586). *Context:* No provenience; Unknown; Found in sieve.*Type:* Varia (drop pendant); XXII.B.2.b. *Dimensions:* L 19.20, D 7.90 mm. *Material:* Carnelian. *Condition:* Complete. *Perforation:* Type IV; PD 1.10 mm.

No. F3.pr, KM 1683 (fig. 587). *Context:* Trench X; 3B/4B; Between level 8.85 and 8.66; Found in sieve. *Type:* Varia (cone pendant); XXII.B.5.b. *Dimensions:* L 17.30, W 16.60, H 16.10 mm. *Material:* Agate. *Condition:* Complete. *Perforation:* Type II; PD 1.80-2.00 mm.

No. F6.934, KM 1689 (fig. 588). *Context:* Trench F2; Unknown; 3.00-14.00N/8.00-9.00W. *Type:* Varia (cone pendant); XXII.B.5.b. *Dimensions:* L 17.60, W 14.70, H 13.00 mm. *Material:* Agate. *Condition:* Complete. *Perforation:* Unidentified. PD 0.80-1.40 mm.

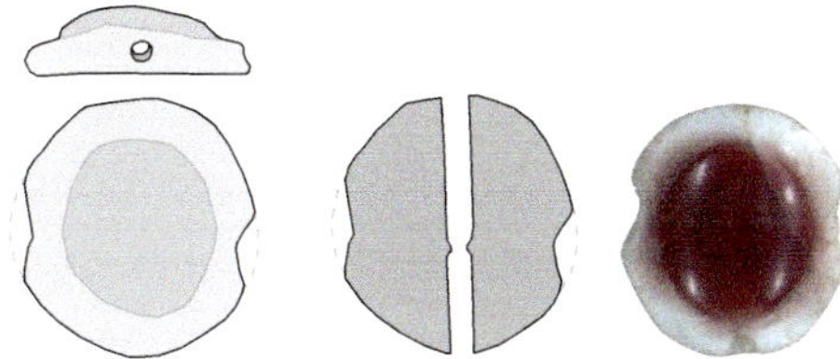

Fig. 572.

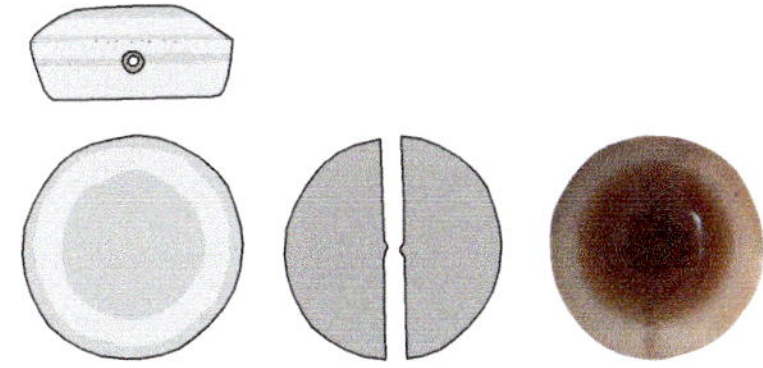

Fig. 573.

Fig. 574.

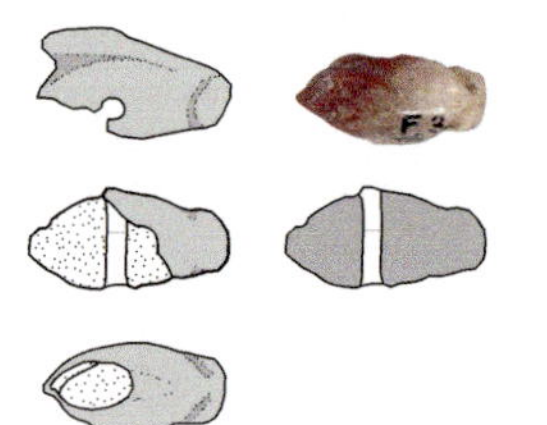

Fig. 575.

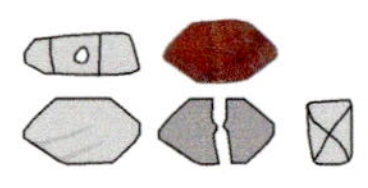
Fig. 576.

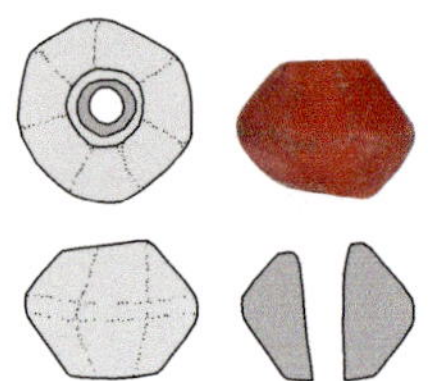
Fig. 577.

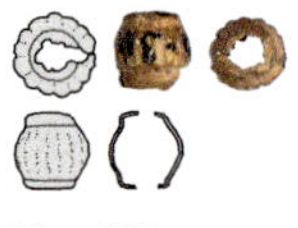
Fig. 578.

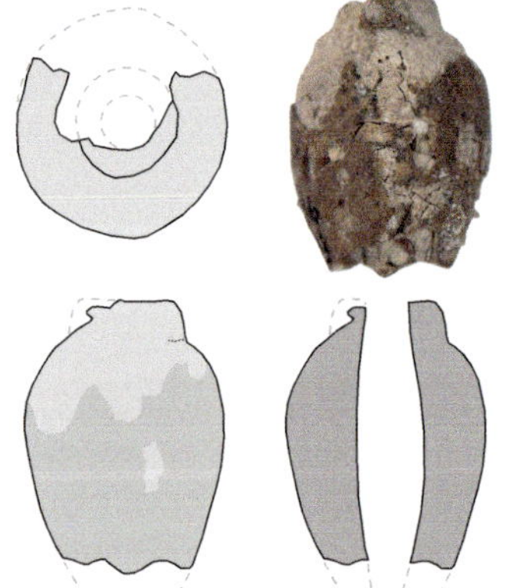
Fig. 579.

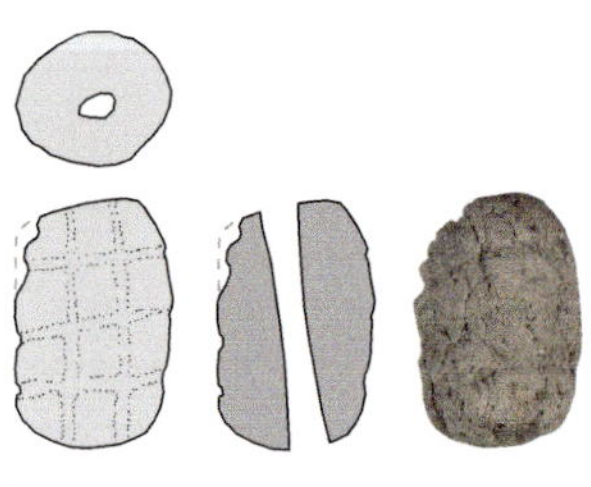
Fig. 580.

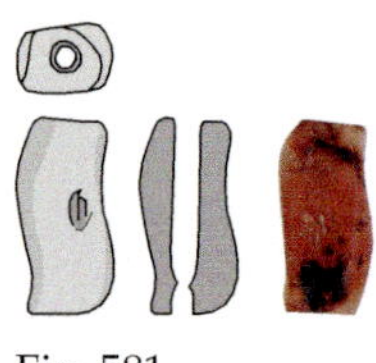
Fig. 581.

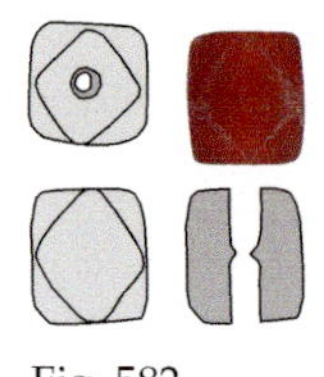
Fig. 582.

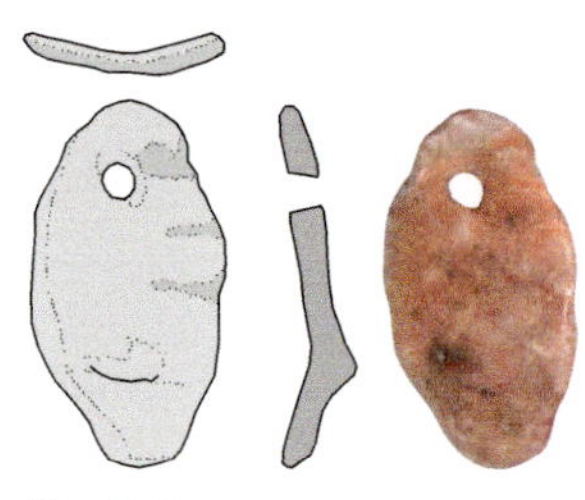
Fig. 583.

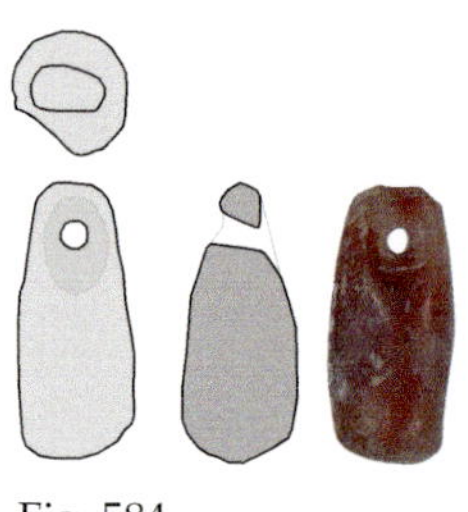
Fig. 584.

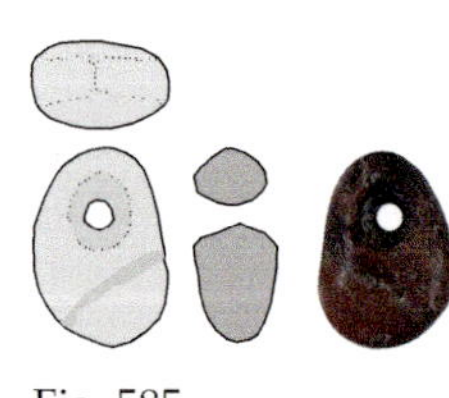
Fig. 585.

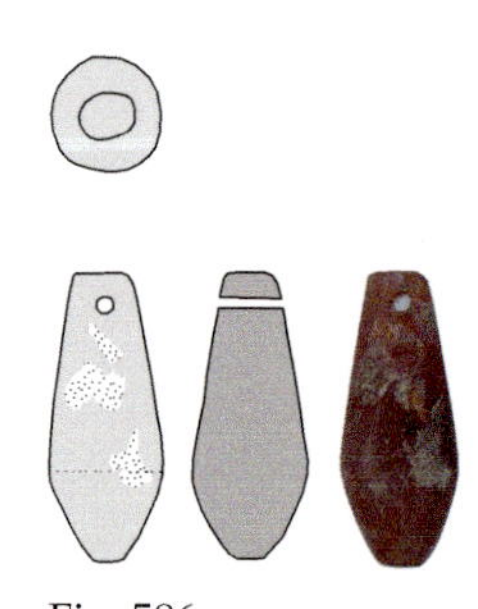
Fig. 586.

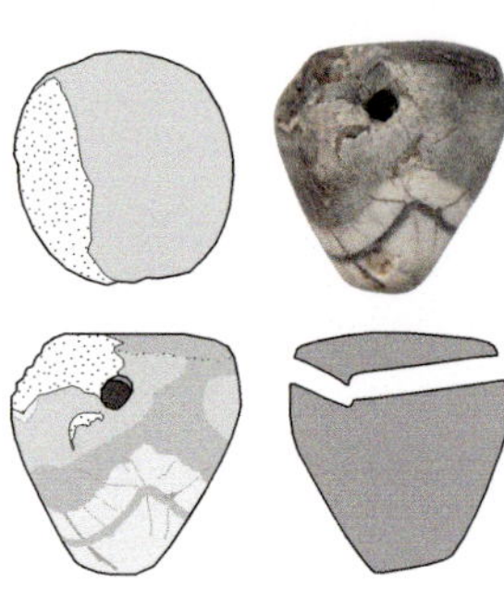
Fig. 587.

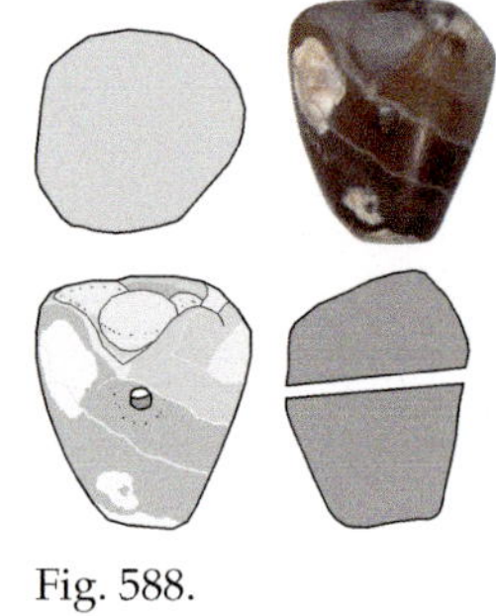
Fig. 588.

Notes

1. A regular bead is a bead of a relatively simple geometric shape, which can be approximately determined by a transverse and longitudinal section (Beck 1928 p. 4).
2. Encompasses Woolley's type 12 (ovoid) and type 13 (ball-shaped) (Woolley 1934 p. 368).
3. Nine fragmentary beads have been excluded.
4. The average measurements are c. 7.00x9.00 mm (LxD).
5. Incised beads include a long barrel with circular cross section (fig. 505) and a long barrel with hexagonal cross section (fig. 441).
6. Barrels with circular cross section may be equated with Woolley's "date-shape" (Type 6) (Woolley 1934 p. 375, fig. 70.6).
7. Thirty-two fragmentary beads have been excluded.
8. The average measurements are 11.90x7.50 mm (LxD).
9. Pulak (2008 p. 327) refers to shell rings worn as belts in burials at Tell Imlihiye (grave 1), Kish and Ur. In the Dilmun sphere, shell rings are also found in settlement contexts at Al-Khidr (Benediková 2010 p. 115, fig. 107c-f), at the Saar settlement (Killick and Moon 2005 p. 180, fig. 5.7s), at Qala'at al-Bahrain (Højlund & Andersen 1994 p. 413-414, figs. 2064, 2067 and 2068) and in grave contexts in Bahrain (Ibrahim 1982 pl. 54:9. Srivastava 1991 p. 29-30, pl. XL).
10. The average measurements are c. 18.20x9.90 mm (LxW).
11. This bead form is best correlated with "a flattened date-shape" (Type 7) in Woolley's terminology (Woolley 1934 p. 366-367).
12. Six fragmentary beads have been excluded.
13. The average measurements are 19.50 and 13.80 mm (LxW).
14. The beads can also be found in the online collections of University of Pennsylvania Museum of Archaeology and Anthropology under their respective catalogue number (no. 30-12-568). Additional parallels come from Ur graves P.G. 1932/51 and T.W., PG 38 (nos. 32-40-229 and 30-12-602), where the former is dated to the Akkadian period (c. 2350-2150 BC). References to online collections will in the following be abbreviated as PM no. (Pennsylvania Museum), LM no. (Louvre Museum), BM no. (British Museum) and MM no. (Metropolitan Museum).
15. LM no. SB 24038.
16. PM no. 32-40-227.
17. The average measurements are 20.00 and 24.30 mm (LxW).
18. One fragmentary bead has been excluded.
19. The average measurements are c. 24.55 and 15.85 mm (LxW).
20. One fragmented bead has been excluded.
21. The average measurements are 22.45 and 14.90 mm (LxW).
22. The average measurements are 20.40 mm and 13.50 mm (LxW).
23. One fragmentary bead has been excluded.
24. The average measurements are 19.30 mm and 13.60 mm (LxW).
25. The average measurements are c. 7.25x13.35 mm (LxD).
26. Comparable to Woolley's type 20 (rhomboid) (Woolley 1934 p. 368 and fig. 77).
27. The average measurements are c. 14.6x15.6 mm (LxW).
28. The average measurements are c. 15x8.5 mm (LxD).
29. Two fragmentary beads have been excluded.
30. The average measurements are 8.20x6.25 mm (LxD).
31. Beck's cylinders with circular cross section (I.A.2.b.–I.D.2.b.) cover Woolley's type 4 (cylindrical) and type 5 (tubular) (Woolley 1934 p. 367).
32. Fourteen fragmentary beads have been excluded.
33. The average measurements are c. 14.00x7.20 mm (LxD).
34. Ur: BM no. 122435 (long cylinder beads, dated to Akkadian or Ur III contexts, c. 2350-2000 BC), BM no. 122448 (short cylinders dated to the Ur III period, c. 2100-2000 BC), BM no. 123158 (short cylinders dated c. 2000-1750 BC). Susa: LM no. SB 23975.
35. Woolley's type 3 (biconvex) (Woolley 1934 p. 367).
36. One fragmentary bead has been excluded.
37. Woolley's type 19 (diamond-shaped) (Woolley 1934 p. 368, fig. 76).
38. The Al-Sabiyah tumuli date between the Ubaid and the end of the Bronze Age and the *"argument is strongly in favor of an Early and Middle Bronze date"* (ca. 3000-1500 BC) (Rutkowski 2015 p. 539-540).
39. Susa: LM no. SB 24038.
40. Susa: LM no. SB 23963.
41. See for instance BM nos. 116774, 120586, 121492 and PM nos. 32-40-236, 35-1-77, 30-12-580.
42. LM no. SB 21853.
43. MM no. 47.1a-h.
44. Beads from the 2008-2012 excavations at Tell F6 do show import of organic materials, such as ostrich eggshell beads and a Conus Ebraeus shell made into a bead (Andersson 2016 p. 182).
45. According to the Mohs hardness scale, hard stone measures 7-10, medium-hard stone 3-6 and soft stone 1-2. The hardness of chalcedony is 6.5 (Bishop et al. 2005 p. 132). The term cryptocrystalline is often used interchangeably with the term microcrystalline (cf. Moorey 1994 p. 93).
46. The find of red ridged Dilmun pottery at Tul e-Peytul (Liyan) suggests that Liyan was an important gateway between the Gulf and the Fars highlands for Dilmun trade (Pezard 1914. Potts 2009 p. 34. Højlund & Andersen 1994 p. 98-99, note 9).
47. A few chlorite beads have been found at Al-Khidr, but they differ from the chlorite beads found at Tell F3 and Tell F6, by being spherical in form, well-made and finely polished (Benediková 2010 p. 103, fig. 90.a).

48. The soft stone pendants (Hilton in prep.) exhibit very different shapes and dimensions than the bead pendants treated in this volume.

49. At Saar and Al-Khidr contexts were sieved, thus the recovery of the beads would reflect their original numbers and distribution (Killick & Moon 2005, p. 6. Benediková et al. 2010 p. 21). Contexts were not systematically sieved at Qala'at al-Bahrain, nor the Barbar Temples and therefore beads may be underrepresented at these sites (pers. comm. Højlund 2022).

50. Maroni: BM no. 1898,1201.52. Enkomi: BM no. 1897,0401.605; 1897,0401.692 and 1897,0401.738.3. Ialysus: BM no. 1872,0315.7 and 1872,0315.8. Ugarit: LM no. AO 24009 (hoard of jewellery found in a Mycenaean vessel), LM no. AO 30799 (c. 1200-1150 BC), LM no. AO 17401. Minet el Beida: LM no. AO 14846 (c. 1550-1150 BC). Emar: LM no. AO 27835 (c. 1200-1150 BC). Mari: LM no. AO 30030 (tomb 208), LM no. AO 19038 (tomb 119) (c. 1392-911 BC).

51. Evidence for stone bead manufacture has been found at large urban centres in Mesopotamia, such as Ur, Ebla, Nippur, Larsa, Abu Salabikh, Babylon, Mari, Jebel Aruda, Uruk and Tell al-Ubaid (Moorey 1994 p. 106-109). Carnelian beads were manufactured at Larsa (Moorey 1994 p. 107), while lapis lazuli beads were produced at sites like Ebla, Jebel Aruda, Larsa, Ur and likely also at Mari during the 2nd millennium (Casanova 2008 p. 68).

Bibliography

Andersen, H.H. & Højlund, F. 2003: *The Barbar Temples*, vols. 1-2. Aarhus. JASP 48.

Andersson, A. 2014: Beads, Pendants and Other Ornaments from the Late 3rd-2nd Millennium BC Dilmun Occupation at Failaka, Kuwait. In: *Beyond Ornamentation. Jewelry as an Aspect of Material Culture in the Ancient Near East.* (eds.) A. Golani and Z. Wygnanska. Polish Archaeology in the Mediterranean XXIII/2. Special studies, pp. 209-224.

Andersson, A. 2016: Beads. In: *Tell F6 on Failaka Island. Kuwaiti-Danish Excavations 2008-2012* (eds.) Højlund, F. & Abu-Laban, A. JASP 92. Moesgaard Museum, Denmark & The National Council for Culture, Arts and Letters, Kuwait. pp. 176-198.

Andersson, A. 2021: Beads. In: *Tell F3 on Failaka Island. Kuwaiti-Danish Excavations 2012-2017.* (eds.) Højlund, F. & Hilton, A. JASP 116. Moesgaard Museum, Denmark & The National Council for Culture, Arts and Letters, Kuwait.

Arnaud, D., Calvet, Y., Huot J.L. 1979: Ilšu-Ibnišu, orfèvre de l'E.Babbar de Larsa. La jarre L.76.77 et son contenu. In: *Syria.* Vol. 56, number 1-2. pp. 1-64.

Aruz, J. 2008: Art and Interconnections in the Third Millennium. In: *Art of the First Cities: The Third Millennium B.C. From The Mediterranean to the Indus.* The Metropolitan Museum of Art, New York. Yale University Press, New Haven and London, pp. 239-250.

Aston, B. G., Harrell, J. A. and Shaw, I. 2000: Stone. In: (ed.) Nicholson, P. T. and Shaw, I. *Ancient Egyptian Materials and Technology*, pp. 5-77.

Beck, H.C. 1928: *The Classification and Nomenclature of Beads and Pendants.* In: *Archaeologia. The Society of Antiquaries of London*, Vol. 77 pp. 1-76.

Beech, M.J. 2010: Mermaids of The Arabian Gulf: Archaeological Evidence for the Exploitation of Dugongs from Prehistory to the Present. In: *Liwa (Journal of the National Center for Documentation & Research)*, Vol. 2, No. 3, pp. 3-18.

Benediková, L. (ed.) 2010: *Al-Khidr 2004-2009, Primary Scientific Report on the Activities of the Kuwait-Slovak Archaeological Mission.* National Council for Culture, Arts & Letters, Kuwait City. Archeologicky ústav Slovenska akadémie vied, Nitra.

Barthélemy de Saizieu, B. 2000: Stone beads from the Nausharo site (Pakistani Baluchistan), 2800-2000 BC. In: *CORNALINE DE L'INDE. Des pratiques techniques de Cambay aux techno-systèmes de l'Indus.* Éditions de la Maison des sciences de l'homme. Paris.

Bibby, G. 1969: *Looking for Dilmun.* Alfred A. Knopf, Inc.

Bishop, A.C., Woolley, A.R. and Hamilton, W. R. 2005: *Guide to Minerals, Rocks and Fossils.* Firefly Ltd.

Bisht, R.S. 2015: *Excavations at Dholavira (1989-90 to 2004-2005).*

Brunet, O. 2009: Bronze and Iron Age Carnelian Bead Production in the UAE and Armenia: New Perspectives. In: *Proceedings of Seminar of Arabian Studies, vol.* 39 pp. 57-68.

Çakırlar, C. & Ikram, S. 2016: 'When Elephants Battle, the Grass Suffers.' Power, ivory and the Syrian elephant. In: *Levant*, vol. 48, no. 2, pp. 167-183.

Calvet, Y. & Pic, M. 1986: Un Nouveau Bâtiment de l›Âge du Bronze sur le Tell F 6. In: *Failaka. Fouilles françaises 1984-1985. Sous la direction d'Yves Calvet et Jean-François Salles*, pp. 66-71.

Campbell Thompson, R. 1936: *A Dictionary of Assyrian Chemistry and Geology.* Oxford, Clarendon Press.

Campbell, S., Moon, J., Killick, R., Calderbank, D., Robson, E., Shepperson, M. and Slater, F. 2017: Tell Khaiber: An Administrative Centre of the Sealand Period. In: *Iraq*, vol. 79, pp. 21-46.

Carter, R.A. 2003: Tracing Bronze Age Trade in the Arabian Gulf: Evidence for Way-stations of the Merchants of Dilmun between Bahrain and the Northern Emirates. In: *Proceedings of the First International Conference on the Archaeology of the U.A.E.* pp. 124-131.

Carter, R.A. 2012: *Sea of Pearls: Seven Thousand Years of the Industry that Shaped the Gulf.* Arabian Publishing.

Casanova, M. 2008: Lapis Lazuli. In: (eds.) Aruz, J.; Benzel, K. and Evans, J. M. *Beyond Babylon. Art, Trade and Diplomacy in the 2nd Millennium BC.* The Metropolitan Museum of Art. Yale University Press, New Haven and London. pp. 68-69.

Ciarla, R. 1990: Fragments of stone vessels as a base material. Two case studies: Failaka and Shahr-i Sokhta. In (eds.) Taddei, M. and Callieri, P. *South Asian Archaeology* 1987. Proceedings of the Ninth International Conference of the Association of South Asian Archaeologists in Western-Europe, held in the Fondazione Giorgio Cini, Island of San Giorgio Maggiore, Venice. pp. 475-491.

Chakrabarti, D. K. & Moghadam, P. 1977: Some Unpublished beads from Iran. In: *Iran*, Vol. 15, pp. 166-168.

Charpentier, V., Brunet, O., Mery, S., Velde, C. 2017: Carnelian, agate, and other types of chalcedony: the prehistory of Jebel al-Ma'taradh and its semi-precious stones, Emirate of Ra's al-Khaimah. In: *Arabian Archaeology and Epigraphy*, vol. 28 pp. 175-189.

Chevalier, J., Inizan M.L., Tixier J. 1982: Une Technique de perforation par percussion de perles en cornaline (Larsa, Iraq). In: *Paléorient*, vol. 8, no. 2. pp. 55-65.

Clayden, T. 2009: Eye-Stones. In: *Zeitschrift für Orient-Archäologie* vol. 2, pp. 36-86.

Crawford, H. 2000. Bahrain: Warehouse of the Gulf. In: *Traces of Paradise. The Archaeology of Bahrain 2500 BC-300 AD.* The Bahrain National Museum.

David-Cuny, H. & Neyme, D. 2016. *Failaka Seals Catalogue, volume 2. Tell F6 "The Palace".* National Council for Culture, Arts and Letters, State of Kuwait.

De Waele, A. & Haerinck, E. 2006: Etched Carnelian Beads from the Northeast and Southeast Arabia. *Arabian Archaeology and Epigraphy* vol. 17:1, pp. 31-40.

Francis, P. Jr. 1989: Beads of the Early Islamic Period. In: *BEADS: Journal of the Society of Bead Researchers*, Vol. 1, pp. 21-40.

Francis, P. Jr. 2002: *Asia's Maritime Bead Trade: 300 B.C. to the Present.* University of Hawai'i Press.

Frenez, D. 2018: The Indus Civilization Trade with the Oman Peninsula. In: Cleuziou, S. & Tosi, M. (eds.) *In the Shadow of the Ancestors. The Prehistoric Foundations of the Early Arabian Civilization in Oman.* Ministry of Heritage and Culture Sultanate of Oman. pp. 385-396.

Frenez, D. 2021: A non-Egyptian «Egyptian» stone vessel from Ras Al-Jinz RJ-2, Sultanate of Oman: Critical review of an entrenched hypothesis. In: *Academia Letters, Article 445.* pp. 1-12.

Frenez, D., Genchi, F., David-Cuny, H. & Al-Bakri, S. 2021: The Early Iron Age collective tomb LCG-1 at Dibbā al-Bayah, Oman: long-distance exchange and cross-cultural interaction. In: *Antiquity*, Vol. 95 (379), pp. 104-124.

Frifelt, K. 1991: *The Island of Umm an-Nar vol. 1. Third Millennium Graves*. JASP 26:1.

Gensheimer, T.R. 1984: The Role of shell in Mesopotamia: Evidence for Trade Exchange with Oman and the Indus Valley". In: *Paléorient*, 1984, vol. 10, no.1. pp. 65-73.

Glob, P.V. 1968: *Al-Bahrain. De danske ekspeditioner til oldtidens Dilmun*. Gyldendal.

Gwinnett, J.A. and Gorelick, L. 1977: The Change from Stone Drills to Copper Drills in Mesopotamia. An Experimental Perspective. In: *Expedition*, vol. 29, no. 3. pp. 15-24.

Gwinnett, J.A. and Gorelick, L. 1978: Ancient Lapidary. A Study using Scanning Electron Microscopy and Functional Analysis. In: *Expedition*, vol. 22, no. 1. pp. 17-32.

Gwinnett, J.A. and Gorelick, L. 1981: Bead making in Iran in the Early Bronze Age. Derived by Scanning Electron Microscopy. In: *Expedition*, vol. 24, no. 1. pp. 10-23.

Gwinnett, J.A. and Gorelick, L. 1998: A Brief History of Drills and Drilling. In: *BEADS: Journal of the Society of Bead Researchers*, vol. 10. pp. 49-56.

Hausleiter, A. 2011. Ancient Tayma': An Oasis at the Interface Between Cultures. New Research at a Key Location on the Caravan Road. In: (eds.) Franke, U., Gierlichs, J., Vassilopoulou, S. and Wagner, L. *Roads of Arabia. The Archaeological Treasures of Saudi Arabia*. Museum of Islamic Art-National Museums of Berlin. Ernst Wasmuth Verlag Tübingen. Berlin.

Hatton, G.D., Shortland, A.J., and Tite, M.S. 2008: The production technology of Egyptian blue and green frits from second millennium BC Egypt and Mesopotamia. In: *Journal of Archaeological Science*, vol. 35, pp. 1591-1604.

Hermann, G. 1968: Lapis Lazuli. The Early Phases of its Trade. In: *Iraq*, Vol. 30, No. 1, pp. 21-57.

Hilton, A. 2014: *The Stone Vessels. Failaka/Dilmun*. The Second Millennium Settlements, vol. 4. JASP 17:4. Aarhus University Press and the National Council for Culture, Arts and Letters, Kuwait.

Hilton, A. 2021: Hard Stones. In: *Tell F3 on Failaka Island. Kuwaiti-Danish Excavations 2012-2017*. JASP 116. Moesgaard Museum, Denmark & The National Council for Culture, Arts and Letters, Kuwait. pp. 123-129.

Hilton, A. in prep. Soft stone amulets. In: Højlund, F. in prep. *Copper, Cuneiform Inscriptions and Other Finds*. Failaka/ Dilmun. The Second Millennium Settlements vol. 6. JASP 17:6.

Hilton, A., Andersson, A. & Højlund, F. 2021. Trenches BD and BC, dating and finds. In: (eds.) Hilton, A. & Højlund, F. *Tell F3 on Failaka Island. Kuwaiti-Danish Excavations 2012-2017*. JASP 116. Moesgaard Museum, Denmark & The National Council for Culture, Arts and Letters, Kuwait. pp. 11-24.

Howard-Carter, T. 1984: *The Johns Hopkins University Expedition to Failaka Island 1973-1974*. Unpublished report on file in the Kuwait National Museum.

Howard-Carter, T. 1986: Eyestones and Pearls. In: (eds.) Al-Khalifa, S.H.A. & Rice, M. *Bahrain Through the Ages: The Archaeology*. Routledge. Taylor and Francis Group. London and New York. pp. 305-310.

Højlund, F. 1987: *The Bronze Age Pottery*. Failaka/Dilmun. The Second Millennium Settlements 2. JASP 17:2.

Højlund, F. 2008: *The Danish Archaeological Expedition to Kuwait 1958-1963. A glimpse into the archives of Moesgård Museum*. Moesgård Museum & The Kuwait National Council for Culture, Arts and Letters (Arabic version 2009).

Højlund, F. in prep. *Copper, Cuneiform Inscriptions and Other Finds*. Failaka/Dilmun. The Second Millennium Settlements vol. 6. JASP 17:6.

Højlund, F. & Abu-Laban, A. 2016: *Tell F6 on Failaka Island: Kuwaiti-Danish Excavations 2008-2012*. JASP 92. Moesgaard Museum, Denmark & The National Council for Culture, Arts and Letters, Kuwait.

Højlund, F. & Andersen, H.H. 1994: *Qala'at al-Bahrain vol. 1. The Northern City Wall and the Islamic Fortress*. JASP 30:1.

Højlund, F. & Hilton, A. 2021: *Tell F3 on Failaka Island. Kuwaiti-Danish Excavations 2012-2017*. JASP 116. Moesgaard Museum, Denmark & The National Council for Culture, Arts and Letters, Kuwait.

Ibrahim, M. 1982: *Excavations of the Arab Expedition at Sar el-Jisr, Bahrain*. State of Bahrain, Ministry of Information.

Ingram, S. R. 2005: Faience and Glass beads from the Late Bronze Age Shipwreck at Ulu Burun, Master's Thesis, Texas A&M University.

Inizian, M.L. 2000: Importation de cornalines et agates de l'Indus en Mésopotamie. Le cas de Suse et Tello. In: *CORNALINE DE L'INDE. Des pratiques techniques de Cambay aux techno-systèmes de l'Indus*. Éditions de la Maison des sciences de l'homme. Paris.

Jasim, S. A. 2012: *The Necropolis of Jebel al-Buhais: Prehistoric Discoveries in the Emirate of Sharjah, United Arab Emirates*. The Department of Culture & Information.

JASP = Jutland Archaeological Society Publications.

Kanungo, A. K. 2008: Glass in India. In: *Encyclopaedia of the History of Science, Technology, and Medicine in Non-Western Cultures*. p. 1023-1033.

Kenoyer, J.M. 1991: Ornament Styles of the Indus Valley Tradition: Evidence from Recent Excavations at Harappa, Pakistan. In: *Paléorient*, 1991, vol. 17, No. 2. pp. 79-98.

Kenoyer, J.M. 1997: Trade and Technology of the Indus Valley: New Insights from Harappa, Pakistan. In: *World Archaeology*, Vol. 29, No. 2, High Definition Archaeology: Threads through the Past, pp. 262-280.

Kenoyer, J.M. 1998: *Ancient cities of the Indus valley civilization*. Karachi: Oxford University Press.

Kenoyer, J. M. 2003: Stone Beads and Pendant Making Techniques. In: A Bead Timeline: Vol. 1 Prehistory to 1200 CE. J. W. Lankton. Washington, DC, The Bead Museum, pp. 14-19.

Kenoyer, J.M. 2005: Bead Technologies at Harappa, 3300-1900 BC: A comparative summary. In: *South Asian Archaeology 2001*, edited by C. Jarrige and V. Lefèvre. Paris, Editions Recherche sur les Civilisations -ADPF. pp. 157-170.

Kenoyer, J.M. 2008a: Indus and Mesopotamian Trade Networks: New Insights from Shell and Carnelian Artifacts. In: (eds.) Olijdam, E. & Spoor, R.H. *Intercultural Relations Between South and Southwest Asia. Studies in Commemoration of E.C.L. During Caspers (1934-1996)*. BAR International Series 1826, pp. 19-28.

Kenoyer, J.M. 2008b: Beads of the Indus. In: *Art of the First Cities: The third Millennium B.C. From The Mediterranean to the Indus*. The Metropolitan Museum of Art, New York. Yale University Press, New Haven and London, pp. 395-396.

Kenoyer, J.M. 2013: Eye Beads from the Indus Tradition: Technology, Style and Chronology. In: *Journal of Asian Civilizations*, vol. 36, No. 2, December 2013. pp. 1-22.

Kenoyer, J.M. 2016: Bead Drill Hole SEM Analysis. In: (eds.)

Højlund, F. and Abu-Laban, A. *Tell F6 on Failaka Island: Kuwaiti-Danish Excavations 2008-2012*. JASP 92. Moesgaard Museum, Denmark & The National Council for Culture, Arts and Letters, Kuwait. pp. 198-206.

Kenoyer J.M. & Frenez, D. 2018a: Stone Beads in Oman during the 3rd to 2nd Millennia BCE: New Approaches to the study of Trade and Technology. In: *BEADS: Journal of the Society of Bead Researchers*, vol. 30, pp. 63-76.

Kenoyer, J.M. & Frenez, D. 2018b: Carnelian and Agate Beads in the Oman Peninsula during the Third to Second millennia BC. In: Cleuziou, S. &Tosi, M. (eds.) *In the Shadow of the Ancestors. The Prehistoric Foundations of the Early Arabian Civilization in Oman.* Ministry of Heritage and Culture Sultanate of Oman. pp. 397-410.

Kenoyer, J.M. & Vidale, M. 1992: A new look at stone drills of the Indus Valley Tradition. In: (eds.) Vandiver, P., Druzick, J.R., Wheeler, G.S. and Freestone, I. *Materials Issues in Art and Archaeology, III,* Vol. 267. Materials Research Society, Pittsburgh, pp. 495-519.

Killick, R. & Moon, J. 2005: *The Early Dilmun Settlement at Saar.* London-Bahrain Archaeological Expedition. Saar Excavation Report 3. Archaeology International Ltd, Ludlow, UK.

Kjærum, P. 1994: *Stamp seals, seal-impressions and seal blanks.* In: Højlund & Andersen 1994, pp. 319-350.

Kjærum, P. & Højlund, F. 2013: *The Bronze Age Architecture.* Failaka/Dilmun. The Second Millennium Settlements 3. JASP 17:3.

Lankton, J.W. (ed.) 2003: *A Bead Timeline, Vol. 1: Prehistory to 1200 CE.* Washington D.C.: The Bead Society of Greater Washington, Publishers Press Inc.

Laursen, S.T. & Steinkeller, P. 2017: *Trade, Cultural, and Historical Contacts between Babylonia and the Gulf Region during the Third and Early Second Millennia: Archaeology and Texts.* Eisenbrauns. Winona Lake, Indiana.

Law, R. W. 2011: *Inter-Regional Interaction and Urbanism in the Ancient Indus Valley: A Geologic Provenience Study of Harappa's Rock and Mineral Assemblage, Occasional Paper 11.* Kyoto, Research Institute for Humanity and Nature.

Law, R. W. 2014: Evaluating the Potential Lapis Lazuli Sources for Ancient South Asia Using Sulfur Isotope Analysis. In: (eds.) Lamberg-Karlovsky, C.C., Genito, B. & Cerasetti, B. *'My Life is Like the Summer Rose' Mario Tosi E L'Archaeologia Come Modo De Vivere.* Papers in Honour of Maurizio Tosi for his 70th Birthday, BAR International Series 2690, pp. 419-430.

Lilyquist, C. 1994: The Dilbat Hoard. In: *The Metropolitan Museum Journal*, Vol. 29. pp. 5-36.

Limper, K. 1988: *Uruk. Perlen, Ketten, Anhänger.* Grabungen 1912-1985. Ausgrabungen in Uruk-Warka Endberichte. Band 2. Verlag Philipp Von Zabern. Mainz Am Rhein.

Ludvik, G., Kenoyer, J.M., Pieniążek, M. 2014: Stone Bead-making Technology and Beads from Hattusa: A Preliminary Report. In: (ed.) A. Schachner. *Die Arbeiten in Boğazköy-Hattuša 2013. Archäologischer Anzeiger* 2014, Vol. 1, pp. 147-153.

Ludvik, G., Kenoyer, J.M., Pieniążek, M. & Aylward, W. 2015: New Perspectives on Stone Bead Technology at Bronze Age Troy. In: *Anatolian Studies*, Vol. 65, pp. 1-18.

Lui, Robert. K. 1995: Middle East and North Africa. In: *A Universal Aesthetic: Collectible Beads.* Ornament, Inc. California.

Mackay, E. J. H. 1938: *Further Excavations at Mohenjo-Daro.* New Delhi.

Mackay, E. J. H. 1943: *Chanhu-Daro Excavations 1935-36.* New Haven, Connecticut.

Maxwell-Hyslop, K.R. 1971: *Western Asiatic Jewellery c. 3000-612 BC.* Methuen & Co. Ltd. II New Fetter Lane London EC4.

Melein, M. M. 2018: *Iron Oxide Rock Artefacts in Mesopotamia C. 2600-1200 BC: An Interdisciplinary Study of Hematite, Goethite and Magnetite Objects.* Archaeopress Archaeology.

Moorey, P. R. S. 1994: *Ancient Mesopotamian Materials and Industries.* Oxford, Clarendon Press.

Mughal, M.R. 1983: *The Dilmun Burial Complex at Sar. The 1980-82 Excavations in Bahrain.* Ministry of Information. Bahrain.

Oguchi, K. 1992: Shells and Shell Objects from Area A of 'Usiyeh. In: *Al-Rafidan* vol. XIII, pp. 61-81.

Oguchi, K. 1998: Beads from Area A of 'Usiyeh. In: *Al-Rafidan,* vol. XIX, pp. 75-111.

Oppenheim, A.L., 1954. The Seafaring Merchants of Ur. *Journal of the American Oriental Society* 74 pp. 6-17.

Parpola, S., Parpola, A. & Brunswig, R. H. Jr. 1977: The Meluhha Village: Evidence of Acculturation of Harappan Traders in Late Third Millennium Mesopotamia? In: *Journal of the Economic and Social History of the Orient*, vol. XX, part II, pp. 129- 165.

Peyronel, L. 2015: A Long-Barrel Carnelian Bead from Ebla. A New Evidence for Long-Distance Contacts between the Indus Valley and the Near East. In: (ed.) Matthiae, P. *Studia Eblaitica. Studies on the Archaeology, History, and Philology of Ancient Syria.* pp. 217-220.

Pézard, M. 1914: *Mission à Bender-Bouchir.* Publications de la Mission Archéologique de Perse 15.

Pieniążek, M. 2012: Luxury and Prestige on the edge of the Mediterranean World: Jewellery from Troia and the Northern Aegean in the 2nd Millennium B.C. and its context. In: (eds.) Nosch, M.L. and Laffineur, R. *Kosmos Jewellery, Adornment and Textiles in the Aegean Bronze Age.* Proceedings of the 13th International Aegean Conference/ 13e Rencontre Ègéenne Internationale. University of Copenhagen,Danish National Research Foundation's Centre for Textile Research, 21-26 April 2010. pp. 501-508.

Pieniążek, M. & Kozal, E. 2014: West Anatolian Beads and Pins in the 2nd millennium BC: Some Remarks on Function and Distribution in Comparison with Neighboring Regions. In: (eds.) Golani, A. and Wygnańska, Z. *Polish Archaeology in the Mediterranean 23/2, Special Studies: Beyond Ornamentation. Jewelry as an Aspect of Material Culture in the Ancient Near East.* pp. 187-208.

Pollock, S. 1985: Chronology of the Royal Cemetery of Ur. In: *Iraq*, Vol. 47, pp. 129-158.

Possehl, G.L. 1996: Meluhha. In: Reade, J. (ed.), *The Indian Ocean in Antiquity.* London, pp. 133-208

Potts, D.T. 2009: The Archaeology and Early History of the Persian Gulf. In: (ed.) Potter, L.G. *The Persian Gulf in History.* Palgrave Macmillan.

Prabhakar, V.N., 2015: Analysis of the Ernestite Stone Drills from Dholavira Excavations. In: Man and Environment in Prehistoric and Protohistoric South Asia: New Perspectives. *South Asian Archaeology and Art 2012*, Vol 1. pp. 257-270.

Prabhakar, V.N. 2018: Decorated Carnelian Beads from the Indus Civilization Site of Dholavira (Great Rann of Kachchha, Gujarat). In: *Frenez et al. (eds.), Walking with the Unicorn. Social Organization and Material Culture in Ancient South Asia. Jonathan Mark Kenoyer Felicitation Volume.* Archaeopress Archaeology. Oxford, pp. 475-485.

Prabhakar, V.N., Bisht, R.S., Law, R.W. and Kenoyer, J.M. 2012: Stone Drill Bits from Dholavira-A Multi-faceted Analysis. In: *Man and Environment. Indian Society for Prehistoric and Quaternary Studies.* Vol. XXXVII, No. 1. pp. 8-25.

Pulak, C. 2008: Inlaid Rings. In: (eds.) Aruz, J.; Benzel, K. and Evans, J.M. *Beyond Babylon. Art, Trade and Diplomacy in the 2nd Millennium BC.* The Metropolitan Museum of Art. Yale University Press, New Haven and London, pp. 326-327.

Robinson, A. 2015: *The Indus: Lost Civilizations.* Reaktion Books.

Roux, V. & Matarasso, P. 2000: Harappan carnelian beads. Technical practices and techno-system. In: *CORNALINE DE L'INDE. Des pratiques techniques de Cambay aux techno-systèmes de l'Indus.* Éditions de la Maison des sciences de l'homme. Paris.

Rutkowski, L. 2015: *Tumuli Graves and other Stone Structures on the North Coast of Kuwait Bay (Al-Subiyah 2007-2012).* Kuwaiti–Polish Archaeological Mission (KPAM) Publications.

Shaw, I. and Nicholson, P. 1995: *The Dictionary of Ancient Egypt.* British Museum Press, London.

Srivastava, K. M. 1991: *Madinat Hamad: Burial Mounds, 1984-85.* Ministry of Information. State of Bahrain. Bahrain National Museum.

Stevenson, A. 2013: Egypt and Mesopotamia. In: Crawford, H. (ed.) *The Sumerian World.* Routledge. pp. 620-636.

Uesugi, A. 2018: Current state of research and issues of Indus Archaeology Focusing on field researches and material cultural studies. In: *Current Research on Indus Archaeology.* South Asian Archaeology Series, vol. 4. pp. 1-55.

Vandiver, P. 1983: Glass Technology at the mid-second Millennium BC. Hurrian Site of Nuzi. In: *Journal of Glass Studies,* vol. 25. International Glass Conference: June 6-12, 1982. pp. 239-247.

Vats, M.S. 1940: *Excavations at Harappa.* Calcutta.

Vogt, B. 1996: Bronze Age Maritime Trade in the Indian Ocean: Harappan Traits on the Oman Peninsula. In: Reade, J. (ed.), *The Indian Ocean in Antiquity.* Kegan Paul: British Museum. pp. 107-132.

Woolley, L. 1934: *Ur Excavations, vol. II. The Royal Cemetery. A Report on the Predynastic and Sargonid graves excavated Between 1926 and 1931.* London.

Wygnańska, Z. 2015: Beads, pendants and other ornaments from tumuli graves and the survey in the Al-Subiyah region. In: *Tumuli Graves and other Stone Structures on the North Coast of Kuwait Bay (Al-Subiyah 2007-2012).* Kuwaiti-Polish Archaeological Mission (KPAM) Publications. pp. 487-532.